THE CAHOKIA ATLAS

University of Illinois at Urbana-Champaign
Studies in Archaeology
Number 2

Thomas E. Emerson, Series Editor
Michael D. Conner, Center for American Archeology, Volume Editor for the First Edition
Barbara E. Cohen, Volume Editor for the Revised Edition

THE CAHOKIA ATLAS

A Historical Atlas of Cahokia Archaeology

REVISED EDITION

Melvin L. Fowler

Illinois Transportation Archaeological Research Program
University of Illinois
Urbana, Illinois

Studies in Archaeology

Series Editor:

Thomas E. Emerson

The Illinois Transportation Archaeological Research Program (ITARP) is the product of a four decade long cooperative effort between the University of Illinois and the Illinois Department of Transportation (IDOT) in the preservation of the state's important archaeological resources. It began under the direction of Charles J. Bareis in 1959 with the newly created Illinois Archaeological Survey, continued in 1980 when the IDOT statewide survey program was transferred to the Resource Investigation Program, up until the present time with the formation of ITARP in 1994. The establishment of ITARP was the result of IDOT's interest in developing a centralized program to facilitate its cultural resources protection efforts.

One of ITARP's primary goals, as a research unit of the University of Illinois, is the dissemination of information on archaeological and historical topics to both professional and public audiences. This externally peer reviewed series, Studies in Archaeology, is designed to bring scholarly works of topical and regional research to the broadest possible audience.

The production of these volumes is accomplished through the efforts of the ITARP Publication Production Office under the direction of Mike Lewis, Publications Manager and Graphic Designer Linda Alexander. Additional copies of this report may be obtained from the Center for American Archeology Press, Box 366, Kampsville, IL 62053.

Library of Congress Cataloging-in-Publication Data

Fowler, Melvin L. (Melvin Leo), 1924–
    The Cahokia atlas : a historical atlas of Cahokia archaeology /
Melvin L. Fowler. – Rev. ed.
      p. cm. – (Studies in archaeology ; #2)
    Includes bibliographical references and index.
    ISBN 0-9644881-3-2
    1. Cahokia Mounds State Historic Park (Ill.)–Atlases.
2. Mississippian culture–Illinois–American Bottom–Atlases.
3. Excavations (Archaeology)–Illinois–American Bottom–Atlases.
4. American Bottom (Ill.)–Antiquities–Atlases. I. Title.
II. Series : Studies in archaeology (Urbana, Ill.) ; #2
E78.I3F69   1997
977.3'89–DC21   97-16031
                              CIP

The publication of the first edition was financed in part with federal funds provided by the U.S. Department of the Interior and administered by the Illinois Historic Preservation Agency. However, the contents and opinions do not necessarily reflect the views or policies of the U.S. Department of the Interior or the Illinois Historic Preservation Agency.

Publication of the revised edition was funded by the Center for American Archeology–Illinois Historic Preservation Agency Book Fund and the Illinois Transportation Archaeological Research Program of the University of Illinois.

CONTENTS

ILLUSTRATIONS

FIGURES

TABLES

PREFACE TO THE REVISED EDITION

This revised edition of the Cahokia Atlas has been a long time in development. In the 1960s and 1970s I received several NSF grants as well as support from the Illinois Department of Conservation and the University of Wisconsin-Milwaukee. The goals of this research were originally:

1. to prepare a physical and cultural map of the Cahokia site.
2. to define the site limits.
3. to define the nature and character of the site as a community.
4. to determine the nature of specialized areas within the site. (Fowler 1974:14)

Although these goals have been expanded and modified, both in terms of specific aims and theoretical bases, they have remained as the basic guideposts of this atlas.

To achieve these goals included the preparation of an aerial photogrammetric map of the Cahokia site, collection of air photographs and maps from earlier researchers, and extensive library and manuscript research to bring together all the published information on the site we could find. Then came the hard part: countless hours adding up to days and months of walking over the area to check and recheck the insights coming from studying the maps, photos, and notes.

The first version of this atlas was submitted to the Illinois Department of Conservation (IDOC) in 1979. This manuscript contained only the materials that are now in Chapters 1 through 8. These are the purely description portions. At the same time I submitted the original manuscript, I also mailed copies to nearly fifty of my colleagues for their review. Many of them responded with emendations, additions, and corrections of factual errors as well as many other helpful suggestions. These were, for the most part added to the original manuscript. If IDOC had had the resources to publish this report at that time, it would have been this purely descriptive document.

When the historic preservation role, including archaeology, was transferred from IDOC to the newly formed Illinois Historic Preservation Agency (IHPA) and Tom Emerson became the chief archaeologist, I was contracted to rework *The Cahokia Atlas* for publication. I set to work preparing maps for publication and making some revisions to the descriptive data of the original manuscript. I realized that the descriptive data needed some interpretation so, in 1989, I wrote and added Chapters 9, 10, and 11 and Appendix I. Emerson solicited the archaeologists at Southern Illinois University at Edwardsville to write Appendix 5 on more recent work in the Cahokia area.

The main goal of my 1989 chapters was to present a model of how Cahokia may have been organized. While these interpretations present a static, or synchronic, model, they were never intended as more than an outline of how the site may have been organized. In the first edition of the atlas I stated:

> [T]he observed distribution of mounds is representative of the prehistoric layout and extent of the community. While all portions of this area may not have been occupied simultaneously, the concepts which dictated the organization of space are indicated by the distribution of the man-made features, primarily the mounds (Fowler 1989:190).

Furthermore, there is indication that this community pattern as indicated by monumental construction "started in the Early Mississippian period, and possibly earlier, during Emergent Mississippian" (ibid). Thus this synchronic view presented the possibility of investigating a processual or developmental model.

A major addition to the 1989 manuscript was Chapter 10, which included a redefinition and updating of a model of Cahokia organization that I first presented in 1974 (Fowler 1974:23-25, Figure 7). In this chapter I proposed that, although most of the data available at that time suggested all parts of greater Cahokia had covered most of the know time range, the site could be subdivided into subcommunities. Ideally, each of these subcommunities had its own plaza and platform and burial mounds, and although some were arranged differently, there was a space between these subcommunities. Again the contemporaneity of these subcommunities was not known. Several of these have been tested since 1989, but much still remains to be done to test this hypothesis and place it in a diachronic model of Cahokia.

Although there are differences among archaeologists in terms of specific definition of plazas and other features of monument groupings, this model of Cahokia has remained a basis upon which further investigations and interpretations have been conducted. In my interpretations I used such terms as *city* and *mar-*

kets, which carry a connotation of state-level sociocultural integration. This was not my intention. The loose usage of such terms is akin to the current usage of terms like "regal" to describe chiefly centers and trappings. It is meant to imply the complexity and social and economic differentiation in Mississippian society at Cahokia and its environs.

A number of changes have been made in this version of *The Cahokia Atlas*. These include much needed editorial revisions to correct inadvertent errors. Other changes are the result of continuing research. Mound 96 was resurveyed with close interval mapping, and this new map replaces the older one. A more detailed description of the Jondro Mound (78) was made, and copies of the profile and plan maps published by Moorehead are included. Further comments by reviewers are also included, as is an updated 1990-1995 research appendix.

Many individuals at the University of Wisconsin-Milwaukee (UWM) have played key roles in the original research and editorial revisions, whether conducting library searches for obscure references, drafting maps, making photographs, or participating in long discussions about Cahokia. Among these I wish to acknowledge Helen Achcynski, James Anderson, Elizabeth Benchley, Marion Mochon, and Barbara Vander Leest.

The research involved was, and is, supported by grants from the National Science Foundation. Extensive support has been and is being provided by the University of Wisconsin-Milwaukee. The 1979 version of this atlas was prepared under a grant from IDOC. The revisions and additions of new data, particularly for this new edition, have been supported by the Archaeological Research Laboratory of UWM, the Research Committee of the National Geographic Society, and the Cahokia Mounds Museum Society. Needless to say, without the considerable support of these institutions this edition would not have been possible.

Finally, I express my gratitude to Thomas Emerson, formerly with the IHPA and now at the University of Illinois at Urbana-Champaign, for seeing to it that the two editions of *The Cahokia Atlas* were published.

To all of the above individuals and institutions, as well as to many others not mentioned by name, must go the credit for whatever merits this document has. I can only hope that I have fairly presented their efforts. Any errors, misrepresentations, or misinterpretations are fully my responsibility.

Milwaukee, Wisconsin
August 27, 1996

ACKNOWLEDGMENTS

This volume has been a long time in the making. Many individuals have been involved directly or have influenced the outcome.

The basic goals are to present a collation, summary, and some analysis of the surface features that make up the Cahokia Mounds State Historic Site. A fundamental assumption of this work is that the forms and surface distribution of such things as mounds, borrow pits, and walls can yield insights into community extent and organization. To complete such a work has required extensive examination of the published accounts of explorations of the Cahokia archaeological site, examinations of maps and artifacts in museum collections, and countless hours, days, and months of walking over the area to check and recheck the information gleaned from the libraries and museums. It is because of the necessity for this latter portion of the research that the late Pedro Armillas referred to the entire approach as "pedestrian" archaeology. It is to him that I owe whatever understanding I have of this method. I belatedly acknowledge here his influence on this work.

When I first submitted this report to the Illinois Department of Conservation in 1979, I also mailed copies to nearly fifty of my colleagues for their review. Many of them responded with emendations, additions, and corrections of factual errors, as well as many other helpful suggestions. Over the years these people and others have sent me pictures that I had not known about and other data regarding Cahokia. All of this has improved this report and added greatly to its content. To these many individuals, far too numerous to list there, I express my indebtedness and gratitude. Without their willingness to share information and to give me the benefit of their insights, this work would not have been possible.

While conducting the original research and making the revisions and additions necessary, many individuals at the University of WisconsinMilwaukee have played key roles, whether conducting library searches for obscure references, drafting maps, making photographs, or participating in long discussions about Cahokia. Among these are Helen Achcynski, James Anderson, Elizabeth Benchley, and Barbara Vander Leest.

The research involved was supported by grants from the National Science Foundation. Extensive support was also provided by the University of Wisconsin-Milwaukee. The 1979 version of this report was prepared under a grant from the Illinois Department of Conservation. The revisions and additions of new data have been supported by the Archaeological Research Laboratory at the University of Wisconsin-Milwaukee. Needless to say, without the considerable financial support of these several institutions, this work would not have been undertaken and completed.

Finally, I express my gratitude to Thomas Emerson of the Illinois Historic Preservation Agency for his commitment to seeing that this book was published, and to Michael Conner of the Center for American Archeology for his editorial commitment above and beyond the call of duty in refining a very difficult and cumbersome manuscript.

To all of the above individuals and institutions must go the credit for whatever merit this document may have. I can only hope that I have fairly presented their efforts. Any errors and misinterpretations are my responsibility.

Milwaukee, Wisconsin
July 30, 1989

FOREWORD

It is fitting that this year, which marks the completion of a new public interpretive center at Cahokia Mounds State Historic Site, also sees the publication of two major scholarly works on the history of Cahokia and its place in the prehistory of the Eastern United States (this volume and *Cahokia and the Hinterlands*, edited by Thomas E. Emerson and R. Barry Lewis, University of Illinois Press [1991]). These events represent the culmination of years of ongoing, difficult struggles by private, professional, and government groups to protect, preserve, and interpret this greatest of North American sites.

The need for a premier interpretive center was recognized by the state of Illinois over two decades ago. During the intervening years, a number of locations and designs were formulated. As the various factors such as access, impact on the archaeological resources, funding, and educational goals were assessed and reassessed, numerous locations were examined and rejected. In 1985, Governor James Thompson created the Illinois Historic Preservation Agency (IHPA) and specifically charged it to preserve, protect, and interpret the history and prehistory of Illinois. That same year, IHPA selected a site for the interpretive center and the preliminary planning began. The mitigation of the impact of the construction of the interpretive center on the archaeological resources represented one of the largest and best-funded episodes of archaeological research ever undertaken at Cahokia. The ongoing analysis of the resulting data has contributed major new dimensions to our understanding of "downtown" Cahokia, just as the new interpretive center will, for the first time, adequately convey to the American public the spectacular Native American civilization that resided there in A.D. 1000 (see Appendix 5 for a summary of this work).

Part of the planning of the new interpretive center and its exhibits was the attempted recovery of the scattered Cahokia collections from various private and public groups that had acquired the material. This fragmenting, scattering, and dispersal of Cahokia collections has been one of the major detriments to scholarly research at the site. The ultimate purpose was not only to gain the return of this material so that it could be used in interpreting the site but also to form a central curatorial repository at the Illinois State Museum where present and future scholars could have easy access to this rich material for analysis and interpretation. Some major holders of Cahokia materials—such as Beloit

College, Washington University, and the University of Wisconsin-Milwaukee—worked with IHPA to bring these important resources together, although unfortunately some out-of-state institutions decided to retain their collections.

As important as the reassembling of the Cahokia collection has been the active effort of IHPA to encourage the description, analysis, and interpretation of this data. Much of the early excavated information at the site was never described or reported due to inadequate funding or the failure of researchers to follow through with their obligations. As part of the site's management, IHPA has attempted to fund, sponsor, co-sponsor, and encourage, within a controlled framework of professional standards, research and publication of information from the existing database. This limited effort has already contributed substantially to increasing our understanding of the construction and evolution of the Cahokia ceremonial precinct with research on Monks Mound, the Grand Plaza, and Tract 15B. This museum-collection research was critical in establishing for the first time the presence of a seventeenth-century French mission at the site.

The systematic analysis and publication of all such previously collected data is a clear priority of IHPA in order to further the goal of better interpretation and management of Cahokia. An important step in this process is the thorough compilation and presentation of all of the myriad of research, testing, excavations, collections, and scientific and not-so-scientific efforts at Cahokia. It was this goal that led to Dr. Fowler's efforts in the late 1970s to compile such a document, culminating with a completed draft in 1979. Through the years various attempts have been initiated to make this information available to a wider audience. When IHPA was organized in 1985, one specific goal of the archaeology program was to gather together the results of previous work. This effort again clearly identified Dr. Fowler's *Cahokia Atlas* as a prime document to be disseminated to the public. Funding and editing delays caused a further five years to pass, but finally the concerted work of many people has brought the volume to fruition.

The publication of this volume bears testimony to the faith and effort of many people, especially to William Farrar, former Deputy State Historic Preservation Officer, who actually believed we could do it, when in 1984 I argued that we should start an archaeology publication series with no funds, no editor, and one manuscript; to Theodore Hild, the current Deputy State Historic Preservation Officer, who I am not sure believed we could succeed, but who did find the money (most of it, anyway); to Evelyn Taylor, Preservation Services Division editor, who graciously allowed me to volunteer her evenings and weekends to edit the massive initial drafts; and finally, to Melvin Fowler, who survived a decade of being "in press" with a smile.

Thomas E. Emerson
Series Editor

FOREWORD TO THE REVISED EDITION

It gives me a great deal of pleasure to have had the opportunity to participate in both the original publication and the republication of what has surely become an Illinois archaeological bestseller. It was obvious in the early 1980s, when I argued for the volume's initial publication in the Illinois Historic Preservation Agency's (IHPA) new series *Studies in Illinois Archaeology,* that it fulfilled a real need. Formal recognition of Cahokia Mounds by the National Park Service with its placement on the National Register of Historic Places and designation as a National Monument and by UNESCO as a World Heritage site signified the international importance of the great prehistoric site. However, before 1989 little had been done to bring the story of Cahokia to either a professional or a popular audience. Fowler's *Cahokia Atlas* admirably accomplished that task. I don't think any of us, however, realized how popular the book would be. Within six years the volume went out of print without satisfying the professional or popular demand.

Despite the demand for the *Atlas*, its reprinting presented a number of problems. As scholarly attention has increasingly focused on the archaeology and history of research at Cahokia, reinterpretations of previously studied materials as well as new data are continually becoming available. It seemed a shame not to have the *Atlas* incorporate the new evidence from these ongoing excavations and analysis. We were also aware that typographical and mapping errors had crept into the original edition. These needed to be corrected. It became apparent that rather than reprint the *Atlas*, we had to undertake a totally updated, revised edition.

More than just the archaeology has changed in the six years since the *Atlas* was published. After 1993, IHPA was no longer able to continue its publication program in archaeology. That program, for which I served as series editor, effectively ended when funds diminished and I left the agency in 1994 to join the staff of the Department of Anthropology, University of Illinois at Urbana-Champaign (UIUC). Luckily, through the kind offices of Evelyn Taylor, William Wheeler, and Mark Esarey of the IHPA, permission was granted to revise and republish the *Atlas*. The mechanism for this effort became available when I became series editor for the *Studies in Archaeology* at UIUC. Funding for this project was generously provided by the Center for American Archaeology – Illinois Historic Preservation Agency Book Fund and

the Illinois Transportation Archaeological Research Program, University of Illinois (ITARP). ITARP's production office handled all the volume formatting, graphics, and production for the book under the auspices of the production manager, Michael Lewis, and graphic artist Linda Alexander, who also designed the striking new cover. Mike and Linda chaperoned the book from manuscript to finished product to ensure that *Atlas* would be a high-quality publication. Barbara E. Cohen undertook the arduous tasks of editing and indexing the work, and the increased accuracy and user-friendly nature of this new edition can be attributed to her efforts.

Fortunately for those interested and concerned about Cahokia archaeology, Dr. Fowler was enthusiastic about the process and agreed to assist with the revisions. We also solicited information, insights, and comments from a number of archaeologists with lifelong interest in Cahokia. These individuals provided vital information that made the revision process considerably more effective and thorough. We would especially like to thank Charles J. Bareis, George R. Holley, John E. Kelly, and Timothy R. Pauketat for contributing considerable time and effort to help with the revised edition.

Cahokia-focused research by Holley, Rinita Dalan, Pauketat, and Kelly has begun to extensively change our understanding of the "Cahokia phenomenon." Much of this new research is included in the body of the *Atlas* as well as in a new appendix by Holley et al. covering research at the site done from 1990 to 1995. This summary underscores the tremendous outflowing of Cahokia research completed in the past decade. Rinita Dalan's investigations on the Cahokian cultural landscape as part of her thesis (1992, 1997) and the continuing related work by her and Holley have altered our perceptions regarding the sheer scale of the human manipulation of the land. Pauketat's recent analyses (1991, 1994, 1997) of the Tract 15A and Kunnemann Mound materials, which lay unexamined since their excavation decades ago, not only gives scholars a vast new database but also provides the evidence to argue for an explosive Cahokian social and political transformation at A.D. 1000 that matched that documented in the early, rapid construction of the great earthen monuments. The pace of acquisition of new information and interpretation has shifted dramatically in recent years and recently culminated in a new Cahokia summary volume of scholarly articles edited by Pauketat and Emerson (1997).

Outside of Cahokia's central core, research as a result of the massive federal- and state-sponsored highway archaeology projects (e.g., Bareis and Porter 1984) has given us a broader perspective on the reach of the Cahokian elite into the immediate hinterlands of the American Bottom. Our information has increased to the level that it can now support conflicting interpretations of the political relationships between the Cahokian elites and the outlying settlements (e.g. Emerson 1995; Mehrer 1988, 1995). This is a far cry from the situation two decades ago when Melvin Fowler first attempted to hypothesize a model for Cahokian rural settlement in the absence of many excavated rural sites.

One of the most positive aspects of the recent archaeological research at Cahokia has been the tendency of scholars to concentrate on the analysis of older, previously unanalyzed collections and small less-destructive excavations to increase out knowledge about the site. Why is this important? In the past a number of large-scale excavations were undertaken that were never adequately analyzed or reported. We must remember that the essential nature of archaeological excavations is to "destroy" the archaeological record. Therefore, such excavations on publicly owned and protected sites, especially internationally renowned sites such as Cahokia, should be extremely limited, closely restricted, and be held to the highest professional standards. While we can be well satisfied with the quality and focus of most of the recent Cahokia research, we must remember of that the few thousand acres that make up Cahokia Mounds State Historic Site comprise a minor segment of the once vast Cahokia political and settlement system.

Most of prehistoric Cahokia lies outside of state-owned lands and is rapidly being destroyed by modern development. This was strikingly demonstrated when John Kelly (1997) discovered intact remnants of the great East St. Louis mound group under the present-day city of East St. Louis. In its heyday this center may have rivalled Cahokia and in fact may have been part of the greater Cahokia center about A.D. 1100. This mound center, long thought destroyed, may have been rediscovered only to be destroyed again by planned urban renewal. While it is fortunate that, in a few cases, there are legislation requirements to take archaeological resources into account prior to development, in most instances nothing is required or done before this precious record of the past is destroyed. Consequently, archaeological research should be concentrated on the endangered parts of Cahokia on private lands rather than on the protected resources in the park. It would be a flagrant neglect of our ethical responsibilities "to preserve the past for the future" if we destroy, through excavation, the publicly owned and protected parts of Cahokia while those outside the park are destroyed without benefit of being recorded.

The publication of this revised edition of Melvin Fowler's *Cahokia Atlas* makes the story of this great prehistoric center available once more to both professional and general audiences. I hope that it also serves to make apparent what a precious historic resource Cahokia is and to remind the public that much of Cahokia lies unprotected beyond the limited park boundaries. Future endeavors must focus on saving those portions of Cahokia that are today subject to loss through the ever-encroaching development that is transforming the American Bottom from a patchwork of small cities and farms to a continuous blanket of urban and suburban sprawl.

Thomas E. Emerson
Department of Anthropology
University of Illinois at Urbana-Champaign

THE CAHOKIA ATLAS

Frontispiece. Artists's reconstruction of downtown Cahokia ca. A.D. 1100. Source: National Geographic Society.

1

INTRODUCTION

For centuries, both in historic and prehistoric times, the area now dominated by St. Louis, Missouri, has been a hub of human travel, economic exchange, and political domination of vast areas of the North American continent. St. Louis is on the west bank of the Mississippi River, and just north of the city the Missouri and Illinois rivers enter the Mississippi. These three rivers provide access to most of the north-central portions of North America. Until the coming of the railroads in the latter half of the nineteenth century, the confluence of these rivers formed a center of commerce and exploitation of the west and northwest. Both precolumbian and historic peoples established communities in this central place to take advantage of this location. In recent years an arch has been built on the riverfront to commemorate the fact that for the past 200 years St. Louis has been the gateway to the West.

About 1,000 years ago, however, prehistoric Indians built their own monuments testifying to the importance of the region. Although much that they left behind has been destroyed by two centuries of urban development and agricultural expansion, many of the great earthen mounds they built remain visible today. The centerpiece of their occupation is what archaeologists have called the Cahokia site, now partially preserved in the Cahokia Mounds State Historic Site across the Mississippi from St. Louis near Collinsville, Illinois (Figure 1.1). At Cahokia lived the elite rulers and religious leaders who governed the thousands of farmers, hunters, traders, and artisans who populated the vast Mississippi floodplain around the site and who provided the labor to build the monumental earthworks. All were supported by the rich natural resources of the Mississippi River Valley and by the crops they grew, especially corn (maize). The area flourished between about A.D. 1000 and 1400, but like all cultures, the Cahokians eventually succumbed to the forces of history and change, leaving behind their mounds and other remains as evidence of their presence, and leaving it to nineteenth- and twentieth-century archaeologists to write their history and tell their story.

Among those who passed through St. Louis in the early nineteenth century were numerous scholars and artists. Many of them have provided us with detailed descriptions of the natural history and antiquities of the area. One of these was Henry Brackenridge, who visited St. Louis in 1811. Brackenridge was a traveler and deeply interested in the ruins that lay about the countryside as silent reminders of the prehistoric past. He was an avid scholar and corresponded with such intellectuals of his day as Thomas Jefferson. One of the collections of mounds that interested Brackenridge was on the banks of the Mississippi near where the Gateway Arch is now located (Figure 1.2). So many mounds were scattered about the area that what is now metropolitan St. Louis was known through much of the nineteenth and early twentieth centuries as Mound City.

In St. Louis, Brackenridge heard about a group of Trappist monks who had a monastery beyond the eastern banks of the Mississippi River. These monks had settled in the area a few years before, first near Florissant, Missouri, and then on the east side of the Mississippi on the banks of Cahokia Creek, a tributary that drains a large area of the Mississippi bottomlands (McAdams 1907:40-41). The monks were reportedly now settled near some large earthen mounds. They were living their life of silence, raising crops to sustain themselves, and making and repairing clocks for the people in the area. Brackenridge's curiosity was aroused and he set forth to find the monks and their mounds (Brackenridge 1962 [1814]:287-288).

Brackenridge crossed the Mississippi on a ferry boat and landed at Illinois Town (now East St. Louis, Illinois), a small but thriving community near the mouth of Cahokia Creek. The Mississippi bottomlands extended north, east, and south of Illinois Town covering an area from "the Kaskaskia to the Cahokia river,

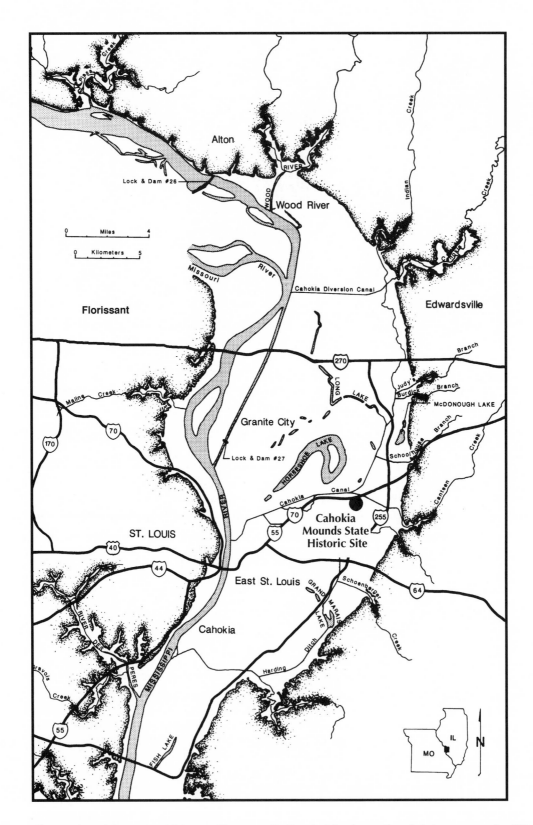

Figure 1.1.   The modern Mississippi River valley near St. Louis. The large floodplain area on the Illinois side of the river is called the American Bottom. Source: Mikels Skele, Archaeology Laboratory, Southern Illinois University at Edwardsville.

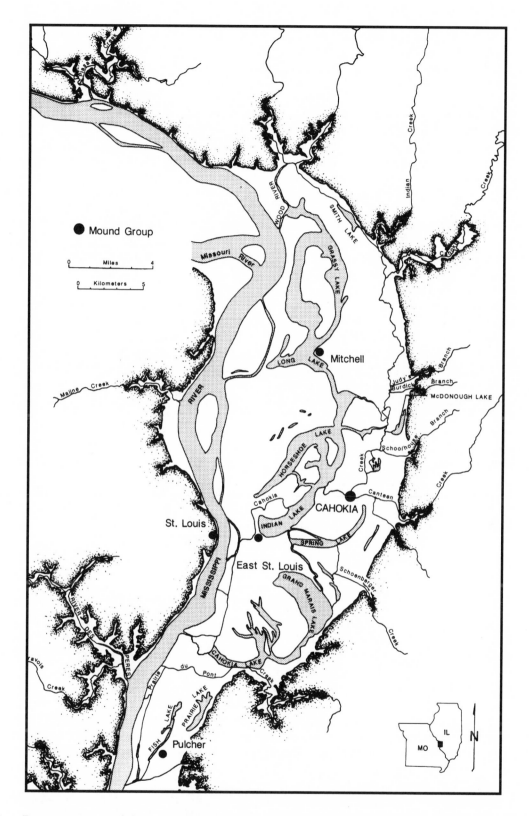

Figure 1.2. Reconstruction of the rivers, creeks, and lakes in the American Bottom ca. 1800, showing locations of the major Mississippian sites. Brackenridge journeyed from St. Louis to the East St. Louis mounds and then along the south bank of Indian Lake to the Cahokia mounds. Source: Mikels Skele, Archaeology Laboratory, Southern Illinois University at Edwardsville.

about 80 miles in length and five in breadth"
(Brackenridge 1962 [1814]:186). This region had been
named the American Bottom because the most intensive settlement there had been by Americans after the
Revolutionary War. The French had earlier settled in
the southern end of the American Bottom but not intensively in the central or northern portions. Today,
the American Bottom is defined as the Mississippi
floodplain from Alton, Illinois, just above the mouth
of the Missouri River, southward to the town of
Chester, Illinois, just below the mouth of the Kaskaskia
River (Figures 1.1 and 1.2).

These bottomlands were first formed by the erosional action of glacial torrents thousands of years ago.
The deeply cut valley was then built up and filled with
rich alluvial sediment by the varying course of the Mississippi River under the impact of the waters of the
Missouri and Illinois rivers, which join the Mississippi
at the north end of the American Bottom.

After crossing the Mississippi, Brackenridge started
on foot toward the monks' settlement, a journey of
several miles. He noted that the area around Illinois
Town was a very wet, swampy lowland. Fortunately
there was a wide ridge along the southern bank of
Cahokia Creek. Along this ridge ran the main trail of
communication from the banks of the Mississippi to
the interior of the American Bottom. For hundreds,
even thousands, of years this ridge supported foot traffic along the edge of Cahokia Creek and across the
swampy west half of the American Bottom.

As Brackenridge walked toward the northeast
along the ridge, undoubtedly along the route of what
is now called Collinsville Road or U.S. Highway 40,
he noted changes in his surroundings. Less than a mile
from Illinois Town the land to the southeast of Cahokia
Creek changed from swampy lowlands to prairie. For
great distances the landscape was made up of waving
grasslands interspersed with oxbow lakes, the remnants of ancient river channels when the Mississippi
flowed closer to the eastern bluffs. On the edges of
these lakes and sloughs willow trees and other lowland vegetation grew. The trees along these sloughs
and the creek beds dotted the landscape and were is-
lands of relief in vistas of waving prairie grasses.

To the northwest of Cahokia Creek the swampy
vegetation continued. In that area were many oxbow
lakes as well—the remnants of more recent
meanderings of the Mississippi channel. In the distance
to the east Brackenridge saw the bluffs rising more than
24 meters (80 feet) above the valley floor. The land at
the base of these bluffs was somewhat higher than the
prairie lands, the result of erosion from the bluff above
and the dropping of sediments by the creeks whose

channels were incised deeply into the bluff and wan-
dered through the bottoms to the Mississippi. This
gently sloping surface was covered with a mixed for-
est of oak, hickory, maple, and other deciduous trees.
The rim of the bluff top was covered with cedar trees,
and behind that the massive upland prairies of Illinois began (Brackenridge 1962 [1814]:186-187).

As he went along he probably encountered small
tracts of land where the natural vegetation had been
cleared and farmers were eking out subsistence from
the land. Many of these land claims went back to the
French settlement of the area. Other than this disturbance of the environment, the main difference between
the early nineteenth century and the time of the peak
of the Cahokia site as a thriving community was the
emptiness of the land. In the twelfth century this had
been a densely peopled area with a city, several towns,
and numerous villages and farmsteads scattered over
the countryside. At the time of Brackenridge's visit
only the mounds and scattered debris remained as
reminders of this splendid past.

A short distance from the Mississippi River, after
about 15 minutes of walking by his estimate,
Brackenridge came upon his first group of mounds,
now called the East St. Louis group (Figure 1.3). This
group, now leveled and buried under late nineteenth-
century landfill, numbered 45 mounds in a semicircle
about a mile in extent (Brackenridge 1962 [1814]:187).

There were other mounds spaced at regular intervals along the ridge between the Illinois Town group
and Cahokia (Figure 1.4). Thus the two groups were
connected by an avenue of communication and
mounds, and they may be considered one community
extending all the way from the east bank of the Mississippi to the main Cahokia site several miles away.
The mounds in St. Louis were directly across the river
and so may be included in the metropolitan area of
Cahokia at the time these groups were inhabited and
thriving towns.

Upon arrival at the Cahokia mounds, about four
miles beyond the East St. Louis group, Brackenridge
went immediately to the largest mound of all, now
known as Monks Mound: "When I arrived at the foot
of the principal mound, I was struck with a degree of
astonishment, not unlike that which is experienced in
contemplating the Egyptian pyramids. *What a stupendous pile of earth!*" (1962 [1814]:187, emphasis added).

His enthusiasm and excitement were apparently
not shared by others, because on July 25, 1813, in a
letter to Thomas Jefferson, he said: "When I examined
it in 1811, I was astonished that this stupendous monument of antiquity should have been unnoticed by any
traveler: I afterwards published an account in the

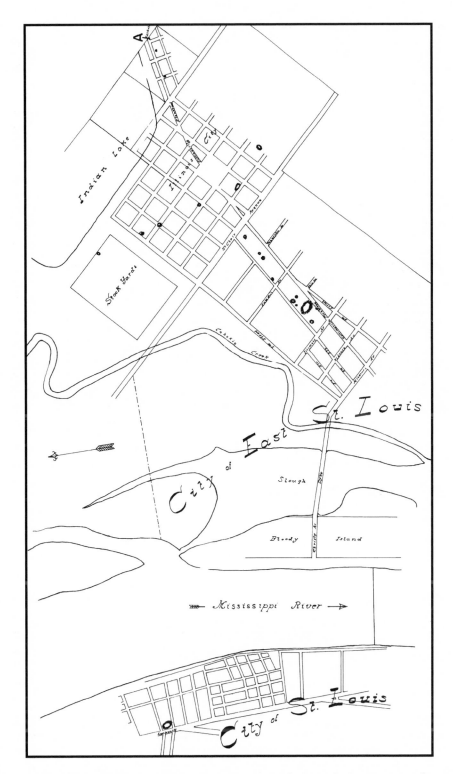

Figure 1.3. A reconstruction of the map of 17 of the mounds in the East St. Louis mound group commissioned by J. J. R. Patrick about 1880. The original map is curated by the Missouri Historical Society in St. Louis. The original was photographed in sections by James Anderson and Melvin Fowler in 1967. This figure is a tracing of the enlarged photographs. The mound on the St. Louis side of the Mississippi River is the so-called Big Mound, the largest mound in the St. Louis mound group. "A" marks the point of connection with Figure 1.4. Source: Missouri Historical Society and the Archaeological Research Laboratory, University of Wisconsin-Milwaukee.

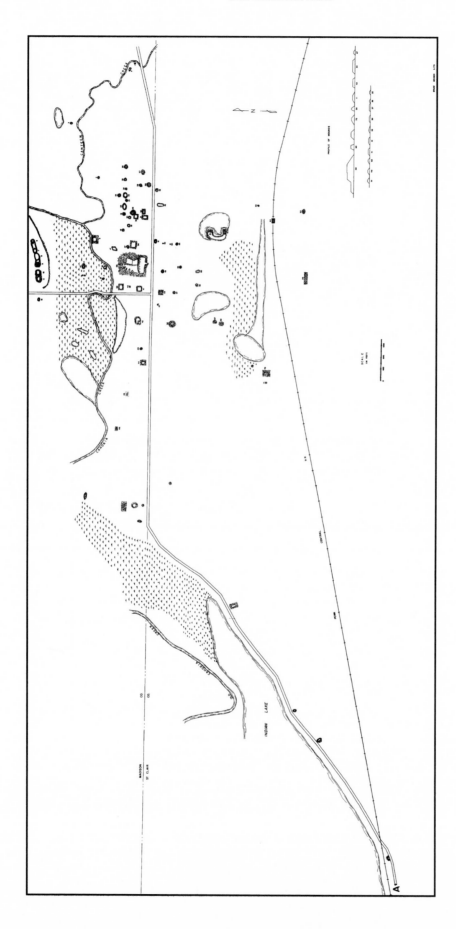

Figure 1.4.   A reconstruction of the complete map of the Cahokia site made by J. J. R. Patrick in 1876, including the series of mounds along the south bank of Indian Lake between the East St. Louis group and the Cahokia mounds. The road indicated on the map is probably the route followed by Brackenridge on his tour from St. Louis to Cahokia. The section on the right-hand page shows the main Cahokia site with Monks Mound in the upper center. The "A" in the lower left is the point of connection with Figure 1.3. Source: Missouri Historical Society and the Archaeological Research Laboratory, University of Wisconsin–Milwaukee.

newspapers of St. Louis, detailing its dimensions, describing its form, position &c. but this, which I . . . considered a discovery, attracted no notice" (1813:155).

Brackenridge also visited the monks' settlement, which was on a nearby mound, but he found them uncommunicative as a result of their vows. Nevertheless, he peered into their cottages and observed their industry (1962 [1814]:287-288).

Seeing the Cahokia archaeological site at a time before any intensive agriculture was practiced in the area, Brackenridge described it in a condition very similar to that in which it may have been when the last precolumbian Native American occupied it; based upon the size of trees growing on the big mound, Brackenridge estimated this had to have been more than 200 years earlier. The mounds must have been only slightly altered.

He visited the many other mounds and walked over the area between them. As he did, he noted "small elevations" at "regular distances from each other" (1962 [1814]:188). Near these he observed quantities of flint, animal bone, and broken pottery. The small elevations he referred to were house mounds or platforms. Thus, in 1811, the locations of the dwellings of the last inhabitants were clearly visible to him, as were the fragments of their tools and utensils. These surface irregularities have long since been plowed away, and the relics visible to Brackenridge have been pulverized or collected by nineteenth-century avocational archaeologists.

The "discoverer" of Cahokia came to the conclusion that "a very populous town had once existed here, similar to those of Mexico" and that it could not have been "the work of thinly scattered tribes" (1962 [1814]:188). In fact, he saw the entire American Bottom as "filled with habitations and villages" and concluded that "if the city of Philadelphia and its environs, were deserted, there would not be more numerous traces of human existence" (1962 [1814]:186).

Brackenridge is the discoverer of the Cahokia mounds in the sense that he was the first to call them to public attention by writing articles for the St. Louis newspapers, sending long letters to his colleagues, and publishing articles in scientific journals of his time. The early French explorers of the area did not note the existence of these mounds. Later French settlers placed a chapel and a trading post on and near the big mound (Walthall and Benchley 1987). In fact, the mound carried the name L'Abbe as a result for a number of years prior to Brackenridge's visit and the presence of the Trappist monks.

Surveyors working for the U.S. government had begun their platting of the American Bottom a few years before Brackenridge's time (Messenger 1808:76).

In laying in and correcting township and section lines they came very close to the large mounds and, in fact, described some of them in their field notes. The notes were not plotted until some years after Brackenridge's visit. However, the land surveyors in St. Louis may well have informed him of the mound locations (Brackenridge 1962 [1814]:184).

Today, the route taken by Brackenridge is called Collinsville Road, and Interstate 55-70 runs parallel to it. Illinois Town has changed its name to East St. Louis, and development has obliterated the first group of mounds that Brackenridge visited. Instead of the prairies, groves of trees, and scattered farmsteads, a modern traveler views intensively cultivated areas of horseradish and corn, oil refineries, factories, shopping centers, and many towns and villages. The landscape has been totally altered in the nearly 180 years since Brackenridge made his discovery.

Most of the traces of the Native American heritage are also gone. The house platforms, "the great number of mounds," and "the astonishing quantity" of artifacts and debris from the past have largely been leveled, plowed away, or covered over. However, some of the mounds, including the largest, remain along the banks of Cahokia Creek. Fortunately this central group was made into a park by the state of Illinois in the 1920s, and in 1982 it was placed on the United Nations World Heritage Site list. The expansion of the park area, now officially known as Cahokia Mounds State Historic Site (Figure 1.5), the archaeological investigations that have gone on, and the excellent program of interpretation and preservation conducted by the state of Illinois now guarantee that this part of Brackenridge's discovery will be available for generations to come.

Persons traveling along Interstate 55-70 might note an unusual hill close to the south side of the highway (Figure 1.6). This "hill" is well manicured and very flat on top. It is actually Monks Mound, the largest precolumbian earthwork in North America and the central focus of the largest Native American city north of central Mexico. Monks Mound was probably a large platform, built and renewed over a period of two centuries, upon which the rulers of the prehistoric city lived.

While it might not be possible to experience completely the awe and wonder that impressed Brackenridge when he first saw this "stupendous pile of earth," the twentieth-century visitor cannot help but be amazed by this prodigious earthwork and its surrounding evidences of precolumbian splendor.

Monks Mound is often referred to in superlative terms and rightfully so. It is the largest precolumbian structure north of Mexico. Only the Great Pyramid at

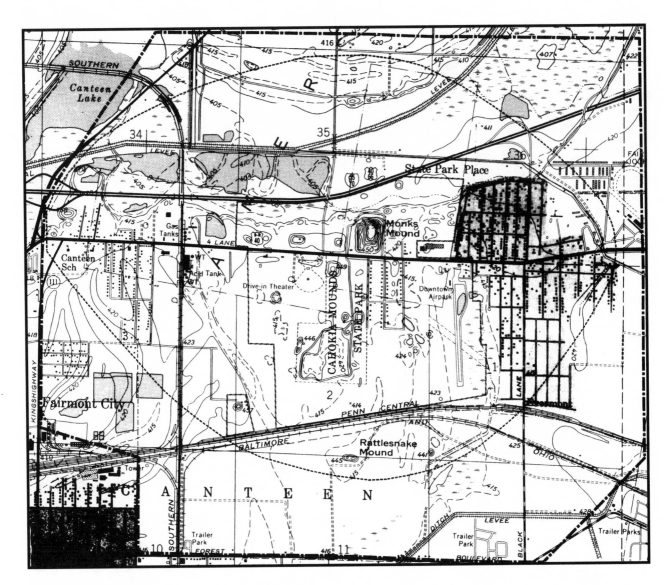

Figure 1.5.   Map of the Cahokia site showing the boundaries of the federally designated National Historic
Landmark (—·—) and the extent of mound distribution (------). Courtesy of Robert Koepke,
Southern Illinois University at Edwardsville.

Cholula in the state of Puebla, Mexico, and the Pyramid of the Sun at Teotihuacan near Mexico City are larger. Like Monks Mound, most of the Mexican structures were built over a period of decades or centuries in a series of stages and cycles of renewal and enlargement. Cholula and the Pyramid of the Sun were built of rubble, stone, adobe, and debris, but each stage was capped with a fine masonry facade. Monks Mound was built totally of earth mined from nearby borrow pits. It is certainly the largest earthen structure in all of North America built before Columbus set sail.

A first-time visitor, or even the experienced archaeologist, is often overwhelmed trying to grasp the enormity of this mound. While the dimensions are but numbers, they may help to convey a feeling for its monumentality. Monks Mound is nearly 305 meters (1,000 feet) long and 236 meters (775 feet) wide. It covers an area of nearly 72,000 square meters or 7.2 hectares (over 17 acres). The mound ascends in a series of terraces, and the highest level is about 30.5 meters (100 feet) above the surrounding ground. It has been estimated that over a 200-year period nearly 624,000 cubic meters (over 22 million cubic feet) of earth were used in its construction (details of these measurements and those made by many different investigators are given in Chapter 5).

The areal extent of Monks Mound itself is larger than many entire archaeological sites contemporary

Figure 1.6. Aerial view of Monks Mound looking toward the northwest. Source: Cahokia Mounds Museum, Illinois Historic Preservation Agency.

with Cahokia. Certainly the volume of earth used in Monks Mound far exceeds that in all the mounds of many contemporary sites.

Another way of attempting to understand this huge earthwork is to step back and view it from a distance, perhaps from the south, and let your imagination go to work. Recreate the mound as it might have been about A.D. 1100, when prehistoric Cahokia was at its peak of grandeur. It probably was much more uniform in shape than now; slumping, erosion, and the destruction caused by trees, grazing cattle, the Trappist monks and others growing crops on its terraces, and the eighteenth-century French chapel built on the southwest corner have all altered its contours. It is possible that the sides and slopes were kept clean by the Cahokians and plastered with special clay mixtures, the Cahokia equivalent to the masonry used in Mexico, which may or may not have been decorated. Looming at the top was a huge building, 30 meters (100 feet) long and 12 meters (40 feet) wide. The crest of the thatched roof may have extended nearly 10 meters (30 feet) into the air. Whether palace or temple can be left to your mind's eye, but it definitely was the central edifice and dominating feature of the ancient city. On the south side of the mound was a stairway, not unlike that which is there today, leading from ground level to the topmost

terrace. Since Monks Mound was undoubtedly the central focus of the city, there was probably a steady stream of people going up and down the stairway to carry out business relating to management of the city, its foreign relations, and public ceremonies on appropriate days.

The big mound is, however, only part of the total, albeit the largest and probably the most important part. Surrounding it are many earthen mounds—the most recent counts indicate over 100—spaced over an area of 5 square miles (ca. 1,400 hectares or 3,300 acres). Since much of that area today is covered with subdivisions, factories, and farms, it is difficult to envision what vista this may have presented in the past. Gone are a large number of the mounds, the residential platforms, and the surface debris "everywhere dug up, or found on the surface of the ground with a thousand other appearances" (Brackenridge 1962 [1814]:186).

An artist reconstructs the city of ancient Cahokia from a bird's-eye view (frontispiece). A visitor to the area might approximate this by climbing the stairs to the top of Monks Mound, 30 meters above the surrounding plain. Looking out over the panorama of that portion of the American Bottom, one must again in the mind's eye ignore recent human activity to imagine the town as it was in the prehistoric period.

The first impression is of clusters of mounds of various sizes and shapes. These mounds are uncluttered and surfaced like the central mound. Some are rectangular platforms with thatched structures on top. These buildings are the residences of subordinates and kin to the ruler of Cahokia. Others may be mortuary storage buildings or charnel houses. Other mounds are conical, the burial mounds or elite cemeteries of the community.

The mounds are organized around plazas or open areas. There are many of these. The largest open space is just to the south of Monks Mound. Around this plaza are some of the largest mounds of the community, including elite residences and the largest conical mound. These in turn are surrounded by a large wall or palisade. The area inside this wall is about 83 hectares (205 acres). Beyond the wall, to the north, south, east, and west, are smaller mound-plaza clusters occupied by chiefs related to the ruler of Cahokia or people from distant areas who have come to take advantage of the boom times Cahokia is enjoying.

Scattered outside the wall are numerous ponds. A particularly large one is just south of the palisade. These are the borrow pits from which the Cahokians scooped the soil for construction of the mounds.

Everywhere there are people carrying burdens; cultivating gardens; preparing meals; striking a bargain for some goods from far away; conducting ceremonial dances; playing games with either sacred or gambling intent, or both; and, in short, living their daily lives in the metropolis. Including those inside their houses, or visiting and trading in neighboring towns, or cultivating more distant large fields of maize, there are tens of thousands.

Archaeologists are attempting to document and refine this picture of ancient Cahokia using the scraps of debris still remaining in conjunction with the tools of modern science. Even though they are confined to studying the remnants of the garbage of the once-thriving city, their incredulousness is akin to Brackenridge's with each project undertaken and each bit of new data uncovered or insight gained.

There are many reasons for this. One of course is the almost overwhelming immensity of the site. No other archaeological complex in the United States comes close to its size and extent. Size alone is not sufficient to incite our amazement. Size is but a reflection of the complexity of the social order that built and governed the community. It is this social complexity that intrigues archaeologists and motivates much of the research directed at understanding what Cahokia was and the processes that caused it to arise in the American Bottom.

An important hypothesis of anthropologists is that a major transformation took place in the long course of human social development from village-oriented folk cultures to city-centered political states. This has been called the "urban revolution." Studies of the processes of this basic revolution in societal values and organization have been carried out in many areas of the world. In the Western Hemisphere studies of this type have focused on Peru and Mexico, where two of the world's pristine civilizations developed. Several explanations for the urban revolution have been offered. Among these are ecological, technological, and ideational or religious explanations. A once popular, but greatly oversimplified, explanation for such change is the migration of people or the diffusion of ideas from single centers of origin.

Although Cahokia may never have developed to the complexity of the Aztecs and Maya in Middle America or the Incas in Peru, it is an example of the independent evolution of a very complex society. Detailed research on the nature of Cahokia's social, political, and economic organization and the development of ideas to answer the question "why" should offer a case history for comparison with other studies. In such a manner our understanding of the total range of the human way can be enhanced.

This book is an attempt to summarize and describe the significant features of the Cahokia Mounds State Historic Site. It summarizes previous investigations, describes some documents that allow us to understand prehistoric Cahokia, presents an atlas of the site's major physical features, and offers an interpretation of prehistoric Cahokia. The author hopes this will provide all interested persons—tourists, avocational and professional archaeologists, hobbyists, and anyone with a curiosity about our Native American heritage—a basic framework to examine this most unusual and significant archaeological zone.

INTRODUCTION TO CAHOKIA ARCHAEOLOGY

This atlas is intended for professional archaeologists and nonarchaeologists interested in this unique prehistoric site. Like all scientific disciplines, archaeology has its own language of terms and jargon. In order to make this volume more accessible to nonarchaeologists, such jargon has been avoided whenever possible, but some background discussion of how archaeologists go about studying and interpreting the past is also useful.

Like people everywhere, the Indians of North America divided themselves into different groups based on cultural and ethnic identities. When Europeans and their American descendants came into contact with native inhabitants on this continent, they began applying names to these groups that they saw as different tribes, nations, confederacies, and the like. These names were generally, although not always specifically, congruent with how the Indians perceived their own ethnically diverse world.

Although archaeologists have gained more knowledge about the precolumbian history of North America, they have found it impossible to connect known historic tribes with archaeologically known ones. As in other parts of the world, American Indians have undergone numerous changes in culture and technology over the approximately 12,000 years that they have inhabited the continent and moved over its expanse. Therefore, archaeologists have developed various taxonomic systems to classify prehistoric times and people.

The most common system used today in eastern North America divides prehistory into a series of major periods (Table 1.1) and into local phases within periods (see Figure 1.7 for a summary of phases and other classifications that have been applied to Cahokia).

TABLE 1.1
Archaeological Periods in the American Bottom Region

Period	Time Range
Historic	A.D. 1600-present
Oneota	A.D. 1400-1600
Mississippian	A.D. 1000-1400
Emergent Mississippian	A.D. 800-1000
Woodland	
Late Woodland	A.D. 300-800
Middle Woodland	150 B.C.-A.D. 300
Early Woodland	500-150 B.C.
Archaic	ca. 8000-500 B.C.

The most important periods at Cahokia are Late Woodland, Emergent Mississippian, and Mississippian. During the Patrick phase of the Late Woodland period between about A.D. 600-800, large, permanent villages were established on the floodplain in the American Bottom. Subsistence for the growing population was centered on the abundant animal resources in the area and the cultivation of various crops such as sunflower, squash, and several other plants native to the area.

Population size and community complexity continued to increase during the Emergent Mississippian period between A.D. 800-1000. For the first time corn became an important part of the diet. As the agricultural system intensified and the population grew, social organization also became increasingly complex. Many of the mound complexes in the American Bottom may have been started during this period. However, it was the Mississippian period, between A.D. 1000-1400, that saw the full florescence of the complex society that gave rise to the many mounds and farming communities in and around Cahokia. The developments at Cahokia also spread their influence to large areas of the midwestern and southeastern United States.

The mounds at Cahokia probably served a variety of functions. They can generally be classified into three main types: flat-topped mounds that usually have square or rectangular bases; round, conical mounds; and oval, ridge-top mounds. Much information has been obtained about the contents and structure of many mounds, and this information is presented in detail in the mound descriptions in Chapters 4-7 and summarized in Chapters 9 and 10 on the organization of Cahokia.

Many names and numbering systems have been applied to the Cahokia mounds over the years. The numbering system used in this atlas is based on that developed by John J. R. Patrick, who in 1876 produced the first accurate and detailed map of Cahokia. Additional numbers have been given to mounds that were not noted by Patrick. The informal names that have been applied to some mounds and groups of mounds are also sometimes used in the atlas, and a full list of mound names and numbers is presented in Appendix 3.

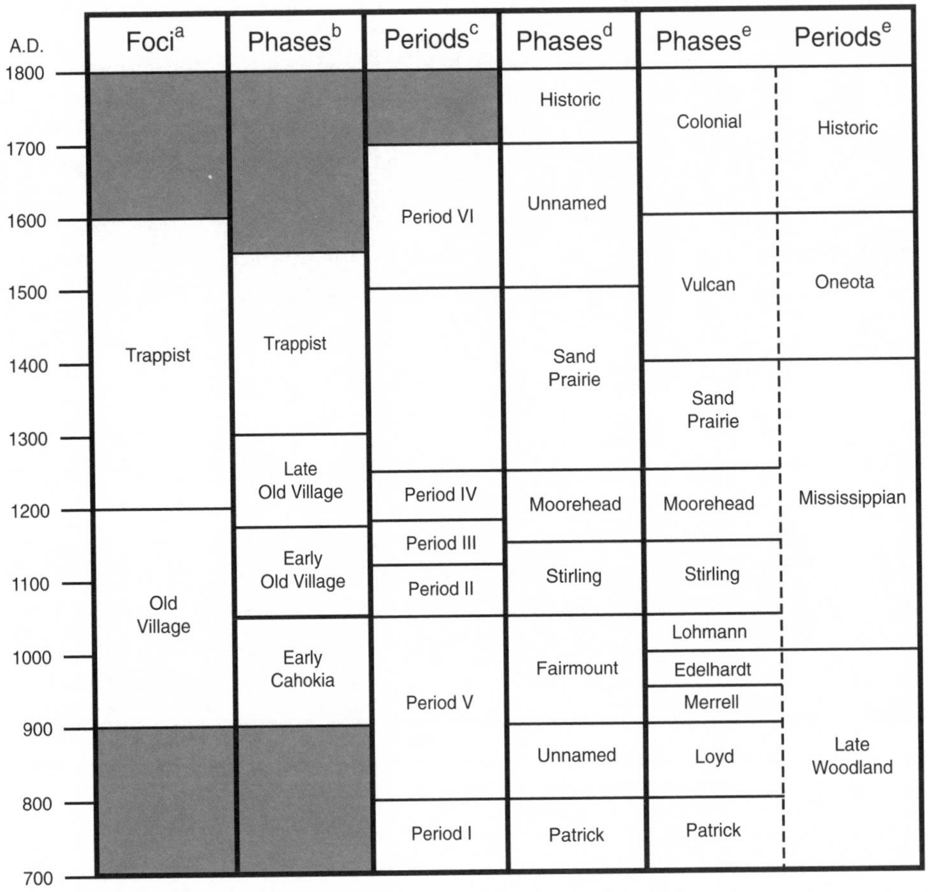

A.D.	Foci[a]	Phases[b]	Periods[c]	Phases[d]	Phases[e]	Periods[e]
1800				Historic	Colonial	Historic
1700						
1600			Period VI	Unnamed		
1500	Trappist	Trappist			Vulcan	Oneota
1400				Sand Prairie		
1300		Late Old Village			Sand Prairie	Mississippian
1200			Period IV	Moorehead	Moorehead	
	Old Village	Early Old Village	Period III	Stirling	Stirling	
1100			Period II			
1000		Early Cahokia	Period V	Fairmount	Lohmann	Late Woodland
					Edelhardt	
					Merrell	
900				Unnamed	Loyd	
800			Period I	Patrick	Patrick	
700						

a. Griffin 1949
b. Hall 1966
c. O'Brien 1972a
d. Fowler and Hall 1972
e. Bareis and Porter 1984

Figure 1.7. Archaeological phases at Cahokia

2

HISTORY OF INVESTIGATIONS

French exploration of the Illinois Country commenced in 1673 when Père Jacques Marquette and Louis Jolliet entered what is now Illinois via the Mississippi River. The journals Marquette kept of his travels have provided a wealth of information on the lower Illinois River bottom, but nowhere does he mention the mounds or the Indian settlement in the area now known as Cahokia Mounds State Historic Site.

In 1682, just nine years after Marquette and Jolliet's expedition, Tamaroa and Cahokia Indians, tribes in the Illinois Confederacy, were living on the banks of the Mississippi below the mouth of the Illinois River. The number of Cahokia Indians is not known, but the Tamaroa had a village of 180 cabins. Later these groups moved near the French settlement of Cahokia (Walthall and Benchley 1987), a still-extant town about 14 kilometers (9 miles) south of the Cahokia mounds. As early as 1660 the Jesuit Relations speak of a large nation of "Ilinouek living on the banks of the great river" (Hair 1866:9-10). However, this statement probably refers to the Kaskaskia village located near LaSalle, Illinois (Brown 1961). One may infer from these tantalizing bits of information that the large Indian population at the Cahokia site and in the American Bottom had dissipated by the end of the seventeenth century.

The earliest known map of the Cahokia area was made by Gen. George Collot, who in 1796 undertook a journey to study the western United States (Figure 2.1). His map indicates a cluster of "Indian Ancient Tombs" about 11 kilometers (7 miles) south of the French settlement of Cahokia. Those mounds are believed to be the group now known as the Pulcher site (Fowler 1969a).

No mounds of any kind directly east of the present location of St. Louis were noted on Collot's map, although the map extends to the eastern bluffs flanking the American Bottom. However, a prairie area lying between two creeks is indicated near the general loca-

tion of the Cahokia mounds. According to the map, no trail ran through that area. It appears that this section of the American Bottom was off the beaten track. During the French period, the main routes were the channel of the Mississippi River and the road that extended from the village of Cahokia south to Kaskaskia by way of Prairie du Rocher and Fort de Chartres. That road undoubtedly continued from the village of Cahokia northward to the river and on to St. Louis. The Cahokia mound site was presumably missed by the French because it was in a wilderness area and the Indian inhabitants had already abandoned the site.

The land around the Cahokia mounds was claimed by families of French descent in the early part of the nineteenth century. The area of Monks Mound was part of Survey No. 628, Claim No. 133, which was the property of "Nicholas Garrot [more often spelled Jarrot] in writ of Gene B. Gonville alias Rapolet" (sketch map made in 1809 found in government survey record for Madison County, Illinois). According to Hair (1866:32), this land was affirmed to Jarrot on December 31, 1809. Ownership of that tract can be traced through land records in the Madison County courthouse through to its purchase by Thomas Ramey in 1864. Much of the land in the vicinity of Monks Mound remained in Ramey ownership until the state of Illinois purchased it in the 1920s.

Public attention first focused on the Cahokia mounds area when Henry Brackenridge visited the site in 1811. Brackenridge toured the Mississippi Valley under a commission from Thomas Jefferson to map, describe, and explore the area. Brackenridge published several descriptions of the general site and of Monks Mound. As far as can be determined, he collected nothing from the site, nor are there any records of his work other than the published records.

When Brackenridge was in the area, a mound near Monks Mound was occupied by the Trappist monastery. "The step, or apron, [for Monks Mound] has been

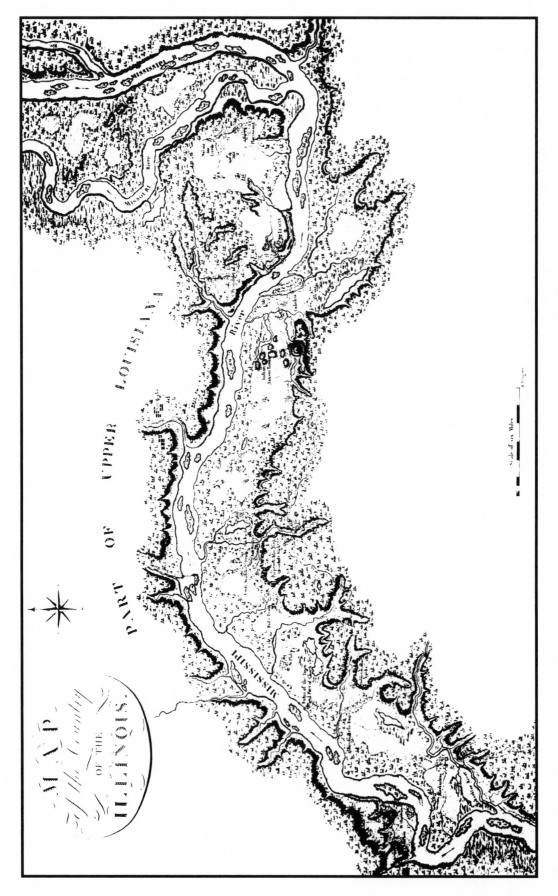

Figure 2.1. A portion of the Collot map of the Mississippi River valley near St. Louis drawn at the end of the eighteenth century. The "Ancient Indian Tombs" south of the French village of Cahokia are probably the mounds at the Pulcher site (see Figure 1.2). The location of the Cahokia mound group is shown as an open area between two creeks, possibly Spring Lake and Indian Lake (see Figure 1.2). Note that the north arrow points west.

used as a kitchen garden, by the Monks of La Trappe, settled near this, and the top is sowed with wheat" (Brackenridge 1962 [1814]:187-188).

> Having spoken of the Trappist in my account of the mounds in the American bottom, I here subjoin a description which was published in the St. Louis paper, and which contrary to my wishes, I have understood gave great offense to the good fathers. The buildings which the Trappist at present occupy, are merely temporary: they consist of four or five cabins, on a mound about fifty yards [?] high, and which is perhaps one hundred and fifty feet square. Their other buildings, cribs, stables, etc., ten or fifteen in number, are scattered about on the plain below. I was informed that they intended to build on the terrace of the large mound; this will produce a fine effect, it will be seen five or six miles across the plain, and from some points of view ten or twelve. They have about one hundred acres enclosed in three different fields, including the large mound, and several others. . . . I ascended the mound which contains the dwellings [of the monks]. This is nearly 25 feet in height: the ascent rendered easy by a slanting road. I wandered about here for some time, in expectation of being noticed by someone; it was in vain that I nodded to the reverend Fathers, or peeped in to their cabins (1962 [1814]:287-288, query added).

The Trappist monks reportedly moved to the Cahokia mounds area in April 1809. They settled on approximately 400 acres of land allegedly given to them by Jarrot, although the land was not officially in the title of Jarrot until December of that year. It is probable, however, that he had a claim to the land prior to its being officially recorded and thus was able to strike a deal with the monks for use of the land. Apparently this was not a satisfactory place for the monks, because they eventually abandoned the area "after considerable reduction in numbers by death" (DeHass 1869:297).

Scholars have debated which of the mounds the monks occupied. Almost all references specifically note that they did not occupy Monks Mound but used it as a gardening place. The only exception is a description by John Francis Snyder:

> In 1808 [sic] a small colony of Monks of the Order of LaTrappe secured from Major Nicholas Jarrot, of Cahokia, a tract of 400 acres of land, on part of which the big mound is situated, with the view of establishing one of their monasteries there. Preparatory thereto they built two log cabins on the broad terrace at the south side of the Mound, and a few other cabins on the small mounds nearby. Owing to the unhealthy malarial climate, and other causes, their colonizing enterprise proved a failure, and in March 1819, those

of them who had not died sold the land, and returned to France. . . . [T. A. Hill] at once built a dwelling house on the terrace where the principal Trappist cabin formerly stood, and sometime later, dug a well on that terrace almost down to its base, nearly thirty feet (1917:257-258).

The T. A. Hill, also known as Amos Hill, referred to bought the property sometime after the monks left and built a house on Monks Mound. The well to which Snyder refers is on the western slope of Monks Mound. Snyder, however, is the only author to mention the monks' building on Monks Mound. Snyder may have based his discussions on the writings of an earlier investigator:

> The buildings which . . . [the Monks] occupied were never of a very durable character, but consisted of about half a dozen large structures of logs, on the summit of the mound about fifty yards to the right of the largest. This is twenty feet in height, and upward of a hundred and fifty feet square; a well dug by the Trappist is yet to be seen, though the whole mound is now buried in thickets. Their out buildings, stables, granaries, etc., which were numerously scattered about on the plain below. Subsequently they erected an extensive structure upon the terrace of the principal mound, and cultivated its soil for a kitchen-garden, while the area of the summit was sown with wheat (Flagg 1838:169-170).

Whereas Brackenridge suggested that the monks planned to build on Monks Mound, Flagg stated that they actually built there. Flagg, however, did not witness the monks' presence at the site. I prefer to accept the descriptions of the eyewitness Brackenridge and conclude that the monks did not build their monastery on the big mound, but on a nearby mound. The name "Monks," however, was given to the largest mound.

Most early writers, both eyewitnesses and later investigators or historians, suggest that the mound upon which the monks built was just west of Monks Mound (Featherstonaugh 1844:267; Flagg 1838; Latrobe 1835:182; Putnam and Patrick 1880:470). Most descriptions of the mound on which the monks built are rather vague and cannot be used reliably to locate their dwellings. The only person who is specific about the location of the "true" Monks Mound is David I. Bushnell, who in both of his publications on Cahokia refers to the mound immediately southwest of the big mound (1904:9, 1922:97). He gives measurements for this mound as "25 feet in height, its base line from north to south was 180 feet and from east to west two hundred feet" (1922:97).

Those dimensions and descriptions correspond to the mound now designated Mound 48, and Bushnell's measurements seem to come directly from a map made by Dr. John J. R. Patrick in 1876 (see Chapter 3). There is something to be said for his description and location of the mound. Mound 48 has a large enough surface area that it could have accommodated the cabins the monks reportedly built. Evidence of a roadway up the south side of Mound 48 corresponds with Brackenridge's description. The road, however, may be the result of more recent construction.

Some earlier references suggest that the mound on which the monks lived was directly west of Monks Mound. This would be Mound 41, which has a much smaller surface area than Mound 48, and with the monks' cabins it would have been very crowded. There is no evidence of a road on this mound, so it is unlikely the monks lived there.

The problem of where the monks lived could be solved by judicious archaeological excavation on the flat surfaces of both Mounds 41 and 48. The surface of Mound 48 was, however, disturbed by construction of a farmhouse.

The monks also disturbed the surface of the mound by digging into "the ground to lay the foundations of their homes, . . . [and] found many bones, idols, arms and materials of war, and many other Indian antiquities" (McAdams 1907:40-41). The monks' collection of antiquities, unfortunately, has not survived.

After Brackenridge, the next record of the Cahokia mounds was made by members of the Maj. Stephen H. Long expedition up the Missouri River in 1819. Its goal was to explore the upper Mississippi River valley. During a layover period in St. Louis to repair their steamboat, Long's party made several visits to the mounds at Cahokia. They also prepared a rather detailed map of the mounds. Of the Cahokia site, Major Long has this to say:

> In the prairies of Illinois, opposite St. Louis, are numbers of large mounds. We counted seventy-five in the course of a walk of about five miles, which brought us to the hill a few years since occupied by the monks of LaTrappe. This enormous mound lies nearly from north to south, but it is so overgrown with bushes and weeds, interlaced with briers and vines, that we were unable to obtain an accurate account of its dimensions (1905 [1823]:120).

There is no evidence that the Long expedition collected any artifacts or prepared any general maps of the village at the Cahokia site.

Several writers commented on Cahokia in the period 1820-1860, but none provided much detailed information (e.g., Flint 1826; Latrobe 1835). J. C. Wild leaves us the best account of the area. His 1841 description of the mounds is most noted for its drawing of Monks Mound and of several other mounds viewed from atop Mound 51 (Figure 2.2):

> From the surface of the small mound from which the view was taken, the artist, and the writer, in the space of a few minutes, picked up about half a peck of broken bones and pieces of pottery and flint. One of the bones, which is nearly perfect, is evidently the arm bone of a human being (1841:52-53).

Wild's drawing gives us an excellent view not only of Monks Mound as it was in the early part of the nineteenth century but also of other mounds that have since been altered and reduced by extensive cultivation. One of these is Mound 56, the Jesse Ramey Mound, which is located about 250 meters (76 feet) south of Monks Mound. His illustration shows this as a high mound with a ridge top. Just south of this mound Wild illustrates what is now called Fox Mound (Mound 60). Other mounds of less specific identification can be seen in the background.

During the same period, Prince Maximilian de Wied conducted an expedition to the upper Missouri River area. The artist Karl Bodmer, an expedition member, made many paintings and drawings on this trip; most were of Indians such as the Mandans of the Missouri River area. Included in his drawings were many landscapes composed while he moved up the Mississippi River from New Orleans to St. Louis. On the return trip the group again stopped at St. Louis, and the artist sketched the nearby mounds. Bodmer's illustrations do not have the vertical exaggeration found in Wild's drawings; rather they represent the mounds from a natural perspective. One of Bodmer's sketches is of Monks Mound viewed from the east (Figure 2.3, top). It appears to have been drawn from the top of a mound, possibly Mound 31. The drawing shows the upper terraces of Monks Mound as well as the first terrace extending to the south. Several buildings depicted on the upper terrace were probably those occupied by Amos Hill, who had moved onto Monks Mound a few years before.

Another of Bodmer's drawings (Figure 2.3, bottom) is a view looking directly south from the first terrace of Monks Mound. Bodmer's sketch illustrates many of the same mounds as Wild's albeit from a different angle. The Jesse Ramey Mound (Mound 56) is drawn with much more regular contours than in Wild's drawing, but he also shows it with a ridged rather than a platform top. Fox Mound is almost obliterated from view by the height of Mound 56. Other mounds are

Figure 2.2. The Wild drawing of the central area of the Cahokia site as viewed from the west (Wild 1841:Plate 10). The artist and his companion are on Mound 51 (Persimmon Mound). Monks Mound is to the right with trees on it; the buildings on top may represent the residence of Amos Hill.

also shown in Bodmer's drawing. Bodmer depicted an area of open pastureland with cattle grazing under the shade of a few trees. Survey records indicate that this land was wet prairie, so these drawings may represent the area's natural state.

G. W. Featherstonhaugh visited the mounds at about the same time. He was greatly impressed with Monks Mound and included a drawing with his description (see Figure 5.1). He visited the owner, Amos Hill, who had constructed a house and garden plot on top of the mound. Hill had laid the foundation of his house on an eminence he found on the summit of his elevated territory, and according to Featherstonhaugh,

"upon digging into it found large human bones, with Indian pottery, stone axes and tomahawks" (1844:264-272).

Featherstonhaugh may have confused the location of Hill's house on the third terrace of Monks Mound with a small mound that was evidently on the southeast corner of the third terrace. Hill apparently had leveled this small mound, but his house was not constructed precisely in its location. Featherstonhaugh's drawing, in fact, is the only one that shows a small mound or conical eminence on the southeast corner of the third terrace.

Figure 2.3. Two drawings of Cahokia from the 1830s by Karl Bodmer: (top) Monks Mound from the east; (bottom) mounds to the south of Monks Mound. Source: Joslyn Art Museum, Omaha, Nebraska.

In the 1840s, Charles Dickens passed by Monks Mound during a visit to the United States. He was unimpressed and, in fact, was dismayed by the territory:

> Looming in the distance, as we rode along, was another of the ancient Indian burial-places, called the Monks' Mound; in memory of a body of fanatics of the order of LaTrappe, who founded a desolate convent there, many years ago, when there were no settlers within a thousand miles, and were all swept off by the pernicious climate: in which lamentable fatality, few rational people will suppose, perhaps, that society experienced any very severe deprivation (1842:131).

Several professional anthropologists visited the Cahokia mounds area beginning about 1860. The first was Dr. Charles Rau, a curator at the Smithsonian Institution in Washington, D.C. He noted evidence that ancient Indian habitation extended 1 mile (1.6 kilometers) east of Monks Mound and 6 miles (9.6 kilometers) west to the junction of Cahokia Creek and the Mississippi. His description indicates that Indians occupied an area from Monks Mound to the mouth of Cahokia Creek into what is now East St. Louis. It is probable that the entire ridge extending along the southern bank of Cahokia Creek into the East St. Louis area, which was also dotted with mounds, was inhabited and is one continuous archaeological zone.

Rau's report is particularly informative because he discovered a site in the American Bottom where prehistoric Indians manufactured pottery: "The locality to which I allude is the left bank of the Cahokia Creek at the northern extremity of Illinoistown, opposite St. Louis. At the point just mentioned the bank of the creek is somewhat high and steep, leaving only a small space for a path along the water" (1867:347).

Rau found abundant evidence of fired pottery. Since clay was available nearby for the manufacture of ceramics, he interpreted this as a manufacturing location. In 1869 Rau also published an article describing a cache of unused tools, 50 flint hoes, and 20 shovels found by workmen grading an extension to Sixth Street in East St. Louis (1869:402-405).

One of the more notable students of the Cahokia mounds area in the late 1800s was Dr. John J. R. Patrick of Belleville, Illinois. Patrick, as Warren K. Moorehead, himself an important figure in Cahokia archaeology, noted, was "one of the pioneers in Cahokia work" (Moorehead 1929:96; see also Warner and Beers 1874:96).

Patrick's major contribution to our knowledge of the Cahokia site was a detailed map of the locations and forms of the mounds made in the late 1870s (see Figures 1.4 and 3.1). Patrick also made many collections of artifacts from the Cahokia area by surface pickup and through some excavation. Patrick's map and his archaeological materials were donated to the Missouri Historical Society in 1891. The collections were carefully cataloged according to the standards of the day and have been very well maintained by the Missouri Historical Society. Many of these artifacts are labeled by county only (St. Clair or Madison County, Illinois), but much of this material is from the Cahokia site. Curiously, many of the items collected by Patrick reflect Late Mississippian occupation (see Figure 1.7), even though Late Mississippian artifacts have not been strongly represented in more recent excavations and archaeological collections. This is understandable when one realizes that most of the site's destruction occurred in the 1900s through extensive cultivation and construction of subdivisions and factories. The latest occupation of the Cahokia site by Mississippian peoples is probably now represented only in the upper levels, that is, in the cultivated zones of the area. Late Mississippian cultural remains were probably abundant in Patrick's time, but since then they have either been carried off by collectors or destroyed by cultivation. The data representing the Late Mississippian occupation of Cahokia, therefore, may be extant only in collections such as Patrick's.

During the 1880s, F. W. Putnam, an associate of the Peabody Museum of Harvard University, visited Monks Mound with Patrick. Together they produced a report on Cahokia for the *Twelfth Annual Report of the Peabody Museum*, which includes two illustrations of models of Monks Mound constructed by Patrick. One model illustrates the appearance of Monks Mound in 1879, and the other represents the two researchers' idea of the mound's original appearance. Cast-iron copies of these two models, both excellent reproductions, are in the Missouri Historical Society collection.

Putnam's and Patrick's reconstruction was the first to represent Monks Mound not with an irregular surface but as an even-sided mound. The worst error in these reconstructions is attributing a uniform second terrace to the west side of Monks Mound. Data that are discussed in the description of Monks Mound (Chapter 5) suggest that the second terrace was deliberately constructed as an irregular area. Resolution of the second terrace configuration can be made only by conducting detailed excavations to establish its prehistoric form and function.

During the 1880s and 1890s, William McAdams was the primary investigator of the Cahokia site. He conducted excavations and published several articles on the area. McAdams wrote the chapter "Antiquities" for the *History of Madison County, Illinois* (1882). He gave a detailed description of Monks Mound and published an engraving that shows details of the mound. The view includes the house on the fourth terrace and the well on the second terrace.

McAdams's most notable discovery was at the base of Monks Mound: "At the foot of the Cahokia temple [Monks Mound] we were so fortunate as to discover a sort of tomb or burial place and in size less than two rods square, amid the crumbling dust of near a score of human skeletons, we found about a hundred vessels of pottery in almost perfect condition" (1882:62).

In 1882 McAdams published a sketch map of the Cahokia site (see Figure 3.2). The map suggested the mounds' configurations and gave the heights of most mounds in his survey area. The map was probably made as part of McAdams's assignment by the Bureau of American Ethnology to explore and survey the Cahokia site.

A few years later McAdams worked with Cyrus Thomas to prepare a map published in the *12th Annual Report of the Bureau of Ethnology* (Thomas 1894:131-134). Like McAdams's earlier map, the Thomas map (see Figure 3.3) provided general locations of the mounds, suggested their forms, and indicated their heights. The map was apparently based upon McAdams' survey, as there is little evidence to indicate that Thomas visited the Cahokia site. There are serious differences, however, between the McAdams map of 1882 and the Thomas map of 1894 (these are discussed in Chapter 3).

Two years before Chicago's Columbian Exposition in 1893, McAdams and his son, Clark, were commissioned to collect materials and prepare the Illinois Archaeological Exhibit for the fair. They collected some items from the Cahokia area. A full report of this exhibit was written by William McAdams and published in *Report of the Illinois Board of World's Fair Commission-*

ers at the World's Columbian Exposition (1895:227-304). Clark McAdams inherited his father's collection and interest in Illinois archaeology, writing several articles about the Cahokia site and the Cahokia area (1907).

Another late nineteenth-century midwestern archaeologist was Rev. Stephen D. Peet, who for many years was editor of *The American Antiquarian*. He also edited a magazine called *Records of the Past*. A lengthy article by Peet entitled "The Great Cahokia Mound" appeared in *The American Antiquarian* in January 1891. Peet reported that shortly before he arrived at Cahokia, workmen digging drainage ditches had come across various artifacts, which they treated with little care. "The object which impressed us most was a sandstone tablet, which contained figures very much like those found upon the inscribed tablets taken from one of the mounds of the Etowah group in Georgia" (1891a:10) (Figure 2.4).

A drawing of this tablet was reproduced in *The American Antiquarian* (Peet 1891b:58-59). Later, in 1891 J. R. Sutter of Edwardsville, Illinois, wrote a letter published in the same journal (1891:351) stating that he now owned the tablet as well as other relics from Monks Mound. The tablet is now preserved by the Madison County Historical Society in Edwardsville, Illinois. The society has other materials from the Monks Mound area, some possibly from the Sutter collection.

After the turn of the century, Clark McAdams, working with Dr. Cyrus A. Peterson, prepared a map of the Cahokia area for private distribution (see Figure 3.5). The map also gave mound locations, general forms, and heights. It differed somewhat from the McAdams and the Thomas-McAdams maps published some 20 years earlier. In general, the heights are somewhat less than those noted on the earlier maps, suggesting that Clark McAdams and Peterson measured the heights of some of the mounds after they had been

Figure 2.4. The engraved sandstone tablet described by Peet in 1891.

plowed down. The Peterson-McAdams map was published in 1949 in the pamphlet *Cahokia Brought to Life*, edited by R. E. Grimm.

At the turn of the century, one of the most vigorous scientists studying the prehistory of Illinois was Dr. John Francis Snyder of Virginia, Illinois. Much of Snyder's writing dealt with the Cahokia mounds and the need to preserve the area. Snyder was born in 1830 on a farm south of the Cahokia site near present-day Dupo. The farmhouse was built on the edge of the major mound at what is known today as the Pulcher site. (In his mapping, Patrick refers to Pulcher as the Snyder's group.) Snyder spent much of his childhood wandering over the area observing the mounds and other remnants of prehistoric peoples. The area's history was a lifetime interest (Walton 1962).

Professionally, Snyder was trained both as a lawyer and as a medical doctor. He practiced medicine in Virginia, Illinois, although archaeology and history were his consuming interests. There is no evidence that Snyder conducted any excavations into the Cahokia mounds, but he is known to have excavated several other mounds in the Illinois River valley. Snyder's writings reveal that he was a careful scholar given to checking original sources of descriptions and summarizing the viewpoints of previous investigators. Many of Snyder's most important archaeological writings and those pertaining to Cahokia have been reprinted (Walton 1962).

One of Snyder's major concerns was preserving the mounds, and he actively promoted the state's involvement with the site. Snyder in particular strongly supported legislation to make the Cahokia area into a park. He was active in forming and sustaining an organization called The Monks of Cahokia, which had as one of its major goals the preservation of the Monks Mound area.

In the early 1900s, David I. Bushnell, Jr., representing the Peabody Museum of American Archaeology and Ethnology at Harvard University, made a detailed examination of the entire American Bottom area, publishing a 20-page report of descriptions of the major sites in the region (Bushnell 1904). Bushnell's report includes a map of the northern portion of the American Bottom illustrating the relationships of several mound groups, including those at Cahokia, East St. Louis, St. Louis, and the Mitchell site near Long Lake. The mounds are located as dots of different sizes on the map. Bushnell's map appears to be one of the more accurate early maps of the area.

Bushnell became affiliated with the Bureau of American Ethnology and in 1922 published another report that provided additional descriptions of these sites, including a map of the entire American Bottom

area. The report also contained a description of the Pulcher site south of the town of Cahokia.

Bushnell's 1922 report also includes aerial photographs of the Cahokia site taken by pilots from the Army Air Service at Scott Field in Belleville, Illinois. A letter on file at the Illinois State Museum dated February 23, 1922, from Maj. Frank M. Kennedy to Dr. A. R. Crook, Chief of the Illinois State Museum, suggests that those photos were taken some days prior to February 23. The photos obtained were not very clear, and Major Kennedy explained their quality:

> We do not think it is entirely our fault for certain unusual local conditions prevent satisfactory pictures of the Cahokia Mounds. ... This condition exists principally of [*sic*] the fact that the mounds are located in the valley near the river and are surrounded by a large number of factories and coal mines using soft coal. We find that there is at all times a layer or blanket of smoke next to the ground for about three or four hundred feet high which prevents our getting satisfactory clear negatives (letter from Kennedy to Crook, February 23, 1922, on file at the Illinois State Museum).

These were the first aerial photos made of an archaeological site in North America.

Some 30 years later an anthropologist was to take note of these air photos and state: "The first air photographs of an American site were taken by Wells and McKinley in 1921-22. The pictures show little that was not equally visible from the ground, and no one was inspired to follow up the technique" (Rowe 1953:907-908). Indeed these photos did not provide much information for the reasons described by Major Kennedy above.

However, at the time these photos were taken Dr. Crook was continuing an effort of several years duration to obtain aerial photographs of the Cahokia mounds. Crook had been on the Springfield reception committee for Gen. John Pershing, and he used that opportunity to request the special aerial-photo flight from the Army Air Service. The photographs were made by Lt. George W. Goddard and his assistant, Lt. H. K. Ramey. Apparently Goddard and Ramey did not encounter the same atmospheric problems that marred the first aerial photos. Goddard must have had an excellent day for the photography because his photos show much more detail of both the Cahokia site and the surrounding region. The low, oblique photos give excellent views of soil patterns not visible at ground level, and the photos remain today some of our best records of the subsurface features at the Cahokia site (Figures 2.5 and 2.6). The Goddard-Ramey photos also document the shape and location of many mounds that have since been destroyed. One can even see

Figure 2.5.   A 1922 Goddard air photo of the west half of the Cahokia site viewed from the east. Monks
Mound is in the right center. The large white area in the left center is a borrow pit. Source:
Illinois State Museum and Crook (1922:Figure 6).

Moorehead's excavations into Mound 20 (see below),
which were in progress by April 1922 (Fowler 1977;
Goddard 1969:93; Hall 1968).

There were two periods of intensive archaeological investigations at the Cahokia site, the first of these
in the 1920s, and the second in the 1960s (Figure 2.7).
Warren K. Moorehead (Figure 2.8) conducted archaeological investigations first under the auspices of the
Illinois State Museum and then the University of Illinois (Moorehead 1921, 1922a, 1922b, 1923). Moorehead
appears to have investigated the literature on all the
previous work at the Cahokia site and based his first
map of the mound group (see Figure 3.7) on Patrick's
map. Moorehead's mound-numbering system basically follows that of Patrick (see Chapter 3).

Unfortunately, there is no detailed list of the
mounds that Moorehead excavated. Between 1921 and
1929, Moorehead published descriptions of work at
several mounds. There are indications that Moorehead
tested in additional mounds but did not describe these
investigations in his published reports. Some recent
archaeological investigations have found traces of
Moorehead's unreported excavations. Gregory Perino,
working for the Thomas Gilcrease Foundation in
Mound 34 and the habitation area east of Monks
Mound (called the Ramey Field), reports that
Moorehead:

excavated parts of Mound 34 or at least tested it. There
was a well like pit down through the center of the

Figure 2.6.   A 1922 Goddard air photo of the east half of the Cahokia site viewed from the west. The city of Collinsville is on the bluff at the top center and Monks Mound is in the lower left. Source: Illinois State Museum and Crook (1922:Figure 7).

mound reaching to the bottom. Then on the terraces we found post hole pits about eight inches in diameter. . . . One had a rusty tobacco can in it but . . . I did not know that Moorehead was in the habit of dropping tobacco cans or bottles with notes in these holes. In minor excavations of the Ramey Village site we found at least one of Moorehead's test trenches (Perino, personal communication, 1980).

A similar tobacco can was found by J. W. Porter in excavations at the Mitchell site 11 kilometers (7 miles) to the north of Cahokia. Preserved in the can was a note with Moorehead's signature on it. Moorehead's most extensively reported excavations are those at the Kunnemann Mound (Mound 11), the Harding or Rattlesnake Mound (Mound 66), and Mounds 20 and 33 (Figure 2.7).

Although Moorehead is well known for the published descriptions of his excavations and mapping Cahokia, he also worked avidly to promote the preservation of the Cahokia mounds as a state park. While working at the site, Moorehead engaged in a dispute over whether the mounds were natural formations or the work of Indians. He took the position that the mounds were all man-made and that even discussing the possibility of the mounds being natural formations would greatly injure attempts to make the area a state park. Moorehead presented many papers and reports to the state legislature and wrote numerous letters on the need for a park to preserve the site. Moorehead's strong preservation efforts are undoubtedly one of his major contributions to Cahokia archaeology.

The period 1930–1931 was a busy one at the Cahokia site. The Powell family, owners of one of the larg-

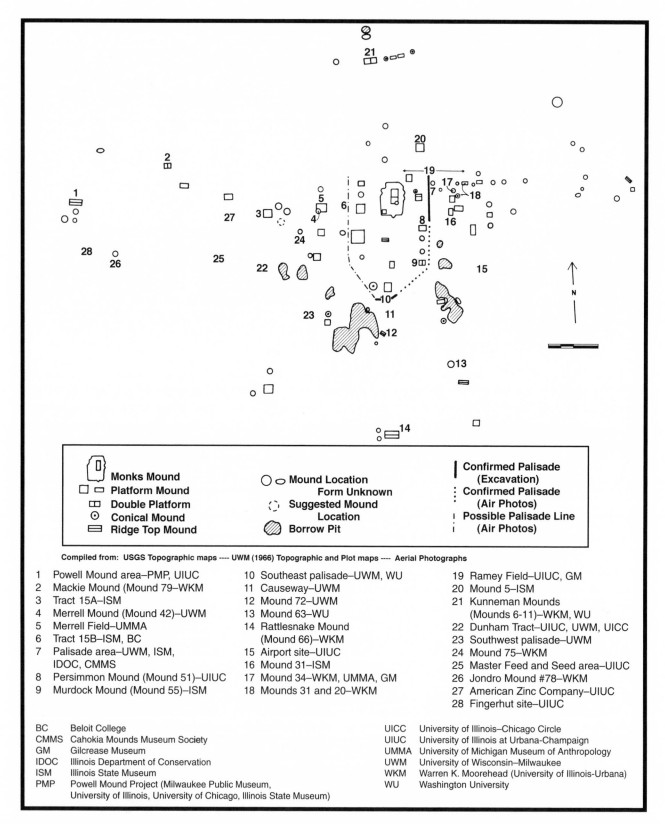

Figure 2.7. A schematic map of the Cahokia site showing the locations and forms of mounds, borrow pits, and other cultural features. The numbers represent the general locations of various excavation projects at Cahokia.

Within the figure, the legend reads:

- Monks Mound
- Platform Mound
- Double Platform
- Conical Mound
- Ridge Top Mound
- Mound Location / Form Unknown
- Suggested Mound Location
- Borrow Pit
- Confirmed Palisade (Excavation)
- Confirmed Palisade (Air Photos)
- Possible Palisade Line (Air Photos)

Compiled from: USGS Topographic maps ---- UWM (1966) Topographic and Plot maps ---- Aerial Photographs

1 Powell Mound area–PMP, UIUC
2 Mackie Mound (Mound 79–WKM
3 Tract 15A–ISM
4 Merrell Mound (Mound 42)–UWM
5 Merrell Field–UMMA
6 Tract 15B–ISM, BC
7 Palisade area–UWM, ISM, IDOC, CMMS
8 Persimmon Mound (Mound 51)–UIUC
9 Murdock Mound (Mound 55)–ISM
10 Southeast palisade–UWM, WU
11 Causeway–UWM
12 Mound 72–UWM
13 Mound 63–WU
14 Rattlesnake Mound (Mound 66)–WKM
15 Airport site–UIUC
16 Mound 31–ISM
17 Mound 34–WKM, UMMA, GM
18 Mounds 31 and 20–WKM
19 Ramey Field–UIUC, GM
20 Mound 5–ISM
21 Kunneman Mounds (Mounds 6-11)–WKM, WU
22 Dunham Tract–UIUC, UWM, UICC
23 Southwest palisade–UWM
24 Mound 75–WKM
25 Master Feed and Seed area–UIUC
26 Jondro Mound #78–WKM
27 American Zinc Company–UIUC
28 Fingerhut site–UIUC

BC Beloit College
CMMS Cahokia Mounds Museum Society
GM Gilcrease Museum
IDOC Illinois Department of Conservation
ISM Illinois State Museum
PMP Powell Mound Project (Milwaukee Public Museum, University of Illinois, University of Chicago, Illinois State Museum)

UICC University of Illinois–Chicago Circle
UIUC University of Illinois at Urbana-Champaign
UMMA University of Michigan Museum of Anthropology
UWM University of Wisconsin–Milwaukee
WKM Warren K. Moorehead (University of Illinois-Urbana)
WU Washington University

Figure 2.8. Warren K. Moorehead. Source: Department of Anthropology, University of Illinois at Urbana-Champaign.

est mounds at the west end of the site (Figures 2.9 and 2.10), wanted to level the mound for farming and to fill in a low area. It is reported that the Powells had a standing offer of $3,000 for any scientific or educational institution that would excavate the mound and move the soil. Apparently no institution was willing to undertake the work, and the Powell family commenced leveling the mound without the presence or aid of archaeologists. Dr. Paul F. Titterington, a St. Louis physician, alerted archaeologists to the problem (Figure 2.11).

The first archaeologist to arrive on the scene was Professor A. R. Kelly of the University of Illinois. He spent December 1930 and January 1931 observing the mound's destruction and examining some burials that were exposed in the process. Kelly did not remain for the entire project. After the upper portions of the mound were removed, a cooperative program of the University of Illinois, the University of Chicago, and the Milwaukee Public Museum was established to in-

vestigate the remaining portions of the Powell Mound further. Will C. McKern, Director of the Milwaukee Museum, coordinated the program. Most of the fieldwork was carried out by Thorne Deuel, then at the University of Chicago and later the Director of the Illinois State Museum. Deuel spent most of February 1931 excavating trenches into the lower portions of the Powell Mound. Approximately 2 meters (7 feet) of fill remained, and Deuel excavated through these into the village material underneath.

In the summer of 1931, Mound 84, a small mound to the south of the Powell Mound, was investigated under the field supervision of Gene W. Stirling. Under the mound he found evidence of a habitation site, although its ceramic material differed from that found in the upper portions of the mound. On the basis of these stratigraphic differences, a two-period division of the occupation at the Cahokia site was established. The more recent occupation was called Trappist and the earlier occupation was called Old Village (Kelly 1933; Griffin 1949).

In 1933 Lt. Dache Reeves of the U.S. Army Air Service secured the first vertical aerial photographs of the Cahokia site. Photographing archaeological sites was an avocational interest of Lieutenant Reeves, and he photographed the earthworks at Newark, Ohio, Macon Plateau in Georgia, and Marksville in Louisiana as well as at Cahokia (Reeves 1936; Fowler 1977:68). The negatives for all of these are now in the archives of the U.S. National Museum of the Smithsonian Institution. Permission to obtain copies of these was secured from Colonel Reeves, USAF Ret., in 1967. The late Clifford Evans, then Curator of Anthropology at the U.S. National Museum, arranged for the University of Wisconsin-Milwaukee Archaeological Research Laboratory to acquire the necessary prints.

The Reeves photographs are exceptionally valuable for understanding the Cahokia site. The flight pattern was planned in such a way that stereoscopic coverage was obtained of the entire area of the Cahokia site. Because these are vertical photographs, they provide an excellent photographic map of the site. In 1933, when the photos were taken, much of the Cahokia site was still farmland so many features now destroyed were still visible. Both Goodard and Reeves made valuable and unique contributions to our understanding of Cahokia with their pioneering aerial archaeological work.

One of the Cahokia area's most avid avocational archaeologists was the above-mentioned Dr. Paul Titterington of St. Louis, who over the years visited the mounds many times and made collections of materials. In 1938 he published a book that illustrated much of the material from the Cahokia site and sum-

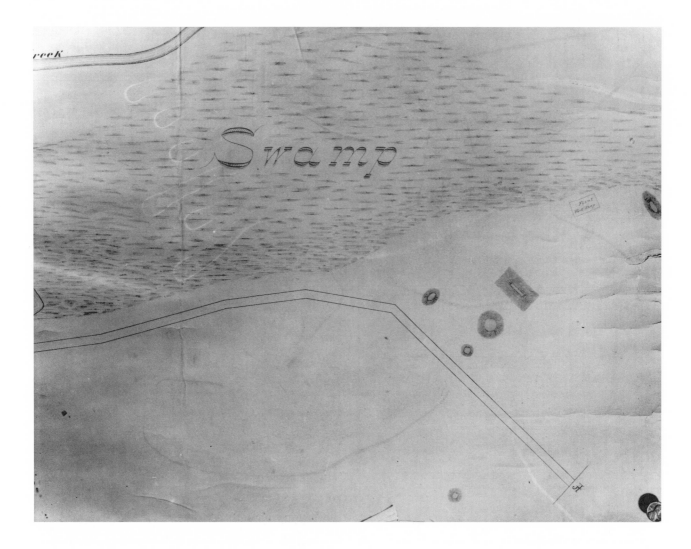

Figure 2.9.   The Patrick map of the Powell mound group on the west end of the Cahokia site. The large, rectangular mound is Powell (Mound 86); it was nearly completely destroyed in 1931. Source: Missouri Historical Society and the Archaeological Research Laboratory, University of Wisconsin-Milwaukee.

marized some of the earlier investigations, including those on the Powell Mound. Unfortunately, near the time of Dr. Titterington's death, his collection was divided and dispersed and much data on Cahokia was lost. Portions of it were given to the Museum of Anthropology at the University of Michigan. Other parts were purchased by collectors and cannot be located at the present time.

In 1940 Titterington learned that construction of a subdivision southeast of Monks Mound would destroy several mounds. Titterington contacted Thorne Deuel of the Illinois State Museum, and Deuel arranged for a WPA project to work at Mound 55 (Murdock Mound) before it was leveled. The investigations were conducted under the field supervision of Harriet M. Smith,

who has since described these excavations in some detail and published much of the results of her work (Smith 1969). The Mound 55 project ended with the bombing of Pearl Harbor on December 7, 1941. No further work was conducted at the Cahokia site until the mid-1950s, when two major projects were begun.

The first, a study of the American Bottom that included site survey and test excavations, was conducted by James B. Griffin and Albert Spaulding of the University of Michigan with a grant from The Viking Fund (later known as the Wenner-Gren Foundation). Excavations were carried out at the Pulcher site (Griffin 1977). Major excavations were also conducted at the Cahokia site, including Mound 34 and habitation areas northeast of Monks Mound and to the north of

Figure 2.10. A low, oblique air photo of the Powell Mound viewed from the west. This 1922 photo was made by Lt. George Goddard of the U.S. Army Air Service. Source: Illinois State Museum.

Mound 42 (Merrell Mound). Unfortunately, the University of Michigan project stopped due to lack of financing, and only preliminary investigations were completed. The materials and records from the surveys and the various excavations are curated at the Museum of Anthropology at the University of Michigan.

In 1956, Gregory Perino, working for the Thomas Gilcrease Foundation of Tulsa, Oklahoma, initiated several excavations at the Cahokia site. He opened a large test trench underneath Mound 34 and conducted excavations at the north end of the Ramey Field.

In the 1950s, Preston Holder of Washington University conducted various excavations in the Cahokia area. One of his earliest tests was southwest of the Powell Mound toward East St. Louis. A number of mounds in the vicinity extend between the Powell Mound and the East St. Louis group, and there appears to be continuous habitation material throughout the area. In excavations conducted by Holder about 1952, he dug into what he called the "junk yard site," which is the present location of the Indian Mounds Motel just to the south of Highway 40 (Collinsville Road). During that excavation Holder uncovered what

appeared to be a status burial with a number of accompanying retainers.

In the center part of the Cahokia site, Holder conducted excavations in Mound 10, part of the Kunnemann group, just north of Monks Mound. He excavated on the west end of the mound, clearing off a profile through it. At the base of the mound was a large burned structure covered with thatch. A few oral reports on Holder's work in Mound 10 have been presented, including one by Joyce Wike at the Central States Anthropological Society meetings in 1969 in St. Louis. Holder conducted other excavations in the general Cahokia area. Most were of a salvage nature when materials were threatened with destruction by modern construction or erosion.

In 1958 and 1959, a new discount store was built directly to the southeast of Monks Mound, and Mounds 30 and 31 were leveled. Since the area was not owned by the state of Illinois, construction could not be stopped. Joseph Caldwell, Curator of Anthropology at the Illinois State Museum, arranged to perform test excavations in Mound 31 before its destruction. He accomplished the work with the cooperation of local avocational archaeologists. A large

Figure 2.11. The leveling of the Powell Mound in January 1931. Source: Department of Anthropology, University of Illinois at Urbana-Champaign.

trench was cut through the edge of Mound 31, providing a rather complete stratigraphic profile. Caldwell's excavations were followed by a dig with a volunteer crew composed of Joe Berta, Leonard Blake, Jack Bower, Ray Bieri, and William Fecht. They excavated a portion of the northern edge of the mound before it was destroyed.

In the 1960s, impending construction of Interstates 55, 270, and 255 prompted extensive archaeological work at Cahokia. This was some of the first large-scale archaeological salvage work carried out in the United States under the federal highway program, and it initiated the second period of intensive investigation at Cahokia.

The salvage financing program of the federal government provided up to one-tenth of one percent of the budget of federally constructed projects for the recovery of archaeological and paleontological data. I first became aware of this program in the late 1950s when I was sent to the Cahokia site by the Illinois State Museum to examine the area. John McGregor of the University of Illinois, as president of the Illinois Archaeological Survey (the organization of professional Illinois archaeologists) also conferred with the Illinois Department of Transportation (IDOT). The two of us reported to the Illinois Archaeological Survey (IAS), identifying the nature of the fieldwork needed.

There was much discussion about the necessary work and the ways in which it could be organized. It was proposed that the overall direction of the work would be through the Illinois Archaeological Survey. The three cooperating institutions of the IAS would participate in excavating threatened areas. It was decided that the Illinois State Museum would be responsible for what came to be called Tracts 15A and 15B, those areas closest to Monks Mound. The University of Illinois at Urbana-Champaign (UIUC) would be responsible for excavations at the western end of the site in the Powell Mound area (the Powell Tract), and Southern Illinois University at Carbondale (SIUC) would conduct excavations at the Mitchell site to the north of Cahokia. Work commenced on these projects in 1960 (see Figure 2.7).

Although this was salvage archaeology under the worst conditions, several significant features and much data about the Cahokia site were revealed that otherwise would have gone undiscovered. The Illinois State Museum crews, under the direction of Warren Wittry, found in Tract 15B many indications of habitation and sites where houses were built over several generations (Figures 2.12 and 2.13). In this area they also discovered what appeared to be a large walled compound, three sides of which were within the area of excavation. The excavation possibilities were limited by the

extent of the right-of-way of Sand Prairie Lane, which was being relocated as part of the construction of highway overpasses.

Wittry also conducted some excavations into Mound 5, which was being partially removed by the edge of the highway right-of-way and slated as earth fill for the highway's construction. After much discussion and negotiations, the divisional office of the Illinois Department of Transportation gave IAS archaeologists the right to veto the use of such areas for fill (the contractor's sources of fill had to be approved by the highway department). We naturally rejected the use of Mound 5 as fill, much to the irritation of the landowner involved.

In Tract 15A, another series of house features and architectural complexes was found, once again indicating the rather intense use of this area for habitation (Figure 2.14). A major and most interesting feature was a large series of stains in the soil indicating where posts had been placed in the ground. When mapped, these features turned out to be portions of large circles, and Wittry called them Woodhenges. He interpreted these as calendrical circles. During the 1977 and 1978 summer seasons, Wittry excavated other portions of the circles under the sponsorship of the Illinois Department of Conservation and the University of Illinois at Chicago Circle (Figures 2.15 and 2.16).

The first salvage excavations at the west end of the Cahokia site in the 1960s were under the direction of Elaine Bluhm of UIUC. She conducted a short excavation just to the west of Mound 45 and to the south of Mound 46. This excavation was primarily in the area where the overpass was being built over the Alton and Southern Railroad, but it also involved a local manufacturing concern in that area.

Work began in the Powell Tract in 1960 under the direction of Donald Lathrap of UIUC. When Lathrap returned to the university for teaching in the fall of 1960, Charles Bareis took over supervision of the project. Extensive residential evidence was found in this area as well as data suggesting a sequence of the occupation. Many of the pits and house remains uncovered were analyzed by Patricia J. O'Brien for her doctoral dissertation (1969a), which was later published as a monograph of the Illinois Archaeological Survey (O'Brien 1972a). The University of Illinois concentrated its efforts in the area designated for the Highway 111 interchange. Just to the north, the Groves Construction Company removed earth north of the highway for fill dirt for highway construction.

The University of Illinois at Urbana-Champaign has continued research at Cahokia. When a large discount store was proposed in the area, Charles Bareis arranged for some salvage archaeology before construction be-

Figure 2.12. Excavations in Tract 15B. Source: Illinois State Museum.

Figure 2.13. Remains of houses found in Tract 15B. Source: Illinois State Museum.

Figure 2.14. Excavations in Tract 15A. Source: Illinois State Museum.

gan. Some remaining portions of the Powell Mound were excavated, and test trenches were dug through three smaller mounds to the south and southeast. Excavations were also carried out northeast of Powell Mound on property owned by the company constructing the discount store. Extensive and detailed residential compounds were uncovered in the area. Bareis has continued his excavations in this area with the archaeological field schools of the Department of Anthropology at UIUC.

Washington University continued its work at the Cahokia site with excavations on Monks Mound in 1964 (Figures 2.17 and 2.18). This project was a cooperative project of Washington University and the University of Illinois at Urbana-Champaign. Nelson Reed and John Bennett represented Washington University, with James Porter doing the fieldwork. The University of Illinois excavations were directed by Charles Bareis. That year and later, Washington University archaeologists concentrated their work on the third and fourth terraces of Monks Mound, while Bareis worked at the interface between the first terrace and the slope leading up to terrace three. He also conducted a small test on the third terrace.

The project on the fourth terrace was intended to determine the nature of activity there (Figure 2.19). After the first two seasons (1963 and 1964), John Bennett, Nelson Reed, and James Porter decided in 1965 to do a solid-core testing of the mound (Figure 2.20). They wanted to determine the nature and stages of its construction (Reed, Bennett, and Porter 1968). The solid-core drilling project continued in 1966. Then a large excavation was opened which cross-sectioned one of the core sections so the core data could be compared to data recovered in the broader area. More detailed discussion of this work is presented in the discussion of Monks Mound in Chapter 5. The work of Washington University was carried out under the auspices of the Illinois Archaeological Survey, with financial support from Washington University, the

Figure 2.15. Students from the University of Illinois at Chicago Circle excavate the remains of a cedar log from a Woodhenge post pit. Source: Cahokia Mounds Museum, Illinois Historic Preservation Agency.

Figure 2.16. A reconstructed Woodhenge at Cahokia Mounds State Historic Site. Source: Cahokia Mounds Museum, Illinois Historic Preservation Agency.

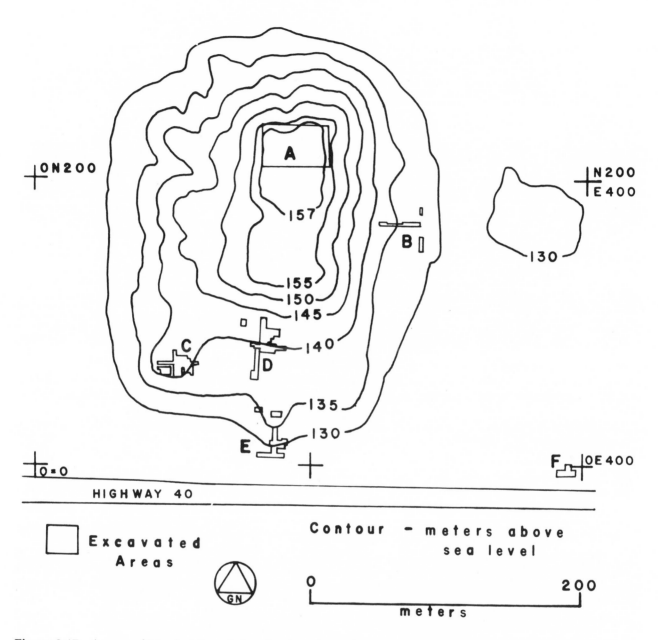

Figure 2.17. A map of Monks Mound showing locations of various excavations during the 1971 cooperative archaeological project. A: fourth terrace, Washington University; B: east lobes, University of Wisconsin-Milwaukee; C: southwest corner of first terrace, University of Wisconsin-Milwaukee; D: first terrace, University of Illinois at Urbana-Champaign; E: south ramp, Washington University; F: Ramey Field, University of Illinois at Urbana-Champaign.

Figure 2.18. Vertical air photo of Monks Mound and the surrounding area taken on June 22, 1971. The various excavations on Monks Mound are visible (see Figure 2.17). Source: Surdex Corporation, Photo 660-224, University of Wisconsin-Milwaukee Archaeological Research Laboratory.

Figure 2.19. Washington University excavations on the fourth terrace. Source: Illinois Department of Conservation, Cahokia Mounds Museum, and Illinois Historic Preservation Agency.

Collinsville Illinois Chamber of Commerce, private sources, and a grant from the National Science Foundation. In 1971, further excavations were conducted on the fourth terrace by Washington University archaeologists under the sponsorship of the Illinois Department of Conservation and the Illinois Archaeological Survey. The final season of this work was carried out in 1971, when much of the fourth terrace was excavated and a plot made of its features.

From the late 1960s to 1971, Monks Mound was the focus of other excavation projects (Figure 2.17). In 1968 the University of Wisconsin-Milwaukee (UWM), as part of its work sponsored by the National Science Foundation, determined that it was important to dig the southwest corner of the first terrace. Previous test excavations by James Porter had obtained stratigraphic cross sections near one of the core borings. Basically the UWM project proposed that a marker point for a north-south axis for the Cahokia site existed on the southwest corner of the first terrace of Monks Mound. Excavations were carried out in 1968, 1969, and 1971

(Figure 2.21). This work was conducted under the supervision of Elizabeth Benchley for the University of Wisconsin-Milwaukee. Detailed stratigraphic data obtained from the dig demonstrated that this had been a focal point of activity through much of Monks Mound's construction. It was only possible, however, to excavate in the upper portions, because this area of Monks Mound is 10.6 meters (35 feet) above the present ground level. Charles Bareis continued his interest in the interface area between the first and third terraces of Monks Mound, directing projects there in 1971 and 1972.

In 1971 the IAS, with funds from the Illinois Department of Conservation, excavated Monks Mound to obtain data that might be used for developing an interpretive program. The excavations included areas already mentioned, the first and fourth terraces, and some new excavations. One of these, carried out by Washington University, was intended to determine details of the so-called south ramp, or the approach to the first terrace.

Figure 2.20. Solid-core drilling on the fourth terrace by Washington University researchers. Source: Illinois State Museum.

The University of Wisconsin-Milwaukee was interested in excavating what are called the east lobes of Monks Mound, irregular protrusions on the east side of the mound (Figure 2.17). James Porter speculated that the lobes were possible ramps leading from the ground level to the fourth and third terraces (Reed et al. 1968:158). The University of Wisconsin-Milwaukee project on the east lobes, carried out under the direction of Kenneth Williams, suggested that these were late features of the site dating to the Sand Prairie phase (see Figure 1.7). One of the main contributions of the east lobes excavations was the discovery of a deep stratigraphic sequence dating from the Patrick through the Sand Prairie phases. This is the only well-documented, continuous stratigraphic sequence for the entire occupation of the Cahokia site area.

In 1966 the University of Wisconsin-Milwaukee began an extensive project at the Cahokia site under my direction. No one since Moorehead's time had at-

tempted to deal with the Cahokia site in its entirety, nor had anyone since Patrick attempted to work out a detailed map of the site. We started with three goals: to prepare a detailed map of the Cahokia site, to collect all of the available historical information, and to assemble aerial photographs of the site.

First, aerial photogrammetry was employed to prepare a map of the entire Cahokia site (see Chapter 3). The aerial photographs were made in the late spring of 1966 and a draft map was prepared by fall. This map was checked, revised, and a final version completed by the summer of 1967.

Assembling the many aerial photographs of the Cahokia site was another goal. Early photographs from the 1920s and 1930s, as well as all of the more recent ones, were collected. We now have a rather complete set that includes the Soil Conservation Service aerial photographs of the area, the UWM aerial photographs taken for mapping purposes, and many of the photographs taken over the years by the Surdex Corporation of St. Louis.

This atlas presents the compilation of historical information on Cahokia and reflects the wealth of information obtained from the site map and the aerial photographs.

After analysis of maps and other data, a series of excavations commenced. In the first season of the project, 1966, an area east of Monks Mound, where all early air photos and most recent ones showed a white north-south line, was examined. Archaeologists assumed it was a prehistoric feature, and excavations confirmed that it was a palisade or fortification line along the east side of Ramey Field (Anderson 1969). Excavations continued on the palisade line in the 1967-1970 seasons. This work was continued by the Illinois State Museum and then later by the Illinois Department of Conservation. In recent years, continued excavations on the palisade line in the Ramey Field have been carried out under the sponsorship of the Cahokia Mounds Museum Society for their summer field school (Figure 2.22).

A second project carried out in 1966 and 1967 by the University of Wisconsin-Milwaukee involved what appeared to be a causeway running from Fox Mound (Mound 60) in a southerly direction toward the railroad tracks. It is possible that this line continued south of the railroad tracks and tied into the Rattlesnake Mound (Mound 66) area. A trench through this area suggested that what appeared to be the causeway may have been fill for a railroad spur, but it is also possible that the railroad spur was built on top of an aboriginal causeway. Further excavations are needed to test this hypothesis.

Figure 2.21. Archaeologists from the University of Wisconsin-Milwaukee excavate on the southwest corner of the first terrace. Source: Illinois Department of Conservation, Cahokia Mounds Museum, and Illinois Historic Preservation Agency.

A third UWM project was excavating portions of Mound 72, 850 meters (930 yards) south of Monks Mound. Excavations were conducted there for several reasons. One, it appeared to be at the southern end of a north-south center line of the Cahokia site, which suggested it was related to the area on the southwest corner of the first terrace of Monks Mound. Second, this was a ridge-top mound, the placement of which suggested that it had been used by the Indians as a marker for the site limit or axis. Excavations into Mound 72 were carried out by the University of Wisconsin-Milwaukee during the years of 1967-1970. The

UWM continued this work in 1971 under the financial sponsorship of the Illinois Department of Conservation.

The UWM program also attempted to locate the palisades in the southwest portion of the Cahokia site. Lines on air photos suggested some sort of feature ran from the northwest to the southeast through the woods in the southern portion of what was then the park area. Excavations commenced after stripping the vegetation and removing a few inches of soil. Features indicated some construction in the area, but it was not as extensive or deep as the constructions in the Ramey Field.

Figure 2.22.   Students in the Cahokia Museum Field School excavate along the palisade east of Monks Mound. Source: Cahokia Mounds Museum, Illinois Historic Preservation Agency.

It appears that a series of small fences or temporary walls had been built, but the dates of these constructions are not known.

Some excavations were carried out on a weekend volunteer basis on the surface of Mound 42 to determine the extent and nature of a small mound on top of Mound 42 that was leveled early in this century. Those excavations were under the supervision of Elizabeth Benchley.

Another project conducted by the University of Wisconsin-Milwaukee was a controlled surface collection in Ramey Field east of Monks Mound. Done in 1967, the goal was to determine the distribution of surface materials that might indicate subsurface features. The surface survey was conducted before excavations began to determine the distribution of cultural features throughout the Cahokia site.

A cooperative project with Beloit College, under the auspices of the University of Wisconsin-Milwaukee, was carried out in 1969, 1971, and 1972 in the Merrell Tract just east of Mound 42 and west of Sand Prairie Lane. Archaeologists searched for a western palisade line comparable to that in Ramey Field and the continuation of the walled compound found by Wittry in Tract 15B. The project began with a controlled surface collection of the field. Beloit College conducted excavations in selected areas and found a rather extensive and detailed occupation pertaining to the Early Mississippian phases of the Cahokia site.

Another major project was carried out in 1966 in the Dunham Tract south of Tract 15B under the direction of Charles Bareis of the University of Illinois at Urbana-Champaign. The path proposed for Interstate 255—south from Interstate 55-70 between the areas of

Mound 44 and 46, continuing south of Highway 40 in a slight southeasterly direction through a large field and crossing the railroad tracks near Rattlesnake Mound—was examined. Excavations were also conducted to examine the subsurface features, particularly in the northern end of the tract, where surface materials were the most extensive. Archaeologists found many pits and houses in the area, although they were far less common at the southern end. Archaeologists also examined a white line that ran diagonally through this area that was visible on air photos to determine if it was a palisade or some other feature. The results of this are inconclusive at the present time. Fortunately, the path of Interstate 255 was relocated, and the highway does not run through this portion of the site.

In 1961 Mound 51, known locally as the Persimmon Mound, was sold by the owner to a local contractor to use as landfill. Fortunately, during that summer Charles Bareis had a UIUC field school at the adjacent Collinsville Airport site while Warren Wittry (with crews at Tract 15A) and James Porter (at the Mitchell site) were doing salvage work nearby. When they became aware of the danger to the mound, they initiated a series of volunteer efforts to collect information before it was totally destroyed. Bareis's 1961 UIUC field school crew, with help from Wittry and Porter and their field supervisors, placed a trench along the top of the mound. Even as the testing proceeded, the western and southern sides of the mound were being removed by the contractor. Four years past before further work could be carried out, by which time most of the mound had been hauled away. During 1965 Porter and Glenn Freimuth undertook backhoe testing of the remaining low remnant of the mound. In 1966 and 1967 Bareis returned to the work with his UIUC field schools, and in 1968 he organized a group of Collinsville High School students to help with the final excavations.

Archaeologists discovered that the area had been an ancient borrow pit. Centuries before, it had been filled in with garbage and other debris, and later Mound 51 was built over the old borrow pit. Plant and animal remains in this garbage fill were preserved better than in many areas at the Cahokia site. A doctoral dissertation on the borrow pit, written by William Chmurny (1973), is one of the more complete ecologically oriented discussions of the Cahokia site.

Since 1971, archaeological work at the Cahokia site has concentrated on contract work as the site developed. Exceptions have been Charles Bareis's continued work in the Powell Mound area with field schools from UIUC. Bareis has concentrated in an area northeast of the Powell Mound, uncovering intensive habitation debris. Another exception has been the adult

field school sponsored by the Cahokia Mounds Museum Society. This educational program, primarily under the field direction of William Iseminger, has focused on the palisade area first excavated by the University of Wisconsin-Milwaukee in the late 1960s.

In 1977 and 1978, Robert L. Hall of the University of Illinois at Chicago Circle obtained a contract to conduct further excavation on the Woodhenges discovered in Tract 15A. Warren Wittry returned to the site to conduct this work, which was necessary to permit the reconstruction of one of the Woodhenges.

In the 1970s the Illinois Department of Conservation placed significant emphasis on land acquisition and development of the Cahokia site area. Much of this emphasis was on developing a new museum. Several projects were contracted to test possible museum locations. In 1975 and 1976 Elizabeth Benchley, representing the University of Wisconsin-Milwaukee, and Robert Hall of the University of Illinois at Chicago Circle extensively tested the Dunham Tract south of Tract 15B. This project added to previous highway salvage work in the area. Surface collections, phosphate testing, magnetometer studies, soil coring, and test excavations were conducted.

The location of the proposed museum was moved to a new position south and east of Monks Mound. This area was chosen because little or no archaeological data had been recovered there by Moorehead and other earlier investigators. Controlled surface collections, topographic mapping, air-photo studies, and other investigations were carried out during the summer of 1979 by an archaeological crew from the University of Wisconsin-Milwaukee under the direction of the author (Fowler, Benchley, and DePuydt 1980). These studies found traces of what might have been aboriginal cornfields along with other cultural features.

In 1980 Elizabeth Benchley conducted test excavations of the proposed museum tract based upon the findings of the previous years (Benchley and DePuydt 1982). Many of the features suggested by the 1979 work were tested and confirmed, and she also found deeply buried evidence of a Late Archaic occupation (see Table 1.1). Whereas similar data had been obtained from other sites in the American Bottom, such evidence had not been previously encountered within the Cahokia site. In 1981 archaeologists from Southern Illinois University at Carbondale received a contract from the Department of Conservation (Nassaney et al. 1983). They conducted more extensive excavations in this area, further documenting the finds of the earlier seasons.

Because the proposed museum tract was on low-lying ground and flooded during many months out of several years, it was decided to move the museum somewhat to the north on higher ground. William J. Woods and Christy Wells of Southern Illinois University at Edwardsville conducted preliminary archaeological excavations in the new museum tract in the fall of 1984. Archaeological investigations to examine the tract in more detail were carried out in the spring and summer of 1985. The Interpretive Center has now been built on this tract.

During the late 1970s and 1980s, archaeological investigations related to Cahokia, but not on the Cahokia site proper, have been conducted on the right-of-way of Interstate 270, the eastern interstate beltline around the St. Louis area. The work was sponsored by the Illinois Department of Transportation, and the prime contractor was the University of Illinois at Urbana-Champaign. Portions of the fieldwork were subcontracted to the University of Illinois at Chicago Circle, Southern Illinois University at Edwardsville, Illinois State University, and Western Illinois University. The archaeology was under the general direction of Charles Bareis, with James Porter coordinating the fieldwork. The contribution of this enormous project to Cahokia archaeology has largely been in demonstrating the complexity of the smaller communities that supported Cahokia; it has also refined our understanding of the evolution of Cahokia and contributed to fundamental and refined changes in the chronology of the area (Bareis and Porter 1984).

A series of Cahokia Conferences in the late 1960s and early 1970s contributed greatly to the understanding of Cahokia archaeology. The first was organized by James Porter and Charles Bareis, and attended by myself, the late Glen Black, Warren Wittry, David Baerreis, James Griffin, and Pedro Armillas. Later conferences were organized by the author while the UWM National Science Foundation project was under way at Cahokia. Archaeologists from all over the Midwest attended these field conferences to discuss the work at Cahokia as well as related work in the Mississippi Valley.

In 1971 the author and Robert Hall convened a special Cahokia Conference with an emphasis on developing a refined ceramic chronology for the site. In 1973 a second Cahokia Ceramic Conference was held to check and make minor revisions in the sequence worked out in 1971. These conferences established a series of phases covering the growth of Cahokia from about A.D. 800 to at least A.D. 1400 (Fowler and Hall 1972). Although based largely on ceramics, these phase designations also included other factors, such as mound construction, in their descriptions. (See Figure 1.7 for a summary of the various temporal phases defined at Cahokia.) Since that time there have been revisions of the Cahokia Conference phases. These revisions have mainly been based upon the extensive work on the Interstate 270 project (Bareis and Porter 1984) and have produced a more refined ceramic chronology. Since this volume is primarily concerned with a discussion and description of the surface features, such as mounds and borrow pits, extensive discussion of these ceramically derived chronologies is not germane. Whenever it is necessary to discuss time, reference is made to calendrical dates or years A.D., based upon the considerable number of radiocarbon assays that have been run on materials from Cahokia (see Appendix 1).

The years of archaeological research at Cahokia culminated in 1982 when the Cahokia site was entered on the World Heritage Site list by UNESCO. This recognition was the result of inquiries by Brackenridge and others in the nineteenth century, Warren K. Moorehead in the 1920s, and many archaeologists in the Midwest in the 1960s and 1970s. After 170 years of curiosity and inquiry, the world took note of Cahokia. It is one of the five natural, historical, and archaeological sites in the United States to be included on this international register, and the only property on the list that is not federally owned.

3

THE MAPS OF CAHOKIA

Over the years, many maps of the Cahokia site have been published. They vary in their accuracy and detail, but most provide some information useful for understanding the site. This chapter reviews these maps and discusses their usefulness and limitations. As noted in Chapter 1, the map made by John Patrick in 1876 is one of the best and most complete. His system of mound numbering is followed in this atlas and on the most recent and detailed map of Cahokia made by the University of Wisconsin-Milwaukee (UWM) in 1966. The UWM map also includes many mounds not identified by Patrick.

Since the Cahokia site was "discovered" in the early nineteenth century, many have attempted to illustrate the Cahokia mounds. Drawings concentrated mostly on Monks Mound, but a few attempted to show other mounds in the central area. These are not actual maps but rather two-dimensional representations of the mounds. The one that comes closest to being a map is an illustration published by J. C. Wild showing two visitors viewing the area from Monks Mound south through the Round Top and Fox mounds (see Figure 2.2). The view is apparently from the east, from on top of Mound 51 (Persimmon Mound). Although done in a style that tends to exaggerate vertical heights, this drawing does give an impression of the mounds as they appeared early in the nineteenth century. However, the relationships and sizes of mounds cannot be scaled from this drawing.

True maps of the Monks Mound area were not made until the 1870s, when a detailed plan view of the entire Cahokia site was sponsored by Dr. John J. R. Patrick. Moorehead described the map and the procedures used as follows:

> Dr. J. J. R. Patrick, Belleville, Illinois was one of the pioneers in Cahokia work. The survey called on his widow who is now Mrs. John Bauman. She showed us some field notes written by Dr. Patrick, in 1877.

November 18 of that year he visited Monks Mound and did some exploring in the vicinity (1923:43).

> The best and most complete map of the Cahokia group I have observed is the result of a survey made by county surveyor Hilgard under the direction of Dr. J. J. R. Patrick assisted by B. J. Van Court of O'Fallon, Illinois and Wm. J. Seever of St. Louis. The work done about 1880 and the original map owned by the Missouri Historical Society was loaned us. . . . Manifestly the survey of 1875 is accurate and if Mr. Hilgard or Mr. Patrick drew a certain mound as a pyramid and today it appears as an oval or oblong mound, it should be classified as a pyramid (1922a:13).

> Mrs. Bauman has in her possession several field maps, and a profile survey of the group. She says that the first survey was executed November 5, 1876, and that the profile survey was made July 5, 1879, and that Louis Gainer Kahn, a surveyor, either made this survey, or assisted in it. She thinks there were several surveys, more or less thorough, made of the Cahokia Mounds in the period between 1870 and 1888 (1929:97-98).

The Patrick map is part of the Patrick collection, now under the guardianship of the Missouri Historical Society at the Jefferson Memorial Building in St. Louis, Missouri. The director and staff of the Missouri Historical Society have been very generous in allowing archaeologists to examine and photograph this map. In 1962 the Patrick map was photographed under the direction of Warren Wittry of the Illinois State Museum and Nelson Reed, a St. Louis businessman and archaeologist. In 1967 further photographs of the map were made by James Anderson and the author, both from the University of Wisconsin-Milwaukee. Enlarged prints were made and used in redrafting the Patrick map. The University of Wisconsin-Milwaukee produced a copy duplicating the original map. While the details of draftsmanship on the reproduced map are not as precise or as well done as the original, it faithfully gives the feeling of the map, accurately locates the mounds, and illustrates their size and shape as shown by Patrick and his surveyors (Figure 3.1).

The Patrick map was made in two units to encompass the entire Cahokia site. The first section extends on an east-west axis from where Canteen Creek intercepts the Collinsville Road to the west as far as Mound 46, and from the Kunnemann group (Mounds 6-11) to the north to Mound 66 (Rattlesnake Mound) to the south.

The other section includes the Powell mound group at the western limits of the Cahokia site where Collinsville Road turns to the southwest toward East St. Louis. It is obvious that Patrick intended these two sections to be united as he provided a key for connecting them; a section through Collinsville Road is labeled "A" on both maps (see Figures 1.3 and 1.4).

Patrick also assigned numbers to the mounds he mapped in the main portion of the site. He did not assign numbers to the Powell group. In all, Patrick assigned numbers to 71 mounds. Working from east to west on the north side of Collinsville Road are Mounds 1 through 46, and, from west to east on the south side, Mounds 47 through 71.

The original Patrick map was expertly surveyed and drawn. The locations are almost certainly precisely given because the surveyor recorded them in the field. Most of the mound drawings show the heights in a shading technique that was common at the time. The original map was prepared in color with the water areas shown in blue and the main features shown in black ink. Each mound, shaded to show its approximate height and shape, is covered with a gray wash to make it stand out.

Moorehead's analysis of the Patrick map is an accurate one. Archaeological investigation has generally confirmed both the locations and shapes of mounds illustrated by Patrick. His map predated intensive cultivation of the area, so the mounds in Patrick's time probably were much closer to their original form than they are today.

There are a few exceptions. For instance, what Patrick labeled Mound 61, in the site's southeastern quadrant, is shown with its major axis north-south, whereas modern maps and examination of this mound indicate its major axis is east-west. This seems to be an error by Patrick and not the result of modern cultivation.

Accompanying Patrick's map of the Cahokia site are maps of other area mound groups. A detailed map of the East St. Louis mound group (see Figure 1.3) shows the street outlines of East St. Louis and the lo-

cations of mounds in relation to them. That map also shows the St. Louis side of the river and one of the St. Louis mounds. Patrick also shows the intervening area between the Cahokia group and the East St. Louis group with mounds more or less evenly spaced along what is now Highway 40. All of the maps are keyed for connection into one map that extends west from Cahokia Creek to St. Louis.

Another map is included of the group of mounds—the Pulcher site—near the modern town of Dupo. Patrick labels this the "Snyder's group" after Dr. John Francis Snyder, who was born in a house built on the edge of the major mound.

Also part of the Patrick collection is a detailed map of Monks Mound dated 1876 (see Figure 5.3). This map provides specific measurements of Monks Mound as well as the heights of the terraces. It was apparently based on work by Mr. B. J. Van Court, a surveyor from O'Fallon, Illinois. William McAdams commented on the map in 1882:

> As the size of the Cahokia Mound has been given variously, we applied to Mr. B. J. VanCourt, a practical surveyor living in the vicinity, at O'Fallon, and whom we knew had made a regular survey of the mound. Mr. VanCourt sent us the following: 'In my survey I did not follow the irregularities of the mound but made straight lines enclosing the base. The largest axis from north to south and . . . is 998 feet, the shortest from east to west is 721 feet. The height of the mound is 99 feet. The height of the structure covers 16 acres, two roods, and three perches of ground' (1882:59).

This, however, contradicts the data given on the map, which gives the length at the base of the mound as 307.8 meters (1,010 feet), the width as 216.4 meters (710 feet), and the area of the base of the mound as 5.6 hectares (13.85) acres.

Until the last few decades, the Patrick map was the most detailed and precise map made of the Cahokia site. In fact, many of the maps made between 1880 and 1930 were based to some extent on it.

The next known map of the Cahokia site was published by McAdams in 1882 (Figure 3.2). No numbers were given the mounds so they correlate to the Patrick map only in a very general way, in terms of their locations and forms. It is obviously a sketch map, not an accurate measurement of locations of the mounds. The mounds are shown, however, in relationship to each other, and their shapes are indicated by outline drawings. Tick lines extending from the drawings show the general height of each mound, which is stated in feet and labeled either next to the mound or on the mound drawing. For example, the map shows Monks Mound

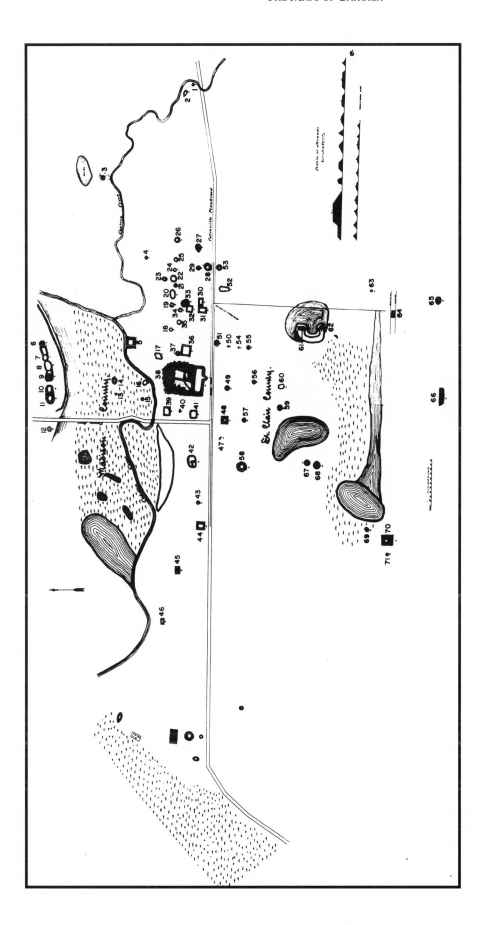

Figure 3.1. A reconstruction of the 1876 Patrick map now at the Missouri Historical Society. The original map was photographed by James Anderson and Melvin Fowler in 1967. The two sections were then enlarged and pieced together. A tracing was made from this mosaic. This map includes the 70 mounds of the central section of Cahokia assigned numbers by Patrick as well as the unnumbered mounds of the Powell group to the west. The original Powell map was on a separate sheet but its juncture with the main map was clearly indicated. Larger mound numbers have been added by the author. Source: Missouri Historical Society and the Archaeological Research Laboratory, University of Wisconsin-Milwaukee.

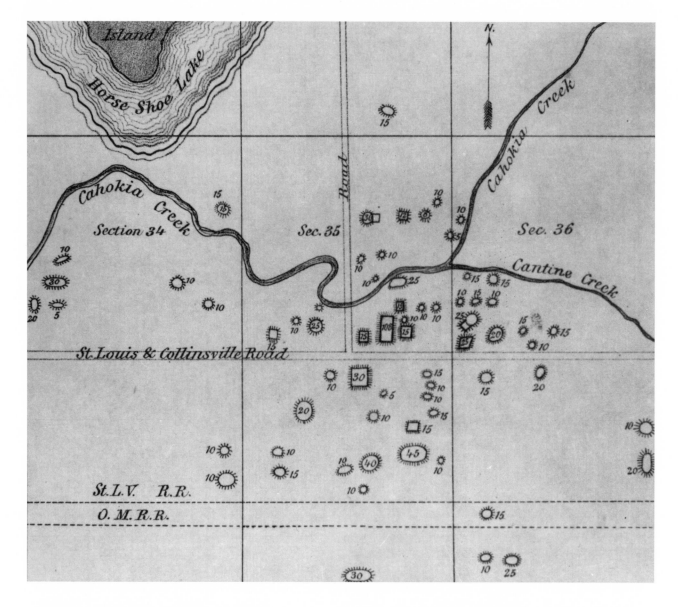

Figure 3.2.   The 1882 McAdams map. The numbers beside the mounds give their heights in feet. Source:
                    McAdams 1882:61.

with a height of 108 feet. McAdams illustrates the entire Cahokia site, including the Powell group at the
west end of the site. However, he does not show all
the mounds that Patrick shows. For example, Mounds
1 and 2, shown by Patrick on the banks of Canteen
Creek at the eastern limits of the site, are not illustrated
by McAdams. McAdams also shows a few mounds
not mapped by Patrick but later documented by
Moorehead; Mound 79 (Mackie Mound) is one example.

It is difficult to appraise the accuracy of the heights
on McAdams's map. Patrick drew cross sections of
some mounds and gave the scale to suggest their

heights. In some cases, the McAdams map corresponds
rather closely with Patrick's heights and in other cases
there is sharp disagreement. For example, Patrick indicates a height of 25 feet for Mound 48, while
McAdams shows it as 30 feet.

Another map of the Cahokia site was published by
Cyrus Thomas in 1894 (Figure 3.3). It is very similar to
the McAdams map in the nature of its drawings, suggesting that it was copied from that source. The Thomas map is more finely drawn and more precise than
the McAdams map. Once again, the entire area of the
site is shown, including the Powell Mound area. The
forms of the mounds on the Thomas map are shown

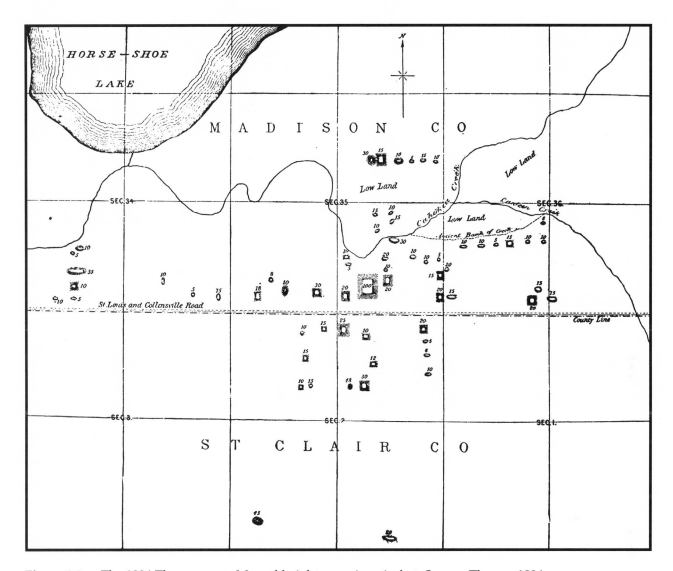

Figure 3.3. The 1894 Thomas map. Mound heights are given in feet. Source: Thomas 1894.

in the same way as on the McAdams map, with outline and hatching to show the height. As with McAdams's map, the heights are shown as numbers either next to or on the mound. In many cases the heights on the Thomas map are less than those shown on the McAdams map. The Thomas map also omitted the railroads at the south end of the site that were shown on the earlier McAdams map.

The U.S. Army Corps of Engineers made a contour map of the area at about the same time Thomas made his map (Figure 3.4). Their 1888 USGS quadrangle—the first topographic map of the area—uses 2-foot (0.6-meter) contours. However, the detail is so general that it is difficult to believe the contours are really in such small intervals. It is interesting that the mounds are illustrated not in contour lines, but by the old tech-

nique of shading the slopes in parallel lines to show their configuration. Only a few mounds are shown, and their forms are very generalized. As mentioned before, Mounds 1 and 2 are omitted from the McAdams and Thomas maps, but Mound 2 is very clearly shown on the USGS map. The value of this map is its illustration of the general nature of the swamps, the location of Cahokia Creek, and the proposed locations of the drainage ditches and canals intended to straighten out the channels of Cahokia and Canteen creeks.

In 1906 Dr. Cyrus A. Peterson and Clark McAdams, the son of William McAdams, privately printed a map of the Cahokia site with mound heights (Figure 3.5). This map is sketchier in some ways than the earlier maps. It attempts to show the mounds with hatching or shading in a sort of a three-dimensional perspec-

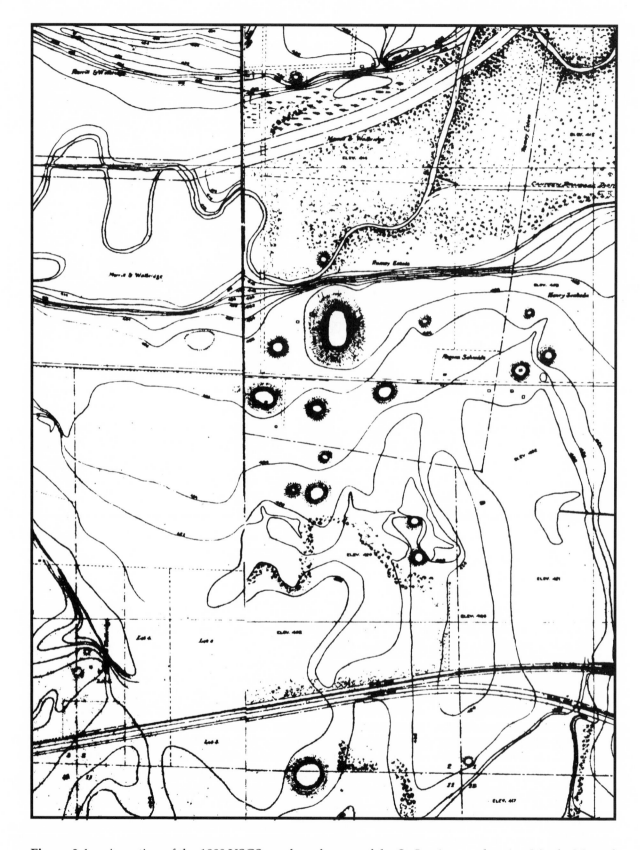

Figure 3.4. A portion of the 1888 USGS quadrangle map of the St. Louis area showing Monks Mound and other mounds at Cahokia. Source: U.S. Geological Survey.

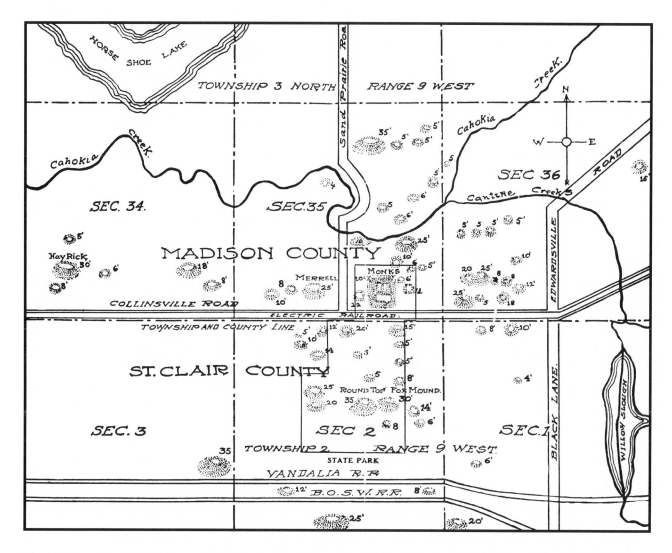

Figure 3.5. The 1906 Peterson-McAdams map. Mound heights are given in feet. Source: Throop 1928.

tive, as if viewed from the south. More detail is shown for Monks Mound, and all four terraces are all indicated. Mounds 1 and 2 are omitted from this map.

The arrangement and locations of mounds in the Peterson-McAdams map conform more closely to the earlier McAdams map than to the more recent Thomas map. It was undoubtedly prepared from the map and notes made by Clark McAdams's father. There are discrepancies between heights given for some mounds on this map—Monks Mound, for example—and the earlier maps of William McAdams and Cyrus Thomas. Unfortunately, these discrepancies are not consistent. One would assume that over time the mounds were plowed down and eroded; however, some of the 1906 heights are greater than those reported by William McAdams in 1882.

The Peterson-McAdams map was reprinted in 1928 by A. J. Throop, with the following comment:

The above map of the Cahokia Mound Group was privately printed in April, 1906, by Dr. Cyrus A. Peterson and Mr. Clark McAdams, St. Louis, with the view of preserving a recollection of the group as it remained at that time. By courtesy of Mr. H. M. Braun we are enabled to reproduce it for 'Mound Builders of Illinois'. The elevations were determined by Mr. Louis Greiner, Belleville; the locations by Mr. J. Schmidt Brooks (1928).

The next map on record is apparently a land-survey plat. Charles Bareis located the map—which he originally believed was made about 1923 by highway personnel—in the files of the district office of the Illinois Department of Transportation in French Village, Illinois (Figure 3.6). The map shows the property designations and owners. The main area of Monks Mound is listed as U.S. Survey 628, Claim 133, and the property owner is listed as T. T. Ramey. The channel of Cahokia Creek is included, as are the locations of railroads, streams, and property lines. The bluff line and mounds along it are designated at the east edge. Mound contour lines are sketched for the central portion of the Cahokia site, and the Ramey farmhouse and outbuildings are depicted on the west side of Monks Mound.

The proposed line of the Springfield and Central Illinois Traction Company is an important feature on the map. The presence of that line suggests that this map may be even earlier than the date noted on it. In 1912 Moorehead gave a lecture before the Illinois Historical Society that was summarized in a publication with direct quotes from Moorehead's talk: "A few years ago one of the great Street Railway lines of the western part of your state proposed hauling away the Cahokia Mound and using that magnificent monument as it would an ordinary gravel bank to procure material for filling lines of track that were to be built across certain low and swampy grounds" (1912:185).

In 1916 the Ramey family, the owner of the central portion of the Cahokia site including Monks Mound, published a bulletin called *The Mound Builders: The Greatest Monument of Prehistoric Man*. In it they made a plea for the site's preservation. Nineteenth-century descriptions of Monks Mound and the Cahokia site by Brackenridge, DeHass, and others comprised the major portion of the bulletin. The land-survey map of the Cahokia site was included in the report. It is apparent that the map was made sometime before 1916, perhaps before Moorehead's 1912 lecture; between 1900 and 1910 is probably accurate.

The mounds on this map are drawn as though contoured, although they seem to be merely sketches of the mounds' shapes. The only contours labeled are those for Monks Mound, which is assigned a base elevation of 430 feet above sea level (131.1 meters above sea level). The contours are then at irregular intervals, apparently to indicate major changes in the slope of the mound. The next contour above 430 is 437 feet (133.2 meters), above that 438 feet (133.5 meters). The top elevation is 526.5 feet (160.5 meters), indicating a total height of approximately 96 feet (29.3 meters). Not all of the mounds that were surely visible at the time are shown. The contours of Mound 66 to the south conform rather well to the general shape it retains today. The east and west limits of the site are shown, but the mounds there are not marked. I conclude that this map was probably done for the Rameys because it shows the mounds generally known in their area but not mounds in the rest of the site.

Another map of the Cahokia site was published by Bushnell in 1904. It is included in a map of the entire American Bottom area that shows the major known mound sites: Cahokia, East St. Louis, St. Louis, Mitchell, and Pulcher site. The mounds in each group are shown as dots, and the most shown are for the Cahokia group. It is likely that the positions of the mounds at the Cahokia site were based on the Patrick map and on more detailed examination of the area by Bushnell. It is difficult from the small scale of this map and the dots to determine if there is much added that Patrick did not show. It shows the layout of the Cahokia site and its relationship to many other sites, including the row of mounds that continues from the Powell mound group of the Cahokia site down to the East St. Louis group. Bushnell's map is similar to a map of western Madison County, Illinois, published by Thomas in 1894 showing the Mitchell group in relationship to the Cahokia group. However, Thomas's map does not show the locations of the mounds as precisely and extensively as Bushnell's does. The Bushnell map is of a different scale and sort than the rest of the maps of the area that refer specifically to the Cahokia site.

A series of maps of the Cahokia site was published by Moorehead as a result of his work in the 1920s. Moorehead published three separate reports on the Cahokia site, the first in April 1922, the next in 1923, and another in 1929. Each contained a map of the site. In 1922 Moorehead stated that "the original map [by Patrick] owned by the Missouri Historical Society was loaned us. We made a copy which is herewith reproduced [as] Figure 1" (1922a:13).

Examination of this map (Figure 3.7) shows that it is indeed a copy of the Patrick map. It is a rather precise tracing; the quality of the lines, the lettering, the locations of ponds, shapes of mounds, and so forth are all very much as Patrick shows them. However, the shading on Monks Mound is not as complete as on the Patrick map; it appears that reproducing the map was stopped before the work was completed. Moorehead's Figure 1 in his 1922 publication includes the mound numbers 1 through 71 assigned by Patrick. Moorehead follows the numbers precisely and includes the cross sections of the mounds that Patrick published on his map. This is the best map of the Cahokia site that Moorehead published. The caption on it says it is a "reproduction of the map drawn by J. J. R. Patrick about 1880. From apparently an accurate survey." Moorehead, however, did not realize that the Powell mound group was part of the Cahokia site and that Patrick had intended for the two map sections to

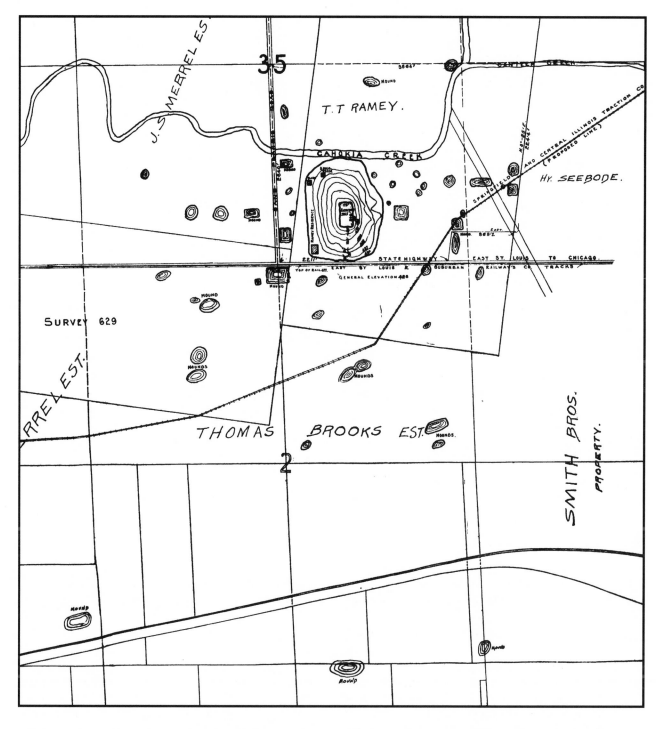

Figure 3.6. Land survey map of the central portion of Cahokia published by the Ramey family in 1916. Source: Ramey Family 1916.

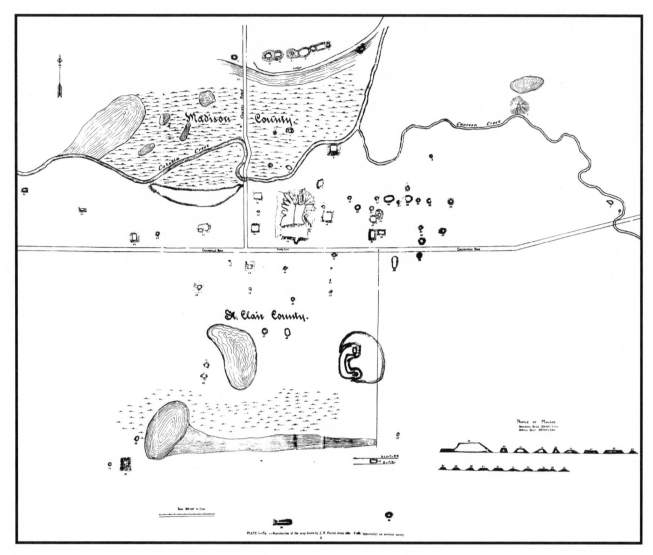

Figure 3.7.   The 1922 Moorehead map. Source: Moorehead 1922a: Figure 1. Used by permission of the University of Illinois at Urbana-Champaign.

be attached. Moorehead's lack of understanding of the Patrick map is noted in his discussion of the Powell Mound: "A survey of this mound (which I have not been able to identify positively by number on the Patrick map) shows a major axis 310 feet long and running south 89° east . . . and a height of 40 feet" (1929:84).

In his 1923 publication, Moorehead reproduced not his original copy of the Patrick map, but a much cruder sketch taken from his copy of the Patrick map (Figure 3.8). The mounds are shown in roughly the same form, although with less precision. Moorehead added some mounds he had discovered that Patrick had not included. He also changed the numbering system from that used on the Patrick map; there are not only additional numbers (72 through 84), but the numbers 1 to

71 are sometimes assigned to different mounds. Also, Moorehead noted sites where there were surface indications of habitation, which he labeled village sites. Burial sites are also indicated. In the heading for this map, Moorehead gives the following description "Based on map of J. J. R. Patrick, 1880. Camp sites and burial sites are indicated showing results of 1921-22 field work" (1923:Figure 1). (See Appendix 3 for a table showing the various numbers assigned to mounds at the Cahokia site by Patrick and Moorehead, as well as additions made in the last two decades.)

The final map of Cahokia published by Moorehead in 1929 is yet another version of the Patrick map, but it is a little more neatly drawn than the 1923 version (Figure 3.9). It is similar in many ways to the 1923 map,

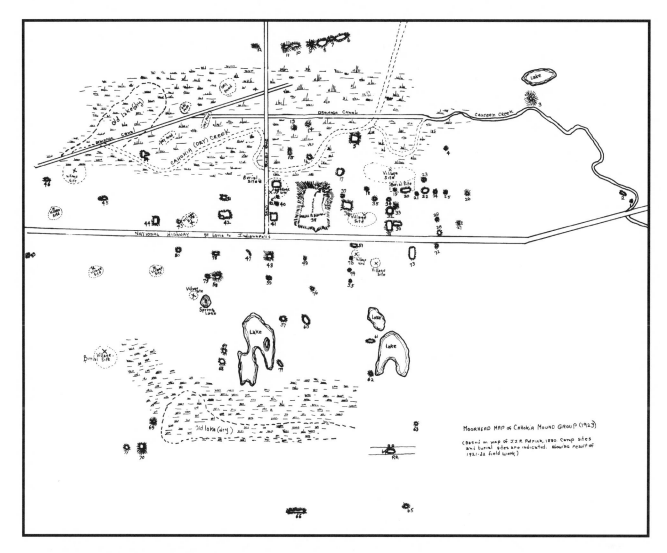

Figure 3.8. The 1923 Moorehead map. Source: Moorehead 1923. Used by permission of the University of Illinois at Urbana-Champaign.

but includes 85 mounds and the locations of village and burial sites. Moorehead returned to Patrick's numbering for Mounds 1-71 and he added Mounds 72 through 85. He also resolved the question of the location of the Powell Mound on the Patrick map to his satisfaction. He assigned Patrick's number 46 to the Powell Mound even though he claimed he could not accurately locate this from the Patrick map and numbers. It is an error on Moorehead's part because he did not recognize the section of Patrick's Cahokia map that pertains to the Powell group. There is no question that Mound 46 is a distinct mound and that the Powell Mound and its two associated mounds, numbered by Moorehead as 84 and 85, are further to the west and surely easily recognizable in the 1920s when Moorehead worked in the area.

In using the Moorehead maps of the Cahokia site, one should ignore the 1923 map and focus on the 1922 and 1929 maps. The 1922 map is the more faithful copy of the Patrick map and the more accurate map of the Cahokia site. The 1929 map is an accurate reflection of Moorehead's final interpretation of the site and the areas in which he worked.

The next map of record is one prepared by the U.S. Geological Survey in 1930 and 1931, when the basic plane-table surveying for the Monks Mound 7.5' quadrangle map was completed. Included in the Monks Mound quadrangle is the Cahokia mound group. Based on a photostatic copy of an apparent compilation of field-survey notes from which the final map was made, it appears that the mounds were surveyed in 5-foot (1.5-meter) contour intervals and with a great

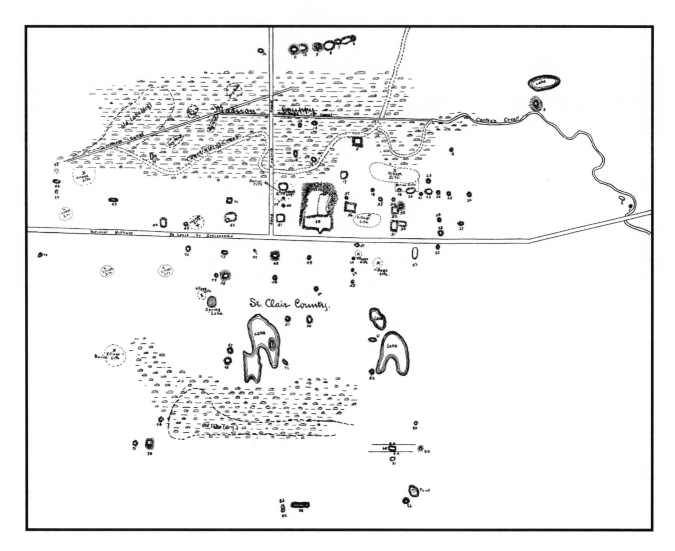

Figure 3.9.   The 1929 Moorehead map. Source: Moorehead 1929. Used by permission of the University of Illinois at Urbana-Champaign.

amount of detail. Many mounds shown on the quadrangle map do not appear on other maps. Figure 3.10 is a copy of this map showing the Monks Mound area. One can note details of Monks Mound, such as the east lobes and the south ramp on the front of Monks Mound, and many of the other mounds in the area are shown. The mound numbers on this map are based on the Patrick and Moorehead maps, and it includes additional mounds at Cahokia located on the 1966 UWM map. Mounds 1 through 71 retain Patrick's numbers, 72 to 85 are Moorehead's additions, and numbers 86 and 88 are the UWM additions. Not all of the mounds noted by Patrick and/or Moorehead are visible on the contours of this map; therefore, there are some gaps in the numbers.

As the Monks Mound quadrangle map was prepared for publication, many lines indicated by the field surveyors were smoothed off and many of the 5-foot intervals omitted. The published version shows much less detail than the field-note compilation upon which Figure 3.10 is based. Part of the published USGS Monks Mound Quadrangle is shown in Figure 1.5. Both are excellent maps of the Cahokia site, but the original field-note compilation map is more valuable for locating the mounds and interpreting the area.

Many of the mounds not recorded by recent investigators but noted by Moorehead are indicated on the USGS topographic maps. For instance, Mound 79 is clearly indicated as a contour where Moorehead located the mound. Mounds 45 and 46, which caused

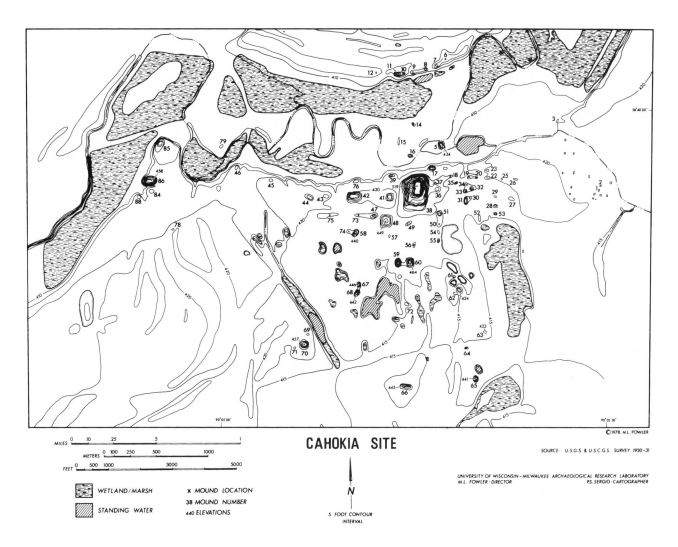

Figure 3.10. Map of Cahokia based on the field notes for the USGS survey in 1930 and 1931. Source: U.S. Geological Survey.

Moorehead some confusion, are shown clearly on the topographic map where Patrick located them. Other contours indicate the presence of mounds not noted by any of the earlier investigators. These should be numbered as mounds as well. For instance, to the east of Mounds 61 and 62 is a distinct contour that is observable in the field. What appears to be a relatively large mound was not numbered by either of these early investigators.

A schematic map of the Cahokia site published by Paul Titterington in 1938 described the mound group: "In 1922, Mr. George D. Higgins of St. Louis completed a survey of the group. He spent several years in his spare time making measurements and gathering data, and then constructed a model of scale showing the size and location of the various mounds. A photograph of Higgins' model is shown in Figure 2" (1938:1, Figure

2). That map shows the locations of mounds in the Cahokia group and their relative sizes and shapes. It appears, however, to be less accurate than some of the earlier maps.

Although many investigators worked at the site from the 1950s to the mid-1960s, there are no other known published maps of the Cahokia site from this period. In 1966 the Anthropology Department of the University of Wisconsin-Milwaukee began a thorough study of the Cahokia site. The goal was to make a detailed map of the entire Cahokia site from Mound 1 on the east to the Powell Mound area on the west, and from the Kunnemann mound group on the north to the Rattlesnake Mound area on the south. These were generally considered as the limits of the Cahokia site. This map was made through aerial photogrammetry and produced at a scale of 1:2,000 with a 1-meter (3.3-

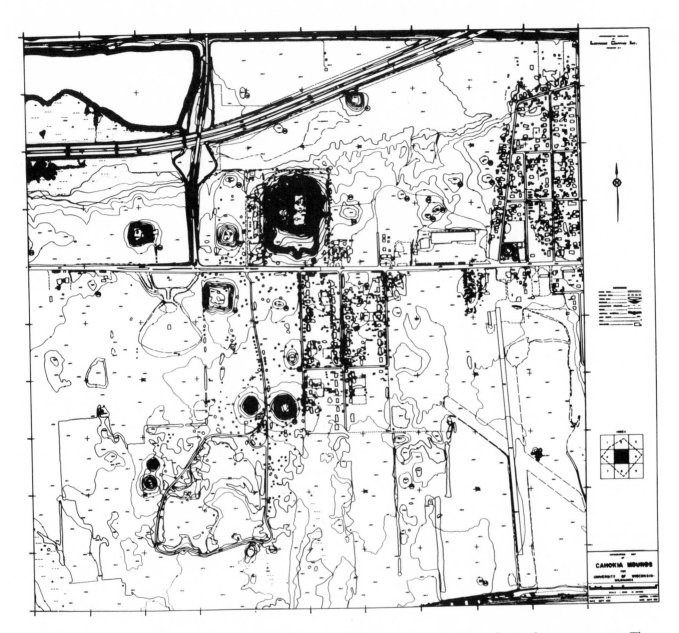

Figure 3.11. The central section, Section 5, of the 1966 UWM map. Monks Mound is in the upper center. The outside boundaries of the section are 2,000 meters. Source: Archaeological Research Laboratory, University of Wisconsin-Milwaukee.

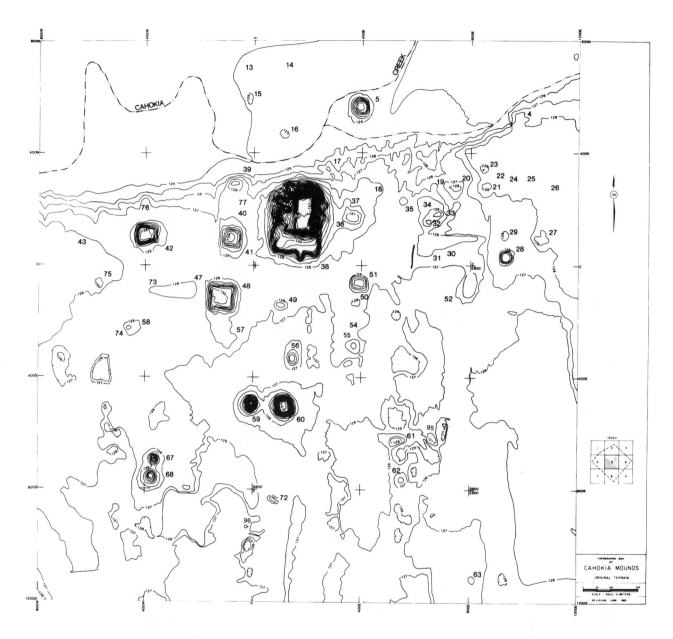

Figure 3.12. The central section of the UWM map with streets, houses, and other modern features removed. Contours of some mounds, such as Mound 51, have been reconstructed based on earlier maps, photographs, and descriptions. The outside boundaries are 2,000 meters. Source: Archaeological Research Laboratory, University of Wisconsin-Milwaukee.

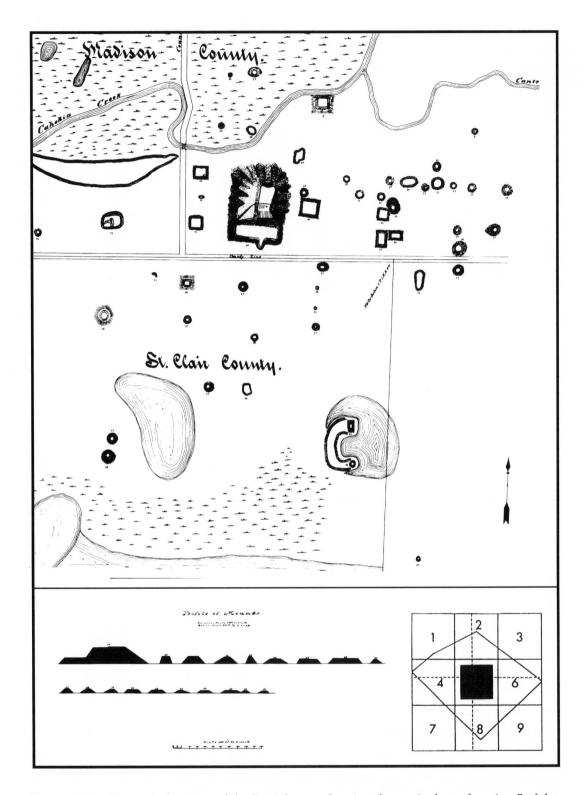

Figure 3.13. The central section of the Patrick map showing the equivalent of section 5 of the UWM map. The outside boundaries are 2,000 meters. Source: Missouri Historical Society and the Archaeological Research Laboratory, University of Wisconsin-Milwaukee.

foot) contour interval (Figure 3.11). The base map was made in several segments since at this scale it was too large to include on one sheet. The UWM map is divided into nine numbered sections, each 2,000 x 2,000 meters; each section is further divided into 25 400 x 400-meter subsections that are given letter designations. For example, Section 5H is 400 x 400-meter block in Section 5. (See Appendix 2 for a completed discussion of the UWM map.) A grid established by James Porter and his crew in 1962 is used on the map. The 0N0E point of this grid is just to the southwest of Monks Mound.

When the original grid was surveyed, it was intended to align with true north. However, an error was made in compensating for magnetic declination. Therefore, grid north ended up being 1°18'5" east of true north. By 1966, when we started making the topographic map, many archaeological projects had been carried out using this grid. It was decided to retain the grid orientation on the 1966 UWM map. The north arrow on the 1966 UWM map is grid north.

That basic grid was expanded and projected over the entire site for the 1966 UWM map. Recent surveying has placed concrete monuments at many locations in the central portions of the site, and as new projects develop such monuments are surveyed and placed in convenient locations.

A further refinement of the UWM map has been made in that modern buildings, streets, and highways were removed and an interpolation made of contours as they might have appeared before modern construc-tion (Figure 3.12). The interpolations are based on detailed study of aerial photographs and old maps of the area, including the many maps described above (Figure 3.13). Although it is probably impossible to reconstruct the contours, this map suggests both the locations of the mounds and the nature of the topography as they might have appeared in the nineteenth century.

Work is continuing on the mapping of the Cahokia site, and refinements of the UWM map are contemplated. For example, the 1933 aerial photographs of the Cahokia site indicate mounds being destroyed in the vicinity of Mounds 1 and 2. Surface examinations suggest that there are contour elevations in those points where mounds stood before their destruction in the 1930s. Further investigations in these areas may confirm these mound locations, and their reconstructed contours can be added to the map. Interestingly, more elevations are shown in the same general area in the 1930 and 1931 surveys than are indicated in the 1933 aerial photographs. Examination of these areas will determine whether they represent aboriginal mounds or are more recent soil disturbances.

All of the maps discussed here help us to interpret the full extent of the Cahokia site. They also document the topographic changes since Europeans and Americans first explored the area. By combining examination of the Patrick map with modern maps and air-photo interpretation, most of the original shapes of the mounds can be platted.

4

DESCRIPTIONS OF MOUNDS 1–37

Chapters 4, 5, 6, and 7 present detailed descriptions of the 104 mounds currently identified within the Cahokia mound group. The descriptions include discussions of the mounds' size and shape, both as they appear today and as they looked in the past, and how the mounds have been shown on the various maps of the site. Any known excavations or disturbances are also discussed. Grid coordinates are given for the center of each mound; these coordinates refer to the grid on the UWM map, which has its 0N0E point just southwest of Monks Mound. Discussions of mound morphology sometimes include reference to elevations of the base and/or tops of mounds as they appear on the various topographic maps of the site. These elevations are given in the standard format of feet and meters above sea level, although this is not always explicitly stated. Height refers to the distance from the base to the top of the mound.

Mound 1 (N200E2066)

This easternmost mound within the presently defined Cahokia mound group is a small rectangular or squarish platform mound just off the bank of Canteen Creek. There is some local discussion that this mound was built in recent times as a platform for a modern house. However, this does not appear to be the case, as the 1876 Patrick map shows a roundish contour mound where the present Mound 1 is located (Figure 4.1). One can conclude that the present mound, although somewhat modified by recent construction, is the location of the original Mound 1.

The base of the mound is approximately 129 meters above sea level (423.2 feet above sea level). The top elevation is about 129.8 meters (425.85 feet), making the mound 0.8 meters (2.6 feet) high. It is approximately 33 meters (108.3 feet) by 27 meters (88.6 feet) at the base and covers an area of approximately 800 square meters (0.20 acres). No excavations have been conducted on this mound; our only knowledge of it is from contour maps and its present appearance.

Mound 2 (N252E2028)

Just to the north of Mound 1, the Patrick map shows Mound 2 as elongated with a northwest-southwest axis. His drawing suggests that it had a tear-drop shape, rounded at the southeast end and pointed at the northwest end. The mound is shown as almost twice as large as Mound 1. The shape of Mound 2 is unique. Only Mound 52 shows any similarity in shape to Mound 2, but Mound 52 has its narrow end to the south and the wider end to the north. On the UWM map (Figure 4.1), this mound is not indicated by a distinct contour. The base of the mound is approximately 128 meters above sea level (419.9 feet above sea level) and at its highest point is 128.7 meters (422.2 feet) or 0.7 meters (2.3 feet) high. There was a house located on the northern boundary of what must have been Mound 2, and the UWM map suggests a shape similar to Mound 1, that is, square and flat-topped. There are two possible explanations for the dissimilarity between the Patrick map and Mound 2's modern appearance. First, the shape of Mound 2 may have been modified greatly since Patrick's time. Second, some other nearby mound is the Mound 2 indicated on the Patrick map. The 1933 Dache Reeves aerial photos do show what may be an oblong form north of Mound 2; the longer axis runs northwest-southeast parallel to Canteen Creek. This second alternative, however, is not supported by the USGS maps, which do not indicate any other mound in the immediate area of Mounds 1 and 2. The locations of those two mounds on the USGS maps is very close to those indicated on the Patrick map. No reported excavations have been conducted in Mound 2.

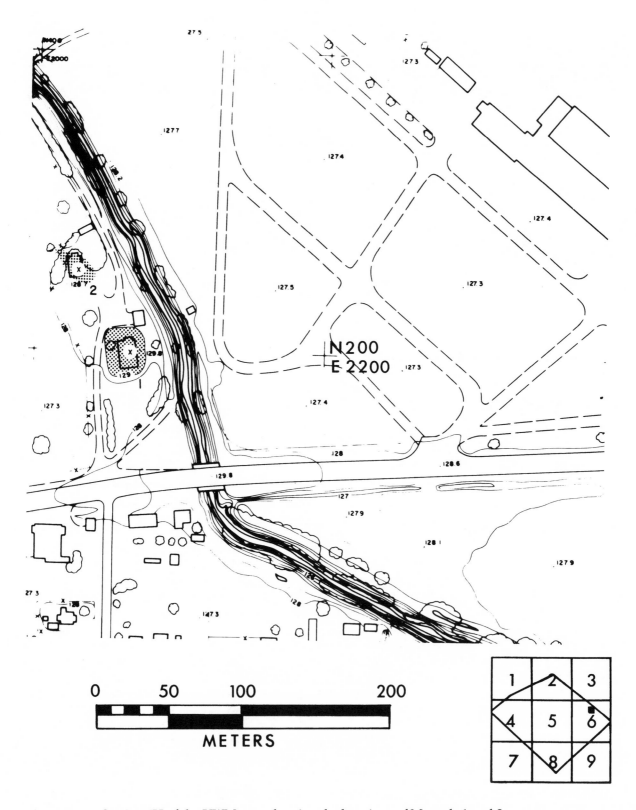

Figure 4.1.   Section 6H of the UWM map showing the locations of Mounds 1 and 2.

Mound 3 (N852E1628)

The Patrick map locates what appears to be a large, conical mound, which is numbered Mound 3, to the north of the Canteen Creek and to the northwest of Mounds 1 and 2 (Figure 4.2). Although there is some difficulty ascertaining the exact location of this mound, plotting it from the Patrick map indicates that it was near the present approach of the overpass on Interstate 70. If that is the case, Mound 3 was likely destroyed by highway construction in the 1960s.

Mound 4 (N524E992)

Patrick shows Mound 4 to the west of Mound 3 but to the south of Cahokia Creek (Figure 4.3). Present contours suggest the mound is approximately 38 meters (124.7 feet) by 34 meters (111.5 feet). The base of the mound is 128 meters above sea level (419.9 feet above sea level) and its highest point is 128.6 meters (421.9 feet), giving a height of 0.6 meters (2.0 feet).

Previous descriptions of Mound 4 have suggested it was much higher. Thomas (1894) gives a height of 8 feet (2.4 meters). The Patrick map shows it as a small, round mound comparable in size to Mound 1 and located directly north of Mound 25 and east of Mound 5, south of Canteen Creek. The mound is hard to detect in early aerial photographs, and no early USGS maps show it. The UWM map shows a northward extension of the 128-meter contour line in the area where Mound 4 should be, which suggests the mound was obliterated by modern construction. Moorehead makes brief mention of Mound 4 (Moorehead 1929). However, there are no published reports of excavations in it.

Mound 5 (N568E392)

This is one of the larger mounds shown on the Patrick map. It is located on the bank of Cahokia Creek immediately west of the point where Canteen Creek flows into Cahokia Creek. Generally, the Patrick map suggests an east-west, north-south orientation. Mound 5 appears to be one of the better-preserved mounds at Cahokia, as it still resembles the rectangular platform present in Patrick's time (Figures 4.4 and 4.5).

If one assumes that the base line of this mound is 126 meters above sea level (413.4 feet), its north-south limits are N520 and N586, and the east-west limits are E358 and E426. This gives a north-south dimension of approximately 66 meters (216.5 feet) and an east-west dimension of 68 meters (223.1 feet). Using the base of

126 meters (413.4 feet), the highest elevation on the mound is 131.8 meters (432.4 feet), giving a present height of 5.8 meters (19 feet). These figures are compatible with the previously reported dimensions of the mound. McAdams, in 1882, reports a height of 25 feet (7.6 meters). Cyrus Thomas, in 1894, gives a height of 30 feet (9.1 meters), and the Peterson-McAdams map of 1906 notes a height of 25 feet (7.6 meters). The difference between the 25 feet given by McAdams, which is probably more accurate, and the present 19-foot height could be due to siltation around the base or slope wash that has obscured the true base of the mound.

McAdams described Mound 5 in 1882: "One large oval mound stands directly on the bank of Cahokia Creek . . . and the side of the mound is so washed away as to give an excellent opportunity to examine the material and manner of its construction. It is composed of black loam, nothing different from the great pyramid" (McAdams 1882:60).

It appears that this mound was not excavated by previous investigators. Moorehead only refers to it in his 1923 volume (Moorehead 1923:48). In 1960 and 1961, during the Highway Salvage Program, the Illinois State Museum dug a stratigraphic trench into the north side of Mound 5. Mound 5 is an excellent representative of a square to rectangular platform mound. This was probably a substructure mound upon which a building once stood.

Mound 6 (N1288E360)

The easternmost mound of what is presently called the Kunnemann group (Mounds 6-11) was designated Mound 6 by Patrick (Figure 4.6). Mound 6 is associated with Mound 7, to its west. Patrick's map indicates that Mound 6 was conical in shape, whereas Mound 7 is apparently a rectangular platform mound. Connecting the two mounds on Patrick's map is a platform elevation. Traces of this platform do not appear clearly on the modern aerial photographs or on current maps. This is probably due to the road that now cuts through this area, which has also been extensively cultivated and is presently covered by three farm buildings.

Taking 128 meters (419.9 feet) as the base elevation for Mound 6, it is located between N1274 to N1296 and E348 to E378, giving a north-south dimension of approximately 22 meters (72.2 feet) and an east-west dimension of 30 meters (98.4 feet). The top of the mound is at 129.8 meters (425.8 feet), giving a contemporary height of 1.8 meters (5.9 feet). McAdams (1882) records a height of 10 feet (3 meters), Cyrus

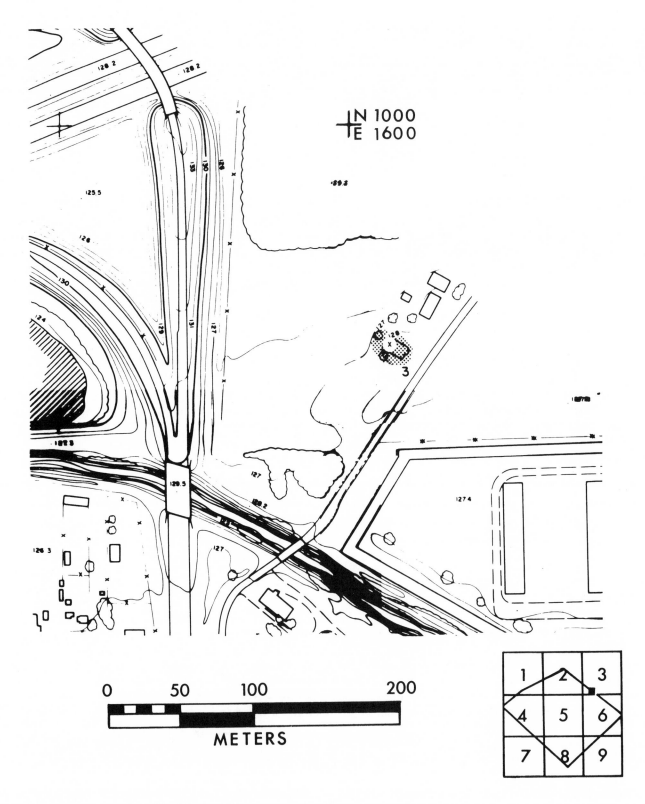

Figure 4.2. Section 3V of the UWM map showing the location of Mound 3.

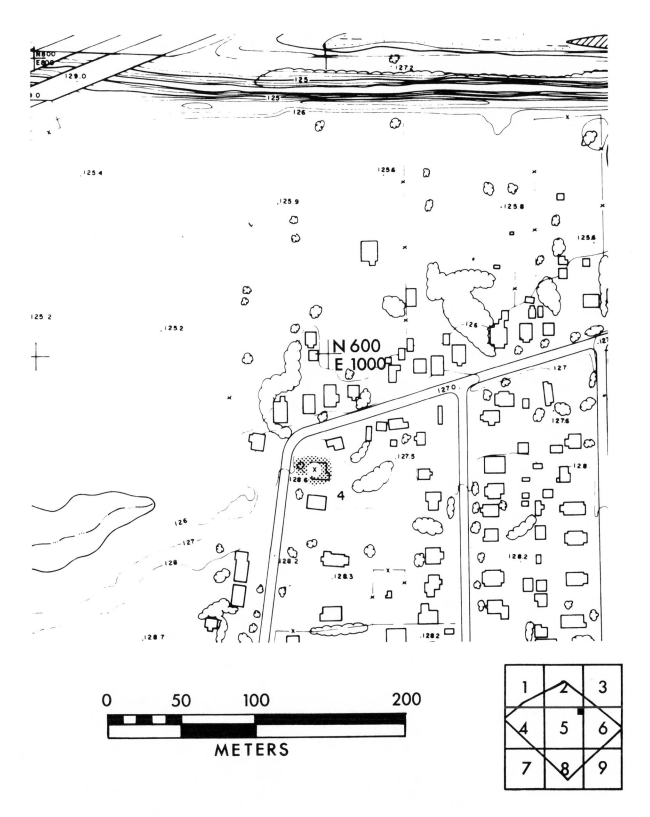

Figure 4.3. Section 5E of the UWM map showing the location of Mound 4.

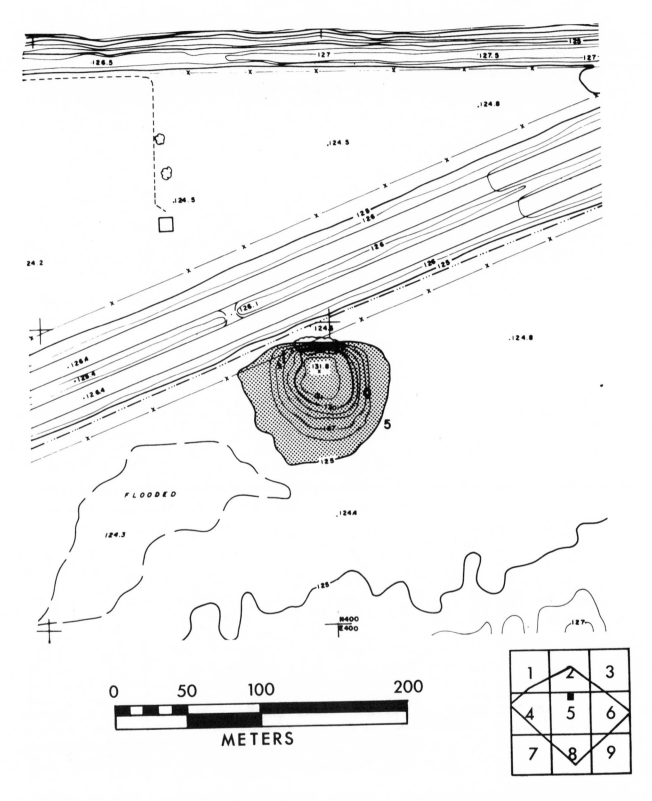

Figure 4.4.   Portions of sections 5C and 5D of the UWM map showing the location of Mound 5.

Figure 4.5.   Photograph of Mound 5. Source: Illinois State Museum.

Thomas (1894) 10 feet, and the 1906 Peterson-McAdams map about 5 feet (1.5 meters). These discrepancies suggest that the major deterioration of the mound took place between the early 1890s and about 1906, since the Peterson-McAdams height corresponds rather closely to the present height.

Mound 7 (N1243E266)

On the Patrick map, Mound 7 is in direct association with Mound 6. It indicates a somewhat oval, flat-topped shape for Mound 7, as compared to the more steep, conical shape of Mound 6. Taking 127 meters (416.7 feet) as a base elevation for Mound 7, it is located between coordinates N1244 to N1276 and E232 to E282 (Figure 4.6). This gives a north-south dimension of 32 meters (105 feet) and 50 meters (164 feet) east-west. The top elevation is 128.6 meters (421.9 feet), for a total height of 1.6 meters (5.2 feet). The McAdams map of 1882 gives a height of approximately 10 feet (3.05 meters) for this mound; the Thomas map of 1894, 15 feet (4.6 meters); and the 1906 Peterson-McAdams map, 5 feet (1.5 meters). These discrepancies are due to the lack of accurate observation by earlier investigators, and to the erosion caused by years of cultivation and other modern disturbances. The early height was probably above 10 feet, as suggested by the McAdams map. Some discrepancies in the heights cited above may also be due to the failure of the 1882 and 1906 maps to identify and separate Mounds 6 and 7 from Mound 8.

There are no indications that Mound 7 has been excavated, although Mounds 6 and 7 are referred to by Moorehead (1923:70, 1929:23, 117). These references, however, merely relate the Kunnemann mound group

to other features of the Cahokia site. It is interesting to speculate on the association of Mounds 6 and 7: one is a platform (Mound 7) and the other conical (Mound 6) with a connecting platform between them.

Mound 8 (N1236E190)

On the Patrick map, Mound 8 is indicated as a large, oval mound with a flat top. It is very close to Mound 7, but it seems to be connected by a small platform to Mound 9, thus bearing the same relationship to Mound 9 that Mound 7 bears to Mound 6. The contours on the 1966 UWM map suggest the same general shapes and relationships between mounds for these pairs of mounds (Figure 4.6).

Assuming an elevation of 127 meters (416.7 feet) as the base of the mound, Mound 8 is located between N1230 to N1248 and E172 to E218, giving a north-south dimension of 18 meters (59.1 feet) and an east-west dimension of 46 meters (150.9 feet). The top of the mound presently is at 127.5 meters (418.3 feet), making a total height of 0.5 meters (1.6 feet). Earlier maps show this mound as much higher. For example, the McAdams map (1882) indicates a height of 8 feet (2.4 meters); the Thomas map (1894), 5 feet (1.5 meters); and the Peterson-McAdams map of 1906, 5 feet (1.5 meters). The difference in height from the late nineteenth century to the present is probably due to the extensive cultivation that has taken place on this mound. At present it is in an open field and obviously has been plowed over the years. There appear to have been no excavations in Mound 8. Moorehead refers to it, as he did Mounds 6, 7, and 9, in reference to its relationship to other archaeological features in the site.

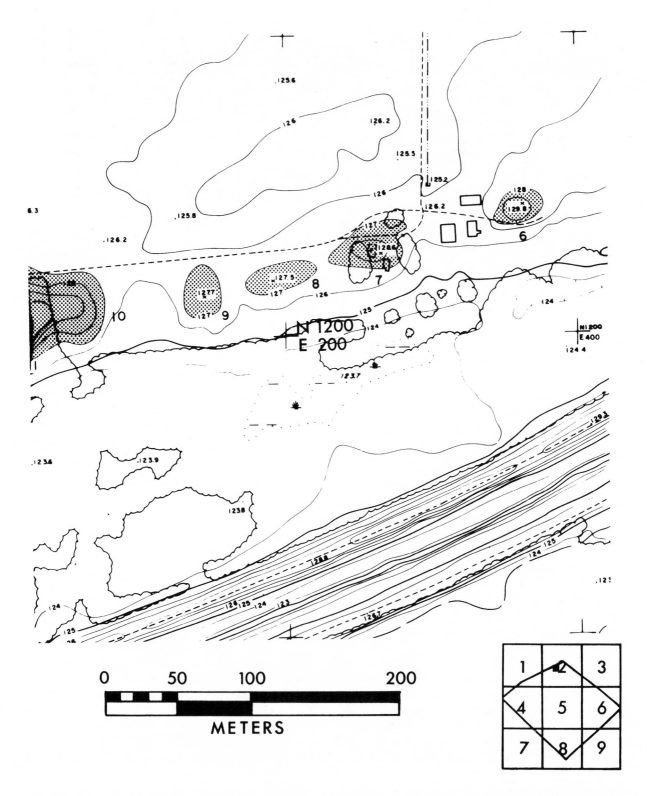

Figure 4.6. Section 2R of the UWM map showing the locations of Mounds 6, 7, 8, 9, and a portion of 10.

Mound 9 (N1226E144)

Located between N1214 to N1249 and E130 to E156 (Figure 4.6), Mound 9 has a north-south dimension of 35 meters (114.8 feet) and an east-west dimension of 26 meters (85.3 feet). Its present height is 0.7 meters (2.3 feet). On the Patrick map, Mound 9 has a squarish base and a conical top and it rises from its base to a rounded point. On this map it is also connected to Mound 8 by a platform. None of the recent photographs or contour maps provide a clue to the existence of the platform between Mounds 8 and 9. Cultivation and habitation may have obliterated the platform, and it is possible that Patrick confused the platform with the slight natural levee or ridge that underlies the entire Kunnemann mound group. The earlier maps show greater heights than the UWM map. McAdams (1882) gives a height 12 feet (3.7 meters); Thomas (1894), 10 feet (3 meters); and the Peterson-McAdams map (1906), 5 feet (1.5 meters).

No known excavations have been conducted in Mound 9.

Mounds 10 (N1222E52) and 11 (N1216E10)

Although these two mounds are numbered separately on the Patrick map and are shown as two separate structures on the Moorehead and UWM maps, I consider them two levels of a single structure. Mound 10 is a lower platform to the east, and Mound 11 is a large, conical, higher eminence on the west half of this location (Figure 4.7). For convenience, however, I will discuss them separately and then discuss their overall configuration.

Using 127 meters above sea level (416.7 feet) as the base, the Mound 10 portion extends from coordinates N1198 to N1244 and from E40 to E75. The E40 line, where Mound 11 begins, is taken as the division between the two areas. The Mound 10 section measures 46 meters (150.9 feet) north-south and 35 meters (114.8 feet) east-west.

With 127 meters as the base line, it appears that the Mound 10 portion is 2.0 meters (6.5 feet) high. That figure varies greatly from previous heights for these mounds, but it appears that even in earlier days there was confusion over their configuration. The McAdams map of 1882 shows a square-shaped Mound 10 extending from the east side of Mound 11. No height is given. The Thomas map of 1894 shows Mound 10 as a square platform mound larger than Mound 11 in area but 15 feet (4.6 meters) lower in height. The Peterson-

McAdams map of 1906 merges Mounds 10 and 11 into one large, oval mound.

The Mound 11 portion of this structure (Figure 4.8), from a base elevation of 127 meters, is 7.5 meters (24.6 feet) high. That figure corresponds with the McAdams map of 1882 and the Thomas map of 1894, both of which give a height of approximately 30 feet (9.1 meters). Moorehead, in 1921, thought that the base line of this mound was about 35 feet (10.7 meters) below the summit. He also believed it had been a conical mound approximately 50 feet (15.2 meters) in height before 15-16 feet (4.6-4.9 meters) were removed around 1900. Moorehead further indicates that the mound was probably about 400 feet (121.9 meters) in diameter with the top platform area about 75 x 56 feet (22.9 m x 17.1 meters). The 1966 UWM map shows the top to be 22 x 17 meters (72 x 56 feet), which corresponds rather closely with Moorehead's measurements. Mound 11 was extensively excavated by Moorehead in 1921 when he cut into the north side with a trench 60 feet (18.3 meters) long and 30 feet (9.1 meters) deep (Figure 4.9). References to Moorehead's excavations can be found in his 1923 and 1929 publications. In the mid-1950s, Preston Holder of Washington University excavated extensively on the west side of Mound 11 and into the area of Mound 10, which he considered a platform extending eastward from Mound 11.

I consider Mounds 10 and 11 to be a single unit, namely a large circular platform on the west (Mound 11) with a platform extending to the east (Mound 10). This structural unit appears to be one of the few mounds with more than one terrace at the Cahokia site. This is contrasted with the other mounds in the Kunnemann group (Mounds 6-9), which are combinations of oval or circular platforms and cone-shaped mounds with an intervening or connecting platform.

Mound 12 (N1230W164)

Mound 12 is illustrated on the Patrick map as a small, conical mound west of both Mound 11 and Sand Prairie Lane. Unfortunately, this mound does not appear as a distinct contour on the 1966 UWM map. Consequently, there is little data on Mound 12 except Patrick's suggestion of its conical shape and the appearance in that area of a small, oval rise on the UWM map (Figure 4.7). Mound 12 is reported by Moorehead (1923:45, 1929:98). His comments were summarized by Titterington: "There is a small mound about 1/4 of a mile north of Monks Mound from which a large number of unfinished celts were taken about 30 or 40 years ago. All were pecked out into a fairly good shape ex-

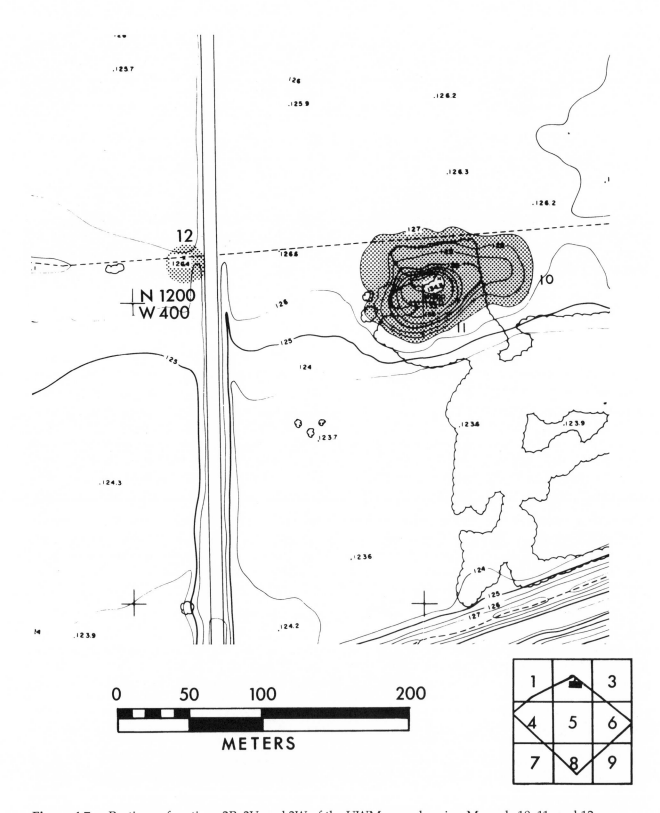

Figure 4.7.   Portions of sections 2R, 2V, and 2W of the UWM map showing Mounds 10, 11, and 12.

Figure 4.8. Photograph of Mound 11. Source: Illinois State Museum.

Figure 4.9. Excavations into Mound 11 in 1922 by Moorehead. Source: Illinois State Museum.

cept for some on which the bit had not been formed. The largest weighed about 25 pounds" (1938:7).

Mounds 13 (N702W16), 14 (N722E122), 15 (N592W18), and 16 (N472E110)

These four mounds, as numbered on the Patrick map and followed by Moorehead, must be considered as a group (Figure 4.10). There are major discrepancies between the Patrick locations of these mounds and indications on current aerial photographs and contour maps of the area. Patrick shows these basically as two pairs (13-14 and 15-16) just north of Monks Mound.

Mound 14 is a large, oval-shaped mound, and 13 is a small, apparently conical mound. Mound 16 is a large oval with a platform top, and Mound 15 is a large (compared to 13) conical mound. Recent maps and field studies indicate, however, that there are remnants of two mounds in the positions Patrick numbers Mounds 14 and 16, and another mound to the west, approximately halfway between what Patrick labels Mounds 13 and 15. I can identify only three mounds in this group, not the four that Patrick has numbered.

On some aerial photographs, a soil disturbance to the east of the line between Mounds 14 and 16, and approximately in a line with Mound 5, might indicate a fourth mound in the group. Whether this fourth mound's location is accepted or not, it is still quite a different arrangement from Patrick's. For now, Mounds 14 and 16 are considered two positively identified mounds.

Mound 14 (Figure 4.10) as mapped by Patrick is the northernmost mound of the group. It does not appear as a distinct contour on the UWM map. Field observations indicate a contour rise in a roughly round and dome-shaped form in this area. Patrick indicates that Mound 14 had a conical summit and oval base with the east-west axis longer than the north-south axis. He located this mound directly north of Mound 15 and south of Mound 9. The McAdams map of 1882 also places it north of Mound 15 and south of Mound 9 and indicates a height of 10 feet (3.1 meters), as does the Thomas map of 1894. Moorehead reports trenching this mound in April 1922, giving its dimensions as 180 feet (55.5 meters) north-south, 110 feet (33.9 meters) east-west, and a height of 5 feet (1.5 meters). He states that a road ran through the area along the crest of Mound 14. He also "saw a sunken depression in the center of the mound from end to end." In his probing Moorehead found "a few pieces of stone, no pottery and some broken bones." Directly to the south of Mound 14 is Mound 16 (Figure 4.10), which is clearly

defined on the 1966 UWM map. Assuming its base is at 125 meters (410.1 feet), it is located between N452 to N482 and E96 to E128, giving a north-south dimension of 30 meters (97.3 feet) and an east-west dimension of 32 meters (103.8 feet). The top of the mound is at 125.7 meters (412.4 feet), indicating a height of 0.7 meters (2.3 feet). The McAdams map of 1882 gives a height of 10 feet (3.1 meters) as compared to the Thomas map of 1894, which gives 15 feet (4.6 meters). The Peterson-McAdams map of 1906 gives a height of 6 feet (1.85 meters). The discrepancies between the late nineteenth century and the present are probably due to extensive cultivation of the area and flooding that has deposited silt in this region. This mound group is located in the lowest-lying land of the whole Cahokia site, an area indicated on most maps as swamp. It is possible that the bases of these mounds are buried and that their true height is somewhat greater. The locations of these mounds suggest that the area may have been drier at the time of their construction. The Patrick, McAdams, Thomas, and Peterson-McAdams maps show great discrepancies in the locations of these mounds. Swampy conditions and the difficulties of surveying the area in those early days may account for the differences.

Another contour and mound elevation on the 1966 UWM map is located approximately halfway between Mounds 14 and 16, directly west of a line that aligns it with Mound 5. This is designated Mound 15 on the UWM map, although it may not be Patrick's Mound 15. Assuming a base elevation of 125 meters (410.1 feet), Mound 15 is located between N472 to N510 and W5 to W25, giving a north-south dimension of 38 meters (124.7 feet) and an east-west dimension of 20 meters (65.6 feet). The top elevation is 125.4 meters (411.4 feet), giving a height of 0.4 meters (1.3 feet). The height given by the McAdams and Thomas maps is 10 feet (3.1 meters), while the Peterson-McAdams map of 1906 gives a height of 5 feet (1.5 meters). Since this may not be the same Mound 15 referred to by Patrick, I cannot comment on its change in shape and form. The Mound 15 on the 1966 UWM map is oval with the long axis north-south. This shape is confirmed by aerial photographs taken from 1933 to the present that show a soil mark of approximately this shape and dimensions.

There is no evidence of Patrick's Mound 13 on the UWM map. There is a possible mound to the east of the axis between Mounds 14 and 16 in a location that would be comparable to the presumed location of Mound 13, but it shows up on only on a few aerial photographs and cannot be confirmed in the field. Present information suggests that this group is represented by three mounds in a basically triangular pattern with its north-south line from Mounds 14 to 16.

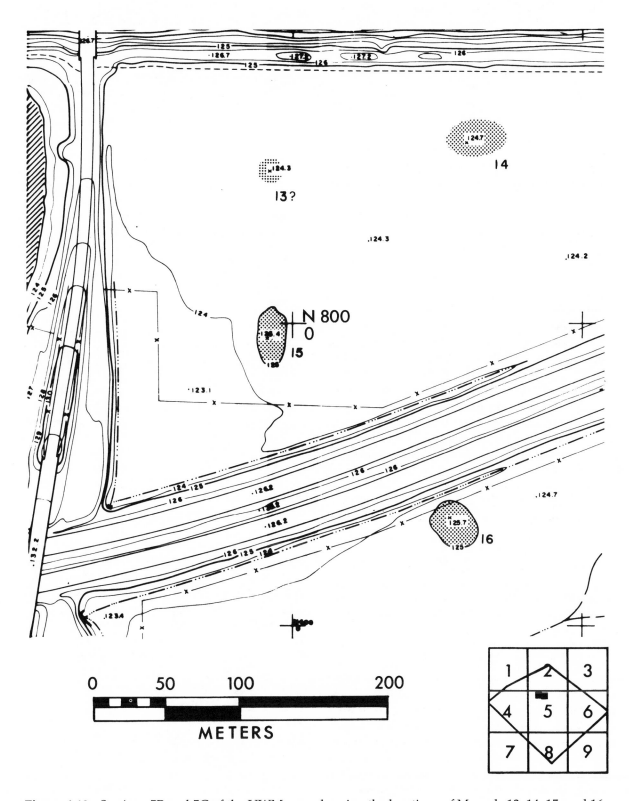

Figure 4.10. Sections 5B and 5C of the UWM map showing the locations of Mounds 13, 14, 15, and 16.

West of the median point of this line stands Mound 15. The number 13 is retained to represent a mound indicated by Patrick that cannot be identified today.

Mound 17 (N342E324)

The Patrick map shows Mound 17 as an irregularly shaped mound to the northeast of Monks Mound (Figure 4.11). The Patrick map shows the mound with straight east and west sides, but the north and south sides progress from northeast to southwest in a step-like pattern. On the McAdams map (1882), Mound 17 is shown as a square mound 15 feet (4.6 meters) high and in the same relative position indicated on the Patrick map. Thomas (1894), however, shows Mound 17 to be conical, small in area, 20 feet (6.2 meters) high, and much further north than the two previous maps. The Peterson-McAdams map (1906) shows Mound 17 as circular, 10 feet high (3.1 meters), and further to the west than either Patrick or McAdams indicate.

The USGS topographic map, which is based on surveys conducted in the early 1930s, shows a circular elevation in the area indicated by both the Patrick and McAdams maps, suggesting that the mound still existed in the early part of this century. The contours indicated on the USGS map suggest an oval mound with its major axis east-west and a height of 10 feet (3.1 meters). Today there is no major elevation in that area, the mound has disappeared. There is, however, a small elevation just to the north of the northeast corner of Monks Mound that may be a remnant of Mound 17. Since the area in question has been owned by the state since 1930, it is doubtful that Mound 17 was bulldozed during road building or other construction, although a small road encircling Monks Mound does make a turn in the general vicinity.

Gregory Perino (personal communication, 1989) has several times mentioned a flood in the 1940s that cut through low-lying land behind Monks Mound, carrying away several feet of earth in that region. It is possible that the area of Mound 17 has been eroded by flooding. Charles Bareis of the University of Illinois at Urbana-Champaign, digging just to the east of where Mound 17 should have been, did find indications of fill and construction work building up the level of the ground. Whether this is a remnant or basal portion of Mound 17 or some other phenomenon remains undetermined.

Because Mound 17 was apparently located near the northeast corner of Monks Mound, it might have been associated with the burial discovered by William McAdams in 1882:

We were working at our investigation, one beautiful day in the early spring, in a field at the base of the great Cahokia mound, when our probe struck something which proved to be one of these burial vases.... The next day, beneath the grateful shade of the great temple mound which towered a hundred feet above us, we took from that ancient tomb, which was not two rods square, over one hundred perfect vessels (McAdams 1895:179).

Moorehead further excavated the area nearly 40 years later and described the burials found:

Both of Mr. McAdams' sons, as well as W. J. Seever, Esq., visited the scene of our operations and indicated where they thought Mr. McAdams had excavated. During that season (1921) we had a crew of twenty-one men at work and we examined the ground some 600 feet northeast of Monks Mound where the witnesses thought McAdams made the discovery. We also extended operations, working rather intensively here and there for a radius of three hundred yards. Some of the trenches were fifty feet in length. Broken human skeletons were found scattered here and there, probably where Mr. McAdams had made finds. We recovered one flexed burial accompanied by half of a bowl. There was another partial burial a few feet to the west. The ground about it was much disturbed. Above both burials was a layer of hard baked red earth some two feet from the surface. The disturbed earth extended from three to as much as five feet in depth (1929:28).

Mound 18 (N262E500)

Just northwest of Patrick's Mound 35 is what appears to be a small, round mound with a flat top. Mound 18 is indicated on the UWM map as a lobe in a contour line, and it has the appearance today of a low dome approximately 1 meter (3.3 feet) high (Figure 4.12). The change in appearance since Patrick's time is undoubtedly due to cultivation over the last 100 years. Earlier maps estimate Mound 18's height as from 6 to 10 feet (1.85 to 3.05 meters), the McAdams and Thomas maps both give a height of 10 feet (3.05 meters). Early maps do not agree on the location of the mound. However, the Patrick map was more carefully surveyed than either the Thomas or Peterson-McAdams maps, and the location indicated by Patrick corresponds more closely to contemporary aerial photos and contour data.

Early excavations were conducted in the vicinity of Mound 18 and the mounds that form a line heading east from it, Mounds 19 to 26. Stephen Peet made the following reference in The American Antiquarian:

Figure 4.11. Section 5H of the UWM map showing the locations of Mounds 17, 36, 37, and 38.

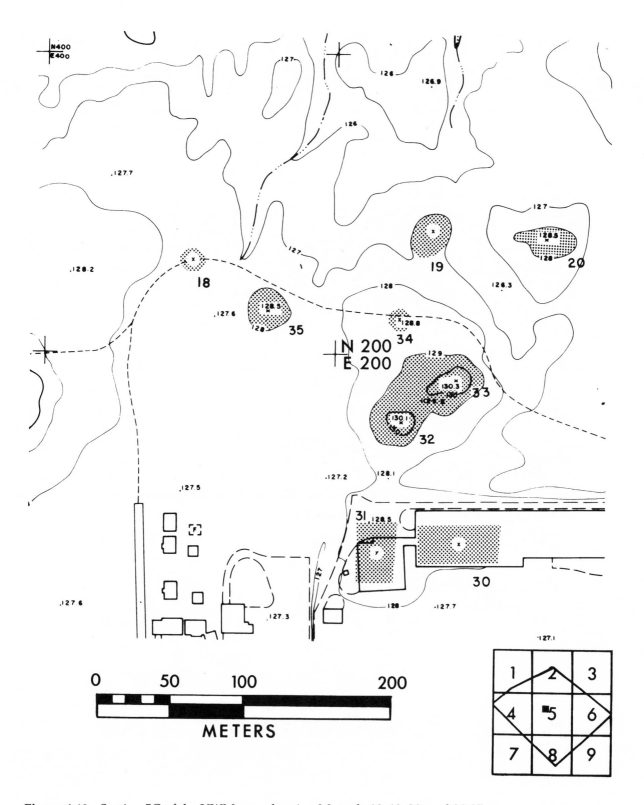

Figure 4.12. Section 5G of the UWM map showing Mounds 18, 19, 20, and 30-35.

Mr. Ramey, the owner of the mound, speaks about digging in one part of the field and finding heaps of bones eight feet deep, and says that the bones are everywhere present. The workmen who were engaged in digging ditches for under draining had a few days before come upon large quantities of pottery and skeletons of large size, but had carelessly broken them instead of preserving them. As to the character of the pottery and the patterns contained in them, we noticed some remarkable resemblances between the pieces exhumed here and those which are found in the stone graves of Tennessee. One specimen was especially interesting. It represented a squirrel holding in its paws a stick, the teeth placed around the stick as if gnawing it, the whole making a handle to the vessel. We noticed also a frog shaped pipe made from sandstone and many other animal-shaped and bird-shaped forms. The object which impressed us most was a sandstone tablet, which contained figures very much like those found upon the inscribed tablets taken from one of the mounds of the Etowah group in Georgia (1891a:9-10).

Mound 19 (N290E664)

To the east of Mound 18 on the Patrick map of 1876 is a line of mounds numbered 19 to 26. The first of these is Mound 19, which is located to the northeast of Mound 34 (Figure 4.12).

The remnant of Mound 19 today appears as a lobe in the 127-meter (416.7 foot) contour line. It is a very small rise in the ground, reduced greatly by plowing. Patrick indicates that Mound 19 is a conical mound with a very small area on top. The McAdams (1882) and Thomas (1894) maps both give a height of 10 feet (3.05 meters), but later maps give only 5 feet (1.5 meters) (Peterson-McAdams map of 1906, Moorehead map of 1923). There are some discrepancies in the location of Mound 19 on the earlier maps, but once again Patrick's location is accepted due to the care of his survey and because it corresponds with the UWM map and aerial photographs.

Moorehead excavated in this area, reporting that because of cultivation, the edges of these mounds overlap. He also reports excavating a trench "of over 250 feet from the center of Mound 19 well into Mound 21" (1923). However, on the UWM map 250 feet (76.2 meters) would cover only the distance from the center of Mound 19 to the center of Mound 20 and would definitely not extend to Mound 21. It is possible that Moorehead may have assumed that Mound 20 actually included Mounds 20 and 21, since the distance between Mounds 19 and 20 on the UWM Map is about 79 meters. If that is the case, Moorehead's description

of material found in Mounds 19, 20, and 21 would only apply to Mound 20. For example, Moorehead makes the following comment:

> About 150 feet from the west end of our trench, at a depth of three feet, were many fragments of spades and hoes, or digging tools of reddish chert. Why these were all broken we do not know. There were enough fragments to comprise fifteen or twenty of the tools, and about them were ashes and burnt earth. Fifteen feet beyond was a mass of pulverized galena lying in ashes (1923:17-19).

Assuming that the west end Moorehead's trench was in Mound 19, 150 feet east of that would be Mound 20. Therefore, this cache of chert hoes would pertain to Mound 20. Other remains found by Moorehead are discussed in the description of Mound 20. Perino, who excavated in the Ramey Field northeast of Monks Mound in the 1950s, mentions a burial "just west of the adjoining Mound 19" (1959:132). This was a female with notched-edge filed teeth.

Mound 20 (N278E744)

As mapped by Patrick, Mound 20 is an oval-shaped platform mound with the long axis east-west. It has the same general shape on the UWM map (Figure 4.12). Assuming the 127-meter (416.7-foot) contour as the base elevation of this mound, it is located between N236 to N300 and E704 to E772. This gives a north-south dimension of 64 meters (210 feet) and an east-west dimension of 68 meters (223.1 feet). The elevation on the top of the mound is 128.5 meters (421.6 feet), a height today of 1.5 meters (4.9 feet). The earlier maps indicated a much greater height. The McAdams map of 1882 gives a height of 15 feet (4.6 meters) and Moorehead, in 1923, 4 feet (1.2 meters). The latter height conforms rather closely to present data, suggesting that most of the disturbance of this mound took place in the late nineteenth century.

As discussed above, Moorehead's excavations were probably largely into Mound 20. The following summarizes some of Moorehead's findings. Most notable were a number of burials. The depths of the skeletons varied from 2.5 to 6.5 feet (0.8 to 2.0 meters), and except for one or two, all were extended. One-third were accompanied by pottery vessels. One skeleton was buried with four pots: a bowl, a jar, a dish, and a dipper-like object with a long, slender projecting handle decorated with sun symbols, a typical bean pot of the Cahokia area. Identification of the sun symbols is based upon the illustration published by Moorehead

(Moorehead 1929:Plate 17). Other pottery vessels, mussel shells, and rough flint objects were also buried with skeletons. None of the skeletons were well preserved. All the interments appeared to be on the same level or base line and were possibly buried in the village debris rather than in the mounds. Moorehead also mentions that most of the burials appeared to be women; unusual, he thought, since both sexes should be found in the cemetery areas (Moorehead 1923:17-19, 1929:41-49).

In regard to the Mound 20 burials, Perino (1959) mentions that two burials on the fringe of Mound 20 and one burial beneath Mound 20 had horizontally filed teeth. Perino was surprised that Moorehead made no mention of notched or filed teeth among the Mound 20 burials, since he is certain some skulls exhibited that type of filing. On the basis of the kind of pottery uncovered with these burials, Mound 20 is considered to be of a late date in the sequence of mound building at the Cahokia site. Mound 20 was one mound cited by Reed et al. (1968:146-147), who stated that most of the mounds were built after the completion of Monks Mound.

Mound 21 (N260E810)

Mound 21 is one of the smaller mounds in this east-west alignment (Figure 4.13). Patrick indicates that it was a small, conical mound. Visible on some of the recent aerial photographs, it appears today as a very minor contour elevation, one apparently partially covered over by slope wash or disturbed by plowing from Mound 22 to the east.

Mound 22 (N280E858)

Mound 22 is shown on Patrick's map to be a large, conical mound; it is part of a triangle made by Mound 22 on the west, Mound 24 on the east, and Mound 23 on the north (Figure 4.13). He suggests that Mound 22 was a large, oval-to-round platform mound. The base of Mound 22 is at an elevation of 129 meters (423.2 feet) and is located between N268 to N298 and E841 to E876 on the UWM map. Its north-south dimension is 30 meters (98.4 feet) and its east-west dimension is 35 meters (114.8 feet). These measurements conform very well with Patrick's description of a slightly oval form with its major axis east-west. The top elevation of the mound today is 129.5 meters (424.8 feet), giving it a height of 0.5 meters (1.6 feet). Both McAdams and Thomas show 15-foot (4.6 meters) heights, while the

Peterson-McAdams map of 1906 shows only 5 feet (1.5 meters).

Mound 23 (N344E850)

According to Patrick's map, Mound 23 is a small, conical mound (comparable in size to Mound 19) directly north of Mound 22. It appears on the UWM map (Figure 4.13) with a base elevation of 129 meters (423.2 feet) between N330 to N360 and E834 to E866. which indicates a north-south dimension of 30 meters (98.4 feet) and an east-west dimension of 32 meters (105 feet). The height shown by the UWM map is 1.1 meters (3.6 feet). The earlier McAdams, Thomas, and Peterson-McAdams maps are not helpful in identifying Mound 23. Mound 23 is a conical mound that is apparently related to Mound 22. There are no records of excavations in Mound 23.

Mound 24 (N286E910)

Moorehead describes Mounds 24 and 25 in his 1929 report as the Edwards mounds. Mound 24 is shown on the Patrick map as a small, conical mound in the east-west line of Mounds 19-26. It is almost equally distant from Mound 22 to the west and Mound 25 to the east. Mounds 24 and 25 may be associated with Mound 22, which is a larger, oval-shaped platform mound. Patrick's is the only early map that locates Mound 24. Ground surveys indicate that the base of what appears to be Mound 24 is in part of a yard of 3209 West Point Street in State Park Village (Figure 4.13). Portions of the mound extend into adjoining lots. Moorehead reports that he excavated in Mound 24, where he found an extended skeleton at a depth of 4 feet (1.2 meters). Near its head were some flint chips, two or three flint knives, and pot sherds. His report suggests that he dug a trench 60 feet (18.3 meters) long and 20 feet (6.1 meters) wide through the mound and that throughout this excavation were fragments of broken pottery. According to Moorehead (1922a), the preliminary Cahokia survey was made in September to October 1921, and it was at this time that he explored the Edwards mounds (particularly Mound 24). He did not identify them by number until writing later reports (Moorehead 1922a:21-22).

In April 1922, aerial photos of the Cahokia site were taken by Lieutenants Goddard and Ramey (Hall 1968), and Moorehead was once again actively engaged in archaeological investigations at this time. However, the aerial photos (Crook 1922:Figure 6) do not show any

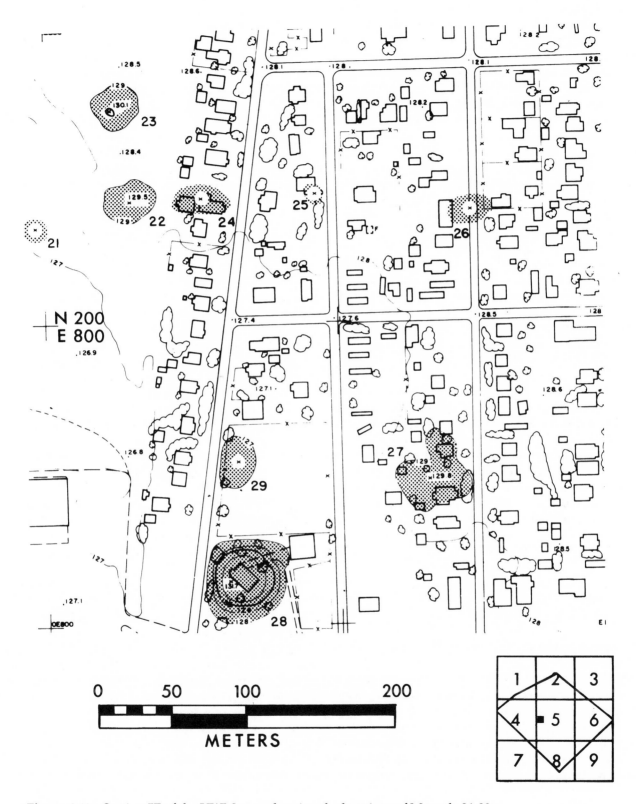

Figure 4.13. Section 5F of the UWM map showing the locations of Mounds 21-29.

excavations in what appears to be Mound 24 but do show large areas of excavations in what must be Mound 26. The large, round excavated area appears to almost completely cover the mound, and slightly to the northeast there appears to be a rectangular excavation. There is a possibility Mound 25 is disturbed, as there is a whitish line running east-west along its southern edge. Moorehead does mention the possibility of an excavation in what may have been Mound 26, although he calls it Mound 25: "East of this [Mound 24], distant about 400 feet, is another mound, Number 25, about 7 feet in height. We dug a trench through the center and sunk 8 or 10 test pits, finding no burials but discovered scales of copper on the base line. About one-third of this mound remains to be explored" (1922a:22).

The aerial photographs and the above citation suggest that he returned and again excavated into Mound 26 in 1922. However, in his later publication (1929:37), Moorehead identifies this as Mound 25 and says that it remains to be explored. Through all of this Moorehead apparently had Mounds 24, 25, and 26 confused, since in his early work he had not applied the Patrick numbers to the mounds. It is my assumption that he started excavations in the fall of 1921 and only later utilized the Patrick map of the site and applied its numbering system. There is some confusion in Moorehead's notes with regard to locations of mounds and which mounds he actually excavated.

The aerial photos explicitly illustrate excavations on Mound 26 and trenching in Mound 25. Hence, Moorehead's reference to Mound 24 may apply to Mound 25, and his testing of a mound 400 feet to the east may refer to Mound 26. Scaling from the Patrick map, the distance between Mounds 25 and 26 is much closer to 400 feet than is the distance between Mounds 24 and 25.

Mound 25 (N286E988)

Patrick shows Mound 25 as a small, conical mound slightly larger than Mound 24. The USGS map shows a circular elevation in the same relative position, which probably represents Mound 25. Field surveys indicate that the base of Mound 25 is intact and accounts for a rise in the street in the middle of the 300 block on Yale Street in State Park Village (Figure 4.13). Available information on this mound has already been discussed with Mound 24.

Mound 26 (N276E1094)

This is the last mound in the east-west row extending from Mound 19 (Figures 4.12 and 4.13). Patrick represents it as a conical mound slightly larger than Mound 25. It is about twice the distance from Mound 25 as 25 is from 24. Field surveys indicate that Mound 26 is partially in the yard of the lot at 3210 Amherst Street in State Park Village; the remainder is in the adjoining property and extends to the east side of the street (Figure 4.13). A contour representing this mound is shown at that same location in the USGS Monks Mound quadrangle. Details on Mound 26 were discussed in the section on Mound 24.

Mound 27 (N96E1062)

Just south of Mounds 24-26 is a group of four mounds—53, 28, 29, and 27. Three of these—53, 28, and 29—form a north-south line (Figure 4.13, see also Figure 6.12). Mound 27 is east of Mounds 28 and 29. Whether these mounds are related as a group is not known, and the details of each are discussed separately. Patrick's map shows Mound 27 as a conical mound with a bulge on the west side, which gives the overall mound an oval base. Mound 27 appears larger than Mound 29 but smaller than Mound 28. Moorehead makes no reference to this mound in his discussions, and he probably did not excavate into it. The Thomas map (1894) indicates a height of 15 feet (4.6 meters), as does McAdams's earlier map (McAdams 1882). Remnants of this mound are indicated on the UWM map with the base at an elevation of 129 meters (423.2 feet) and a peak elevation of 129.8 meters (425.85 feet), suggesting that all that remains is a mound 0.8 meters (2.6 feet) in height. On the 1922 aerial photograph (Crook 1922:Figure 6), the area of Mound 27 shows a square-shaped patch of disturbed soil with what appears to be an elevated center. This squarish outline is especially apparent on the west, north, and south sides, while the east end appears to be more diffuse. The general oval shape indicated by Patrick suggests the possibility of weathering and reshaping of the mound by this time. The aerial photos and the way Patrick draws this mound imply that it may be a multiple-level mound similar to Mounds 10 and 11.

Mound 28 (N34E924)

Shown by Patrick as a large, circular-based, flat-topped mound north of what was then called the Collinsville Plank Road (now Business Route U.S. 40), this is one of the better-preserved mounds in that area (Figures 4.13 and 4.14). A house standing on Mound 28 since the 1870s probably accounts for its preservation. *The Illustrated Encyclopedia and Atlas Map of Madison County* (Anonymous 1873) shows a house in this area on land owned by a Thomas Kent. The aerial photographs of 1922 show a house and other buildings, as do 1933 and more recent aerial photographs. A brick house stood on this property as recently as 1969, when the state of Illinois purchased it and demolished the house. On the UWM map, using a 128-meter (420 feet) elevation as the base of the mound, Mound 28 extends from N1 to N56 and E908 to E962, giving a north-south dimension of 55 meters (180.4 feet) and an east-west dimension of 54 meters (177.2 feet). The contours on the base map suggest the original squarish outline. Taking a base elevation of 128 meters (420 feet), the top of the mound is 131.7 meters (432.1 feet), representing a height of 3.7 meters (12.1 feet). The earlier maps give varying heights; the McAdams map of 1882, 10 feet (3.0 meters); the Thomas map of 1894, 20 feet (6.1 meters); and the Peterson-McAdams map of 1906, 18 feet (5.5 meters). Undoubtedly there is a certain amount of slope wash around the base that obscures the true base of the mound. There are no published records of excavations in Mound 28. When the house on Mound 28 was destroyed, the basement was left intact and filled so that it could be easily cleaned out and the basement walls removed for stratigraphic study.

Mound 29 (N116E932)

The smallest of a group of three mounds (27, 28, and 29), Mound 29 is north-northwest of Mound 28 and west-northwest of Mound 27 (Figure 4.13). The Patrick map illustrates it as a small, conical mound. On the UWM map, this mound is noted as a slight rise partially cut through by the modern street and delineated by the 127-meter (416.7 feet) contour line. If this is indeed the base, the mound is less than 1 meter (3.3 feet) in height since no other contours are mapped in the area. The earlier maps indicate heights ranging from 8 to 15 feet (2.4 to 4.6 meters) for this mound, illustrating the considerable amount of erosion and reduction resulting from intensive cultivation and modern construction. Using the 127-meter contour as the base, Mound 29 is located between N91 to N126 and E919 to E943, giving a north-south dimension of 35 meters (114.8 feet) and an east-west dimension of 24 meters (78.7 feet). This is probably larger than the original mound due to the amount of slope wash that has expanded the area. There are no indications of previous excavations on this mound.

Mounds 30 (N76E686) and 31 (N70E630)

These mounds are closely associated with each other (Figure 4.12). On the Patrick map, Mound 30 is an oblong platform mound with the long axis east-west; Mound 31 is a rectangular platform with the long axis north-south (Figure 4.8). Mound 30 extends eastward from the north half of the east side of Mound 31.

Figure 4.14. View of Mound 28. Source: Cahokia Mounds Museum, Illinois Historic Preservation Agency.

It appears to be somewhat smaller than Mound 31. Unfortunately, Mound 30 was completely obliterated by construction of Grandpa's Department Store in the 1960s, and no contemporary size or exact grid location can be documented. Estimates of height from earlier maps vary from 20 feet (6.1 meters) (McAdams 1882) to 5 feet (1.5 meters) (Peterson-McAdams 1906). The latter estimate coincides with Moorehead's observations in 1921 (Moorehead 1922a), when he describes Mound 30 as an extensive elevation on the east side of Mound 31 not over 5 feet in height. Unlike Patrick, Moorehead describes this mound as square, 180 feet (54.9 meters) on each side.

Given the above figures, Mound 30 was probably reduced in height during the early 1900s since a 1903 photo (by Baum) seems to show a road east of Mound 31 and Smith's Inn. This north-south road might account for the separation between Mounds 30 and 31 that both McAdams (1882) and Patrick illustrated. Moorehead thought Mound 30 was composed of earth taken from a village habitation area.

On October 3, 1921, Moorehead began a long trench at the extreme eastern end of Mound 30 into Mound 31. He wanted to excavate a terrace, or apron, leading up to one of the larger mounds. Moorehead's trench extended due west for 55 feet (16.8 meters). At 35 feet (10.7 meters) west he sunk a test pit 10 feet 5 inches (3.2 meters) deep and found disturbed earth, charcoal, and small pottery sherds at 7 feet 3 inches (2.2 meters). He dug another pit at 55 feet and found the disturbed area extended to 7 feet 8 inches (2.3 meters). During the excavation he found animal bones, broken artifacts, and pottery. He also discovered lumps of burnt clay containing impressions of reeds or rushes, probably from the building of aboriginal houses in the area. Nearer the base of Mound 31, he excavated, by means of a horse team and scraper, a pit 30 feet (9.1 meters) square and 8 feet (2.4 meters) deep. He noted a hard, burned layer of floor beneath the base line similar to the formation noted in the hand-dug trench. On the basis of his excavations, Moorehead was unable to determine whether Mound 31 was a burial structure or merely a foundation for houses or ceremonial lodges.

Slightly larger than Mound 30, Mound 31 is included in Patrick's profile of mounds, where he depicted it as a platform approximately 25 feet (7.6 meters) high. McAdams, in 1882, showed Mound 31 as a square platform mound about 25 feet in height, but Mound 30 does not immediately adjoin it in his drawing. Thomas (1894) showed Mound 31 to be a platform 20 feet (6.1 meters) high. The latter height

conforms with Moorehead's observation that Mound 31 was a pyramid with a flattened summit and Mound 30 was an extensive elevation on the east side of Mound 31 not over 5 feet (1.5 meters) high. Moorehead determined that Mound 31 was 7.5 feet (2.3 meters) higher than Mound 30, or 22.5 feet (6.8 meters) above the surrounding area. Because the southern edge of Mound 31 was much disturbed, he did not measure it, but suggested that the north-south axis was approximately 270 feet (82.3 meters). A Dr. Higgins was reported to have dug a small mushroom cellar in the north end of Mound 31, from which he secured a number of artifacts, including broken pottery, other objects, and soft, dark mound earth. A. E. Postmueller (in Grimm 1949) has reported that a storm or cyclone cellar was dug into the side of this mound and closed by a large wooden door. It may be the same cellar that was ascribed to Dr. Higgins. DeHass observed (1869:300-301) that a farmer living near the great mound excavated an icehouse in another mound and uncovered more than a dozen handsome vessels, mostly ornamented with animal-shaped handles.

A photo taken around 1900 (Baum 1903) indicates that Mound 31 was covered with a grove of trees and, therefore, was relatively untouched for a number of years. This is borne out by both the McAdams's and Moorehead's heights, which coincide rather closely. In 1915 Smith's Inn was located directly east about a quarter of a mile from Monks Mound. In Baum's photograph, Smith's Inn appears as a large, two-story building facing south toward the highway. Behind the inn is a grove of trees and on the surface of the mounds is a picnic ground and grandstand. Later the inn became the Mounds Club, a large casino and night spot. The casino was later occupied by a store, and in the early 1960s, Mound 31 was leveled and Grandpa's Department Store built. Grandpa's Department Store and parking lot now occupy the sites of Mound 31 and Mound 30.

As part of the work of salvage archaeology before the construction of Grandpa's Department Store, Joseph Caldwell, for the Illinois State Museum, conducted a stratigraphic excavation into Mound 31 (Figure 4.15). It revealed a rather complete stratigraphic sequence of the various phases of Cahokia development. The material from these excavations is currently in the Illinois State Museum.

Moorehead (1923:47) thought that Mound 30 was really a part of Mound 31. All of the earlier maps, however, treat them individually. He perhaps based his interpretation on the effects of erosion, cultivation, and use attendant with the casino and farm buildings.

Figure 4.15. Caldwell's excavations in Mound 31. Source: Illinois State Museum.

Mound 32 (N156E648)

Mounds 32 and 33 form one of the associations of square platforms and conical mounds (Figure 4.12). On the Patrick map, Mound 32 is indicated as a square, flat-topped platform of about the same area or size as Mound 5. Mound 33, at the northeast corner of Mound 32, appears to be a conical mound. Directly to the north of Mound 32 is Mound 34, which is another conical mound that may be associated with Mounds 32 and 33. However, it does not appear to be connected to them. Mounds 32 and 33 are pictured close together or connected on the early maps. Stephen Peet apparently was referring to Mounds 32 and 33, as well as to Mound 31, in the following description: "About a half mile to the east of the great pyramid, there was a high platform or pyramidal mound [Mound 31?], and immediately adjoining it on the north was a large platform [Mound 32?], but at the lower level and on the northeast corner of this platform, was a large conical

mound [Mound 33], the three parts being in close proximity" (Peet 1891a:7).

These two mounds probably were associated with each other and may have had, as Moorehead indicates, a connecting platform from the northeast corner of Mound 32 to the base of Mound 33. In 1882 McAdams showed them as a single unit with the platform to the southwest and the conical or larger mound to the northeast. This area has been so disturbed by cultivation that the mounds are now just low elevations in the area; they are completely surrounded by the 129-meter (432.2-foot) contour line.

Using the 130-meter (426.5-foot) contour line, which seems to delineate it, Mound 32 is located between grid coordinates N147 to N162 and E635 to E655, giving a north-south dimension of 15 meters (49.2 feet) and an east-west dimension of 20 meters (65.6 feet). The current top elevation is 130.3 meters (427.5 feet), giving a height of 0.3 meters (1 foot). This cannot be taken as an indication of the true height of this mound, as there must be a tremendous amount of slope wash or fill around the base. Excavation in the margins of this mound would delineate its true shape and suggest its height. The earlier maps, perhaps, give a better indication of its true height. McAdams combined Mounds 32 and 33 and gave a height of 25 feet (7.6 meters). Thomas (1894) listed a height of 15 feet (4.6 meters), and Peterson-McAdams (1906), 20 feet (6.1 meters).

While exploring Mound 33 in September-October 1922, Moorehead dug a deep pit to the bottom of Mound 32 (1923:Figure 2:25). This pit, 14 feet by 18 feet (4.3 meters by 5.5 meters), was 25 feet (7.6 meters) west of the western edge of the north-south trench in Mound 33 (see below). Moorehead reported that he found the base line about 17 feet (5.2 meters) below the surface. Village debris, he observed, extended clear to the bottom of his trench. A heavy deposit of ash and dark soil a few inches thick was found on the base line. He also thought that there was more village site material in Mound 32 than in Mound 33. He assumed, therefore, that Mound 32 had been erected over a site occupied by a "wigwam," since the mound had been built directly on this part of the village and none of the refuse had been cleaned up. Some 37 1-inch (2.54-centimeter) auger holes were drilled to the bottom of Mound 32. They revealed decayed bones and burnt earth at several points. In this general area Moorehead reported finding several pottery bird heads of exceptional form and finish (Moorehead 1929:29).

Mound 33 (N184E684)

This large, conical mound stood on the northeast corner of Mound 32 (Figure 4.12). Using a 130-meter (426.5-foot) elevation as an estimate of the base of the mound, it is located between coordinates N173 to N192 and E669 to E693. This gives a north-south dimension of 19 meters (62.3 feet) and an east-west dimension of 24 meters (78.7 feet). However, the base of the mound is probably buried and covers a greater area since the mounds in this portion of the site have been extensively plowed and their heights greatly decreased. Moorehead reported that the mound was reduced even before his study; witnesses said that Mound 33 was at one time 15 feet (4.6 meters) higher than when he visited the site. Moorehead points out that there was originally:

> a deep depression between Mounds 33 and 34, so the Rameys informed me, which had been filled in by dragging the earth from the summit of the mound down the steep slopes into this depression. The mound was conical originally, and according to all

witnesses probably fifteen feet higher than at the time of our exploration. This would give it a height of thirty-five feet (1929:44).

McAdams's estimate of the height in 1882 combined Mounds 32 and 33, giving a height of 25 feet (7.6 meters); Thomas (1894) estimated 20 feet (6.1 meters), and Peterson-McAdams (1906), 25 feet (7.6 meters). Modern contours indicate a height only 0.3 meters (1 foot) above the 130-meter contour line. Since the base is probably below the 130-meter contour line, much more of the mound is undoubtedly present but is obscured by the slope wash around the base.

In the spring of 1922, Moorehead began excavations on the north side of Mound 33, where the height was 4 or 5 feet (1 or 1.5 meters) above the general surface (Moorehead 1929). Even so, he found it necessary to excavate to a depth of 23 feet (7 meters) to reach the base line. By the end of his dig in the fall of 1922, the trench was about 120 feet (136.6 meters) north-south by 55 feet (16.8 meters) east-west. Moorehead's observations on the mound and its contents can be summarized as follows: (1) All bones recovered below the 18-foot (5.5 meters) level were coated and discolored (brownish green); (2) In the first 10 feet (3.05 meters) below the summit, the majority of the pottery fragments indicated ordinary cooking vessels. Fifteen to 20 feet (4.6 to 6.1 meters) below the surface, red ware and other sherds indicated thin, well-made vessels. Near the bottom of the trench there was a greater abundance of village material; and (3) At the bottom of Mound 33, 23 feet (7.0 meters) below the summit, were found shells, pottery fragments, and one or two ocean shells.

In the center of the cut on the base line 23 feet (7.0 meters) beneath the summit, Moorehead found the following: (1) A circular trench, nearly a true circle, 3 inches (7.6 centimeters) wide and 20 feet 6.1 meters) in diameter (Figure 4.16). There were no ashes or charcoal in the trench; (2) Crossing the center of this circular trench and extending slightly south of it was a circle of postmolds 2 to 3 inches (5.1 to 7.6 centimeters) in diameter (Figure 4.16). Many of these were preserved as charred stubs and charcoal; (3) In the center of the post-hole circle was a burnt basin or altar, and northwest of the circle's center was another basin. Ashes from these two basins were analyzed and apparently included bone and tobacco. Another basin south of the circle contained nothing; northeast of the trench circle were two additional basins shaped like "crude pans with handles." West of the trench circle was another basin filled with charcoal. The basins were 17 to 26 inches (0.4 to 0.7 meters) in diameter and 4 to 7 inches (10.2 to 17.8 centimeters) in depth; (4) The basins were

Figure 4.16. The circular trench and the circle of postmolds at the base of Mound 33. Source: Department of Anthropology, University of Illinois at Urbana-Champaign.

centered on a floor area 25 square feet in area and not very burnt; and (5) By auger testing, the area east and south of the circle was tested to a depth of 15 to 20 feet (4.6 to 6.1 meters); no burials were detected.

In the spring of 1922, on the western end of the trench about 14 feet (4.3 meters) below the summit, Moorehead found a number of post holes 3-5 inches (7.6-12.7 centimeters) in diameter. The posts were decayed but traces of wood remained. There was no indication of fire. He assumed that they were part of a large, circular structure. In the fall of 1922, the trench was widened and extended westward another 20 feet (6.1 meters). In his 1929 report, Moorehead apparently elaborated on this series of posts when he made the following comments:

In the west face of the trench was found a linear series of holes, about thirty in number in a distance of twenty-three feet, most of them less than six inches in diameter and about two feet in depth. Although they had been completely covered over by at least nine feet of earth the holes were only partly filled with dirt. In the bottom of many of them occurred brown decayed bone.... The series ended nearly due north-south and while most of the holes were vertical, a few slanted 10 degrees from vertical (1929:129).

The circular structures underneath the James Ramey Mound, as Mound 33 is referred to by Moorehead, are similar to other circular structures at the Cahokia site. For example, Harriet Smith found such structures underneath Mound 55 (Smith 1942, 1969). Moorehead sometimes referred to them as "sun circles," but there is no reason to accept this terminology.

Much of the pottery Moorehead illustrated came, he said, from the James Ramey Mound and appeared to be the Ramey Incised type, which belongs to the Moorehead phase of Cahokia development (see Figure 1.7). Based on his observations, Reed et al. (1968:146) suggest that this pottery came from under Mound 33 and that this mound was started while Monks Mound was in its final stages or had already been completed. However, it is not clear from reading Moorehead's reports that this pottery indeed came from underneath Mound 33; therefore, suggestions as to the time period when the mound was constructed may not be correct. On the other hand, from the illustrations, one potsherd allegedly from the base of the mound is an excised and engraved type that is not Ramey Incised (Moorehead 1929:Plate 21, Figure 1). It should be recalled that Moorehead thought that the characteristic pottery of the lower portions of the James Ramey Mound was red, thin pottery. Although he provided no details, this sounds similar to the types characteristic of the Early Mississippian period. Without proper illustrations, however, it is difficult to draw conclusions. Other interesting artifacts found by Moorehead include a Ramey knife (Moorehead 1929:Plate 26, Figure 1) and a large flint hoe (Moorehead 1929:Plate 26, Figure 5). A detailed discussion of the artifacts from Mound 33 can be found in Robert Wagner's study entitled *An Analysis of the Material Culture of the James Ramey Mound* (Wagner 1959).

Mound 34 (N224E644)

On Patrick's map, Mound 34 is a conical-shaped mound north of Mound 32 (Figure 4.12). The diameter of Mound 34 is shown as about half the north-south dimension of Mound 32. The location of this mound is unclear on later maps because of cultivation. Today the outline of Mound 34 is blurred, indicated only by an elevation point of 128.8 meters (422.6 feet). Excavations have been made in and around the area of Mound 34.

In 1950 a University of Michigan crew excavated in Mound 34 and, among other things, obtained charcoal from which a radiocarbon date of A.D. 1152 ± 200 years was obtained (Griffin and Spaulding 1951). This material came from a feature 4 feet 3 inches (1.3 meters) below the surface and from the submound village debris.

In 1956 the Thomas Gilcrease Foundation of Tulsa, Oklahoma, carried out a project under the direction of Gregory Perino. A large trench was made in Mound 34, and a huge refuse deposit north of the mound was excavated. Perino found that Mound 34 had a terrace, or apron, on its west side. From this he obtained a great deal of material indicating some of the background of the site. Some Caddoan influence from the lower Mississippi River valley is seen in a number of decorated sherds found under the terrace of Mound 34. Also indicating southern influence were two Alba barbed points and one Arkansas novaculite knife (Perino 1957:86). Charcoal from a prehistoric fire was found at the point where the ramp joined the mound on the west side. Perino's suggestion is that this postdates the construction of both the ramp and the mound. Artifacts in association with this included plain and serrated triangular two-notched and three-notched arrowheads, celts, a flint spade, several beads, effigy shark's teeth, fragments of wooden bowls, a negative painted sherd, an Alba barbed point, and two destroyed marine-shell vessels. The radiocarbon date obtained from this material (M-635) gave an age of A.D. 1290 ± 200 years (see Appendix 1).

Mound 35 (N228E554)

On Patrick's map, Mound 35 is indicated as a conical mound west-northwest of Mound 34 (Figure 4.12). On the basis of Patrick's map, it appears that there is a larger surface on Mound 35 than on Mound 34. The McAdams map of 1882 and the Thomas map of 1894 both give a height of 10 feet (3.05 meters) for this mound. The Peterson-McAdams map of 1906, however, indicates a height of only 5 feet (1.5 meters). Using the 128-meter (419.9-foot) contour line as the base elevation, this mound is located on the UWM map between grid coordinates N215 to N243 and E536 to E569, giving a north-south dimension of 28 meters (91.9

feet) and an east-west dimension of 30 meters (98.4 feet). The top presently has an elevation of 128.5 meters (421.6 feet), giving a contemporary height of 0.5 meters (1.6 feet) for this mound. Although there is no record that Moorehead excavated in Mound 35, he probably did because he refers to the type of "brown sandy soil" of which this mound is made (Moorehead 1929:104).

Mound 36 (N172E366)

Comparable to the pairing of Mounds 32 and 33 is that of Mounds 36 and 37 (Figure 4.11). Mound 36 is a large, square, flat-topped mound located directly east of the central section of Monks Mound. While Patrick's map shows quite a number of rectangular or square mounds with a fairly consistent east-west or north-south orientation, Mound 36 is aligned slightly east of north, as is Monks Mound. McAdams confirms the Patrick delineation of this mound, because he illustrates Mound 36 as square with straight, well-defined sides, about 15 feet (4.6 meters) high, and with a summit area of 1-2 acres (0.4-0.8 hectares).

When DeHass reported on the mound in 1869, he stated that the elevated square defending Monks Mound on the east was itself defended by a mound at the southwest corner. Today no significant elevation appears at the southwest corner; instead, Mound 37 is at the northwest corner. This may have been a typographical error.

With a base elevation of 130 meters (426.5 feet), Mound 36 is located between coordinates N148 to N196 and E330 to E398. This gives a north-south dimension of 48 meters (157.5 feet) and an east-west length of 68 meters (223.1 feet). The current top elevation of this mound is 131.7 meters (432.1 feet), indicating a height today of 1.7 meters (5.6 feet). This mound has been extensively plowed and spread out, implying that the base is probably at a lower elevation than the 130 meters indicated by the UWM map. McAdams (1882) gave a height of 15 feet (4.6 meters) for this mound; Thomas (1894), 20 feet (6.1 meters), and Peterson-McAdams (1906), 12 feet (3.7 meters). The square-to-rectangular outline of this mound is abundantly clear on recent aerial photos. Whereas Mound 36 appears to be nearly square on the earlier maps, the present contours suggest a more rectangular shape with the long axis east-west. This is true of other mounds, such as Mound 32, and this lengthening of the east-west axis may be due to predominant plowing in an east-west direction over the years.

Mound 37 (N225E346)

Shown as a small, conical mound adjoining the northwest corner of Mound 36, Mound 37 appears not only on the Patrick map but on all later maps of the site (Figure 4.11). It has been seriously deflated by plowing and constant use so that its height today is barely discernible on the UWM map contours and on recent aerial photographs. However, in earlier times, it apparently had a much greater height, as the McAdams map of 1882 and the Thomas map of 1894 both give 10 feet (3.05 meters) as its height. In 1906 the Peterson-McAdams map recorded a figure of 6 feet (1.8 meters). In any case, the height is always shown to be less than Mound 36. This contrasts with the other paired mounds, such as Mound 32 and 33, where the conical mound was taller than the associated platform mound. No excavations have been reported in either Mound 36 or 37.

5

MONKS MOUND

The largest mound at the Cahokia site and the largest man-made earthen mound in North America is Monks Mound (Mound 38) (Figure 5.1). It received its name from the group of Trappist monks who lived on one of the nearby mounds. The monks never lived on the biggest mound but gardened its first terrace and nearby areas.

There is undoubtedly some slope wash around the base of the mound; only excavation can reveal its true base. One can use the 1966 UWM map to estimate the mound's size (see Figure 4.11). Taking the 130-meter (426.5 foot) contour as the base elevation, the mound has a north-south dimension of 291 meters (954.7 feet) and an east-west dimension of 236 meters (774.3 feet). This increases, of course, if you use a lower elevation. For example, using the 128-meter (419.9 foot) contour as the base gives a north-south dimension of 320 meters (1,049.9 feet) and an east-west dimension of 294 meters (964.6 feet).

Using the 130-meter contour line for the base, the height is 28.1 meters (92.2 feet); using the 128-meter contour gives 30.1 meters (98.8 feet). It is possible that the north-south and east-west dimensions shown by the 130-meter contour are closer to the true dimensions of the base of the mound. McAdams (1882) reported a height of 108 feet (32.9 meters), Thomas (1894), 100 feet (30.5 meters), and Peterson-McAdams (1906), 104.5 feet (31.8 meters). It seems from these various data that the height currently is in the vicinity of 100 feet (30.5 meters). In the 1968 report on solid-core drilling of Monks Mound, Reed, Bennett, and Porter gave an approximate north-south dimension of 1,037 feet (316.1 meters), 790 feet (240.8 meters) east-west, and a height of 100 feet (30.5 meters).

Monks Mound is also the only mound with more than two terraces at the Cahokia site, and indeed throughout much of eastern North America. All maps and reconstructions of the mound illustrate four terraces or levels (Figure 5.2); the first terrace is the lowest and the fourth the highest. The most extensive

terrace, the first, extends across the southern end of Monks Mound. This first terrace rises an average of approximately 35 feet (10.7 meters) above the surrounding ground level. Patrick had a special detailed map of Monks Mound made (Figures 5.3 and 5.4); it is dated November 5, 1876. He showed the first terrace covering 1.75 acres (0.71 hectares), with the front face running at an angle of "North 83° West." Using the 129-meter contour line, the UWM map suggests a height above the surrounding area of approximately 9.8 meters (32.1 feet).

A unique feature, not shown on the Patrick map, but apparently always a part of the first terrace, is shown on the UWM map (see Figure 4.11). On the west side of the first terrace a bridge-like projection from the rising slope leads up to the third terrace. The projection was probably once more regular on its north-south side, since a roadway cuts through what would be its northwest side. The road was apparently built in the early 1800s when T. A. Hill took up residence on the fourth terrace. Excavations into the southwest corner of the first terrace have shown that a portion of this ridge was built by the Native Americans and was the site of a small platform mound.

The main feature of Monks Mound's first terrace is a projection extending southward in a position that aligns with the center of the third and fourth terraces. The Patrick map (Figure 5.3) shows this projection in some detail, and an axis is drawn through the third and fourth terraces at a heading "North 6° East." This projection is not centered in the front of the first terrace. Patrick shows it 310 feet (94.5 meters) from the west edge of the first terrace and only 185 feet (56.4 meters) from the east edge. The 1966 UWM map (see Figure 4.11) in general agrees with the Patrick map in this regard, although it shows a much more irregular projection.

This projection has often been interpreted as a ramp or stairway leading from ground level to the first terrace, and it is referred to as the south ramp. Excava-

Figure 5.1.   Featherstonhaugh's 1844 drawing of Monks Mound viewed from the south. It shows the first, second, and third terraces. This is the only drawing that shows a small mound on the southeast corner of the third terrace.

tions conducted in 1971 by Washington University suggested that this is indeed the case, since impressions of what may have been log steps were found in that area.

Most reconstructions of Monks Mound show it as composed of four very level and well-constructed terraces. Patrick made two models of Monks Mound, one showing it more as its contours were at the time he observed it and another with the contours straightened. Cast-iron copies of these models are in the Missouri Historical Society at the Jefferson Memorial Building in St. Louis and at the Peabody Museum at Harvard University. Most of the terraces are probably correctly restored in these models.

However, the second terrace in no way matches those reconstructions. Patrick's map shows the northwest quadrant of Monks Mound relatively uniform in slope and curvature. It is difficult to define any terrace in that area based upon his map. His model, however, shows the northwest quadrant of Monks Mound much as we see it today, that is, as a series of projections. These project almost as though they extend from a central point, like radii of a circle in that portion of the mound.

Putnam described the models in 1880:

I am glad to be able to state that Dr. J. J. R. Patrick, a careful and zealous archaeologist, residing in the vicinity of this interesting monument, has, with the assistance of other gentlemen, not only made a survey of the whole group of which Cahokia is the prominent figure, but has also prepared two accurate models of the mound itself. . . . One of these models represents the mound as it now appears, with its once level platform and even slopes gullied, washed, and worn away; and the other is in the form of a restoration, showing the mound as it probably existed. Before the plough of the white man had destroyed its even sides and hard platforms, and thus given nature a foothold for her destructive agencies. (Putnam and Patrick 1880: 470-475).

Putnam suggests that plowing the mound had contributed to the irregular nature of Monks Mound. John F. Snyder suggested that this portion of Monks Mound is irregular because:

the tribe became demoralized and abandoned the work. The arrest of their labors may have resulted

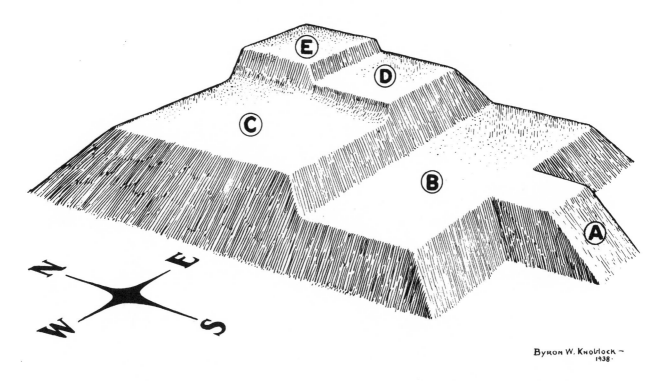

Figure 5.2.   Monks Mound as drawn by Byron W. Knoblock in 1938. This drawing was published by Titterington (1938: Figure 1) with the caption "Diagrammatic sketch of Monk's Mound as it is thought to have been originally: A, ramp; B, first terrace; C, second terrace; D, third terrace; E, fourth or top terrace."

from one or two causes. They were, perhaps, overwhelmed and dispersed by an incursion of wild savages; or, owing to the incoming herds of buffalo, they relapsed from their higher development of semi-sedentary life and agricultural pursuits back into nomadic savagery and subsistence by the chase (1909:91-92).

Moorehead, in the 1920s, suggested that some of these earlier ideas may not have been correct. After quoting McAdams (1887) to the effect that the protrusions on the northwest side were probably the result of erosion and rainstorms, Moorehead said:

It should be added that on the north side, there are projecting spurs, 50 to 100 feet long and 30 to 50 feet high. Some have horizontal summits, while others are sloping and have the form of approaches. This is the most abrupt side and some gullying has no doubt taken place. . . . The present writer's impression of the form of this huge mound with its platform and approaches is in harmony with that of Dr. Fenneman that it 'plainly indicates the work of man and not of geological processes' (1923:68).

Another suggestion is that of these irregularities on the northwest side of Monks Mound were deliberate. They do seem to project with irregularity, and as Moorehead suggests, some have flat surfaces while others appear almost as approaches or ramps leading up to the mound. The protrusions radiate around this section of Monks Mound as if from a central point somewhere on the third terrace. Further argument for their deliberate manufacture is presented by Reed et al.:

The second terrace is an irregular mass on the western side of the mound with a partially level area 65.5 feet high. It has long been assumed that this structure was largely destroyed by erosion, but our photogrammetric map . . . suggests that there is not enough wash at the base to account for the deep gullies. Moreover, excavation in the wash area near the base of the mound revealed a Mississippian house structure 18 inches beneath the present surface (1968:137).

That this Mississippian house was built on a sloping surface and appeared so close to the modern surface

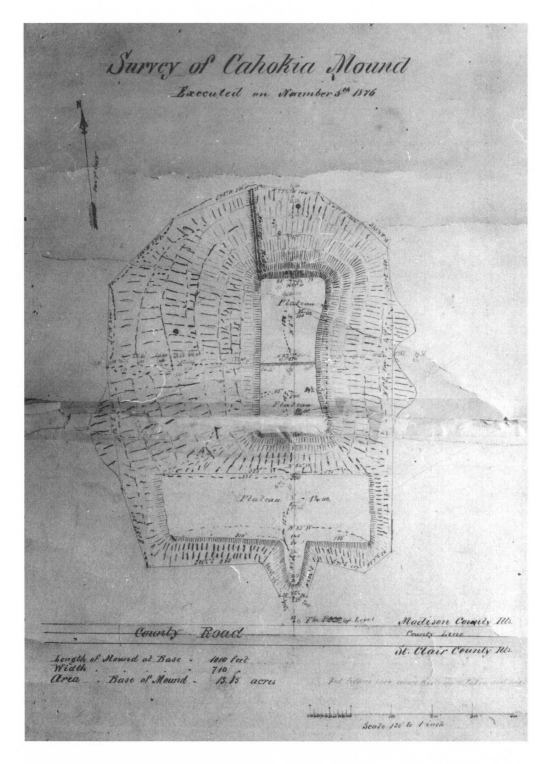

Figure 5.3.   Map of Monks Mound made in 1876. This is basically a survey map showing the details of the traverses around the mound at different elevations and showing the dimensions measured by the surveyor. Source: 1976 photograph of the original (in the Missouri Historical Society) by James Anderson and Melvin Fowler.

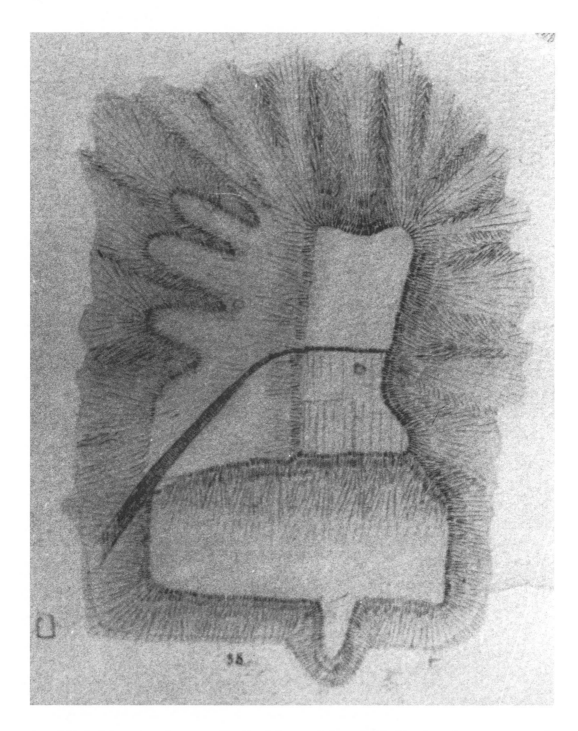

Figure 5.4. Monks Mound as drawn on the Patrick map. It is probably based on the survey map shown in Figure 5.3, although this map shows more details of the second terrace on the northwest corner of the mound. Source: 1967 photograph of the original (in the Missouri Historical Society) by James Anderson and Melvin Fowler.

suggests that the gullies were not caused solely by wash created since the Mississippian period.

Irregular though it is, there is certainly evidence that the second terrace represents a deliberate construction feature of unknown function as a part of the building up of Monks Mound to its present form. However, only detailed excavation can determine conclusively whether it is erosional or deliberate, or if there is some other explanation for the second terrace.

The third and fourth terraces occupy a central location in the eastern half of the main mass of the mound. In terms of the structure of the mound, they occur in the uppermost level of the northeast quadrant. The steepest slopes of Monks Mound are on the north and east sides. Altogether the third and fourth terraces encompass an area approximately 100 meters (328.1 feet) north-south by 50 meters (164.0 feet) east-west. The entire area is encompassed in the 155-meter (508.5-foot) contour line on the UWM map (see Figure 4.11). The fourth terrace, which is higher, is encompassed basically within the 157-meter (515.9-foot) contour line.

The fourth terrace was apparently the residence of T. A. Hill. According to DeHass "[Hill] moved on the property in 1831 and erected a cabin upon the very summit. He there lived many years, died and lies buried at the north-west corner of the great tumulus" (1869:297). Hill's residence is illustrated in McAdams's (1887) drawing of Monks Mound (Figure 5.5) as well as in the 1834 drawings by the artist Karl Bodmer (see Figure 2.3).

In the 1960s and again in 1971 excavations were carried out on the third and fourth terraces of Monks Mound by archaeologists from Washington University. They discovered the remains of a very large building—30 x 12 meters (100 x 40 feet)—partially enclosed by a wall and with a large upright post in front on the fourth terrace.

What locals call the "east lobes" of the mound are noted on most of the maps and drawings of Monks Mound. The Patrick map of 1876 (Figure 5.3) shows two rather large protrusions extending from the east side, more-or-less due east of the fourth terrace. These same types of protrusions are shown quite clearly on the UWM map (see Figure 4.11).

Alternative explanations for the east lobes have been given. One is that they represent a natural slumping of material from the steep east side of Monks Mound. Moorehead may have been referring to these lobes and to this phenomenon in 1923 when he wrote: "On the east side there is some evidence of creep of considerable masses of material and deposition at the base of the mound of material washed down from above" (1923:68).

Excavations into the lobes were conducted in 1971 by crews from the University of Wisconsin-Milwaukee. They found that the lobes were made up of basket-loaded clay laid over very late Mississippian archaeological material (see Figure 1.7). This suggests that, whatever their original purpose or source, they covered the area in the late fourteenth century.

The winter of 1984 was a particularly wet one in the Cahokia area, and there were major slumps of the north and east faces of Monks Mound. The eastern slump was very near the northernmost east lobe. This slump was tested by archaeologists of the Illinois State Museum and found to be made of disturbed basket loading (McGimsey and Wiant 1984). The 1984 slump looks very much like the existing lobes, suggesting that the east lobes were not ramps but slumps as Moorehead thought.

There are many other unique mound features mentioned in the early literature, but they are neither confirmable nor substantiated by later data. Early reports on the dimensions and appearance of Monks Mound are fairly uniform in their reporting of size and shape; however, various writers have offered unique comments on one or another particular feature of the mound. Their comments could be based either on acute observation or fanciful speculation. They cannot be accepted at face value, but are provocative and interesting nonetheless.

Several people comment on a general terracing of Monks Mound other than the four major terraces mentioned here. A general comment of this type was made by Wild: "Monks Mound, when viewed from the west, presents strikingly, the appearance of a strong castle or fortress, which time has just begun to mark with ruin, . . . while the terraces, which rise on this side, rise with considerable regularity above each other, look as if they were intended for armed host to parade upon" (1841:53). Wild was probably referring to the standard first, second, third, and fourth terraces of the mound, although his description suggests a step-terrace appearance.

Photographs of Monks Mound taken in 1892 and in the possession of the Missouri Historical Society indicate a sort of step-terracing on the east face of Monks Mound (Figures 5.6-5.9). These terraces may be the result of vegetation that checked erosion, producing a terrace-like appearance, or they could be cattle paths along the side of the mound. On the other hand, the photos may demonstrate the early appearance of the mound and the nature of its construction before erosion and vegetation changed its profile. Evidence that Monks Mound may have been terraced in this nature comes from data from the 1964 excavations

Figure 5.5. McAdam's drawing of Monks Mound. Source: McAdams 1882:58.

of Charles J. Bareis in the area where the first terrace meets the slope of the third terrace:

> Perhaps the most significant data obtained from the excavations conducted on the first terrace was the exposure of five minor terrace levels in plan and profile in the test trench. These levels constitute the original south side of the third terrace and indicate that at least a portion of this side was constructed in a series of plateaus or ramps rather than built from top to bottom in a steeply inclined sloping manner. The levels do not appear to represent the steps of a stairway, but an adequate functional explanation cannot be offered at the present time because only a very small

section of the original south side of the third terrace has been exposed (Bareis 1964b:5).

Another author suggested that Monks Mound may have been surrounded by a moat at one time. In 1843 William Oliver, author of one of the many popular advice-to-immigrant books, made the following observations:

> The earth for the construction of this huge mass has been lifted from the circumference of its base, as is evident from the regular ditch-like depression intervening between it and the surface of the prairie. On the north side, which I could not get at, it appeared

Figure 5.6.   An 1892 photograph of Monks Mound viewed from the south. Source: Missouri Historical Society.

Figure 5.7.   An 1892 photograph of Monks Mound viewed from the southeast. Source: Missouri Historical Society.

Figure 5.8. An 1892 photograph of Monks Mound viewed from the west.
Source: Missouri Historical Society.

Figure 5.9. An 1892 photograph of Monks Mound viewed from the northeast.
Source: Missouri Historical Society.

to me that the ground naturally fell away towards a creek in the immediate neighborhood. It is not unlikely that the immense ditch contained water, which has either been drained away artificially or by the natural depression of the creek (1843:170-171).

Examination of recent contour maps provides no clue to the location of this moat.

The Cahokia mounds area was flooded several times after 1843. According to Moorehead:

The highest known flood level of the Mississippi River at St. Louis was in 1844, when the waters rose 7.58 feet above the city directrix, reaching an altitude of 420.31 feet above sea level. According to the topographic map of the St. Louis quadrangle, published by the U.S. Geological Survey, involving the site of the Cahokia Mounds, there are considerable levels above the 420 foot level along the foot of the east valley wall and in the vicinity of Granite City. Monks Mound and few others nearby are on a slight swell a little above 420 feet, but the surface surrounding most of the others appears to be somewhat under that level. Hence, it is thought that many of the mounds were surrounded by this flood. The flood of 1903, two or three feet below that of 1844, reached and covered the low sags in the vicinity of the mounds (1923:71).

Another extensive flood since 1903 is described by Gregory Perino. Perino (personal communication, 1989) has stated that large areas of the ground just northeast of Monks Mound were washed away and the ground level lowered 2 or 3 feet. Such flooding could have alternately filled in and/or removed the evidence of the moat described by Oliver. However, Oliver is the only writer who makes mention of a ditch surrounding Monks Mound.

Variations in topography have also been examined. A rough comparison of elevations on Patrick's 1876 map with those of the 1966 UWM map suggests that elevations of the south edge of the first terrace projections and elevations of the north and east edges of the mound are comparable. However, Patrick's survey showed the area slightly east and west of the borders of the central portion of the mound about 6 feet (1.8 meters) higher than present data. Again, archaeological excavations are necessary to resolve this question of the moat and erosion from flooding.

Several investigators report secondary mounds on different terraces of Monks Mound. William McAdams reported: "to the northwest corner of the base of the structure [Monks Mound] there seems to be a small mound attached, in exact imitation of the small mounds attached to the base of the pyramids of Egypt as well as those of Mexico" (1882:58-59). No map shows

any definite outline of a mound in this area, but buildings located near the northwest corner of Monks Mound are on a slight rise of land.

Other early observers did not note the ridge of land on the west side of the first terrace mentioned above. Wild, for example, says: "On the south side of this mound is a terrace, about two hundred and fifty yards along and ninety in width, perfectly level, and elevated about forty-five feet above the surface of the prairie" (1841:52). As discussed above, excavations into this ridge indicated that a small platform mound occupied by public buildings had been constructed at the southwest corner of Monks Mound's first terrace.

Since the visit to Cahokia Mounds by Featherstonhaugh (see Figure 5.1) in 1834-1835, the existence of a mound on the third terrace has been reported.

Mr. Hill laid the foundation of his dwelling upon an eminence he found on the summit of this elevated territory, and upon digging into it found large human bones, with Indian pottery, stone axes and tomahawks; from whence it would appear that these mounds not only contained a sepulcher at their base, but have been used for the same purpose in aftertimes at the summit (Featherstonhaugh 1844:266-267).

DeHass also described this mound:

The great mound was originally surmounted by a conical mound 10 feet in height. This peculiar feature characterizes one of the square elevations west of the great tumulus [Mound 42]. Removal of the small mound revealed numerous interesting relics—human bones, stone implements and weapons, vases of unburnt earthen ware, etc. These with a large collection of ancient art were long kept by Mr. Hill, former proprietor of the mound (1869: 296).

Although McAdams does not refer to the mound, he observed traces of Hill's former home in the 1880s: "On the top of the pyramid are the remains of a house, said to have been commenced by the monks, but afterwards added to and finished as a comfortable residence for the family of a man named Hill" (quoted in Moorehead 1929:19). The UWM contour map shows a circular-like extension of the contours in the southeast corner of the third terrace of Monks Mound. This may represent remnants of the mound after it was torn down and leveled by Hill.

Another unique feature was mentioned by only one person. Randall Parrish in 1906 said:

A Mr. Hill, who once lived upon it, while making excavation near the northwest extremity uncovered human bones and white pottery in considerable quantities. The bones, which instantly crumbled to dust on exposure to the air, appeared larger than ordinary, while the teeth were double in front as well as behind (1906:22).

Unfortunately, no other reference to this burial is found in other writings about Monks Mound. Therefore, it is difficult to determine whether Parrish obtained it from local hearsay, or whether he confused direction and is referring to the mound Hill excavated on the third terrace.

The following tantalizing bit of information was obtained by DeHass in an interview with Hill's widow:

Many of the larger tumuli are believed to have contained secret entrances which were used after the structure had been completed. This was the case of the great mound at Grave Creek, Virginia, a mound near New Madrid, and it is a notable feature in the Pyramids. Mrs. Hill, who resided a quarter of a century on the great mound, informs me that a large entrance was at one time discovered, but filled up to prevent wild animals making therein their dens (DeHass 1869:295).

Patrick's 1876 map noted a "narrow ridge" on Monks Mound's north side that extends from the northwest corner of the fourth terrace down to the base of the mound at a very slight angle to the west. This ridge is also apparent on some of the Missouri Historical Society photographs taken in 1892. A contour on the 1966 UWM map suggests a ridge in approximately the same location. No other maps show this ridge nor is there an explanation as to what it might represent.

Although not directly on Monks Mound, the burial group discovered by McAdams seems to be associated with the mound:

In excavating near the base of the great temple mound of Cahokia, whose towering height of over 100 feet gave a grateful shade for our laborers, we found in a crumbling tomb of earth and stone a great number of burial vases, over one hundred of which were quite perfect. It was a most singular collection, as if the Mound-Builder, with patient and skillful hand, united with artistic test in shaping the vessels, had endeavored to make a representation of the natural history of the country in ceramics. Some of these were painted, and there were also the paint pots and dishes holding the colors, together with the little bone paddle for mixing, and other implements of the aboriginal artist (McAdams 1887:57).

A further discussion of this burial is found under the discussion of Mound 17, in Chapter 4.

HISTORY OF OBSERVATIONS AND EXCAVATIONS

Monks Mound is located on the banks of Cahokia Creek, Section 35, Nameoki Township, Madison County, Illinois. That statement is about the only one regarding Monks Mound that has gone unchallenged. Authorities have disagreed over whether Monks Mound is artificial or natural. Various dimensions have been given for its shape and size, and many speculations made on the source of its material. One of the biggest debates has been whether Monks Mound is a geological remnant or is totally man-made. The latest investigations seemed to indicate the mound was built in stages and current radiocarbon dates place the time of its construction between A.D. 900 and 1150 (Reed et al. 1968:137).

Two of the early commentators on Cahokia Mounds had no doubt about its artificial construction:

My astonishment was inexpressibly excited when I came to the foot of the large mound, as it is called. It is certainly a most stupendous pile of earth, and were it not for the strongest proof, no one would believe it the works of hands (Brackenridge 1811).

But it is no use to doubt the fact. The big mound on the Cahokia, large as it is, is the work of man, and of that we became convinced, beyond all doubt, by an hour's careful and zealous inspection. Its position with others on a wide level plain of alluvial formation, its uniformity of soil throughout, wherever exposed-its regularity of figure, which is that of a parallelogram, lying north and south, with a broad apron to the southward, and a second, yet lower, . . . and its evident connection with the other mounds in the vicinity, all confirm the fact, though no tradition informs us who was its architect, or for what purpose it was erected (Latrobe 1835:181-182).

Yet, somewhat earlier the artificial nature of the mound was questioned:

But it is now seriously questioned whether these mounds are the work of art. I know not that any writer ever ventured to attack this supposition until John Russell, esq. sent forth his essay in the Illinois magazine, of March, 1831. Mr. Russell is a citizen of this state, and well-known as a writer of considerable talents and literary acquirements. He has had opportunity of examining for himself, many of those mounds, of various dimensions. He maintains they are not artificial, and offers objections to their being productions of human art, not easily obviated (Peck 1834:54).

And in 1873, in the local history of Madison County, Illinois, the following statement appeared:

Along the southern border of the county the Canteen Mounds, large, natural formations occur. The origin of these remarkable phenomenon of nature has excited much comment among our best minds, many attributing the mounds to artificial origin. The most prominent of these formations is Monks Mound (Anonymous 1873:9).

Those who proposed that Monks Mound was a natural phenomenon were probably influenced by racist attitudes. Many believed that the ancestors of the American Indians did not have the capacity to apply themselves to any task as time consuming and elaborate as the building of Monks Mound. (See, for example the description given by John Francis Snyder of the northwest section of Monks Mound, in 1909). Consequently, popular opinion either declared the mounds to be of natural origin or built by some pre-Indian race of mound builders (Silverberg 1968).

In 1915 Dr. A. R. Crook, a geologist and Director of the Illinois State Museum, concluded:

Chemical and mineralogical study of the soil, as well as paleontological and physiographical investigations, indicate that the mounds are the remnants of the glacial and alluvial deposits which at one time filled the valley of the Mississippi River and this region.It may be well to inquire if all so-called mounds in the Mississippi Valley are not natural topographic forms (1915:74-75; quoted in Moorehead 1929:115).

Another geologist earlier suggested that the mounds, and particularly Monks Mound, were of natural origin but had artificial constructions placed on the natural features:

To a height of 35 feet above its base the material of Monks Mound shows assortment and stratification, which is evidently natural. Above that height it affords no structural evidence bearing on the question whether it is of natural or artificial origin; but the form plainly indicates the work of man, and not of geological processes. It is highly probable that the mound in its natural condition was much lower and broader than at the present, and was a rounded, almost drumloidal form, similar to the smaller ones of the group which now surround it. By cutting down its margin to the level of the surrounding plain its builders obtained material to raise the mound to perhaps two or three times its former height without making excavations beneath the level of the plain and without carrying material from the bluffs, 2 1/2 miles dis-

tant. There is no evidence that material was obtained by either of these latter means (Fenneman 1911:12).

Crook changed his mind after observing archaeological excavations into the mounds, viewing the core borings done by M. M. Leighton (a geologist) and Moorehead, and examining aerial photographs from the U.S. Army Air Service taken by Lieutenant Goddard (Goddard 1969; Hall 1968; Fowler 1977) (Figure 5.10).

The debate, though, was finally settled by archaeological excavation. The first of these excavations, although not carefully controlled, was conducted by the property owner, Mr. Ramey, in the late 1800s. McAdams described Ramey's excavation in his 1883 publication:

About midway, on the north side, or face of the pyramid, and elevated 25 or 30 feet above the base, in a small depression, stands a pine tree, singularly enough, since this tree is not found in the forests in this locality. There was a story rife among the early settlers that this tree stood at the mouth of an opening or gallery into the interior of the mounds. To ascertain the truth of this matter, Mr. Thomas Ramey, the present owner of the mound, commenced a tunnel at this tree and excavated about ninety (90) feet towards the center of the mound. When fifteen feet from the entrance to the tunnel a piece of lead ore was discovered but no other object of interest was found. The deposits penetrated by the tunnel are very plainly shown to be the same as seen in the cellar mentioned above (McAdams 1883:2-3).

McAdams had previously commented that the excavations on the third terrace revealed black "cumulus" or mold interspersed with yellow clay, sand, or marly loess. It is interesting to compare his statement with Dr. J. F. Snyder's, written about 20 years after the event; Snyder reported that he detected nothing but "solid bluff clay."

Several years ago its proprietor, Hon. Thomas T. Ramey, dug a tunnel 90 feet in length in direction of its center, on the north side, about 30 feet above the base. In that exploration a small cube of lead ore was discovered, but no charcoal or ashes; nor a flint, pot sherd or bone was found to indicate that the solid bluff clay excavated had ever previously been disturbed. But in that clay taken out of the tunnel I afterwards detected and secured several specimens of small semi-fossil fluvialtial shells, often occurring in the drift deposits of the bluffs. . . . In the same drift deposits fragments of galena are not uncommon (Snyder 1909:90-91).

Figure 5.10. A 1922 Goddard air photo of Monks Mound viewed from the east. Mound 36 is the white rectangle in the center foreground. Source: Illinois State Museum and Crook (1922:Figure 9).

Because of the enormous volume of earth in this "stupendous pile of dirt," elaborate excavations and tunneling have been discouraged. The Ramey family did not permit such excavations to take place. After the turn of the century, occasional probes attempted to determine the mound's structure and content in order to decide the question of its natural or artificial origin. This was certainly an issue when the mounds area was proposed for a state park. Dr. A. R. Crook made 25 borings in the north face of the mound. Warren K. Moorehead and M. M. Leighton, in the 1922 season, also made auger borings on the north end: three on the summit and two on the east slope. Pits were dug 3 feet (0.9 meters) deep and auger bored to a depth of 17.5 feet (5.3 meters), assuring penetration to a depth of more than 20 feet (6.1 meters). Moorehead concluded that the auger borings definitely showed the mound to be man-made. Crook, despite his initial disbelief, later came to accept this interpretation.

No other excavations were conducted on Monks Mound until the 1960s, when Washington University sponsored excavations on the fourth terrace, and in 1965 and 1966 a solid-core drilling technique was employed to determine the nature of Monks Mound's construction. In all, nine holes were cored, one on the first terrace, one on the second terrace, and seven on the third and fourth terraces. Analyzing the limonite bands and soil changes in the cores, the investigators speculated that Monks Mound was built in a series of 14 stages. They further suggested that a population of 10,000 people could have provided the labor force necessary to build the mound. By dividing the number of stages into the time span indicated by radiocarbon dates—A.D. 900 to 1150 (250 years)—it was calculated that the average life of each stage of construction was approximately 18 years (Reed et al. 1968:146).

Analysis of the cores suggests the following major stages:

Stage A: Primary flat-top mound, 20 feet (6.1 meters) high, composed of black organic clay and rising from a natural sand floor. This black organic clay was similar to the gumbo mentioned in Moorehead's many descriptions and to the type of fill that was in Mound

72. This is the natural occurring substratum just below the A horizon in the area surrounding Monks Mound and may indicate that, indeed, the first mound built was of the soil closest to the surface.

Stage B: Flat-top mound rising 6 feet (1.85 meters) above Stage A.

Stage C: Roughly 10 feet (3.05 meters) above Stage A, extending from the north part of the fourth terrace to the south part of the third terrace.

Stage D: This stage was found only in the center and north cores about 8 feet (2.5 meters) above Stage C. It suggests that Stage D might be a terrace on the north half of Stage C.

Stage E: This extends from the south edge of the fourth terrace to the south edge of the third terrace.

Stage F: This is considered the "largest recognized construction stage, with a known thickness of seventeen feet, a north-south range of at least two hundred feet, and an east-west dimension of 175 feet" (Reed et al. 1968:143). At this stage, the mound is roughly 65 feet (19.8 meters) high. The typical black fill of Stage F is not found on the northern half of the mound, however, the sandy clay shows the same limonite bands found on the black fill and may be part of Stage F.

Stage G: Extends from the middle of the fourth terrace to the middle of the third terrace. Investigations suggest that it may be part of Stage F or a raised terrace on Stage F continuing the pattern indicated in Stages B and C.

Stages H through N: These stages average 4 feet (1.2 meters) in height. Their presence or absence in the various cores may suggest terracing (Reed et al. 1968:142-144).

Thus the 1960s work on Monks Mound seemed to confirm the idea of artificial construction, except that Stage A might be an erosional remnant in place before the other work was done. It also seemed to confirm earlier reporters' concepts that the mound was built up by successive additions.

> That no tribe of Indians ever did, would, or could devote five years of constant labor to the erection of a single tumulus, would probably be admitted by everyone acquainted with Indian character. . . . It would seem, therefore, that the only reasonable supposition is that the mound was built by successive additions. How often these were made and how much was added at one period, must be wholly conjectural if we suppose the tribe living at this point to have been a populous one, which is probably the case—say ten or twelve thousand—it is not probable that they would have added more than the equivalent of the great terrace in any season (Thomas 1907:364).

Albeit for all of the wrong reasons, it seems that Thomas was probably right in both his conjectures about the stages of Monks Mound and the number of people living in Cahokia needed to support the construction of Monks Mound.

Other excavations on Monks Mound were conducted during the 1960s and 1970s. Those excavations contributed a great deal to our understanding of the complexity of this great earthwork. Among the most extensive were the excavations on the fourth terrace conducted by Washington University and the Illinois Archaeological Survey. Much of the fourth terrace was completely excavated down to at least 1 meter in depth. The major find was evidence of a large structure at the north end of the terrace. The structure covered much of the north half of the terrace and was probably one of the largest structures at the Cahokia site. Its location on top of the big mound suggests it was certainly the most important building in town. No evidence was recovered as to its function, but it could have been a residence for the principal person of Cahokia or a public building.

The dating of the structure comes from several sources. First of all, it was not built during the last stage of construction of Monks Mound as there was approximately 1 meter of fill on top of it. The fill puzzled archaeologists at first because it contained no evidence of basket loading. The profiles through this fill present a typical soil profile, that is, a humic or A horizon and sterile-looking B and C horizons. The latter gave rise to the short-lived concept that a sterile zone had been placed on top of the remains of the last structure. However, this last stage was probably built up the same as the other stages—by basket loading. There may even have been a structure on top of it. If there was, it has probably been a few hundred years since the last structure and final stage were built. The process of soil formation has undoubtedly obliterated all traces of human activity.

This structure on the fourth terrace is also dated by ceramic vessels found at the site. The vessels are polished black bowls with incised decoration, the famous Ramey Incised type, which is most diagnostic of the Stirling phase of the Cahokia sequence. A radiocarbon date for this structure was estimated at A.D. 1150 (see Table 1.1 and Appendix 1).

The University of Wisconsin-Milwaukee conducted excavations on the southwest corner of the first terrace, to determine the nature of a rise or small mound located in that area. Trenches through the area indicated that it was made up of a series of platform mounds with buildings on the surfaces of these mounds. Below the platform mounds was a series of extensive superimposed floors suggesting that this part of the first terrace had been built up by adding floors for intense activities. On these floors large structures were sometimes built around a courtyard or patio. All of these structures and patios showed evidence of intense activity, and most of the structures had been burned *in situ*. Extending northeastward from the southwest corner of the third terrace was a ridge of fill that appeared to have been covered since Late Mississippian times.

The UWM archaeologists also excavated the southwest corner of the first terrace for evidence of a post marking the north-south centerline of the Cahokia community. As predicted, at that point they uncovered a series of superimposed post pits on the slope of the platform mounds. These posts were not part of any structures, so their presence strengthens the hypothesis of a marked north-south centerline.

Radiocarbon determinations indicate that much of the first terrace mound building occurred during the twelfth century, or during the Stirling phase. Thus this activity must have been contemporary with the construction and utilization of the building excavated on the fourth terrace.

The University of Illinois at Urbana-Champaign conducted excavations on the first terrace, which focused on the central part of the first terrace and especially on the interface between the first and third terraces. That project indicated the great complexity of the construction of these terraces.

Washington University, in cooperation with the Illinois Archaeological Survey, dug some trenches in the ramp projecting from the first terrace. These excavations revealed that there had been steps up the slope of the ramp, indicating it was probably the major access to the first terrace.

The University of Wisconsin-Milwaukee excavated in the east lobes of Monks Mound in 1971 in cooperation with the Illinois Archaeological Survey. Financing was provided by the National Science Foundation and the Illinois Department of Conservation. Significant excavations were conducted under the lobes and adjacent to them. The excavations indicated that the surface under the lobes had been occupied in Sand Prairie times and determined that the slumping that produced the lobes took place some time in the past 400 years. They also recovered a striking engraved sandstone tablet (Figure 5.11). Furthermore, the excavations extended deep into the ground below the Sand Prairie surface, giving a stratigraphic section beginning in Patrick phase times. All the currently defined phases of Cahokia were represented in this profile.

Figure 5.11.   Obverse (left) and reverse photographs of the sandstone table recovered from east lobes area by the University of Wisconsin-Milwaukee in 1971.

Similar stratigraphic excavations were carried out by Washington University crews under the south ramp area.

In conclusion, the area of Monks Mound was apparently occupied by a group of farmers at least as early as A.D. 800. The first stage of Monks Mound was probably built in the Fairmount phase, or about A.D. 950. The Monks Mound area was probably the focal point of the Fairmount phase community, as it was in later times. During the late Fairmount phase and through the Stirling and Moorehead phases, Monks Mound was added to and enlarged several times, possibly as many as 18, until about A.D. 1200, when it achieved the form roughly as we see it today.

Whether Monks Mound was used during the Sand Prairie phase is not known, but there was evidence of Sand Prairie utilization of the area under the east lobes.

Evidence of the use of Monks Mound by historic Indians was found in the southwest and central sections of the first terrace during excavations by the University of Wisconsin-Milwaukee and the Univer-

sity of Illinois at Urbana-Champaign, respectively. Walthall and Benchley (1987) analyzed the material recovered and suggested that the first terrace had been the site of a French colonial mission and a settlement of the Cahokia Illini between about 1735 and 1752. The excavations produced historic Indian burials, house remains, and the remains of a small French chapel (Figure 5.12).

More recent historic utilization of Monks Mound began when Trappist monks who owned the area built their monastery on a nearby mound and farmed the terraces of Monks Mound in the early 1800s. Amos Hill acquired the property in the 1830s. Hill built his house on top of Monks Mound, graded a road up the west side of the mound, dug a well on the second terrace, and leveled a small mound that had been on the southeast corner of the third terrace. More recent owners have built their houses and farm buildings below Monks Mound and have only occasionally attempted to farm the terraces.

Figure 5.12.   Artist's conception of the French chapel constructed on Monks Mound in the 1700s. Source: Walthall and Benchley 1987:Figure 9.

6

DESCRIPTIONS OF MOUNDS 39–88

Mound 39 (N294W77)

Located just west of Monks Mound is Mound 39, a small, rounded mound (Figure 6.1). Originally it was probably rectangular; that is how it is illustrated on the Patrick map of 1876. A straight line can be drawn from the supposed north edge of Mound 39 to the north boundary of Monks Mound. Both the McAdams map and the earlier Thomas map show a mound in a slightly different location than this, but they probably refer to Mound 39. The latter two maps were just sketch maps of the site, and their locations for Mound 39 should not be taken as seriously as the Patrick map. The USGS map confirms the location of this mound as it appears on the Patrick map, as does the 1966 UWM map.

There is some question as to the original size of Mound 39. The Patrick map suggests that it was a large, flat-topped platform mound equal in size to Mound 41. The other maps show it to be somewhat smaller. Moorehead's map suggests the north-south and east-west dimensions were both about 240 feet (73.15 meters). The 1966 UWM map shows an east-west dimension of approximately 48 meters (157.5 feet) and a north-south dimension of approximately 42 meters (137.8 feet).

Thomas gave the height of this mound as 10 feet (3.05 meters). The later surveys suggested that on the north side, toward the slope of the bank of Cahokia Creek, the mound had a height of around 19 feet (5.8 meters) and on the south side a height of 7 to 8 feet (2.1 to 2.4 meters). The overall average height of this mound on the UWM map is 1.1 meters (3.6 feet). The data suggest that the considerable alteration of the shape of this mound is probably due to modern construction and agricultural practices. The height data also conform to the changes in form suggested by comparing the Patrick map illustration of Mound 39 with its appearance on the 1966 UWM map.

The alteration may be partly due to the sawmill located on this mound in the 1800s; it is often called the Sawmill Mound. Moorehead reports that in the period 1850-1860 an explosion in the sawmill killed several workmen. They were apparently buried in one of the nearby mounds, possibly Mound 73 or Mound 47 (Moorehead 1929:39). As Moorehead suggested, that should be kept in mind should future archaeologists find skeletons with traces of wood coffins about them.

The only excavations into this mound were conducted by Moorehead in the early 1920s. His reports do not include any maps of those excavations because material was too irregularly distributed in the mound, he said, to make a map worthwhile. His reports did include the following information: (1) Eight burials accompanied by some grave goods were located along the southern slope of the mound; (2) No burials were found in a 35-foot-long (10.7 meters), 5-foot-deep (1.5 meters) trench dug along the east side; and (3) A center pit 14 by 15 feet (4.3 by 4.6 meters) wide and 16 feet (4.9 meters) deep was dug into the mound (Moorehead 1929:38-40).

An auger was used to probe an additional 3.5-4 feet (1.1-1.2 meters) to a base of heavy, wet clay. That probing revealed that: (1) The mound was stratified, with strongly marked series of alternating bands of dark earth and yellow earth. The dark bands were 3-10 inches (7.6-25.4 centimeters) wide and the yellow bands were 12-24 inches (30.5-61 centimeters) wide; (2) The layers were not even. A conically formed deposit in the northwest corner dipped from the east to the southeast, whereas, according to Moorehead, 10 feet (3.05 meters) down the layers appeared to be more horizontal. It is possible that this formation represented a slope of an earlier construction stage; (3) A heavy black layer was found on the south side of the trench and auger borings on the south side of the pit showed

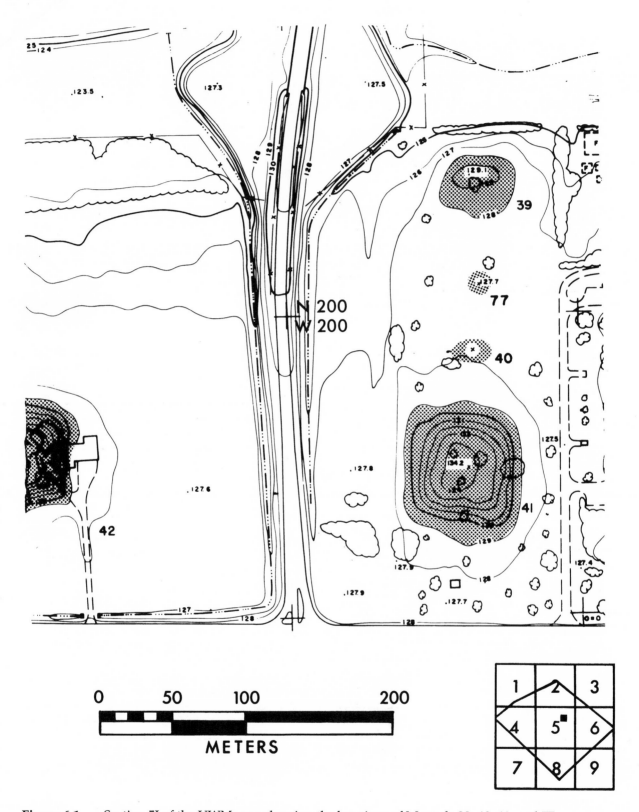

Figure 6.1. Section 5I of the UWM map showing the locations of Mounds 39, 40, 41, and 77.

a heavy blue clay mixed with a grayish clay. A heavy blue clay, the natural deposit just below the soil-development horizon, has been found by more recent excavators throughout much of the site area. This may just be another indication that heavy blue clay is universal throughout the Cahokia site area; (4) Scattered throughout the mound were bits of pottery fragments, chips, spawls, a ceramic mammal-head effigy, an awl from a deer jaw, and a human head effigy cut from a freshwater mussel shell; (5) Moorehead's workmen found a number of disturbed burials, but no indication is given of their location. These were apparently scattered throughout the area. Since the soil was soft and disturbed, Moorehead assumed the burials were in an area where either Patrick or McAdams had dug; (6) Moorehead thought that extensive habitation areas once surrounded this mound. Black pottery predominated, but a few fragments of red pottery were also found; and (7) Furthermore, it was Moorehead's interpretation that a long, low platform existed between Mounds 39 and 77 directly to the south (see Moorehead 1929:38-41).

Skeleton No. 11, in Moorehead's terminology, was the most extensively described and illustrated of the burials found in Mound 39. It was an extended burial with the head to the northeast (Moorehead 1929:Plate 29, Figure 2) and apparently was well preserved; there were two ceramic vessels near the right hand, and another bowl near the left knee (Plate 17, Figure 6). A shell gorget and a bone knife were also found with this skeleton (Plate 23, Figure 1; Plate 25, Figure 8).

Mound 39 appears to have been a platform mound, though indication of earlier building stages are present. Several burials were noted throughout the fill, but their position within the mound structure is not documented sufficiently to indicate their nature.

Mound 40 (N177W74)

Mound 40 was identified by Patrick as a small, conical mound located halfway between Mounds 39 and 41 (Figure 6.1). However, there is confusion in the later maps regarding Mound 40. McAdams indicated neither a Mound 40 or 39. Thomas, though, showed a 5-foot (1.5-meter) mound considerably north of Mound 41, and on his map, it appears that Mound 40 and Mound 39 are placed considerably to the north of Monks Mound's northern edge. I have already noted that the Thomas map is not an accurate locational map, but merely shows the relative relationship of the various mounds.

Moorehead's 1929 map indicated four mounds in this area; from south to north they are Mound 41, Mound 40, Mound 77, and Mound 39. Since Moorehead's map also is not one in which precise locations are noted, it is possible that Moorehead's Mound 77 is Patrick's Mound 40. It is also possible that what Moorehead indicates as Mound 77 is a mound not noted by Patrick. The Ramey map (see Figure 3.6) shows this area with two small mounds between Mound 39 and 41, as does Moorehead. The 1966 UWM map shows no mound contours between Mounds 30 and 41, but an elevation of 127.7 meters (419 feet) between the two mounds may indicate the location of Patrick's Mound 40. Mound 40 is retained in the final mound enumeration because it is shown on the Patrick map, the Moorehead map, and there is some elevation data on the UWM map. There is no record of any excavations in this mound, although Moorehead's report indicates that a variety of excavations were conducted in its vicinity.

Mound 41 (N99W76)

This mound is directly west of the south half of the Monks Mound (Figure 6.1). Approximately 100 meters (328.1 feet) separates them. Mound 41 is unusual in that its contemporary height is greater than the height given in some of the earlier records. McAdams indicates that it had a height of 15 feet (4.6 meters), whereas Moorehead suggests a height of 25 feet (7.6 meters). These discrepancies, however, can probably be attributed to lack of engineering skill on the part of both of these observers.

According to the UWM map, the mound is approximately 5.2 meters (17.1 feet) high based upon the 129-meter (423.2-foot) contour, or 6.2 meters (20.3 feet) high based upon the 128-meter (419.9-foot) contour. All of these heights taken together, however, indicate that this mound has shown little or no change from its original shape. Moorehead described Mound 41 as oval. The Patrick map suggests that it is nearly square, and the UWM map supports this. Earlier writers also suggested that it was also square: "This gigantic tumulus [Cahokia Mound] was defended by four elevated squares placed respectively, one on the east, two on the west, and one on the southwest. They vary from twenty to thirty feet in height, and from 250 to 300 feet square" (DeHass 1869:297).

Although the 128-meter contour of Mound 41 is blurred today, it is possible that there is a small mound directly north of Mound 41. Moorehead's 1923 and 1929 maps and the Ramey map are the only maps indicating two small mounds between 39 and 41; one of these is Mound 40, the other may be a mound no longer discernible (see Mound 40 discussion). There is some evidence that Mound 41 is "the true Monks Mound," the mound on which the Trappist monks built the majority of their dwellings during their residency in the area. However, Bushnell claims that Mound 48 to the south was the primary residence of the monks. Some earlier writers who observed the site while the monks were there contradict this view. There is no indication of any archaeological excavations having taken place on this mound. In summary, Mound 41 is a large, rectangular-to-square platform mound that is relatively unchanged from its original form and shape. It may also have been the site of buildings constructed by the Trappist monks who occupied the area in the early nineteenth century.

Mound 42 (N100W414)

Known as the Merrell Mound, this is one of the largest and best preserved mounds in the entire archaeological zone (Figure 6.2). It is also unique because an oval platform mound is built on its southwest corner. According to Bushnell, this secondary mound was an elevated platform about 75 feet (22.9 meters) in diameter. The main Mound 42 is a rectangular platform approximately 79 meters by 122 meters (260 feet by 400 feet), based upon the UWM map. The Patrick map shows a north-south dimension of 240 feet (73.15 meters) and an east-west dimension of 280 feet (85.3 meters). The various height estimates are fairly consistent, ranging from 25 to 30 feet (7.6 to 9.1 meters) above the surrounding floodplain. The UWM map confirms these estimates.

Fortunately, the mound is well preserved, and it seems to be very near its original form except that the oval platform mound on top was leveled many years ago, making the entire surface relatively level. This mound is preserved probably because a house stood on it for more than 100 years (Figure 6.3). A plat map taken from an 1873 atlas indicates, for example, that there was a building on the mound then (Anonymous 1873). Bushnell described the mound as follows: "Mound E. Rectangular. Elevation 25 feet. The southwest corner is a slightly elevated platform of about 75 feet in diameter dimensions of the base, north to south 240 feet, east to west 280 feet" (1904:10).

The Merrell Mound had not yet been excavated in Moorehead's time. In 1969 Elizabeth Benchley, of the University of Wisconsin-Milwaukee, conducted some test excavations in the southwest corner of the Merrell Mound to examine the nature of the oval platform mound that had been constructed on top of the larger mound.

Mound 43 (N102W673)

Patrick noted a small, conical mound to the west of Mound 42 and directly east of the northwest corner of Mound 44, a large, rectangular platform mound (Figures 6.2 and 6.4). Mound 43 is shown on all later maps, including the Thomas map, Peterson-McAdams map, and a map included in Titterington's publication on the Cahokia site. Mound 43 is indicated on the UWM map by a loop in the 128-meter (419.9-foot) contour line; the elevation of its highest point is 128.8 meters (422.6 feet), establishing its height in 1966 as only about 0.8 meters (2.6 feet) above the surrounding area. Earlier maps give a much greater height for this mound, ranging from 8 to 10 feet (2.4 to 3.05 meters). The height of Mound 43 has decreased considerably because of modern agriculture, though Mounds 42 and 44 show less change over time.

No excavations have been conducted in Mound 43. It seems to be part of a group of mounds that includes Mound 44 just to the west and Mound 91, between Mounds 43 and 44 and to the north of the line between them. Mound 91 went unnoted by earlier investigators, and it is discussed in Chapter 7, which describes the mounds that have been added due to 1960s research. Together these mounds may well form a group surrounding a plaza.

Mound 44 (N80W816)

Apparently this mound was originally a rectangular, flat-topped, platform mound with a north-south axis greater than its east-west axis (Figure 6.4). That configuration is indicated on the Patrick map and is confirmed by the Thomas (1894) map. McAdams, however, represents Mound 44 as a square mound slightly smaller than Mound 41. By the time the UWM map was drawn 70 years later, Mound 44 had assumed a more conical or dome-shaped form due to extensive cultivation. Recorded heights for this mound decreased through time. McAdams (1882), for example, gave a height of 18 feet (5.5 meters); Thomas (1894) recorded 15 feet (4.6 meters); and Peterson-McAdams (1906), 10 feet (3.05 meters). The 1966 UWM map indicates a height of 3 meters (9.8 feet) if the 129-meter (423.2-foot) contour is used as a base line, or 2 meters (6.6 feet) if the 130-meter (426.5-foot) contour is used.

No archaeological excavations have been undertaken in Mound 44. However, in 1961, the Illinois State Museum, in cooperation with the Illinois Division of Highways, conducted archaeological research in the area designated Tract 15A, 3,000 feet (914.4 meters)

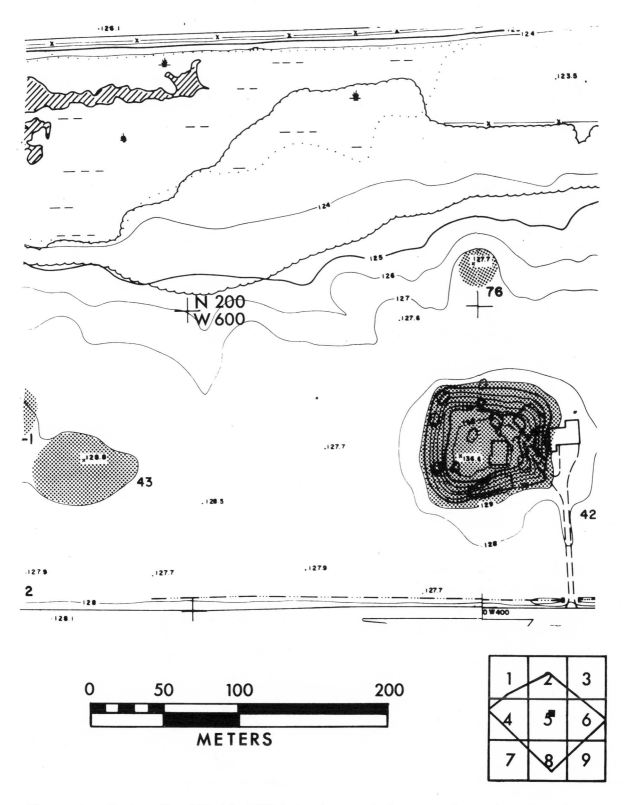

Figure 6.2. Sections 5J and 5I of the UWM map showing the locations of Mounds 42, 43, and 76.

Figure 6.3. Mound 42 in the 1920s (top) and in the 1960s (bottom). Source: Illinois State Museum and Archaeological Research Laboratory, University of Wisconsin-Milwaukee.

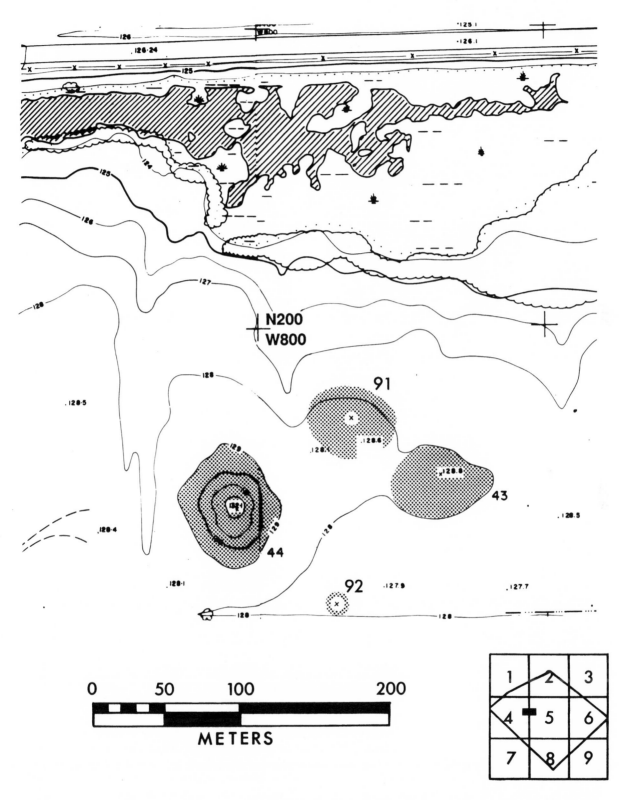

Figure 6.4. Sections 4F and 5J of the UWM map showing the locations of Mounds 43, 44, 91, and 92.

Figure 6.5.   Remains of the palisade wall near
Mound 44 found in Tract 15A in 1961.
Source: Illinois State Museum.

west of Monks Mound and north of Highway 40. This
area is just west of Mound 44. In excavations at the
southern end of Tract 15A just southwest of Mound
44, a long, winding prehistoric trench was encountered
(Figure 6.5).

> In all probability, this trench represents the location
> of a palisade of upright posts. . . . There were no post
> molds evident in the trench indicating that the pali-
> sade had been deliberately razed and did not rot in
> position. It is doubted that the palisade was con-
> structed for defensive purposes. Instead, its relation-
> ship to Mound 44 which lay immediately to the east,
> outside of the right of way, indicated that it may have
> served as a means of setting off the area of the mound
> from other parts of the town. The soil of the mound
> is sandy. The fact that the soil filling the trenches is
> sandy, in contrast to the gumbo of the area, is a fur-

ther indication that the mound and palisade were
related. It is presumed that when the palisade was
taken down, soil which had washed down from the
mound filled the trench. The palisade was traced to
the south as far as the drainage ditch along Highways
40 and 66 (Wittry and Vogel 1962:28-29).

Also unearthed in Tract 15A were the circles of
posts, the Woodhenges, found in the neighborhood of
Mound 44.

> A large circle (480 feet in diameter . . .) is found about
> 100 feet west of Mound 44 and another circle (240 feet
> in diameter . . .) directly north of and overlapping
> Mound 44. Since the area of Mound 44 overlaps the
> area of the projected circle it is possible that this circle
> was an earlier feature than the mound (Wittry and
> Vogel 1962:29).

Mound 45 (N206W1138)

One of the rectangular mounds at the Cahokia site
is Mound 45, shown on the Patrick map with its longer
axis east-west. Mound 45 is located northwest of
Mound 44 and directly west of Mound 40 (see Figure
3.10). McAdams showed Mound 45 as a 10-foot-high
(3.05-meter) conical mound. Thomas, however,
showed a 15-foot (4.6-meter) mound directly west, not
northwest, of Mound 44, which may or may not represent Mound 45. The 1873 plat map (Anonymous
1873) illustrates two large mounds in Section 34, which
are probably Mounds 45 and 46. The Peterson-
McAdams map shows an 8-foot (2.4-meter) mound in
the area that is probably Mound 45.

There is no remnant of Mound 45 left today nor
was there in 1966 when the UWM map was made. The
1934 USGS map shows a building in the area where
Mound 45 was located. The mound was probably destroyed between 1931 and 1966. Plotting its location
from earlier maps onto the UWM map indicates that
the mound was in the northern one-third of the west
side of a large borrow pit situated between Mound 44
and the railroad tracks. This borrow pit was excavated
in advance of a planned interstate highway over the
area of Tract 15A.

Examination of aerial photos provides no clue as
to the location and condition of Mound 45. By 1933,
when the Dache Reeves photos were made, all of Section 34 had been disturbed by construction of both a
canal that straightened Cahokia Creek and a dog-rac-
ing track that probably intersected or cut into Mound
45. The photos do show an interesting soil disturbance
east of the track, apparently where topsoil had been

removed. There is no record of excavations in Mound 45.

Mound 46 (N322W1542)

In 1876, when Patrick was making his map of the Cahokia site, he indicated that a rectangular mound with its long axis east-west stood just south of Cahokia Creek (Figure 6.6). That mound appears to have been, in Patrick's time, very similar to but smaller than Mound 45. Mound 46 is also indicated on both the 1873 plat map for Madison County and the 1931 USGS map of the area as a slight elevation west of the railroad tracks and northwest of Mound 45. The McAdams map shows what is probably Mound 46 as 10 feet (3.05 meters) high.

Moorehead's maps show Mound 46 much as Patrick indicated it, no doubt because Moorehead's map is basically a copy and revision of Patrick's original map. However, what Moorehead did not understand was that Patrick had made a separate map of the Powell group that he did not include in the numbered mounds at the Cahokia site. Moorehead was somewhat confused in that he assumed that Mound 46 was one of the major mounds of the Powell group at the west end of the Cahokia site. With that assumption, Moorehead then added other mounds to the map to show the arrangement of mounds as he saw them at the Powell mound group. He made the main Powell Mound number 46, and the two other mounds in the group he numbered 84 and 85. The UWM map retains Patrick's original numbering.

There are some indications of Mound 46 on aerial photos of the Cahokia site, but it does not appear as a distinct contour on the 1966 UWM map. Mound 46 was apparently buried during construction of Interstate 55-70 and the nearby overpass over the railroad tracks. The mound protrudes slightly from the fill, as indicated by the 130-meter (426.5-foot) contour line and confirmed by inspection in the field. Thus, at least a portion of this mound is still preserved under the fill of the overpass.

Mound 47 (S90W244)

Mound 47 is one of the site's smaller mounds (Figure 6.7). It was mapped by Patrick as a small, irregularly shaped mound, and he showed lines extending from it to the southeast. The lines appear to represent a garden plot or a small cultivated field. However, Moorehead drew the mound as though the striations represented part of the form, giving it a slightly tilted,

comma-shaped configuration. Mound 47 appears on many of the early aerial photographs, although today it is buried under the east entrance to a drive-in theater in the area and is indicated only by a slight rise in elevation.

Maps record varying heights for this mound. The earliest, the McAdams map, indicates that it was 10 feet (3.05 meters) in height; the Thomas map of 1894, 15 feet (4.6 meters), and the Peterson-McAdams map of 1906, 12 feet (3.7 meters). Based on Patrick's indication of the mound's size, these figures seem excessive. The location of Mound 47 seems to be correct and is consistent in all representations. Moorehead suggested that Mound 47 was probably one of the mounds in which the men killed in the explosion at Sawmill Mound (Mound 39) were buried.

Mound 48 (S126W127)

This is one of the larger mounds of the Cahokia site (Figures 6.7 and 6.8). Its modern contours are nearly square with a flat top. An elevation to the south of the platform's center may be the remains of a farmhouse standing there in the early 1920s; when Moorehead and his crew worked in the area in 1921 they used the farmhouse as headquarters (Moorehead 1929:33). The mound is oriented to the cardinal points. There is a slight ledge or step terrace on the east edge, although the west edge is much steeper in grade.

Using the 129-meter (423.2-foot) contour as a base for measurement, the 1966 UWM map indicates that the mound is approximately 112 meters (367.4 feet) north-south and 111 meters (364.2 feet) east-west. The mound's height has been recorded by various mappers and investigators. Patrick showed this mound in cross section with a height of 25 feet (7.6 meters). The McAdams map of 1882 indicated 30 feet (9.1 meters); the Thomas map of 1894, 25 feet (7.6 meters); and the Peterson-McAdams map of 1906, 20 feet (6.1 meters). Using the 129-meter elevation as a base line, the 1966 UWM map showed a height of 7.5 meters (24.6 feet). The 25-foot height recorded by Patrick and Thomas was probably closer to the actual original height. Bushnell also discussed this mound (1904:Figure 3), recording a height of 25 feet (7.6 meters). Mound 48 was probably the mound upon which the Trappist monks built the majority of their buildings.

The rectangular work immediately southwest of Cahokia was occupied from 1810 until 1813 by a small body of Trappist Monks, during which time their garden was on the southern terrace of the great mound. According to the survey of 1875-76 from which all

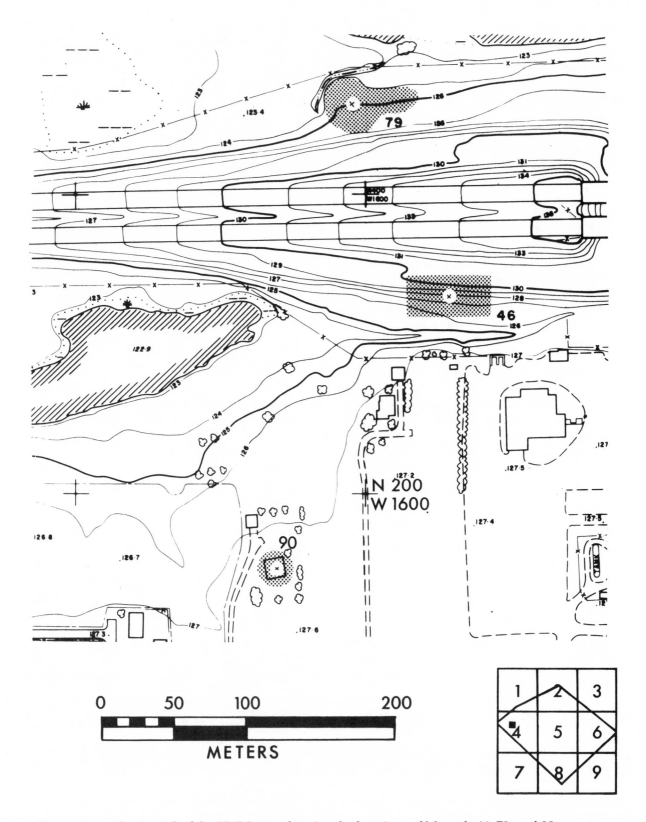

Figure 6.6.   Section 4G of the UWM map showing the locations of Mounds 46, 79, and 90.

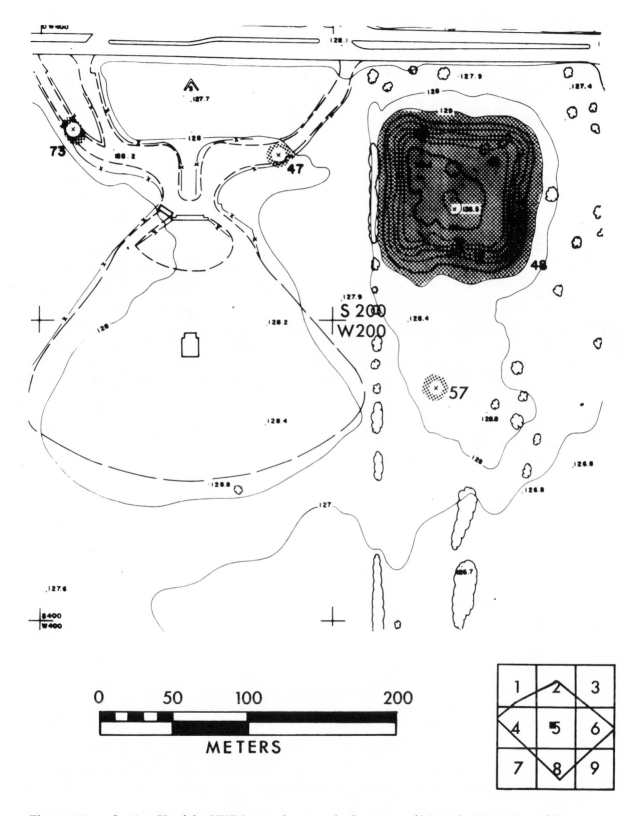

Figure 6.7. Section 5L of the UWM map showing the locations of Mounds 47, 48, 57, and 73.

Figure 6.8.   Photograph of Mound 48. Source: Illinois State Museum.

measurements are now derived, this lesser mound was 25 feet in height, its base line from north to south was 180 feet and from east to west 200 feet (Bushnell 1904:9; 1922:97).

The survey to which Bushnell refers is undoubtedly the Patrick map survey. Several investigators and early travelers locate the monks' building on a mound west of Monks Mound, referring probably to Mound 41. Bushnell, however, very specifically recorded the mound's location, which corresponds with Mound 48. None of the evidence is specific enough to positively locate the position of the mound upon which the monks built. Most agree, however, that the Trappists did not build upon Monks Mound itself.

Excavations into the surfaces of Mounds 41 and 48 would likely determine exactly the location of the monks' structures. The surface of Mound 48 was apparently disturbed by more recent construction of the farmhouse as indicated by Moorehead's description.

The farmhouse on Mound 48 is shown in one of the Goddard photographs (Crook 1922:Figure 8).

Mound 49 (S142E104)

About 100 meters (328.1 feet) south of Monks Mound is a tumulus that was called Red Mound on one of the park's early signs, supposedly because so much red pottery was discovered there (Figure 6.9). Mound 49 appears on the Patrick map as a conical mound of regular form. The contours on the 1966 UWM map, however, suggest a more oval or elongated shape with an east-west axis of nearly 50 meters (164.0 feet) and a north-south axis of approximately 35 meters (114.8 feet).

McAdams showed this mound with a height of approximately 5 feet (1.5 meters) and Thomas, 10 feet (3.05 meters). Using the 128-meter contour as a base elevation, the 1966 UWM map showed a height of 1.7

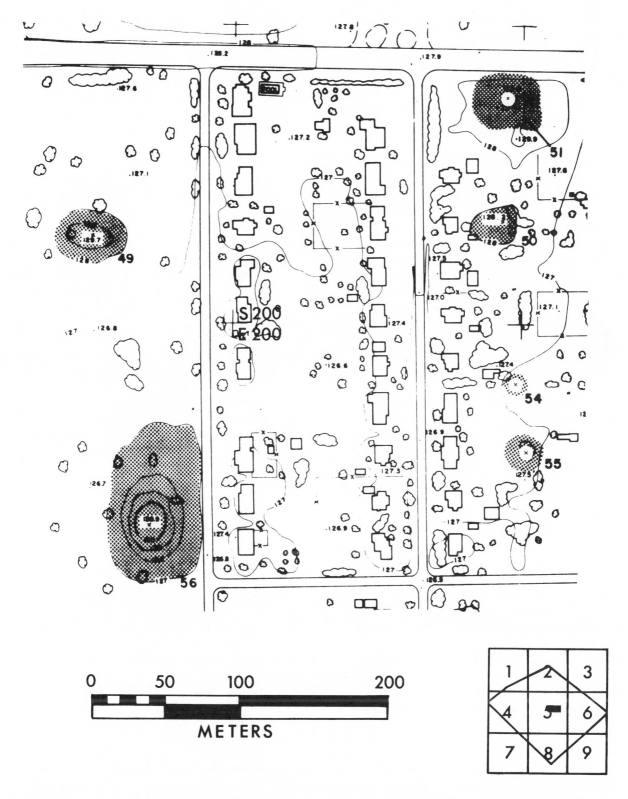

Figure 6.9. Section 5M of the UWM map showing the locations of Mounds 49, 50, 51, 54, 55, and 56.

meters (5.6 feet). No known excavations have been conducted into this mound, which casts doubt on the sign explaining the origins of its name. It is my opinion that this mound was a ridge-topped mound similar to Mound 72 and some of the larger mounds, specifically Mounds 66 and 86.

Mound 50 (S132E385)

This mound is one of a series (Mounds 50, 51, 54, and 55) running in a north-south line just to the southeast of Monks Mound (Figure 6.9). Aerial photographs and archaeological excavations (Anderson 1969) indicate that this row of mounds is just inside the north-south line of a palisade. Patrick recorded it as a relatively small, conical mound. The present contours are so different that they provide little but location.

Published reports indicate that no archaeological investigations were undertaken in Mound 50, although Moorehead said: "Across the National Highway from Monks Mound are the estates of Mr. Cole, Mrs. Tippetts, and Mr. Wells. We did considerable work on Mr. Wells' land in the vicinity of Mounds No. 50, 52, and 53" (1929:31).

Although Patrick assigned the number 50 to this mound, Moorehead incorrectly interpreted this mound in his 1923 map (1923:39) and assigned it a new number, 75. However, in his 1929 version of the map, Moorehead labeled it Mound 50, reassigning 75 to a mound unrecorded on the Patrick map.

The Cahokia Mounds Museum Society Field School conducted text excavations in Mound 50 in 1986 and 1987 (Gergen and Iseminger 1986, 1987), putting trenches in the east and south sides. Results suggest perhaps two phases of construction resulting in a domed, conical mound. Lohmann phase structures, including one probably T-shaped, predate the mound and were truncated by a water-deposited sand layer that may represent a localized flooding episode. Construction of the mound appears to have begun during the Moorehead phase, with subsequent Sand Prairie phase additions (Keller 1996). There are a number of large intrusive pits, including two very large post pits about 3 meters deep, cutting through the mound fill. The eastern edge of the mound fill or wash was cut by the basin of a Sand Prairie phase wall-trench structure.

Mound 51 (S32E388)

Although almost totally destroyed, Mound 51—known locally as the Persimmon Mound—is one of

the better recorded mounds at the Cahokia site (Figures 6.9 and 6.10). Patrick illustrated it as an oval-shaped mound with an east-west axis somewhat longer than the north-south. Moorehead maintained this representation in his various interpretations of the Patrick map. The 1966 UWM map was made after the mound had been largely destroyed and spread out, so it shows little of the mound's nature. The mound apparently was still in good shape in the early 1920s when it was photographed by Goddard (Figure 6.10). It appears on this photo as a well-defined mound with an oval base and a flat top.

There are several contour maps of Mound 51, the first made in 1940 (Figure 6.11) when a survey was made of a subdivision southeast of Monks Mound. The contours on that map are unlabeled and appear to have been sketched in rather than surveyed in detail, but they do show the mound much as it appears in the photograph taken in 1922 (Figure 6.10). This map shows the mound to be approximately 160 feet (48.8 meters) east-west and 140 feet (42.7 meters) north-south.

On the USGS map the base elevation for that area is a contour line of 420 feet (128.0 meters) above sea level, and the mound is outlined by the 430-foot (131.1-meter) contour. This suggests that at the time the USGS map was made the mound was more than 10 feet (3.05 meters) high. The USGS compilation (Figure 3.10) drawings show this mound in much greater detail than the published quadrangle sheet. A base contour of 420 feet (128 meters) encompasses both Mound 50 and 51. The top of Mound 51 is encircled by the 430-foot (131.1-meter) line, indicating Mound 51 was at least 15 feet (4.6 meters) high at that time. The largest of the earlier estimates, on the Thomas map of 1894, is 20 feet (6.1 meters).

If we assume a height of more than 15 feet (4.6 meters), it seems probable that the contour lines on the 1940 map represent a 3-foot (0.9-meter) contour interval. It is likely that this is the contour interval represented since land surveyors often used surveying rods divided into yards rather than feet. Certainly, the map probably doesn't show 5-foot (1.5-meter) contour intervals, the standard practice in topographic surveys, as this would make the top of the mound at least 25 feet (7.6 meters) above the lowest contour line.

During the salvage excavations conducted by Charles Bareis in 1961, a contour map was made of a portion of the mound. From this contours were projected for the total mound as it existed at that time. The datum reference was the top of the mound; it was assigned a value of 100 feet (30.5 meters). The lowest contour mapped was 83 feet (25.3 meters). This indicates a height of about 17 feet (5.2 meters) for Mound

Figure 6.10.   Goddard air photo of Mound 51. Source: Illinois State Museum and Crook (1922:Figure 10).

51 in 1961. This corresponds favorably with data from the other maps.

The mound apparently retained this shape until the 1960s. At that time it was leveled and the mound soil used for fill. Little (a few feet) of the mound remains.

If Mound 51 is the vantage from which Wild's drawing (see Figure 2.2) was made, he was the first to report archaeological data for this mound. Wild apparently did not conduct any excavations but "picked up about a half a peck of broken bones and pieces of pottery and flint" (Wild 1841:52-53) from the surface. This litter on the surface of mounds is similar to Brackenridge's descriptions, three decades earlier, of the ubiquity of archaeological materials over the surface of the entire site. Post-1840s cultivation of the area has wiped out this aspect of Cahokia as well as the forms of the mounds.

Charles Bareis and others, who were conducting nearby highway salvage archaeological work, made test excavations in the mound and below the surface before it was leveled. First, a 60-foot-long, 10-foot-wide trench (18.3 x 3.05 meters) was made across the top of the mound. It was excavated to a depth of about 5 feet (1.5 meters). The testing suggested that the mound had been constructed in at least two stages, and much of

the fill for the mound was a sandy type soil (Bareis and Lathrap 1962:8).

As the mound was further leveled, Bareis worked with crews from the University of Illinois Field School, of which he was director. Portions of the data recovered from those excavations have been reported by William Chmurny in his doctoral thesis (1973).

One can say with assurance only that Mound 51 was built in at least two stages. Two hearths or fire basins that were noted during the destruction of the mound appeared to be on or near the top of the bottom mound stage. A number of other features were also located during the course of the work. An interesting feature was discovered below the mound—a large borrow pit from which earth was taken for mound construction; perhaps it was used for Monks Mound. This borrow pit had then been filled with trash and soil, the area leveled, and Mound 51 constructed over a portion of the former borrow pit.

Mound 52 (S100E798)

Elongate in form, Mound 52 is shown by Patrick to be parallel-sided with rounded ends and, on the basis

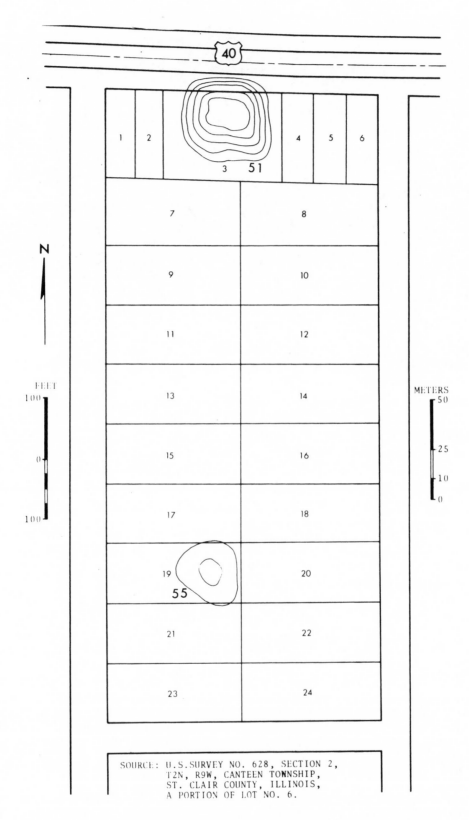

Figure 6.11.   Land survey map showing Mounds 51 and 55 in 1940.

of the shading, not of great height (Figure 6.12). However, the McAdams map of 1882 gave a height of 15 feet (4.6 meters) and the Peterson-McAdams map of 1906, 8 feet (2.4 meters). Using the 127-meter (416.7-foot) contour as the base elevation, the 1966 UWM map showed a north-south dimension of 99 meters (324.8 feet) and an east-west dimension of 83 meters (272.3 feet). However, by 1966 the mound had been greatly disturbed and partially leveled for the construction of a trailer park. Today the mound is only a high elevation in the midst of this trailer park just to the south of Highway 40. It appears, however, that much of the mound is still buried; details of its shape and nature could be determined by excavation.

There are some indications that Moorehead excavated in this mound, as he reported in 1929:

> Mound No. 52, a low structure, appeared to be a house site, and during excavation we observed many lumps of hard burnt clay in which were impressions of reeds and sticks. These gave us information with reference to the walls or methods of construction of the dwellings. Cane, the favorite material used in clay or mud in building wigwam walls in the South, does not occur on Cahokia Creek, so other growths more-or-less cane-like in character were employed by the Indians (Moorehead 1929:31-32).

There are no other details of this excavation. Moorehead does say, however, that they did considerable work in the vicinity of this mound. One assumes this was the excavation in the so-called village site area that he marked on his 1929 map.

Mound 53 (S74E923)

Mound 53 is the southernmost of a row of what were probably conical mounds. The row, which runs north to south, includes Mounds 29, 28, and 53 (Figure 6.12). McAdams (1882) indicated that Mound 53 was 20 feet (6.1 meters) high, while PetersonMcAdams (1906) showed a height of 10 feet (3.05 meters). There is no indication of Mound 53 on the 1966 UWM map because the area on the south side of Highway 40 had been built up into residential and commercial properties. There is no indication that excavations were conducted in this mound, although Moorehead refers to it in reference to excavations in the vicinity. A slightly higher elevation with a contemporary building on it may be the location of Mound 53.

Mound 54 (S238E396)

Mound 54 is indicated by a slight elevation in the subdivision southeast of Monks Mound (Figure 6.9). Patrick showed this mound almost equal in size to Mound 50 and part of the line of Mounds 51, 50, 54, and 55. McAdams (1882) gave a height of 10 feet (3.05 meters), while Thomas (1894) indicated 8 feet (2.4 meters), and Peterson-McAdams (1906) only 5 feet (1.5 meters). By 1940, when excavations were carried out in Mound 55 just to the south and the map made for the subdivision, Mound 54 was so low that it was not noted on the land-survey map (Figure 6.11).

There is no direct reference to excavation in Mound 54, but apparently Moorehead did test in this vicinity and perhaps in the mound as well. In his earlier reports, Moorehead mistakenly numbered this Mound 74 but used Patrick's original designation, Mound 54, in the later publication. In 1923 he noted:

> This fall, the survey did not sink additional pits, but on Mrs. Tippetts' estate, south of Monks, and on the adjoining property owned by Mr. Cole, and Mr. Wells, much work was done. Mr. Allen had leased land of Mr. Wells and he permitted us to work extensively with eight or ten men on an area lying 100 to 200 yards south of Mound 51. Here the village debris was as heavy as at any point on the Ramey lands. There were several low mounds (74 [Mound 54], 75 [Mound 50], and 55). In Number 75 [Mound 50] much burnt clay was discovered, also lumps in which were impressions of reeds and sticks doubtless the walls of dwellings (Moorehead 1923:39).

Mound 55 (S286E404)

Known as the Murdock Mound, Mound 55 was still standing in 1940 and is shown on the plat map for the area made by a local engineer (Figures 6.9 and 6.11). It was to be leveled for the construction of houses, so a WPA crew under the direction of Harriet Smith examined the area from June 11 to December 14, 1941 (Smith 1942, 1969).

Patrick indicated that this was a small, conical mound, but he did not give a height. Various maps give the following heights: McAdams map (1882), 15 feet (4.6 meters); Thomas map (1894), 10 feet (3.05 meters); Peterson-McAdams map (1906), 8 feet (2.4 meters). Smith, in her 1942 summary, described Mound 55 as an oval 9 feet (2.7 meters) in height and 150 feet

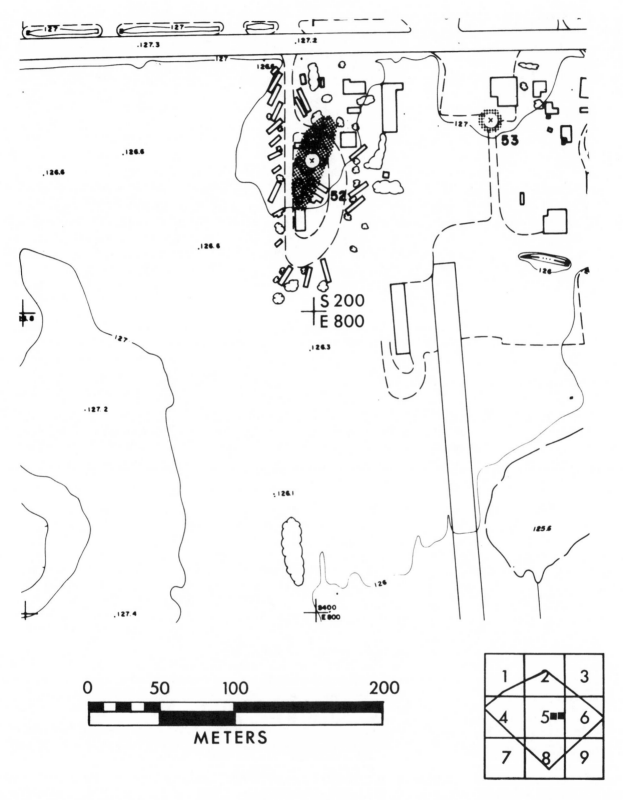

Figure 6.12. Portions of sections 5N and 5O of the UWM map showing the locations of Mounds 52 and 53.

(45.7 meters) by 135 feet (41.15 meters) in base dimensions.

This is one of the most interesting sets of data indicating the deflation of a mound by cultivation. The Goddard air photos of 1922 show this mound in a cultivated field. Mounds 50 and 54 to the north were apparently almost completely destroyed by cultivation by the time these photos were taken. If the heights listed above can be taken as representative of the changes in Mound 55 through time, it is probable that destruction of this mound by plowing took place in the late nineteenth century. Harriet Smith's profile drawings from her 1941 excavations show considerable disturbed or redeposited sediments spread out around the base of the mound. This is probably the result of cultivation. The difference in form as shown by Patrick (conical) and described by Smith (oval with the longest dimension north to south) is also probably the result of plowing. We can conclude that in the 1870s the Murdock Mound was a conical mound perhaps 15-20 feet (4.6-6.1 meters) in height. This is very probably its original form.

Thanks to Harriet Smith's detailed work, this is one of the most completely excavated and examined mounds at the Cahokia site (Smith 1942, 1969). In all, 13 stratigraphic levels were determined, five in a village or habitation area below the mound and eight in the pyramid or mound structure itself.

It is Harriet Smith's interpretation that the Murdock Mound was built as a double-terraced mound with a lower platform extending across the west face; a higher platform, which she labeled the Temple Platform, was on the east half of the mound. She suggested that the northeast and southeast corners of the mound were faceted.

The basal outline of the mound, including the faceted northwest and southwest corners, was found in the excavations. Only a few feet of the height of the mound slopes were actually uncovered. The upper portions had been presumably destroyed by cultivation of the area over several decades. Smith's reconstructions of both the terracing of the mound and its total height were based upon her projections of the slopes and faceted corners and her interpretation of ancient Cahokia engineering principles. On this basis, she projected a height for the west-facing terrace of 16.5 feet (5 meters). The eastern half, or projected Temple Platform, she proposed was 33 feet (10.1 meters) in height. The higher estimate is not consistent with the earlier figures for the precultivation height of the mound, but the height proposed for the western portion, 16.5 feet (5 meters), is very nearly identical to the earliest (1882) value of 15 feet (4.6 meters).

Mound 55 was built primarily of a black gumbo, which made a very compact and stable mound. When the mound was abandoned, materials from the upper levels eroded down, and it was from some of this wash material that a radiocarbon date of A.D. 1350 ± 75 was determined (M-1290). Smith interpreted this as dating the time of the latest utilization of Mound 55.

Mound 56 (S234E144)

Aside from Monks Mound, Mound 56 is one of the most illustrated mounds at Cahokia. Both Wild (see Figure 2.2) and Bodmer (see Figure 1.6) show it as a tall—even accounting for some exaggeration of vertical scale—ridge-top mound. Both of these illustrations were drawn in the 1840s before extensive cultivation of this area. Today the mound is greatly altered from its original form by cultivation and appears as a low, domed rise (Figure 6.9). Mound 56 is shown as conical on the Patrick map. The McAdams map of 1882 gave a height of 15 feet (4.6 meters); the Thomas map of 1894, 12 feet (3.7 meters); and the Peterson–McAdams map of 1906, only 5 feet (1.5 meters). The 1966 UWM map, using a base elevation of 127 meters (416.7 feet), showed a height of 3.9 meters (12.8 feet) for this mound. It is hard to understand how Peterson and McAdams could have given a height of only 5 feet in 1906 unless they confused it with some other nearby mound. However, the location seems to be most closely related to this mound.

In his report, Moorehead described Mound 56, also known as the Jesse Ramey Mound, as follows:

This is about twenty feet in height at the present time, the base diameter some three hundred feet. It is the second mound directly south of Monks. It is not quite clear whether this was originally an oblong mound or of the pyramid type since it has been cultivated for many years. Some twenty-five men were employed in the work and a trench sixty-five feet in length and ten feet deep was extended from near the base on the south side to a line some distance from the center. Then test pits were sunk and post augers used. Five or six feet farther down (a total depth of fourteen or sixteen feet) we came upon rather soft, dark earth quite different from the clay and gumbo of which most of the mounds are composed. It resembled the earth found about burials in the several mounds of the Hopewell group. There were a few scales of copper, and some fragments of a highly finished pottery. That is, fragments recovered indicate the finer pottery such as accompanies burials. This mound was tested during our first season. At a subsequent visit the Ramey family did not care to have it explored. Now that it is state property, it is recommended that thorough exploration be undertaken (Moorehead 1929:37-38).

Mound 57 (S246W128)

There are many points of confusion regarding mound numbers on Moorehead's maps. In the case of the mounds Patrick numbered 57 and 59, Moorehead consistently reversed these numbers. On Patrick's map, what is now called Round Top Mound is clearly marked as Mound 59. Moorehead assigned 57 to Round Top Mound. As stated earlier, this atlas adheres to Patrick's assignment of numbers.

Mound 57 is directly south of Mound 48 (Figure 6.7); it is numbered and shown on the Patrick map as a relatively large, round or conical mound. The McAdams map of 1882 gave a height of 10 feet (3.05 meters), although both the Thomas map (1894) and the Peterson-McAdams map (1906) gave a height of 5 feet (1.5 meters). The 1966 UWM map indicated only an irregular contour in this area with an elevation point, which suggests that the height of the mound in 1966 was only 0.8 meters (2.6 feet). This is indicative of the intense cultivation that has leveled the mound, although there is no record of it being destroyed deliberately to level the ground for farming. Excavations would undoubtedly show the remaining base of the mound and perhaps provide some clue to its original size and date of construction.

Mound 58 (S264W422)

Directly south of Mound 42, Patrick indicated a rather large conical mound that he numbered 58 (Figure 6.13). Patrick recorded no height for this mound. The McAdams map of 1882 gave 20 feet (6.1 meters); the Thomas map of 1894, 15 feet (4.6 meters); and the Peterson-McAdams map of 1906, 14 feet (4.3 meters). Moorehead referred to it only as one "of the very large mounds" (1923:48). The 1930 survey for the USGS Monks Mound quadrangle shows three 5-foot (1.5-meter) closed contours in this area. The elevation of the top of this mound is given as 440 feet (134.1 meters) above sea level. This would indicate a height of about 20 feet (6.1 meters). By 1966 the mound was only 1 meter (3.3 feet) high. Although the earlier maps indicate some lowering of Mound 58 through time, it seems apparent that its major destruction was after 1930. It may have been mostly leveled during construction of the nearby Falcon Drive-In Theater.

This area has been cultivated for many years, and the mound today is indistinct in the contour lines of that area. Based upon those contours, it appears the mound spread to the north and south. In the 1920s, when Moorehead worked in the area, he added a Mound 74 just to the west of Mound 58. It may be, however, that this is just part of Mound 58 disturbed in the 50 years from the time of Patrick to Moorehead. Modern contours in the area show no well-defined second mound but rather an extension to the west that appears to be something like a platform or terrace. Had there been another mound so close to Mound 58, Patrick and his surveyors would surely have indicated it on their map.

Based upon all the previous maps and recorded observations, Mound 58 was a large, conical mound which in the late 1800s was probably 20 feet (6.1 meters) or more in height. There is no reference to any excavation conducted in this mound.

Mound 59 (S496W2)

About 500 meters (1,640 feet) directly south of Monks Mound are two of the more impressive mounds at the site (Figure 6.14). One of these—Mound 60—is a well-formed, flat-top platform mound. Directly to the west of Mound 60 is a conical mound of considerable elevation, Mound 59 (Moorehead's Mound 57), commonly known as Round Top Mound (Figures 6.15 and 6.16). Patrick showed it as a true conical mound about 44 feet (13.4 meters) in height. The height of this mound recorded by map makers is more consistent than for most mounds. The McAdams map of 1882 indicates 40 feet (12.2 meters); the Thomas map, 48 feet (14.6 meters); and the Peterson-McAdams map, 35 feet (10.7 meters). Using the 128-meter contour line as a base, the 1966 UWM map shows a height of 12.1 meters (39.7 feet).

One of the Cahokia site's more imposing mounds, Mound 59 has been photographed many times (Moorehead 1929:Plates 4 and 5; Parrish 1906; Titterington 1938:Figures 2 and 4). Examination of these photographs and height data indicates that this mound is as untouched as any and maintains its original size and form relatively well.

There appears to have been no professional digging in Mound 59. Moorehead refers only to its being unexamined and that, therefore, it is possible that there are interments in it (Moorehead 1923:48). There were, however, other types of excavations in the mound. In one of these it appears that a burial and a hammered copper ornament were found (Moorehead 1929:90;

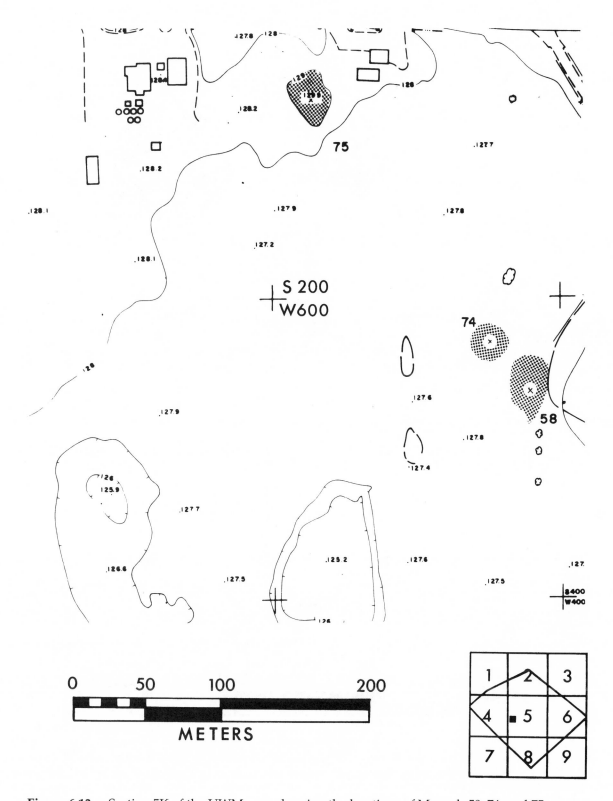

Figure 6.13. Section 5K of the UWM map showing the locations of Mounds 58, 74, and 75.

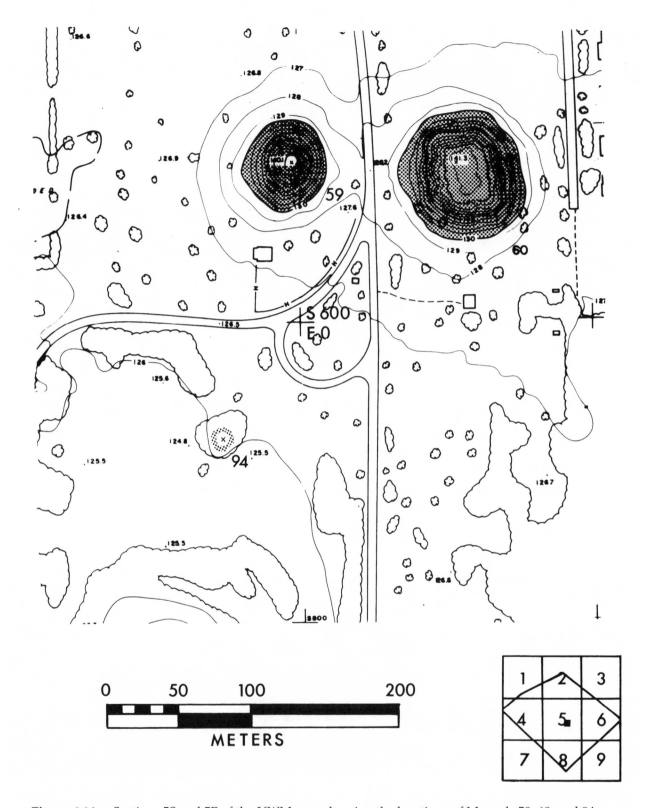

Figure 6.14. Sections 5S and 5R of the UWM map showing the locations of Mounds 59, 60, and 94.

Figure 6.15. Photograph of Mound 59, Round Top, ca. 1911. Source: Cahokia Mounds Museum, Illinois Historic Preservation Agency.

Figure 6.16. Mounds 59 (right) and 60 (left) in the 1960s. Source: University of Wisconsin-Milwaukee, photographed by James Anderson in 1967.

Titterington 1938:11). The person who excavated the object was A. E. Postmueller, and Moorehead recorded the event: "A copper serpent was found by a boy on the surface not far from the Mound No. 76 [Mound 59] in the summer of 1922. The serpent effigy was some four or five inches long, composed of a thin copper sheet with no filigree work" (Moorehead 1929:90, Plate 1).

Postmueller made the following comment about Moorehead's account:

> This statement is not entirely correct. Therefore, the following facts are given. The serpent was found by three boys [one of whom was Postmueller], not on the surface and not near Mound No. 76 [Mound 59], and in the autumn of 1915, instead of 1922. . . . One Sunday late in the autumn of 1915 Bartley Hurst came to my home in Belleville to talk about and see my small collection. He suggested we go to Collinsville to see Oscar Schneider. After early lunch we took the Interurban Electric Line to Collinsville to visit Schneider. He took us to the Cahokia Mounds to do some surface hunting. It was my first trip to the mounds and I was surprised and awed by the immense size and extent of the group. I had never read anything about them and had heard very little of them, so my first visit impressed me profoundly. We roamed over the fields, surface hunting as boys do . . . and worked our way to *Round Top Mound*, which is Number 57 [actually Mound 59] on the map of J. J. R. Patrick of 1880. On the southwest side of the mound we found a trail or rough path so we climbed to the top. There, located in the southwest part of the top was a fair sized hole which had been previously dug . . . about four feet long, three feet wide and three feet deep . . . from two to ten years before or even longer. We started to clean out the bottom of the old hole. We found fragments of pottery, charcal [sic], bone and the usual material. We had nothing to dig with except a trowel that Oscar Schneider brought along. One of us went to the sheds that extended south from the house and barn on Mound 48, finding a broken spading fork which we appropriated for our use. . . . It had been cloudy all afternoon and now the thin mist began to change to a drizzle. We knew that we could not dig long, because it was getting late and would soon be dark. We had moved only a few bushels of earth when we came to a skeleton, and upon the chest lay the figure of a serpent. It was simply a thin sheet of copper, cut or formed in the shape of a serpent's tail. It had a dark green and bluish color with darker pieces of patina. Evidently there was originally more of it at the larger end, but we did not find the missing part or anything else. After we had examined it, I became the owner and have retained it to this day (quoted in Grimm 1949:13-14, emphasis added).

Mound 60 (S498E110)

Associated with Round Top, Mound 60 is a large, rectangular platform mound known as the Fox Mound (Figures 6.14 and 6.16). These two mounds seem to be united by a platform since a contour line surrounds them both on the UWM map. The contour may, however, only represent a blending of the slope wash, or talus slopes, of the two mounds. They probably were a unit since their relationship to each other is matched by other paired mounds at the site. They seem strongly reminiscent of the association of platform charnel-house mounds and conical burial mounds in ethnohistoric period of the southeastern United States.

Mound 60 is shown on the Patrick map as a rectangular mound with the longer axis north-south. Measurements based on the Patrick map suggest a north-south dimension of 160 feet (48.8 meters) and an east-west dimension of 125 feet (38.1 meters). Patrick showed a cross section of Mound 60, noting a height of 46 feet (14 meters). The later maps are consistent with Patrick's measurements: McAdams' of 1882 indicating a height of 45 feet (13.7 meters); Thomas 1894, 50 feet (15.2 meters); and Peterson-McAdams of 1906, 30 feet (9.1 meters). The 1966 UWM map, using a 129-meter (423.2-foot) elevation as a base line, gave a height of 12.3 meters (40.4 feet). Bushnell (1904) referred to this as a rectangular, truncated pyramid with a height of 46 feet (14 meters), a north-south dimension of 160 feet (42.8 meters), and an east-west dimension of 125 feet (38.1 meters).

Photographs of Fox Mound appear in several publications (Bushnell 1922:Figures 1 and 2; Moorehead 1929: Plate 5; Parrish 1906; Titterington 1938:Figures 2 and 4).

There is no indication of excavation in this mound. Moorehead refers to it as one of the larger mounds of the site (1923:48). It has not been cultivated and retains much of its original form today.

Mound 61 (S623E536)

Both Mounds 61 and 62 are in association with a large borrow pit in the southeast quadrant of the site (Figure 6.17). A recent survey suggests that there is a mound (Mound 95) not noted by Patrick or other investigators on the northeast side of this borrow pit. Patrick showed Mounds 61 and 62 linked by a sort of U-shaped causeway. No recent maps have indicated this, so it is difficult to interpret Patrick's map. On the USGS map, particularly the 1930 compilation from the original field notes, there is a U-shaped topographic

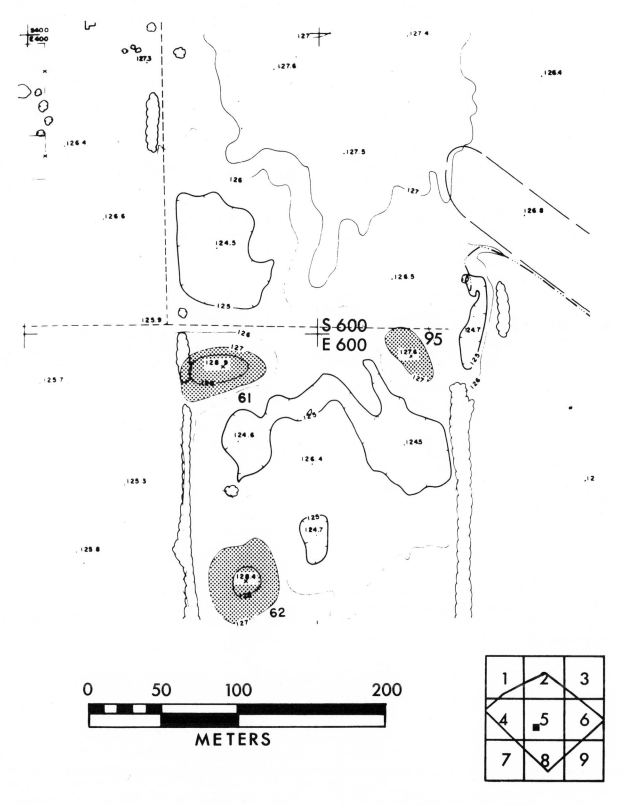

Figure 6.17. Section 5Q of the UWM map showing the locations of Mounds 61, 62, and 95.

feature that may represent Patrick's configuration. In the spring of 1978, I noted a vegetation pattern between these two mounds that almost matched Patrick's description.

Patrick did not give a height for this mound. McAdams in 1882 gave 10 feet (3.05 meters), and Peterson-McAdams in 1906, 14 feet (4.3 meters). The 1966 UWM map, using a 127-meter (416.7 feet) base contour, showed a height of 1.9 meters (6.2 feet). This area has been extensively cultivated in recent years, and the difference between the heights given by the earlier investigators and the 1966 map may reflect deflation from intensive cultivation. As a consequence, the borrow pits in the area have undoubtedly filled in since Patrick's time, although they are still clearly visible in the topography of the area and retain moisture.

The Patrick map showed Mound 61 as rectangular with a much longer north-south axis. The UWM map, however, shows this as a long, oval-shaped mound with a much longer east-west axis. Whether the discrepancy is the result of cultivation or an error on Patrick's map cannot be determined. The east-west orientation is in agreement with Moorehead's rendering of this mound in his interpretation of the Patrick map in 1929.

Moorehead gives some indication of the height of Mound 61: "Two pits were sunk and by means of the augers we tested to the base, a distance of 20 feet" (1923:35-36). Since Moorehead does not define what he considers the base, he may have considered the natural gumbo surface of the area as part of the mound. This might account for the difference in height between the Peterson-McAdams estimate and Moorehead's.

When Moorehead worked in this mound, he reported the following:

This is an oval mound located between the two ponds on land owned by Mrs. William Tippetts. Externally it is rather promising, and as it is shaped not unlike altar mounds of the Ohio Valley, the survey decided to test it. Much to our surprise we found it composed of exceedingly heavy, black gumbo. . . . Very little in the way of material was encountered. The mound appeared to be unstratified (Moorehead 1923:35-36).

Moorehead goes on to comment on the relationship of Mound 61 to village site material—pottery fragments, bone fragments, or broken stone:

The soil around Mrs. Tippetts' Mound is mostly gumbo; the village site indications are not heavy, but several hundred yards north, where there is less gumbo, the village was thickly populated. It does not seem likely that the Indians would go any distance to secure the earth for the construction of No. 61. It

would be more convenient to obtain it from points nearby and the two depressions marked 'lakes' on the map probably represent the places from which the earth was taken for 61 and 62 (Moorehead 1923:49).

Because there was no pottery or other artifacts in this mound, Moorehead suggested that it was one of the earlier ones built at the site (1923:47, also 1929:58 and 105).

Mound 62 (S766E552)

Mound 62 is located near the large series of borrow pits in the southeast quadrant of the Cahokia site and is associated with Mound 61 and Mound 95 (see description of Mound 61 above and Figure 6.17). Mound 61 was shown by Patrick as a round, conical-shaped mound. Patrick showed no height for it, but on the Peterson-McAdams map of 1906 a height of 6 feet (1.8 meters) was given. The UWM map, on the basis of the 127-meter (416.7-foot) contour, showed a height of 1.4 meters (4.6 feet). It appears that this mound has been less affected by destruction from plowing than Mound 61 (see above).

In 1923, Moorehead made the following comment:

On our large map are several areas marked 'Village Site.' Readers should not conclude that wigwams existed merely at those places. Such markings indicate that at certain points we dug pits and found the indications of occupation extended several feet into the ground. We believe that all the area was occupied except a space south of the National road. This is bounded on the west by tumuli 68 and 70, on the south by 66 and 65, on the east by 64 and 62, and on the north by 77 [Mound 72]. We did not test very extensively in this area but where we did so, little was found (1923:38).

There is no evidence, however, that Moorehead dug or tested Mound 62.

Mound 63 (S1114E814)

The Patrick map shows Mound 63 as a small, conical mound in the southernmost portion of the area he mapped (Figure 6.18). There is no indication of the height on the Patrick map, nor is it indicated on the McAdams map of 1882 or the Thomas map of 1894. However, the Peterson-McAdams map of 1906 shows a mound that probably is Mound 63 with a height of 6 feet (1.8 meters). The 1966 UWM map, using a 128-

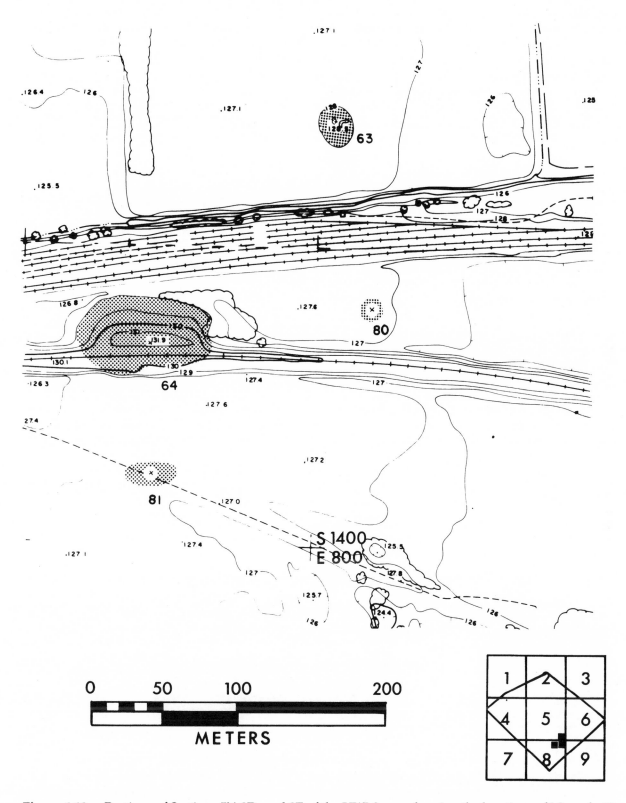

Figure 6.18. Portions of Sections 5Y, 8D, and 8E of the UWM map showing the locations of Mounds 63, 64, 80, and 81.

meter (419.9-foot) contour as a base, shows a height of 0.5 meters (1.6 feet). The contours on the USGS map of the Monks Mound quadrangle show a contour line at 420 feet (128 meters) outlining Mound 63 and an elevation at the top of 423 feet (128.9 meters), suggesting that in 1930 the mound was at least 3 feet (0.9 meters) high, probably higher. Again, this area has been extensively cultivated and the mound probably reduced.

Mound 64 (S1270E688)

Sometimes known as True Rattlesnake Mound, Mound 64 is located between the railroad tracks directly south of Mounds 61 and 62 (Figure 6.18). Patrick showed it as a rectangular mound with the long axis directly east-west. An 1892 photograph in the files of the Missouri Historical Society may be of this mound (Figure 6.19). It is labeled "Hayrick Mound of the Cahokia Group, Madison County, Illinois, 1892. One mile south of Cahokia Mound size 250 feet long, 12 feet wide, 50 feet [?] high." No railroad tracks are visible in the photograph, so the mound may actually be Mound 66, but the dimensions given on the photograph are too short to be Mound 66 and the height too great.

The early maps recording this mound show it much lower. The McAdams map of 1882 gave a height of 15 feet (4.6 meters) and the Peterson-McAdams map of 1906 only 8 feet (2.4 meters). It is difficult to know which of these is correct; for example, the dimension of 12 feet wide given on the Missouri Historical Society photo is not consistent with a mound 250 feet long and 50 feet high. Probably the width and height are reversed on the photo label. The 1966 UWM map, which shows only portions of this mound since it is buried under the railroad tracks, suggests an east-west dimension of 73 meters (239.5 feet) and a north-south dimension of 27 meters (88.6 feet).

Moorehead wrote of Mound 64:

This lies to the extreme south of the group, fully a mile from Monks Mound, and many years ago was considerably damaged by the construction of the Baltimore and Ohio and Pennsylvania Railroads which pass on either side. Some of the earth was utilized in grading tracks. It is stated by older residents that the Baltimore and Ohio construction crew removed some two-thirds of the structure, and found a stone pipe, said to represent an eagle, about 20 inches in length. Diligent inquiry fails to indicate the present location of this specimen. The structure is composed of very heavy dark gumbo and although eight or ten test pits were dug by our crew, no pipes, skeletons, or other objects were uncovered (1929:83-84).

Figure 6.19.   Mound 64 in 1892. Source: Missouri Historical Society.

The dimensions, reported Moorehead, were:

the major axis running N87°W, and from the highest point on which, taken as BM [Bench Mark], base appears at eleven and three-tenths feet. Northward from BM, the minor axis extends sixty feet; southward, the center line of the B.&0. track lies at thirty feet, and the cutting operations necessary to laying this have seriously marred the entire south half of the mound (1929:83-84).

Mound 65 (S1566E772)

Moorehead (1929:83-84) suggested that Mound 65 is "South 9° East, 994 feet" (303 meters) from Mound 64 (Figure 6.20). Patrick recorded Mound 65 as a rather large, conical mound but did not give a height. McAdams in 1882 indicated a height of 25 feet (7.6 meters) and the Peterson-McAdams map of 1906, 20 feet (6.1 meters). Using the 127-meter (476.7-foot) contour as a base line, the 1966 map shows a height of 6.2 meters (20.3 feet). There are several references to Mound 65 in Moorehead's discussion, but usually in connection with other mounds. However, on one occasion, Moorehead said: "Tests on Number 65 were completed by June 20. . . . There is a complete series of thirty-five or more maps on Mounds 65, 66 and other mounds, on file in the Museum of Natural History of the University of Illinois" (Moorehead 1929:76).

He described the shape of this mound as:

The ground plan appears to be almost a circle, but at a point approximately halfway up the slope the outline becomes noticeably rectilinear, and from there to the summit the mound might be described as prismoidal in form or, loosely, as a truncated pyramid of four sides or, but for unequal axial dimensions, as a truncated cone. But farming operations have disturbed the original perimeters, a drainage canal bank has been thrown up against the south-east slope, and the contents of at least two extensive pits, presumably test holes sunk within the last few years, have doubtless altered the original outlines of the summit, so that at this time the mound may for all practical purposes be considered the frustum of a cone (Moorehead 1929:81-83).

Moorehead described a test hole sunk at what he called "BM," in most of his work the high point at a mound's center, which "showed water at twenty-five and eight-tenths feet which is the same level as the surface of the water in a drainage canal to the south of the mound." The water-bearing sand was "entered at from twenty-three to twenty-five feet and . . . was

found in every one of the forty-four test holes put down" (Moorehead 1929:82). Stratigraphy noted within the mound was described as follows:

Above this stratum of sand was found a deposit of stiff multicolored gumbo or clay in which red and yellow and their various shades predominated, and which for want of a better name, has been indicated . . . [in] cross section maps of this mound under its local name of 'shale'. This stratum reached a maximum thickness of two feet under the central portions of the mound, but pinched out and disappeared altogether within from ten to twenty to twenty-five feet of the mound's perimeter. This might lead to some speculation as to whether No. 65 was built on a low natural mound, speculation that is rather encouraged by examination of stratum immediately above the shale. This is a deposit of gray sandy gumbo, averaging less than twelve inches in depth, and always decreasing in every direction toward the perimeter of the mound. At a point within three feet from the east end of the major axis it disappears completely, only to reappear in increased depth two feet higher and twenty feet further east whence it sloped eastward under something more than a foot of pure gray sand.

Extending the entire length of the major axis and across at least the south half of the mound's base, we found a sharply marked deposit of black gumbo, so dry and hard along the minor axis, where we sunk a line of test holes, that it was difficult to cut and so loose after being cut that it could hardly be kept in the augers for removal. At twenty feet . . . the augers went through a foot of hard dry sand, an entirely new formation to us but which was encountered later at eighteen feet under Stn. [station] 6, where it was nearly four feet deep and at about twenty and six-tenths feet under Stn. 18, . . . where it was about two feet deep. . . . [T]hese sand deposits . . . lied at or below base and . . . under extremely dry and very hard black gumbo.

The central portions of No. 65 appear to be a mixed mass of black and yellow gumbo of about equal parts, and the whole was capped with a layer of black gumbo ranging from about one and one-half feet in thickness on the south slope to a maximum thickness of nearly six feet under BM.

No remains of any kind were found within the mound, but twenty feet beyond Stn. D, in the field southwest of the mound, one very small sherd was taken from a depth of about three and two-tenths feet below surface (Moorehead 1929:82).

Mound 66 (S1630E80)

Referred to by Moorehead (1929) as the Harding Mound and by the U.S. Geological Survey as the Rattle-

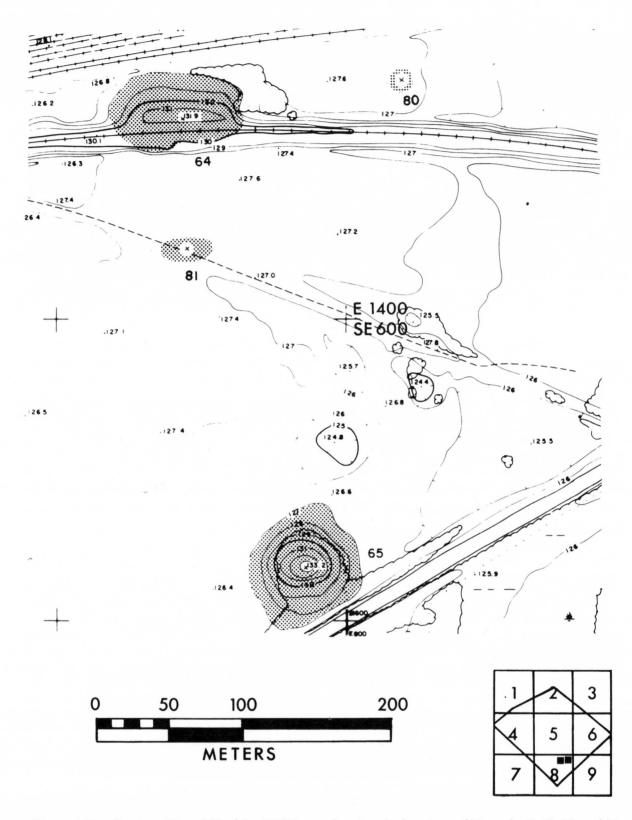

Figure 6.20.   Sections 8D and 8E of the UWM map showing the locations of Mounds 64, 65, 80, and 81.

snake Mound, Mound 66 is one of the largest mounds at the Cahokia site (Figure 6.21). What was locally referred to as Rattlesnake Mound (Mound 64) was partially destroyed by construction of the railroad tracks. The name seems to have been transferred to the Harding Mound by the USGS surveyors, causing some confusion.

Mound 66 is a long, ridge-topped mound, one of the few of this type at the site. Its form is marred by an unfilled trench that Moorehead cut through the mound in the 1920s (Figure 6.22). On recent maps the mound appears to have a notch through the middle. Mound 66 is one of the higher mounds at the site. McAdams, in 1882, gave a height of 30 feet (9.1 meters), whereas Thomas, in 1894, gave 20 feet (6.1 meters), and Peterson-McAdams in 1906, 25 feet (7.6 meters). Using the base elevation as the 129-meter (423.2-foot) contour, the 1966 UWM map shows a height for this mound of 7.4 meters (24.3 feet). Using the same base elevation, the north-south dimension is 51 meters (167.3 feet) and the east-west dimension is 132 meters (433.1 feet). A. J. Throop described the mound in 1928:

> Rattlesnake Mound is approximately five hundred feet long, two hundred feet wide, thirty feet in height. The top is beautifully rounded, furnishing an ideal situation for the four roomy tents of the explorers party. The surrounding ground is very low, with, however, a well-defined graded way running due north. Messrs. Jesse and James Ramey, who called to view the work, stated that this graded pass was extended north through their land toward the mounds immediately south of old Cahokia [Monks Mound].
>
> When Mr. Taylor surveyed the mound he was amazed at the accuracy of the contour maintained by the builders, and expressed himself as puzzled that so great a pile of earth could be made so nearly true to keep its contour throughout the ages. At points two hundred feet east of center and two hundred feet west of center, less than one-tenth of a foot difference in elevation was found (Throop 1928:38-39).

Due to fear that the railroad track just north of this mound would be expanded and destroy the area, Mound 66 was made the focus of intensive excavations sponsored by Moorehead's party. The work was carried out by an engineer, J. L. B. Taylor, and Moorehead's report is mostly a quoting of Taylor's report on the mound excavations. Taylor carefully surveyed the mound in a grid system with the center line of the grid directly through what was thought to be the center of the mound. The plan of excavation was to put a 50-foot-wide (15.2-meter-wide) trench, starting at the edge, through the mound along the north-south, or minor, axis (Figures 6.23 and 6.24). This plan

would allow for a one-to-one slope of the side wall, so that by time the trench reached the bottom of the mound it would be only a few feet wide. This was, however, decided against since opening such a cut would have called "for removal of the office tent which although all four tents had been crowded against each other was nevertheless close against Stn. 16, major axis" (Moorehead 1929:74). Instead the trench was cut 15 to 20 feet to the west, somewhat off the center of the mound.

Excavations through the top of the mound revealed burials:

> About 3 P.M., May 27, the slip team uncovered the knees of a human skeleton at a depth of three feet ... and was then moved to the opposite edge of the cut in order not to interfere with the work of laying this skeleton bare by means of trowels. When the bones had all been cleaned off, they were given a coat of wet Spanish whiting to bring them in relief, and were then photographed, and left in place. . . . As there were traces of wooden coffins and number of nails and metal buttons and buckles found with these, we concluded that these burials were, probably, those of Frenchmen or early settlers.
>
> They were reburied west of the mound, each accompanied by a bottle containing a note from myself telling where and under what circumstances they had been found (Moorehead 1929:74-75).

At a lower level, approximately 3 feet (0.9 meters) below the surface, a large number of burials were found. According to Taylor's estimate, there were remains of at least 140 burials found in a poor state of preservation; traces of bones and teeth were all that remained.

Along with one of the burials was a chunky stone or discoidal, reportedly found on the face of the skeleton. A drawing in Moorehead's report (1929:Plate 36) gives rather specific dimensions for it, although the description of the drawings says it was drawn from memory. It shows a chunky stone approximately 3 inches (7.6 centimeters) in diameter; it was well turned out with flattened edges to the rim and a well-defined and large central depression on both sides. There is no indication of what kind of stone it was.

Besides the excavations, auger holes were drilled into the mound on both its east-west and north-south axes, and Moorehead presented a drawing (1929:Figure 9) to show the nature of mound construction as he could determine it from these tests (Figure 6.24). Moorehead thought that Mound 66 was built mostly of what he called gumbo. As nearly as can be determined, he is referring to a bluish black, very sticky, clay-like soil that is found in the southern portion of

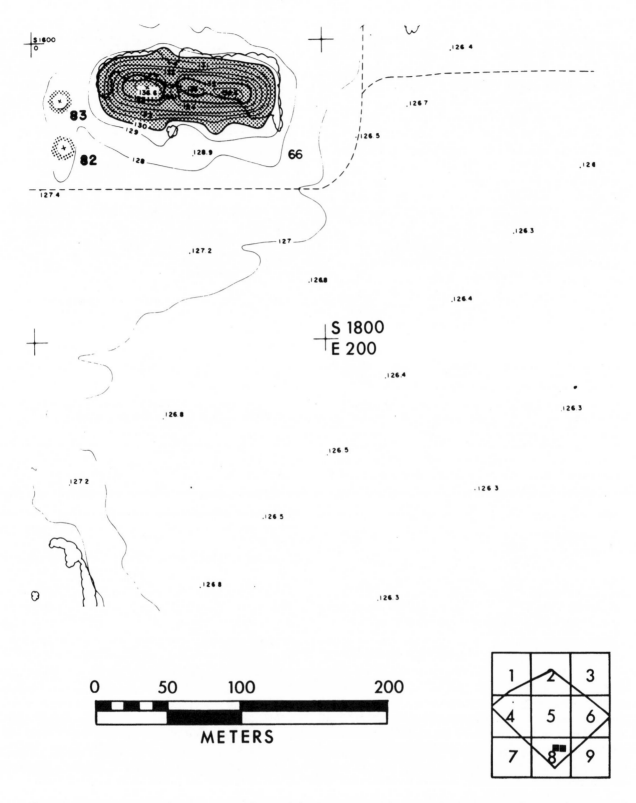

Figure 6.21.   Portions of sections 8I and 8H of the UWM map showing the locations of Mounds 66, 82, and 83.

Figure 6.22. Mound 66. Source: University of Wisconsin-Milwaukee, photographed by James Anderson in 1967.

Figure 6.23. Members of Moorehead's crew use a horse slip to excavate Mound 66 in 1927. Source: Department of Anthropology, University of Illinois at Urbana-Champaign.

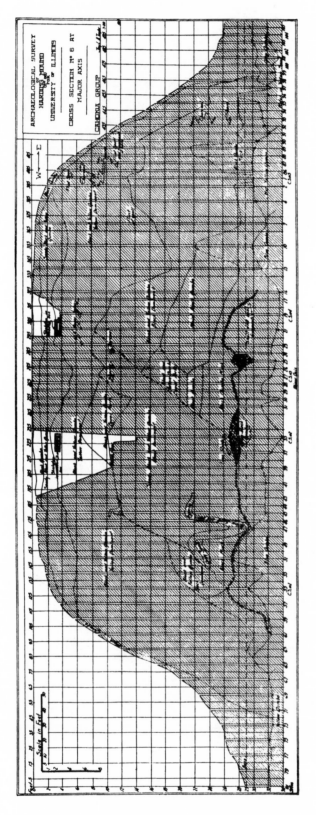

Figure 6.24.   Profile of Mound 66 based on Moorehead's excavations. Source: Department of Anthropology, University of Illinois at Urbana-Champaign, based on Moorehead 1929:Figure 9.

the Cahokia site just under the plow zone. Of this material, Moorehead asked:

> Why were so many mounds built of gumbo? It is difficult to handle-even our own men using modern steel shovels find it heavy and wearisome to remove. Possessed of naught but stone and shell hoes, digging sticks, and baskets or skin bags, the removal and transportation of sufficient gumbo to erect Mound 66 was a herculean task (Moorehead 1929:104-106).

In any given area, mounds made of this so-called gumbo were probably the first built, as this is the material that the Indians came upon first. Using that concept, Moorehead suggested that certain mounds were built earlier than others because no artifacts were found in their fill and because they were chiefly composed of black gumbo.

As to the function of ridge-top mounds in general and of Mound 66 in particular, Moorehead speculated:

> It is too narrow on top for large wigwams or temples. The auger tests—nearly two hundred to the base—did not indicate the level or burnt floor common in mortuary tumuli. Beyond No. 66 toward the north is an elevation flanked by two ponds or depressions. Old observers used to call this a causeway leading to other mounds. There being no village-site worthy of the name around No. 66, why the causeway? The burials found by Engineer Taylor a few feet below the surface, down the southern slope were made after the mound had been constructed. There appear to be no burials, altars, or distinct stratigraphy in the body of the mound. It must remain one of the mysteries of Cahokia and we may be pardoned again for referring finally to the series of complete and detailed maps drawn by Mr. Taylor, which cover every possible fact or circumstance of mound construction of this remarkable tumulus. . . . We have never believed that all these structures were erected within a short space of time, individually or as a group. Number 66 seems to show completion within limited dates, there being no sodlines (Moorehead 1929:104-106).

Mound 67 (S696W360)

Southeast of the largest borrow pit at the Cahokia site is another set of paired mounds similar to Fox and Round Top (Figure 6.25). Mound 67 seems to be the conical mound of the pair (Figure 6.26). Surprisingly, through time the various estimates of height for this mound have increased. The McAdams map of 1882 gives a height of 10 feet (3.05 meters); the Thomas map, 15 feet (4.6 meters); and the Peterson-McAdams map, 25 feet (7.6 meters). Using the 129-meter (423.2-foot)

contour line as a base, the 1966 UWM map shows a height of 6.2 meters (20.3 feet). Using the same base elevation, the north-south dimension is 52 meters (170.6 feet) and the east-west dimension 47 meters (154.2 feet). There are no published indications that any excavations were carried out in this mound, and there are no data about it other than its form, which suggests that it is similar to Round Top Mound.

Mound 68 (S760W376)

Just to the south of Mound 67 is what appears to be a flat-topped platform mound, Mound 68 (Figure 6.25). The McAdams map lists a height of 15 feet (4.6 meters) for this mound and Peterson-McAdams, 20 feet (6.1 meters). Using a 129-meter (423.2-foot) base line, the 1966 UWM map shows a height of 7.4 meters (24.3 feet), a north-south dimension of 72 meters (236.2 feet), and an east-west dimension of 73 meters (239.5 feet). Moorehead referred only indirectly to Mound 68 in a description of the village or habitation area at the Cahokia site.

Mound 69 (S1162W832)

This small mound is part of what is known today as the Rouch mound group in the southwest segment of the Cahokia site (Figure 6.27). It appeared on Patrick's map as a small, conical mound, but today it is only a very slight elevation, and it appears as a light mark in aerial photographs. Nothing else is known of this mound other than its location and that it was visible enough to be mapped in Patrick's time, the air photos confirming its location. The Rouch mounds were included in some of the earliest photographs of the Cahokia site, indicating that at least over the last 40-50 years they have not been altered much in shape.

Mound 70 (S1258W800)

This mound is also part of the Rouch mound group located in the southwest corner of the site (Figures 6.27 and 6.28). It is a very large mound, and Patrick illustrated it as a nearly square, flat-top mound. It is one of the mounds included in Patrick's cross sections, and he gave a height in 1876 of 40 feet (12.2 meters). Thomas in 1894 gave a height of 45 feet (13.7 meters) and Peterson-McAdams in 1906, 35 feet (10.7 meters). Using the 130-meter (426.5-foot) contour as the base, the 1966 UWM map shows a height of 9 meters (29.5 feet). Patrick gave a north-south dimension of 300 feet (91.4

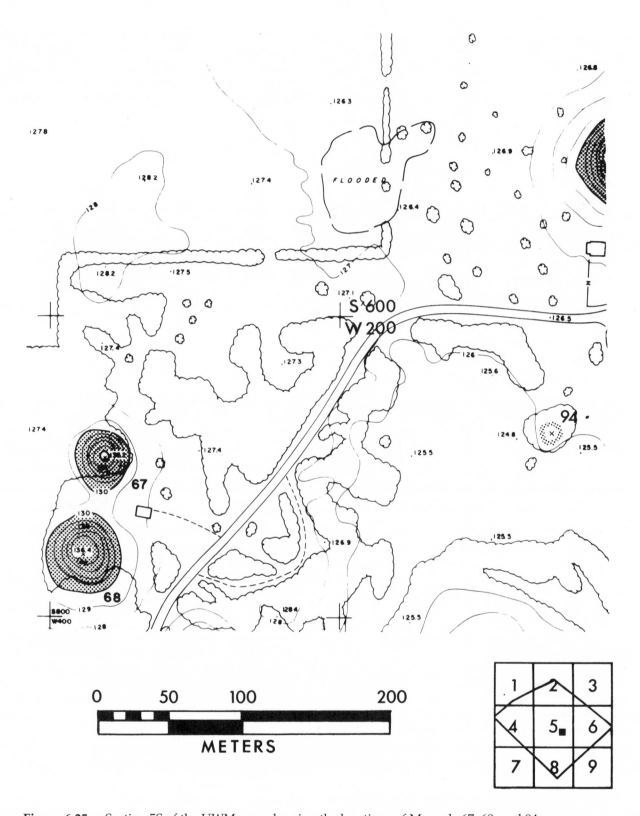

Figure 6.25. Section 5S of the UWM map showing the locations of Mounds 67, 68, and 94.

Figure 6.26. Photograph of Mound 67. Source: Illinois State Museum.

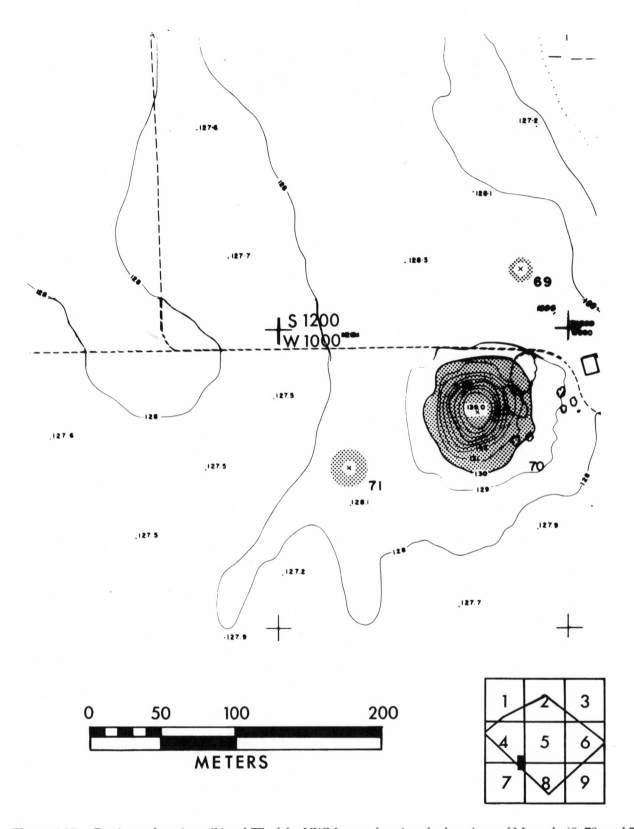

Figure 6.27. Portions of sections 4Y and 7E of the UWM map showing the locations of Mounds 69, 70, and 71.

Figure 6.28.   Goddard air photo of Mound 70 in the 1920s. Source: Illinois State Museum.

meters) and an east-west dimension of about 250 feet (76.2 meters). Again with a 130-meter base elevation, the UWM map shows a north-south dimension of 77 meters (252.6 feet) and an east-west dimension of 75 meters (246.1 feet). The latter map, therefore, is in agreement with Patrick at least in showing the north-south dimension as greater than the east-west dimension, although the 1966 dimensions are less than those given by Patrick.

Bushnell (1904) referred to Mound 70 as a "rectangular truncated pyramid." He apparently based his description on Patrick's as he gave exactly the same height and dimensions, noting that at the time he was writing the mound was cultivated.

Mound 70 has been intensively cultivated and until recent years a farmhouse and other farm buildings were located on it. The mound was purchased for inclusion in the Cahokia Mounds State Historic Site in the 1970s and the buildings removed. There are no published accounts of excavations in this mound.

Mound 71 (S1294W948)

Although noted by Patrick, this small mound does not appear on most of the other maps, and it appears today only as a light spot on aerial photographs (Figure 6.27). It is hardly noticeable in the contours of the area. Patrick suggested that it is a very small circular or conical mound. It is one of three mounds in the Rouch mound group.

Mound 72 (S860E66)

This mound, about 850 meters (2,789 feet) south of Monks Mound, was not included on the Patrick map (Figure 6.29). Patrick numbered 71 mounds, which he included in the main portion of his map of the Cahokia site. The first map Moorehead published (1922a) appears to be a very close copy of the Patrick map. However, in his second publication (1923), he included a very crude sketch obviously based upon the Patrick map but with confused numbering of several mounds. On this one, the first map on which Mound 72 appears, he numbered it 77, and the number 72 he applied to the mound that Patrick numbered 53. In 1929, in his final publication on the Cahokia site, Moorehead returned to the numbering that Patrick used, assigning the number 72 to the mound discussed here. The UWM map retained this number since it represents Moorehead's final publication correcting errors of numbering on his previous map.

Mound 72 is a small, ridge-topped mound (Figure 6.30) that appeared on the McAdams map of 1882 with a height of 10 feet (3.05 meters) and on the Peterson-McAdams map of 1906 with a height of 8 feet (2.4 meters). Using the 127-meter (416.7-foot) contour as a base, the UWM map shows a height of 1.8 meters (5.9 feet).

The mound is oriented differently than most mounds at the Cahokia site in that its long axis is on a northwest-southeast orientation approximately 30° north of east (Figure 6.31). The length of this mound calculated on the basis of the 127-meter contour line is

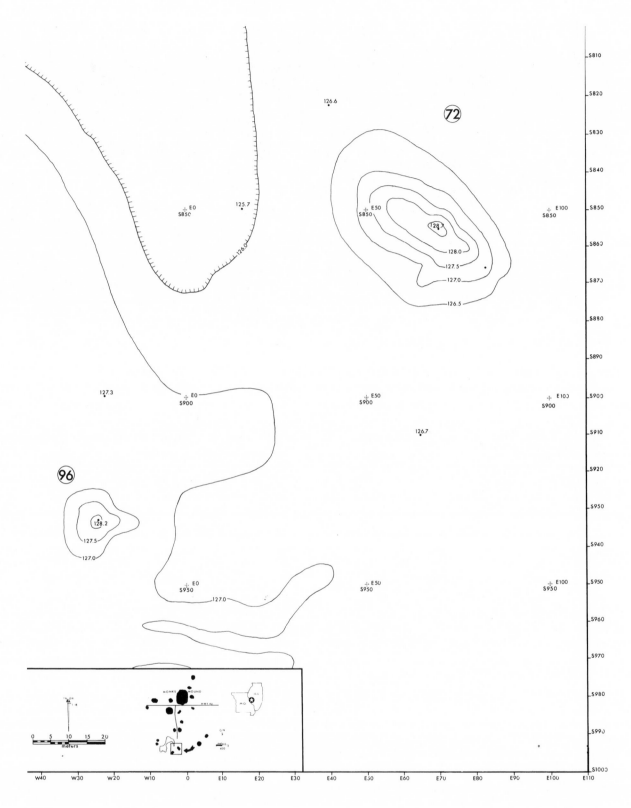

Figure 6.29.   Section 5W of the UWM map showing the locations of Mounds 72 and 96, based on a 1979 resurvey.

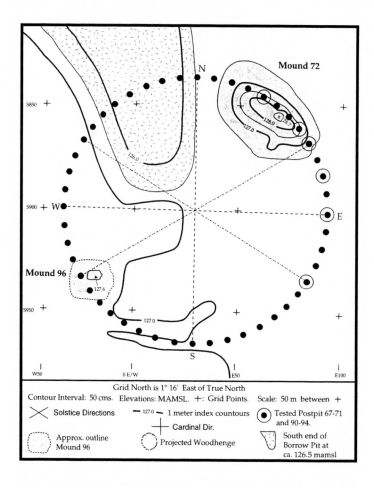

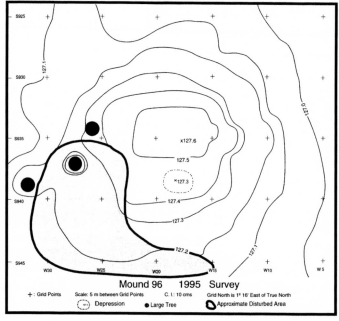

Figure 6.29. (Upper) Map showing the locations of Mound 72 and Mound 96 based upon 1979 and 1995 resurveys of the area. Also shown are projected postpit locations of Woodhenge 72 and the postpit localities tested in 1967-71 and 1990-94 (see Appendix 6:234). (Lower) A 10 centimeter countour map of Mound 96 (see page 163) based upon 1979 and 1995 surveys.

Figure 6.30. Mound 72 in the 1960s. Source: Illinois State Museum.

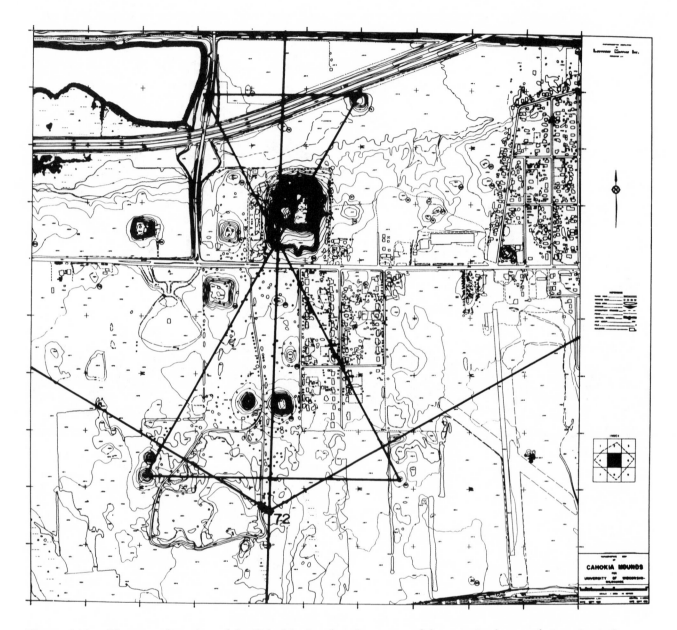

Figure 6.31.   The central section of the Cahokia site showing some of the principal axes of site orientation that converge on the southwest corner of Monks Mound and on Mound 72. Source: Archaeological Research Laboratory, University of Wisconsin-Milwaukee.

42.6 meters (139.8 feet) and its narrow dimension is 21.9 meters (71.8 feet). Because of its orientation and some ideas about the nature of ridge-top mounds at the Cahokia site, this mound was excavated between 1967 and 1971 by crews from the University of Wisconsin-Milwaukee (Figure 6.32).

In the southeast corner of Mound 72 were indications that a large post had been placed in the ground (PP1 in Figure 6.33). The post was later removed but the pit into which it had been placed remained, and impressions of the log were found in the base of the pit. Supporting this log in the bottom of the pit had been two or more smaller logs, which were partially preserved. Radiocarbon dates on these logs give a date of approximately A.D. 950 for the time when the post was placed in the ground.

Excavations through the mound indicated that it had been constructed as a series of smaller mounds that were then reshaped and covered over to give the mound its final shape (Figure 6.33). Within these smaller mounds a series of features was excavated, mainly burial pits and burial deposits. More than 250 skeletons were recovered in various states of preservation.

One burial seemed to be an individual of great importance; he was buried with the remains of other individuals on what appeared to be a platform of shell beads (the central burial in Mound 72 Sub 1 in Figure 6.33). Near him were several retainers with grave goods accompanying them (Figure 6.34). Among these grave goods were several hundred arrowheads of very fine workmanship, separated into distinct categories (Figure 6.35). Among the categories were shapes and materials indicating relationships between Cahokia and areas as far away as Oklahoma, Tennessee, southern Illinois, and Wisconsin. Most of the burials and grave goods accompanying them suggest that many of the people buried in this mound were sacrificed, probably to accompany one or more important individuals. Data recovered from this mound indicate that distinct social stratification was present at the Cahokia site, and extensive economic relationships existed between Cahokia and widely separated areas of the middle portion of North America (Fowler, ed., 1969, 1972).

Figure 6.32.   Crew members from the University of Wisconsin-Milwaukee excavate Mound 72. Source: Archaeological Research Laboratory, University of Wisconsin-Milwaukee.

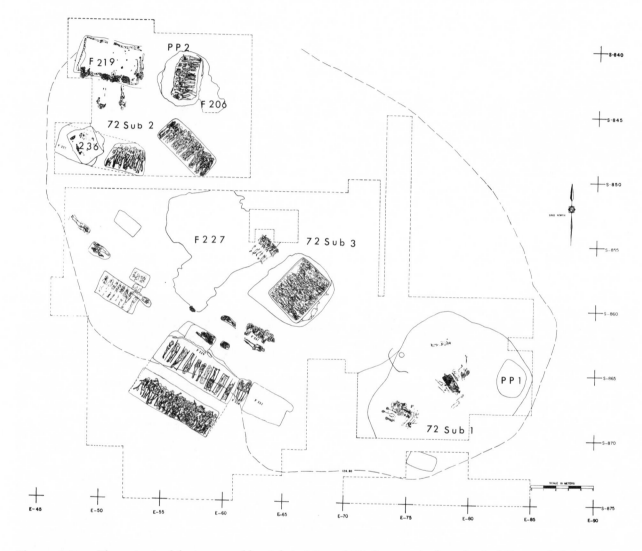

Figure 6.33.   The principal features and burials in Mound 72. Source: Archaeological Research Laboratory, University of Wisconsin-Milwaukee.

Figure 6.34. A group of six burials southwest of the principal burial in Mound 72 located in Submound 1. They are accompanied by caches of projectile points, discoidals, sheet copper, and mica. Source: Illinois State Museum.

Figure 6.35.   Close-up of one of the projectile point caches in Figure 6.34. Source: Illinois State Museum.

Mound 73 (S74W376)

This small mound, directly south of Mound 42, was first noted on the Moorehead 1923 map, although there it is numbered 78 (see Figure 6.7). In his 1929 map, Moorehead changed it to Mound 73. This mound appears to be indicated on the Thomas map of 1894 with a height of 10 feet (3.05 meters), and on the Peterson-McAdams map of 1906 it has a height of 5 feet (1.5 meters). Moorehead described it as a long mound with its east-west axis much longer than the north-south. No dimensions are given. There are no indications of any excavations having taken place in it. It is indicated today by a slight elevation under the area of the west entrance to the former Falcon Drive-In Theater.

Mound 74 (S232W448)

Patrick does not show a mound near Mound 58, but Moorehead does on his 1929 map (Figure 6.13). After 1900, a mound is shown in that location on the Peterson-McAdams map with a height of 10 feet (3.05 meters). Moorehead (1923:39) incorrectly referred to Mound 54 as Mound 74. The UWM map suggests that what Moorehead numbered 74 was a terrace extending toward the west from Mound 58. The earlier air photos and other maps indicate that a house had been

built on Mound 74, and it may be that this mound is merely a reshaping of Mound 58 for construction of the house at the turn of the century.

Mound 75 (S68W570)

Although clearly visible today just south of Highway 40, this mound was noted neither by Patrick, McAdams, Thomas, or Peterson and McAdams (Figure 6.13). Moorehead appears to be the first to have noticed this mound; it is located on both his 1923 map (as Mound 80) and on his 1929 map. Today it is 0.9 meters (3 feet) in height with a north-south dimension of 38 meters (124.7 feet) and an east-west dimension of 30 meters (98.4 feet). Probably substantially higher and smaller in basal dimensions at some earlier date, it had been greatly altered by cultivation by 1966. It may not have been noted earlier because timber obscured it.

Mound 76 (N229W402)

A small, square mound, located on the old bank of Cahokia Creek just north of Mound 42, is another of the mounds noted first by Moorehead (Figure 6.2). In the McAdams map of 1882 there is a mound indicated in this general area but no height is given. In the Peterson-McAdams map of 1906, a mound seemingly located much further north of Mound 42, but perhaps intended to represent this mound, is given a height of 4 feet (1.2 meters). The only reference to excavation in Mound 76 is by Moorehead (1923:47), but he is probably referring to what Patrick numbered Mound 56.

Nearby, the Illinois State Museum conducted excavations in Tract 15B before Sand Prairie Lane was moved in conjunction with interstate highway construction. One of the features found in this excavation was a large, walled compound with circular rooms on its perimeter. Only a portion of the compound was found.

That the compound is located within a plaza strongly indicates that it may have been square, in which case three of the corners would have mounds equidistant from them: Mound 42 to the southwest, 41 to the southeast, and 39 to the northeast (see Figure 3.10). Mound 76 is slightly further south than it should be to complete this pattern on the northwest corner. The deciding factor in its placement most likely was the proximity of a swamp, which prevented the erection of Mound 76 further to the north (Wittry and Vogel 1962:28).

Moorehead also made reference to archaeological finds in this area: "A copper serpent was found by a boy on the surface not far from Mound No. 76 in the summer of 1922. This serpent effigy was some four or five inches long, composed of thin sheet copper with no filigree work. We were unable to secure this object for the university collection" (1929:90). This sounds suspiciously similar to the copper artifact supposedly found in Mound 59 (see discussion of Mound 59) and may merely be a confusion in numbering on Moorehead's part in describing this artifact. In his 1923 map Moorehead assigned the number 76 to Patrick's Mound 56, the Jesse Ramey Mound. This is close to Mound 59, where the copper serpent was most probably found.

Mound 77 (N22FW64)

On Moorehead's 1929 map, four mounds—39, 77, 40, and 41—form a line paralleling the west edge of Monks Mound (Figure 6.1). Mound 77 is Moorehead's addition to this alignment, with 39, 40, and 41 previously noted clearly on the Patrick and other maps. Moorehead stated:

Just south of No. 39 is a small mound (No. 77), on the slope of which, down 2 feet, was discovered a small bowl-like mass of hard, burnt clay. Although broken

somewhat, it appeared to be circular in form, about 20 inches in diameter, or 36 inches around the curvature. No complete measurement could be made, yet the rim was well defined. In the cavity, where the base should have been was a large lump of galena blackened by fire, also some pulverized galena. The lump weighed fully 8 pounds and the powdered galena was about a quart in quantity. There was a pottery bowl, 7 or 8 inches in diameter, and three inches high, with this deposit, and a shallow dish very flat, like a plate, of rather thick clay, also an oval stone on which were distinct markings or lines (Plate II, Figure 5). There were several ordinary hammer stones, and a small jar, almost crucible like. This is dark brown, well made, stands about 4 inches in height, and the base is unusually thick and heavy. The jar is shown in Figure 5, Plate I (1929:39-40).

In his 1923 report, Moorehead described the investigations in this area:

For a number of days, the men probed the area lying between Mounds 23 and 43 east and west and 20 and 62 north and south. . . . These probes indicated burials . . . on the southern slope of Mound 39, and in Mound 82 [77]. . . . We think a long, low platform existed between the Sawmill Mound and the one to the south [77]. . . . Probably a low mound (82) [77] adjoined it (1923:12-14).

Mound 77 was probably connected to Mound 39 by a platform or terrace. Mound 39 is a platform and 77 is possibly a conical or ridge-top mound. This relationship is similar to other paired mounds at the site, such as Mounds 59 and 60.

The map data are not clear on the shape of Mound 77 as it does not appear on the Patrick map. It was located and first assigned a number on Moorehead's 1923 map (see Figures 3.8 and 3.9). The shape indicated by Moorehead is not very clear, but he may have intended to show it as a small, conical mound. Two previous maps show what may be Mound 77. The Ramey map (see Figure 3.6) is the only other map besides Moorehead's 1923 and 1929 maps to show two mounds between 39 and 41. On the Ramey map, an oval mound is positioned just south of 39 with its long axis in a northeast-southwest orientation. The Thomas map of 1894 (see Figure 3.3) has a small, oval mound 5 feet (1.5 meters) in height in the location proposed for Mound 77. This mound is oriented with the long axis east-west. It is probably Mound 77.

Burials were indicated for both the Sawmill Mound (39) and Mound 77. The positioning of these burials is not altogether clear from Moorehead's writings. However, it appears that many of the burials in Mound 39 were on the south slope, that is, toward Mound 77.

On the north slope of Mound 77 was found the clay-lined circular pit described above. Included in the pit was an 8-pound (3.6-kilogram) piece of galena, some pottery vessels, and hammerstones. This could have been an offertory basin dedicated to the burials on the south side of the Sawmill Mound. Moorehead's report on testing these mounds by probing suggested burials in Mound 77, whereas his description of the later excavations do not describe any burials.

Mound 78 (S188W2070)

Mound 78 is also known as the Jondro Mound. In the 1923 map, Moorehead showed a mound to the southwest of Mound 46 that he numbered 83 (Figure 6.36). It is obvious that, in this period, Moorehead confused what Patrick had numbered Mound 46 with the Powell Mound, which in fact was a large mound much further to the west. On the 1929 map, Mound 83 was near Mound 66, but the mound he had numbered 83 in 1923 was numbered 78. There is further confusion in Moorehead's publication of 1929 (pages 51 and 52) in which he referred to the Jondro Mound as Mound 86, whereas he has no number 86 listed on any of his maps. (His highest number on any map is 85.) Because all of Moorehead's maps showed a mound southwest of Mound 46, I assume that 78 and 83 are the same mound and use his last number, 78, for this mound. The only clue that Moorehead gave us as to its location was that "it lies nearly a mile and half west of Monks Mound" (Moorehead 1929:51). It was Moorehead's supposition that the mound was originally conical but was diminished by cultivation. Its height at Moorehead's time varied between 4 and 6 feet (1.2 and 1.8 meters).

In his map of the unnumbered mounds of the Powell group (Mounds 84, 85, 86, and 87 on the UWM map), Patrick showed a mound southeast of the Powell area. The 1931 USGS compilation map shows a mound in the same location, undoubtedly Moorehead's Jondro Mound. It is still visible today, although it is not apparent as a distinct contour on the 1966 UWM map. I am not sure that the mound labeled 78 on the UWM map is indeed the Jondro Mound, but because so much confusion surrounds its location the 1929 numbering is retained.

Moorehead cut a north-south trench through the mound, and another trench at the south end extended 20 feet (6.1 meters) in a northwest direction. Twenty-four whole burials and fragmentary remains, enough to account for 16 or 17 more burials, were found (Moorehead 1929:51). There was a smaller mound covered by the north end of Mound 78. Nothing was found in the smaller mound; the burials were apparently placed in the fill over it. Fragments of a pottery vessel, the only artifact recovered from the mound, were found at the head of one burial. At the opposite end of Mound 78, a pit about 6 feet (1.8 meters) deep was found with a skull in it. It may have been an offertory pit, or perhaps it was a post pit similar to that found in Mound 72.

Moorehead provided other information to more precisely locate Mound 78: "About two hundred feet north of the mound is a depression from which earth and gumbo were taken for this mound: a similar one lies one hundred seventy-five feet south of the mound" (1929:52).

Mound 79 (N462W1610)

Moorehead's 1929 map shows Mound 79, which he named the Mackie Mound, located north of Cahokia Creek and north of Mounds 44 and 45; it forms the apex of a triangle with the latter two (Figure 6.6). This mound was not located on the Patrick map, and locating Mound 79 on other maps is a problem. Moorehead's map of 1929 provides some clue to its location by his placement of the Cahokia Canal crossing the channel of Cahokia Creek, which was also mapped by Patrick, just west of Mound 79. However, Moorehead's configuration is different from the present positions of the canal and creek. Therefore, Moorehead probably mismapped the meander pattern of Cahokia Creek, and his location of Mound 79 relative to the creek is suspect.

Moorehead also omitted the Alton and Southern Railroad tracks that cut north-south through the site just to the west of Patrick's location of Mound 45. The railroad was present in Moorehead's time; it clearly appears in the 1922 Goddard-Ramey photographs. We can assume that Moorehead, in making his sketch map, confused the location of the railroad with the location of Sand Prairie Lane, therefore compressing the scale of the western half of the site. That would have been the result of his misinterpretation of Mound 46 as the Powell Mound. The configuration of the canal Moorehead showed resembles its configuration west of the Alton and Southern Railroad more than it does its configuration near Sand Prairie Lane. If Moorehead did confuse Sand Prairie Lane with the railroad tracks, then Mound 79 should be west of the Alton and Southern Railroad.

A closed contour on the USGS maps suggests a mound on the north side of Cahokia Creek to the northeast of Patrick's Mound 46. The area is now partially covered by Interstate 55-70. Aerial photos, field reconnaissance, and plotting of the location as indicated by

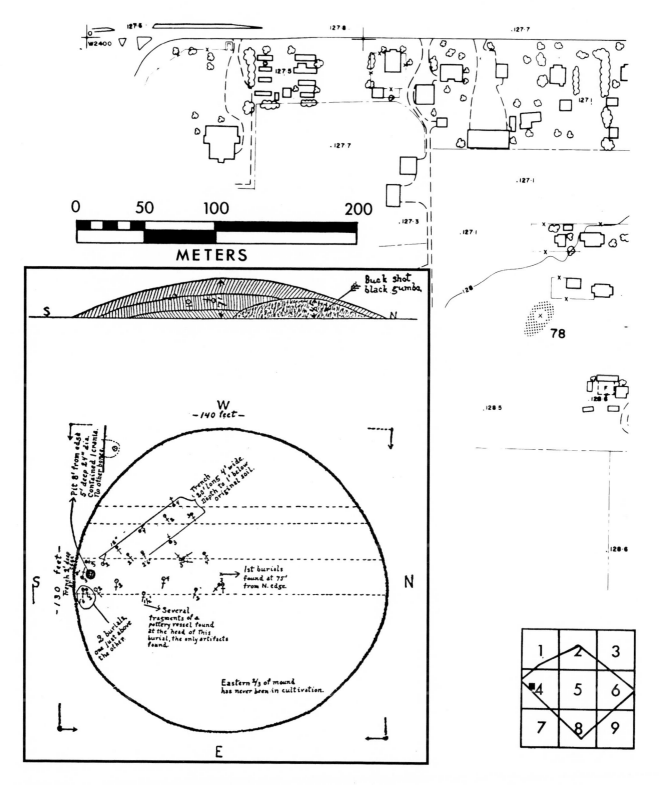

Figure 6.36. Section 4L of the UWM map showing the location of Mound 78. Inset shows a compilation of Moorehead's two illustrations of the Jondro Mound 78 (Moorehead 1929:51-52, Figure 5 and 6). The north-south section (upper) shows the stages of mound construction and the plan view (lower) shows the distribution of burials to the south of the primary mounds constructed of "Buck shot black gumbo".

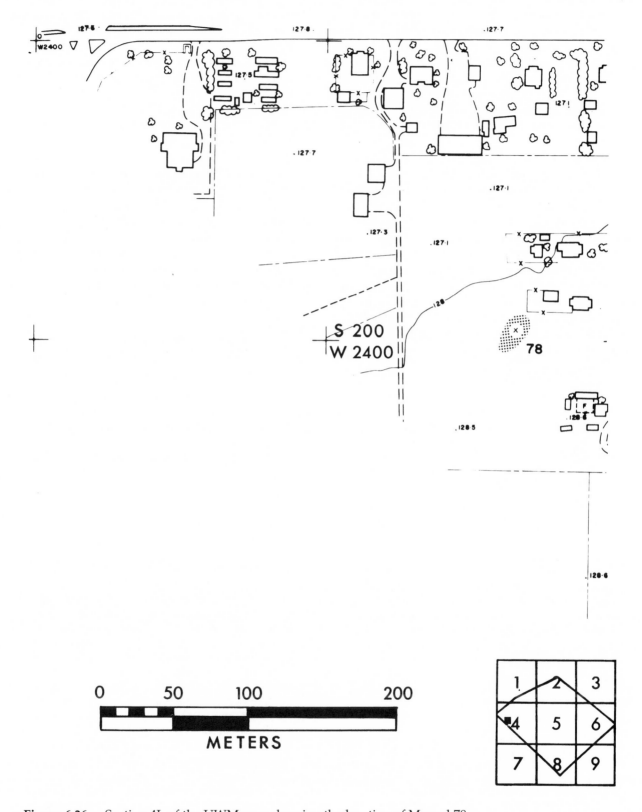

Figure 6.36. Section 4L of the UWM map showing the location of Mound 78.

the USGS maps suggest that the mound is in the embankment of Interstate 55-70 but partially exposed. At exactly that location, remnants of a mound cut through by the ditch bordering the northern edge of the interstate can be seen. I propose that this is the location of Moorehead's Mound 79, a location further confirmed by Moorehead's description that the mound was "about one and one-fourth miles west of Monks Mound and is on the bank of old Cahokia Creek" (1929:55).

Its roughly T-shaped form also conforms to Moorehead's description. It is the only mound on his map with this unique form. Moorehead said that it was 130 feet (39.6 meters) north-south with a long, low platform 3 to 5 feet (0.9 to 1.5 meters) in height extending about 150 feet (45.7 meters) to the east. There is a mound shown in approximately this location on the McAdams map of 1882 that he gave a height of 15 feet (4.6 meters). The only other map to show this mound is Moorehead's of 1929, and his description suggests it was 10 feet (3.05 meters) high at that time.

Moorehead's description of Mound 79 is brief, and it follows in its entirety:

> Mackie Mound, Number 79—This is about one and one-fourth miles west of Monks Mound and is on the bank of old Cahokia Creek. It is covered by a heavy oak grove, has never been plowed, and is about one hundred thirty feet north and south and ten feet high. It is surrounded on three sides by a swamp and there is a long low platform, or apron, extending about 150 feet to the east. This platform varies from three to five feet high. A trench was extended a distance of about thirty feet in the mound down to within a few feet of the base line, then the post augers were brought into service. Numbers of pits were sunk three or four feet in depth. With the exception of a few scales of flint or chert and one pottery fragment, absolutely nothing was found. The mound was composed of the hardest kind of buckshot gumbo, with no sign of stratification. It is clear that no village existed at the point from whence the earth was taken to build this mound as there are no broken artifacts to be observed in to the soil (1929:55-56).

Mound 80 (S1240E840)

Mound 80 on the Moorehead map of 1923 was numbered 75 on the 1929 map (Figure 6.18). In textual references to Mound 80 in his various publications, Moorehead was apparently also referring to what he later numbered Mound 75 (see discussion above of Mound 75). However, on his 1929 map, he showed a mound numbered 80 between the railroad tracks and

Mound 64. It is drawn as a small, circular mound, and the nature of the drafting indicates that it was added after the map's completion. The only indication we have of Mound 80 is on this map. Moorehead's number is retained on the UWM map; perhaps some confirming evidence for this mound can be found in the future.

Mound 81 (S1356E690)

Just south of Mound 64 and the Alton and Southern Railroad tracks, Moorehead located a mound that he numbered 81 (Figure 6.18). He did not refer to it in his publication, so his only record of it is on the map. The McAdams map of 1882 indicated a probable mound in that general location with a height of 10 feet (3.05 meters). There is, however, no way to be sure that this is the same as Moorehead's Mound 81. It is shown as a roughly oval and about half the size of Mound 64.

Mound 82 (S1672E24)

Moorehead showed two small mounds just west of the Harding or Rattlesnake Mound (Mound 66) that he numbered 82 and 83 (Figure 6.21). These are visible in the contours today only as slightly higher elevations. Moorehead conducted excavations in these mounds, which he described as follows:

> a single north-south trench was cut through both and across the narrow neck of low land lying between them. This trench was approximately four feet wide, and was sunk to the yellowish water-bearing gumbo below the mounds, with a maximum depth of five and one-half feet at the apices of the mounds and slightly more than two feet through the strip of ground between them. Midway between them, however, the trench was put down to a depth of four feet in order to examine any changes in formation that might appear, but the yellowish gumbo persisted and water prohibited deeper work. The upper twelve inches of both mounds was a loose, dark, and very sandy loam in which, on the north mound [Mound 83], three very small fragments of pottery were found. Under this, heavy black gumbo prevailed, changing in color as greater depths were reached and blending gradually into the yellowish and extremely wet formation already mentioned. No evidences of stratification or disturbed earth were found.
>
> Two small sherds and a half a dozen unworked flint spalls were picked up on the northeast slope of the south mound [Mound 83], but no remains whatever were found in the trench. Prior to the trenching,

both mounds were thoroughly tested with thirty inch steel probes (1929:84-85).

Recent aerial photographs suggest that Mound 66 is completely surrounded by low, small mounds such as 82 and 83. They show up only as white spots on the aerial photographs, although their intensity on some photographs is similar to Mounds 82 and 83.

Mound 83 (S1640E21)

See discussion of Mound 82 above.

Mound 84 (N148W2310)

As noted previously, Moorehead erroneously equated Patrick's Mound 46 with the Powell Mound at the western end of the site (Figures 6.37 amd 6.38). On his map Moorehead shows two mounds, which he numbered 84 and 85, in the vicinity of what he thought was the Powell Mound; Mound 84 is south of Powell Mound, Mound 85 is to the north. The Patrick map of this section of the site, however, shows two mounds south of the Powell Mound, another mound to the southwest, and a relatively large mound to the north. I believe that Moorehead's Mound 84 refers to the mounds between the Powell Mound and the mound due south, which is Mound 87 on the UWM map. In Moorehead's 1923 report he apparently used the number 84 for the mound that he later numbered 79 and called Mackie Mound. There is further confusion in the numbering, in that Titterington referred to excavations in the Powell Mound vicinity as follows: "Mound 85, which was excavated by the University of Illinois in the summer of 1931 . . . lay just a very short distance south of the Powell Mound" (1938:15).

It seems clear that Titterington was referring to what Moorehead had numbered 84 and not 85, which was to the north of the Powell Mound. The UWM map adhered to Moorehead's number for this mound, and I assume it is the larger of the two mounds south of Powell shown on the Patrick map.

An arrangement of the mounds in this vicinity, very similar to that shown by Patrick, is noted on the early maps of the area. McAdams in 1882 showed Mound 84 with a height of 5 feet (1.5 meters); Thomas (1894), 10 feet (3.05 meters), and Peterson-McAdams in 1906, 8 feet (2.4 meters). The McAdams map differs more from the Patrick map than the others, and it may be that the height he gives is for the smaller Mound 87 just to the south. In that case, his height agrees with the other maps of the area.

Mound 84 was destroyed in the 1930s at the same time as the Powell Mound (Mound 86). There were several efforts to salvage data from these mounds, and though most of the work was concentrated on the Powell Mound, excavations were made into other ones as well. Mound 84 was excavated in the summer of 1931 by a crew from the University of Illinois at Urbana-Champaign under the general supervision of A. R. Kelly and the direct supervision of Gene Stirling. Titterington reported that a burial with beads associated with it was found (1938:Figure 35, J and K). Pottery was found in the mound fill, but of particular significance was a large refuse pit that contained materials stylistically different from that in the mound fill above. This presented for the first time some details of stratigraphy at Cahokia.

On the basis of excavations in Mound 84, a dichotomy was drawn between the earlier Old Village Culture and the later Beanpot, or Trappist, Culture. This two-period division of Cahokia archaeology was elaborated by James B. Griffin in his important paper published in 1949. This basic chronology persisted for many years, but was finally revised in 1971 and 1973 (Fowler and Hall 1975) (see Figure 1.7).

The mound assigned the number 85 by Moorehead lies to the north of the Powell Mound (86). Charles Bareis described the relationships of the mounds in this group as follows:

> According to that portion of the J.J.R. Patrick map . . . which applies to the western portion of the Cahokia site, the Powell Mound group originally consisted of five mounds. . . . The arrangement of this complex included one mound located to the southwest [88], two located to the south . . . [84 and 87], and one situated to the north [85] . . . of the Powell Mound [86], . . . the major earthwork of the group (Bareis 1964b:5).

Mound 85 (N580W2150)

Patrick indicated that Mound 85 was oval in outline with an orientation of the long axis about east-northeast to west-southwest. Using the scale on the Patrick map gives about 225 feet (68.6 meters) for the length and about 100 feet (30.5 meters) for the width. There is no indication of height for this mound.

Other early maps also show a mound in this location. The McAdams (1882) map shows an outline and orientation very similar to the Patrick map. The Cyrus Thomas map of 1894 shows Mound 85 with an oval outline but an east-west orientation. Both McAdams and Thomas indicated the height was about 10 feet (3.05 meters). The Peterson-McAdams map of 1906

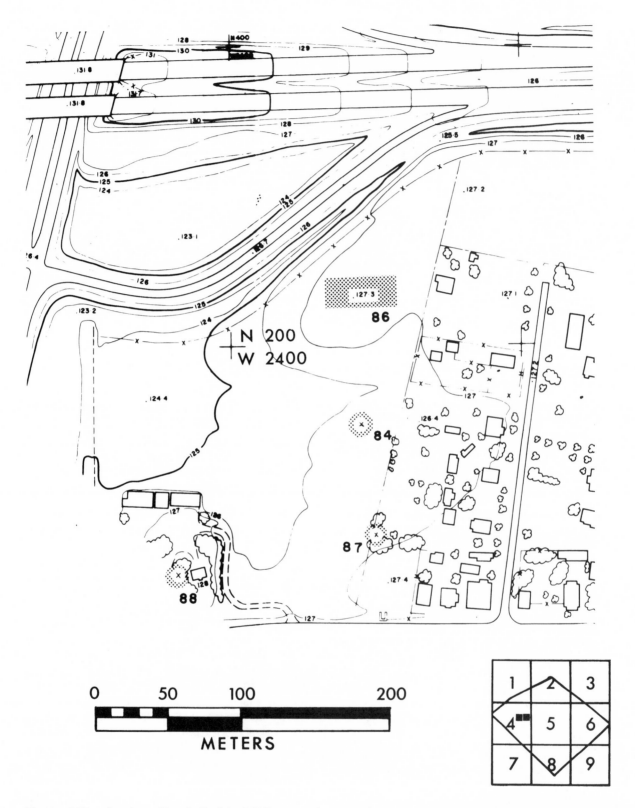

Figure 6.37. Sections 4J and 4I of the UWM map showing the locations of Mounds 84, 86, 87, and 88.

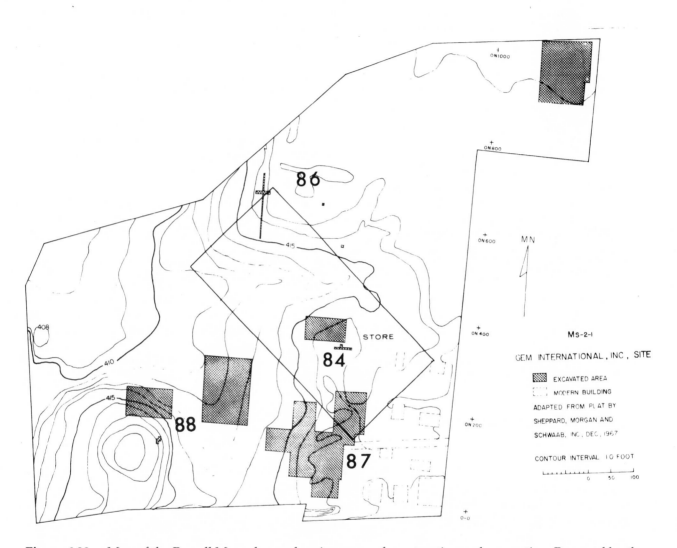

Figure 6.38. Map of the Powell Mound area showing areas of construction and excavation. Prepared by the University of Illinois at Urbana-Champaign. Courtesy of Charles Bareis. (Mound numbers added by author.)

shows only three mounds in the Powell group. The northernmost mound, which may be Mound 85, is assigned a height of only 5 feet (1.5 meters). This mound does not appear on Moorehead's maps until 1929, and he does not give any indication of its dimensions. It is represented as slightly ovoid. The USGS 1931 compilation map has Mound 85 shown clearly by two contour lines. This suggests that in the late 1920s Mound 85 was at least 10 feet (3.05 meters) high. The orientation at that time was northeast to southwest. The difference between the earlier heights and orientations and the later ones may be due to cultivation of the area.

No excavations are reported for this mound. The data presented by Titterington (1938:15) as coming from Mound 85 were actually from Mound 84.

The location of Mound 85 was determined by plotting coordinates derived from the Patrick map on the 1966 UWM map (Figure 6.39). A slight rise in elevation is all that can be seen today. This is the small remnant of this once massive mound.

In summary, Mound 85 was a large mound approximately 70 by 30 meters (250 by 98 feet) and over 3 meters (9.8 feet) in height at the western limits of the Cahokia site on the banks of Cahokia Creek. It had an oval base with the long axis oriented several degrees off an east-west line. It was plowed down over the period from the 1870s to the mid-1900s. It was finally destroyed in 1960 during construction of Interstate 70. Mound 85 was probably a ridged mound rather than a platform.

Mound 86 (N232W2314)

At what is generally considered the western edge of the Cahokia site was a large, rectangular-based, ridge-topped mound that is known as the Powell Mound after the property owners in the 1930s (Figures 6.37 and 6.38, see also Figures 2.8-2.10). The Powell Mound is shown rather distinctly on the additional segment of the map made by Patrick and his surveyors in the late 1870s. Dr. Paul A. Titterington, the St. Louis physician and local archaeologist, saw the mound and later observed its destruction in the 1930s. He described it as follows: "This mound, Number 46 in the Moorehead classification, was 310 feet long, 180 feet wide and 40 feet high. It was the most symmetrical mound in the group and was shaped like a large Hayrick" (1938:15).

Fortunately, the mound was still standing in 1922 when Lieutenant Goddard of the U.S. Army Air Service took oblique photographs of the site (Goddard 1969; Hall 1968; Fowler 1977). One was a low oblique

shot of the Powell mound group. It shows the nature of Mound 86 and its shape, which conforms very well with the description by Titterington (see Figure 2.9).

Scaling data from the Patrick map indicates a north-south dimension of 150 feet (45.7 meters) and an east-west dimension of 300 feet (91.4 meters). Moorehead gave a north-south dimension of 170 feet (51.8 meters) and an east-west dimension of 310 feet (94.5 meters). Various heights have been recorded for this mound: Patrick in 1876 indicated a height of 45 feet (13.7 meters); McAdams in 1882, 30 feet (9.1 meters); Thomas in 1894, 35 feet (10.7 meters); Peterson and McAdams in 1906, 30 feet (9.1 meters); and Moorehead in 1929, 40 feet (12.2 meters). The dimensions are rather consistent, indicating an unchanging size through time. Given Titterington's description and early photos, it appears that the mound retained its primary form.

Because of its outstanding form and shape, the Powell Mound has been photographed and illustrated in many publications (Bushnell 1904:Figure 104: Moorehead 1929:Plate 39; Titterington 1938:Figures 35, 46, 48, 50 and 51).

As discussed at several points in this atlas, Moorehead referred to the Powell Mound as Mound 46, whereas Patrick did not number it and used 46 for another mound. It is unfortunate that the numbering for this mound is confused. I feel it important to maintain Patrick's number 46 for the mound he intended it to represent, which is still partially preserved under the fill of the Interstate 55-70 (see discussion of Mound 46). Therefore, the number 86 has been assigned to the Powell Mound. However, those working at the site in the 1930s followed Moorehead's lead, so that in much of the literature it is referred to as Mound 46.

Unfortunately, the Powell Mound was partially destroyed in 1930 and 1931. Titterington described the event:

> In December of 1930 and January of 1931, all but 5 feet of its base was removed, the object being to fill in an area of low ground 200 to 400 yards to the northwest. By doing this, the owners were able to put their whole tract of about 50 acres under cultivation.
>
> It is regrettable that information from this mound was almost completely lost to science. The loss was due to lack of funds by the scientific institutions, and to the lack of public interest. For a period of several years the Powell brothers had a standing offer of $3,000 and 3 years time open to any institution that cared to study the mound; the only conditional requirement was that the dirt removed be placed in an area of low ground 200 to 400 yards away. The undertaking was too big for those scientifically interested, even with the financial assistance offered

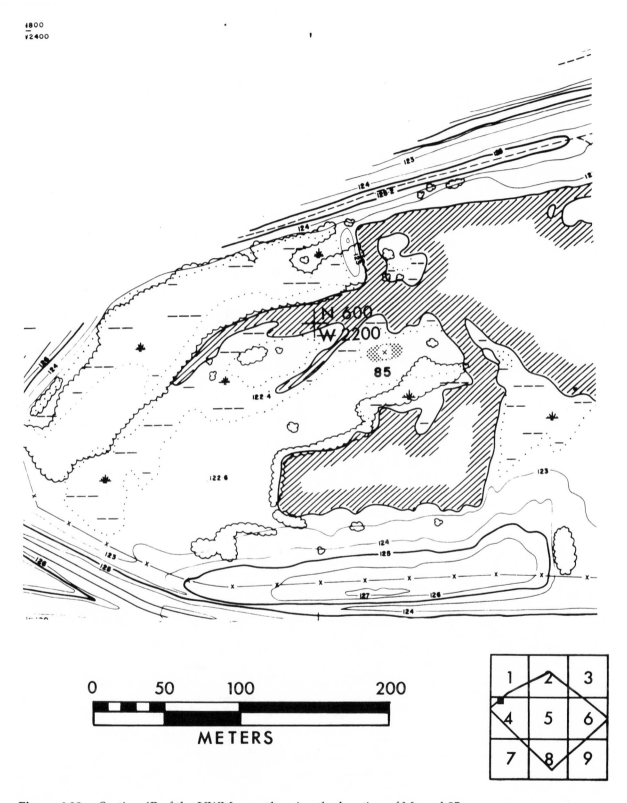

Figure 6.39. Section 4B of the UWM map showing the location of Mound 85.

by the owners. It seems that the state wanted to buy the mound with a 50 foot margin around the base and a road leading to the main highway. This proposition did not appeal to the Powells because it would have taken a mushroom-shaped piece out of one end of their tract of land. They offered to sell their whole farm, but this in turn did not appeal to the state. With this deadlock, there were rumors of condemnation proceedings which precipitated the removal of the mound.

Work was started on the north side of the mound with a large steam shovel, which was hidden from the view of the highway by the large size of the mound [see Figure 2.11]. It was eight days before the public was aware that the mound was being taken down. At this time the Powells gave permission for a scientific man to watch the proceedings, and do what excavating he could as long as he did not interfere with the contractor.

This work was under the supervision of the Archaeological Department of the University of Illinois, but did not get underway until the razing had been in progress for a total of 16 days (1938:13-14).

A. R. Kelly, then of the University of Illinois at Urbana-Champaign, observed the mound's destruction. In February 1931 Thorne Deuel, of the University of Chicago and representing the University of Illinois, conducted excavations into the remaining base of the Powell Mound, or about 5 feet (1.5 meters) of the original mound (Figure 6.40). Kelly observed:

Notes and photographs taken on the profile through the long axis of the large Powell mound by Dr. L. E. Workman of the State Geological Survey during the course of mound removal by steam shovel in 1930, indicate that the mound was constructed in two stages, and consisted of a top layer of mound earth about 18-20 feet in height, brought to an apex in a hogback ridge running along the greater axis of the mound, and underlying an original mound core which is approximately 27 feet high. The older mound was of the rectangular, flat-topped variety familiar in the Cahokia area. No burials or burial furniture were found in the basal mound structure, and the pot sherds and artifacts contained therein were evidently chance inclusions made while the mound builders were obtaining the baskets of mound earth from adjacent camp and village sites.

Later a second mound was built over the original flat-topped structure, but first the mound builders made two unique burial plots on the surface of the basal mound. The first of these burials plots was destroyed by steam shovel: The second was hand trowelled by a member of the University staff and adequate notes were taken. The long bones and skulls of several secondary interments had been placed between alternating sheaths of cedar bark with a blanket or shell covering the bones. A thin cornhusk or grass matting had covered the whole burial plot, approximately 18-20 feet in diameter. Two wooden spools covered with sheet copper, interpreted as ear pendants, fell from the burial level during excavation. . . . Other burials found on the slopes of the mound were without burial furniture. No material of cultural significance was found in the upper 20 feet of the Powell Mound (1933:101).

The materials excavated by Thorne Deuel are stored at the Illinois State Museum. Kelly briefly noted these materials:

Excavations made in February 1931, provided information as to the structure of the seven feet of mound material left at the base of the large mound destroyed by steam shovel. Beneath the mound were extensive village site remains, pot sherds, stone and bone artifacts, and kitchen refuse. The pottery in the underlying camp site was of the same or related type as that accidentally included in the earth used in the mound construction (1933:101).

An analysis of the materials from Thorne Deuel's excavations at the Powell Mound, including sherds, artifacts, and Deuel's notes, was made in 1986 by Steven Ahler and Peter DePuydt (published 1987). Ahler and DePuydt compiled an excavation profile of the north wall of the east-west trench excavated by Deuel (Figure 6.41). The mound section showed three units of cultural activity. There was a premound occupation of the area with ceramics predominately related to the Fairmount phase. A small mound or mound core appeared in the profile; and a later mound fill seems to have been added over the entire mound. The small mound or mound core appears to have been close to 20 feet (6.1 meters) in height. Ahler and DePuydt's analysis of the sherds from the mound fill suggests a Stirling phase association for these activities. Considerable stone chipping debris was found in the premound deposits.

Titterington talked to some who were present when razing of the mound commenced, before A. R. Kelly started his work, and he gives a much more detailed description of the findings, stratigraphy, and construction of the mound (see Titterington 1938:14-15).

In the late 1960s the remaining portion of the Powell Mound was threatened by construction of a large discount store. The University of Illinois Field School, under the direction of Charles Bareis, excavated into the base of the decimated Powell Mound, in the remnants of smaller mounds, and nearby areas (Figure 6.38).

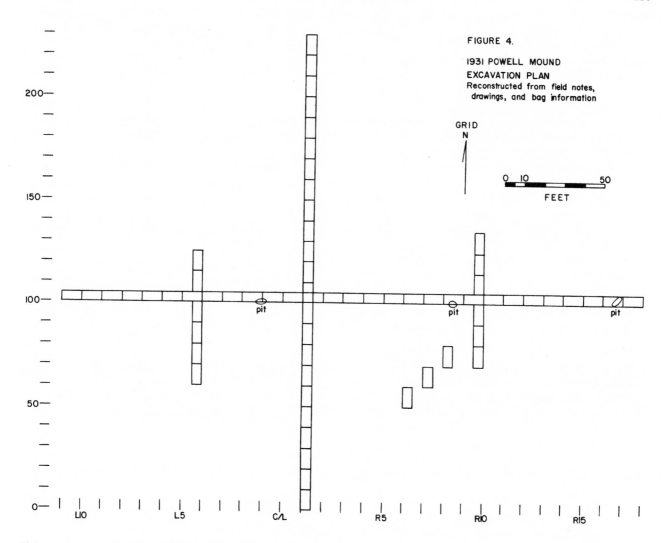

Figure 6.40. Units excavated during the 1931 salvage excavations at Mound 86, the Powell Mound, by Thorne Deuel, University of Chicago and University of Illinois at Urbana-Champaign. Source: Ahler and DePuydt 1987.

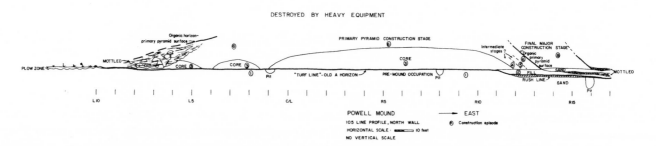

Figure 6.41. Profile through the lower portion of the Powell Mound after the upper portion had been destroyed. Based on the 1931 Illinois State Museum excavations. Source: Ahler and DePuydt 1987.

The razing of the Powell Mound in the 1930s and construction of the Gem Store in the 1960s nearly completed Powell Mound's destruction. Charles Bareis stated:

> The area of the Powell Mound (No. 86) is not totally destroyed. Two or three feet of the mound base remains north of the Venture Store and the parking lot behind the store. In some areas the mound was stripped so low by work for the original Gem International, Inc. Store and parking lot area that the original pre-mound surface has been exposed. . . . Perhaps the northern one third or . . . one half of the bottom two feet of the mound is still there (personal communication, 1989).

Mound 87 (N75W2302)

Patrick showed a small mound that lay in a line from the Powell Mound through Mound 84, south and near the present Collinsville Road (Figure 6.37). This mound was not noted by Moorehead, nor was it apparent on the USGS map. On the 1966 UWM map, there is a slight elevation point shown at the approximate location of this mound just north of Highway 40 (Collinsville Road), and this may represent the remnant of this small mound. It has, unfortunately, been totally destroyed; it is at the entrance and parking lot of the discount store (Figure 6.38).

Mound 88 (N50W2438)

To the southwest of the Powell Mound, Patrick showed a small mound roughly oval in shape with a northwest axis (Figure 6.37). A similar mound is shown on the McAdams map of 1882, with a height of 20 feet (6.1 meters). This is probably the same mound, although the McAdams's location is difficult to confirm because the scale of his map is not as precise as Patrick's. The mound does have the same oval shape with a north-south axis. A mound in a similar location is shown with a height of 10 feet (3.05 meters) on the Thomas map of 1894. There is no indication of this mound on the 1966 UWM map because its location was on the edge of the map and the area was being destroyed at that time.

Workers from the University of Illinois at the Powell Mound made a map with a 1-foot contour interval, and it shows a mound with a height of approximately 6 to 8 feet (1.8 to 2.4 meters) where Mound 88 would be. There are no published references to Mound 88, and it is now totally destroyed; it is in the parking lot of the discount store mentioned above.

7

DESCRIPTIONS OF MOUNDS 89–104

Modern site surveys and surface examinations of the Cahokia site have revealed previously undiscovered mounds, ones not noted by investigators such as Patrick or Moorehead. Other mounds, or what appear to be mounds, have been discovered on aerial photographs and checked in the field, when possible. These mounds have been assigned numbers beginning with 89.

No new mounds have been identified in sections 1 and 3, which include only a small portion of the Cahokia site, and these areas have been greatly disturbed by recent highway construction.

Mound 89 (N1400E0)

This mound appears as an irregular contour in the vicinity of N1400E0, in section 4 just to the north of Mound 11. North of the contour is a borrow pit (Figure 7.1). It was examined by the author several years ago and was designated a mound because of its proximity to the borrow pit, its appearance, and its relationship to other mounds.

To the west of Mound 89 at N1400W200 is a similar contour. Visual inspection suggests that it does not have the regularity exhibited by Mound 89; therefore, it has not been designated a mound.

Mound 90 (N154W1660)

At N154W1660 is a modern house on top of a mound-like structure (see Figure 6.6). Superficially, it appears to be a very well-preserved mound upon which modern residents have built their house. It has been examined quite extensively, although the contours do not show up on the 1966 UWM map. It does, however, appear very clearly on the 1930-1931 compilation for the USGS map. There are other houses in various subdivisions that are on somewhat lower

mound-like elevations, and in most cases these elevations are the result of house construction. That is, soil removed when the foundations or the basements were excavated was mounded up around the foundation, creating a slight contour elevation. Most of these elevations do not appear to be of aboriginal origin, as they fit too neatly the pattern of the distribution of modern houses. Mound 90, however, is much larger than the others, and its location does not fit the modern construction pattern. Because of its size, location, and unique nature, it has been designated a mound.

Another contour with a house on it appears at S800W1600 of section 4, but examination suggests that this mound is the result of modern house construction.

Mound 91 (N140W780)

Several previously unnumbered mounds have been located in section 5. Just to the north of a line between Mounds 43 and 44 is an obvious mound in section 5F that was missed by previous investigators (see Figure 6.4). It is observable from the highway and on foot. It is indicated on the UWM map by an elevation of 128.6 meters (421.9 feet) above sea level and is surrounded to the north by the 128-meter (419.9-foot) contour line, making its height only 0.6 meters (2 feet). This mound has been referred to by some Cahokia investigators as Mound 43A since it is nearest to that mound. Mounds 91, 43, and 44 surround what appears to be a plaza. Washington University crews made a surface collection of the area in 1971, and the presence of a plaza was confirmed by the absence of cultural debris.

Mound 92 (N20W746)

Just to the south of Mound 91 and cut by the modern highway and its ditches is another possible mound

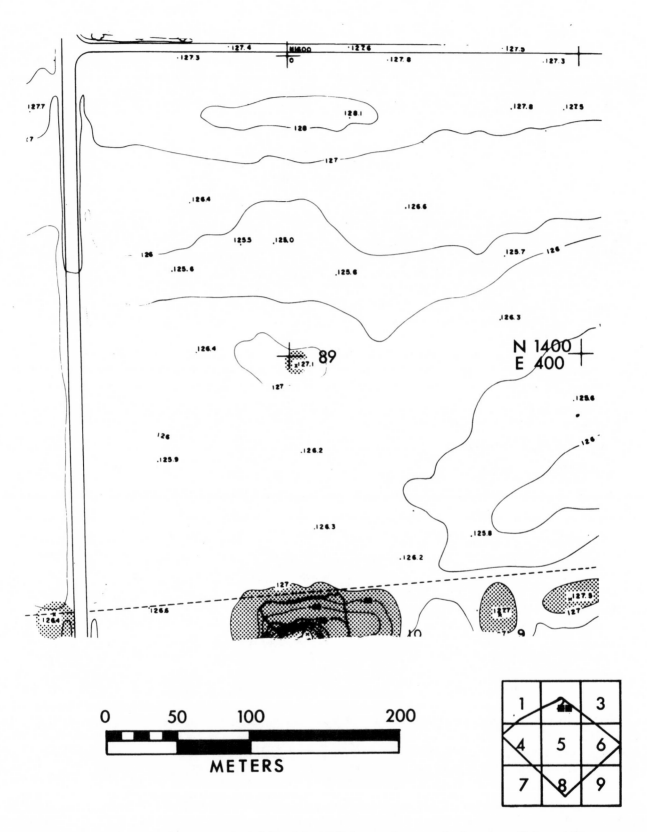

Figure 7.1.   Portions of sections 2Q and 2R of the UWM map showing the location of Mound 89.

(see Figure 6.4). It shows only as a slight elevation just below the 128-meter (419.9-foot) contour line. On some air photos there is a semicircular white area that suggests a mound disturbed by modern construction and cultivation. Its presence could be tested by cutting an east-west trench paralleling the highway ditch starting at about N20W746. If a mound is confirmed here, the four mounds (43, 44, 91, and 92) logically enclose a plaza, designated the West Plaza (Fowler 1978a).

Mound 93 (5665W510)

In section 5P, a contour elevation at 128 meters (419.9 feet) near Borrow Pit 5-4 (see Chapter 8) suggests the remains of another mound (Figure 7.2). This has not been confirmed, though, because the area is wooded today and surface reconnaissance is difficult. It is tentatively labeled Mound 93, but further investigation needs to be carried out to confirm or reject the designation. An elevation there of 128.3 meters (420.9 feet) and a nearby lower point of 127.5 meters (418.3 feet) establishs a height of 0.8 meter (2.6 feet) for Mound 93. It is located across Borrow Pit 54 from Mounds 67 and 68.

Mound 94 (S680W55)

Surrounding the large Borrow Pit 5-1 are several small promontories whose heights give the appearance of mounds, albeit very low ones. Oscar Schneider (personal communication, 1989) suggests that at least one is a mound, here designated Mound 94 (see Figure 6.14). It is located in section 5Q. A very large tree in the area obscures the mound on the UWM map. Mound 94 is tentatively identified as a mound associated with Borrow Pit 5-1.

Mound 95 (S616E665)

To the northeast of Borrow Pit 5-2 is a large mound that previous investigators have not numbered (see Figure 6.17). It is designated Mound 95 on the UWM map. The high point of Mound 95 is at 127.6 meters above sea level (418.6 feet). It is completely surrounded by the 127-meter (416.7-foot) contour line, although the mound is probably higher. Its exact base is not well defined by the contour line.

There is evidence from early aerial photos and surface debris that a structure stood on this mound in the 1920s. It is possible that this mound was created when modern buildings were constructed. However, the

prehistoric pottery found on the surface and the nature of the elevation suggest that it is a prehistoric mound. Its association with a borrow pit as well as its location directly across the borrow pit from Mounds 61 and 62 also support this. This arrangement is very similar to that of Mound 93 with Borrow Pit 5-4 and Mounds 67 and 68. They are almost mirror images of each other in their relationship to other mounds, borrow pits, and to the central portion of the Cahokia site.

Mound 96 (S940W35)

To the southeast of Borrow Pit 5-1 is a small but obvious mound located in Section 5W at grid coordinate S940W35; it is designated Mound 96 (see Figure 6.29). A low elevation is observable in the area. It was not noticeable in the 1960s because of the trees and brush growing in the area. However, in the 1970s, much of the brush was cleared, revealing a low rise. This low mound is probably associated with Mound 72 to the northeast. It may have been the location of a charnel house from which body remains were taken for burial. It should be tested to determine its manmade nature and possible association with Mound 72.

Mound 97 (N520E1584)

Examination of the easternmost aerial photo taken of the Cahokia site in 1933 by Lt. Dache Reeves revealed soil disturbances suggestive of elevations being leveled by team-and-slip operations (Figure 7.3). Although the flight lines of these aerial photos are such that it is difficult to get good stereoscopic examinations of these points, they appear to be mounds that were being leveled at that time. Examination of the 1922 oblique photographs of the same area show no indications of mounds, possibly because of the distorted view that these obliques give of this easternmost area near Canteen Creek. The USGS topographic map indicates some contour-line elevations in the general area, although not in exactly the same spots indicated by the aerial photographs. There was probably a series of mounds in this area.

Only those mounds visible in the Dache Reeves photos are considered in this section. As noted above, other elevations on the USGS maps may indicate mound locations. The data on those locations are, however, insufficient, so I will make no further mention of them here. More intensive examination may confirm details of the topographic map, allowing identification of more mounds. The ones considered here appear on the Dache Reeves photos, on the 1966 UWM

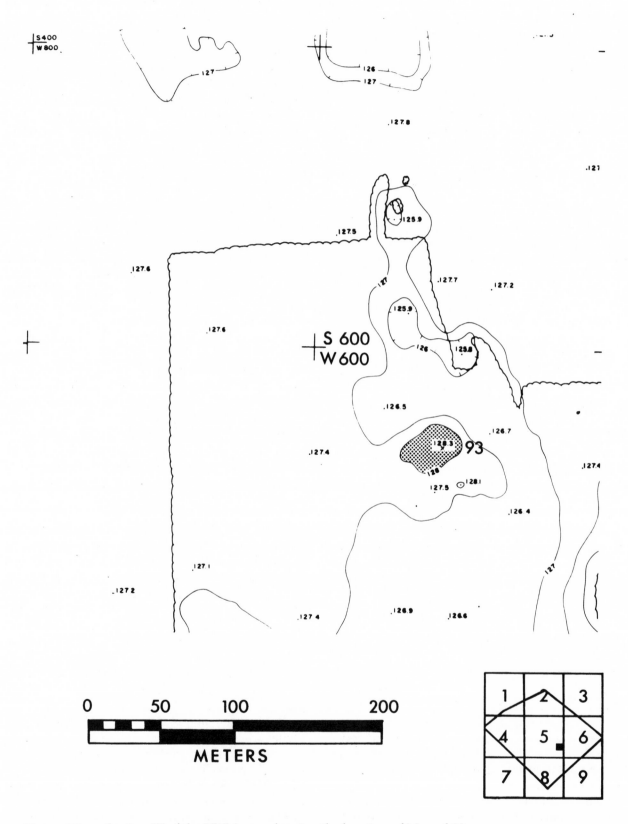

Figure 7.2.   Section 5T of the UWM map showing the location of Mound 93.

Figure 7.3. Mounds 97, 98, and 100-102: (top) a portion of the 1931 Dache Reeves photos of the eastern portion of Cahokia showing Mounds 97, 98, 100, 101, and 102 as they were being destroyed; (bottom) a section of a 1941 USDA air photo of the same area after destruction of the mounds was completed. Source: Archaeological Research Laboratory, University of Wisconsin-Milwaukee.

map, and were identified by surface examination. Together these data make it possible to suggest these are mound locations.

One mound so indicated is located at N520E1584 (Figure 7.4). In 1933 this area was an open field, but it is now intersected by a street paralleling Black Lane. The Dache Reeves photo shows a white soil-disturbance scar at this point. This is Mound 97.

Mounds 98 (N510E1660) and 99 (N634E1610)

Close to Mound 97 are indications of two other mounds (Figure 7.4). Mound 98 is clearly indicated in the 1933 photos. It is enclosed by the 128-meter (419.9-foot) contour line and has a peak elevation of 128.3 meters (420.9 feet). It coincides with the location indicated by the early air photos (Figure 7.3). Northwest of Mound 98 the air photos show another probable mound, Mound 99. Today it is covered with structures and a small street.

Mounds 98 and 99 are near a depression that may be an aboriginal borrow pit. This well-defined depression is 1.7 meters (5.6 feet) deep. It is observable on the 1933 photos, but not on the 1931 USGS map. It should be examined and a test excavation made to determine if it is a prehistoric feature.

Mound 100 (N102E1548)

Mound 100 is located where a church now stands north of the Collinsville Road (Highway 40) and to the east of Black Lane (Figure 7.5). The mound is difficult to observe today because of the modern construction and grass. No surface examination of this area is possible under the present conditions.

Mounds 101 (N165E1652) and 102 (N218E1658)

These two mounds are surrounded by the 128-meter (419.9-foot) contour line, which was probably created by the leveling of the mounds (Figure 7.6). There is a high point, more or less in the center of this general area, at 128.2 meters (420.6 feet). Walking over the area, one detects slight rises in elevation at approximately the coordinates given for the mounds, indicating their remnants. Trenches would help determine if mounds had stood there prior to 1933. It would also suggest what data remain to determine the time of their

approximate construction and their relationship to other mounds at the Cahokia site.

Mound 103 (N355E1715)

Mound 103 is located partially under and in the yard of an elementary school (Figure 7.6). Except for a slight elevation, there are no modern indications of this mound. However, there is sufficient elevation at the 128-meter (419.9-foot) contour line to suggest that the base of the mound may still be present.

Mound 104 (N410E1914)

At the present location of a motel at coordinates N410E1914 is Mound 104 (Figure 7.6), based upon evidence still visible behind the motel. The elevation and the Reeves aerial photographs suggest that this was a mound. Oscar Schneider (personal communication, 1989), however, believes it is not a mound.

Other Possible Mounds

The contours on the USGS 7.5' Monks Mound quadrangle suggest mound locations very similar, or very close, to the ones proposed in this chapter. A close examination of the compilation sheets for this map reveals many more closed contours. It is possible that the contours on both of these maps represent many mounds that were in existence in the 1930s but not noticeable in Reeves's photographs. These locations need to be further investigated, although no numbers are assigned.

Present data suggest no other mound locations in section 6, although there are closed contour lines in almost all of the subsections of section 6. Most, however, are probably the result of house construction and the mounding up of soil around houses. There is one elevation in section 6V that looks suspiciously like a mound since it is not where the house was built but in the backyard. This area was examined in November 1978, but observers could not confirm the mound's presence in the accumulation of debris.

Nearby in this section are two depressions that appear to be aboriginal borrow pits. It was not possible to examine these, but a more detailed examination of section 6V should be made to locate possible man-made features.

The USGS maps also show a mound on the border between section 5 and section 6 at approximately the

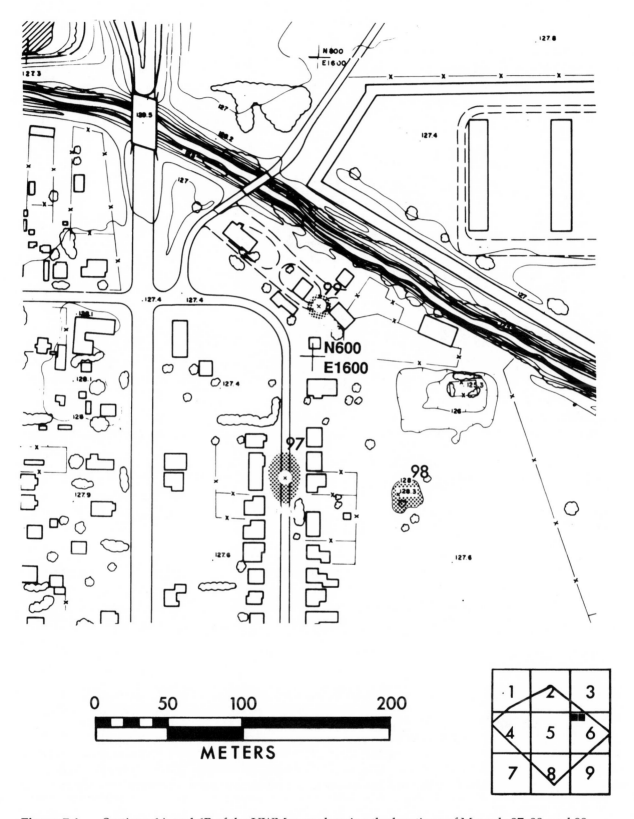

Figure 7.4. Sections 6A and 6B of the UWM map showing the locations of Mounds 97, 98, and 99.

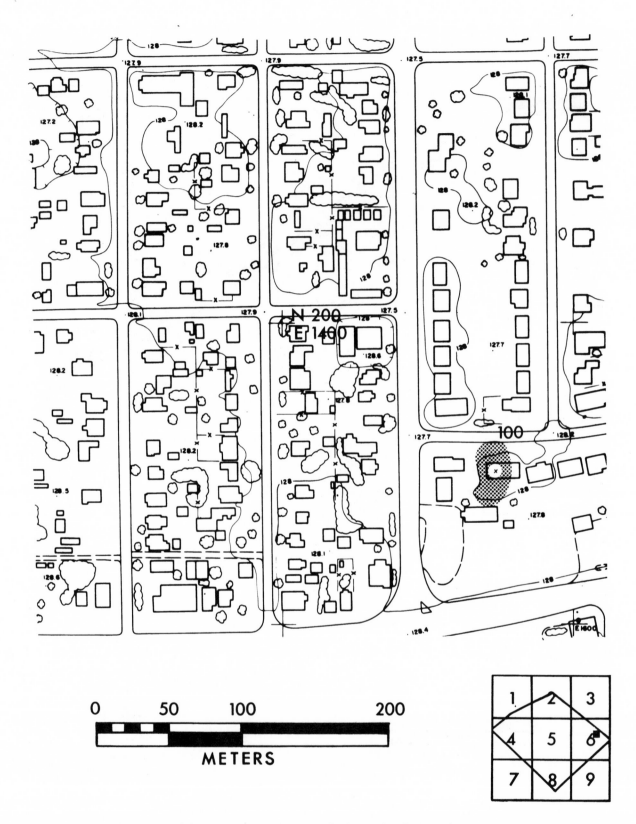

Figure 7.5. Section 6J of the UWM map showing the location of Mound 100.

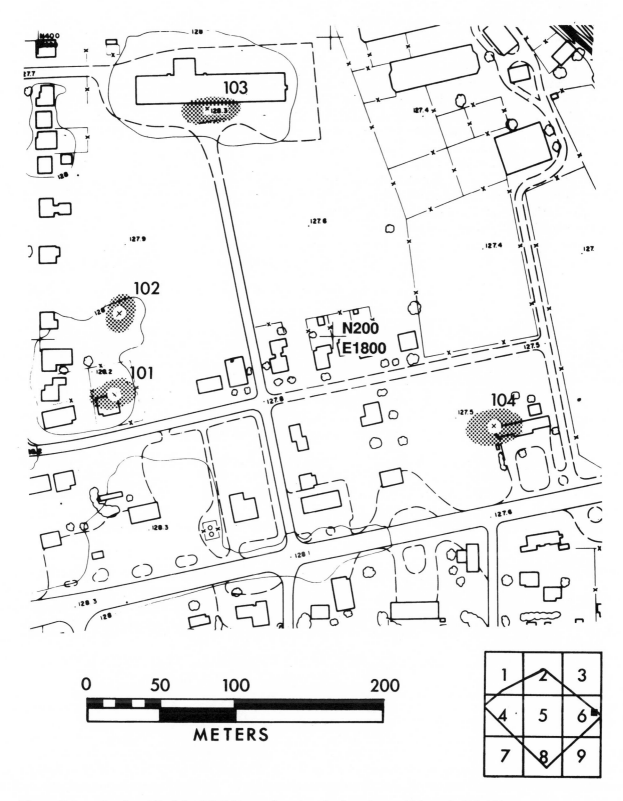

Figure 7.6.   Section 6G of the UWM map showing the locations of Mounds 101-104.

S400 grid line. This appears as a closed contour, and it is not in a location where a house has been built. Reconnaissance in November 1978 could not confirm a mound.

No new mounds have been noted in sections 7, 8, or 9, although future surveys should be carried out to search for possible mounds. For example, a 1973 air photo shows some interesting features surrounding Mound 66 in section 8H at the south end of the site. The photographs were taken during a period of extensive flooding and supersaturation of the soil. The features show up in locations where Moorehead recorded Mounds 82 and 83, indicating what may be a ring of small mounds surrounding Mound 66; further studies should be undertaken here and numbers then assigned to these features.

8

BORROW PITS

Besides the mounds, the most obvious features of the Cahokia site are the large depressions where earth was scooped up by the Indians for the construction of mounds. Today these appear as irregular areas that either have water standing in them or are low and wet and, for the most part, unusable for cultivation. Similar borrow pits exist today along the margins of Interstate 55-70, modern ones created when dirt was used for fill in highway construction.

Borrow pits, literally pits where earth is "borrowed" for construction projects, are common in Mississippian archaeological sites throughout the southeastern United States. These communities required great quantities of earth for construction of platform mounds, plaster for house walls and fortifications, and other uses. After excavation these pits remained as ponds or even moats and as integral parts of the town.

According to Garcilaso de la Vega, Hernando de Soto was originally buried in a borrow pit at a site somewhere in the Mississippi Valley hundreds of miles south of Cahokia.

> For this reason, therefore, they agreed to bury him at night with sentinel so placed that the Indians would not see him or know where he was. Thus they selected as a sepulchre one of the large and broad excavations on a plain near the town where the Indians had removed dirt for their dwellings, and here they interred the remains of the illustrious Adelantado Hernando de Soto amidst the abundant tears of priests and cavaliers. . . . Then to conceal their grief as well as the place where he lay, they spread news among the Indians on the following day that the Governor's health was improved; and with this falsehood they mounted their horses and, galloping across the plains through the holes and over the sepulchre itself, made a show of great festivity and rejoicing. . . . And that all evidences of the sepulchre

might be completely obliterated, they were not content just with trampling it, but before the celebration, gave orders for much water to be thrown on the plain and in the excavations with the excuse that otherwise the horses on running would raise dust (1951:503).

Even with those precautions, the Spaniards worried that the Indians knew where de Soto was buried. Fearing that they might desecrate the corpse, it was disinterred and placed in the Mississippi River, where it probably was carried downstream, disappearing forever.

There are many aboriginal borrow pits scattered over the Cahokia site area; many more probably existed at an earlier period. Many were filled in by the ancient Cahokians in the process of building their city as well as by later erosion and sedimentation. For example, the area under Mound 51 and just to the southeast of Monks Mound apparently was an aboriginal borrow pit, perhaps utilized in the early days of Monks Mound's construction. Charles Bareis's work in this area indicated that the pit was apparently filled in with trash by the prehistoric inhabitants and a mound built over much of it.

Only extensive excavation can reveal the number of borrow pits dug in the central area of the Cahokia site. There are, however, many borrow pits visible today. They can be seen on the contour maps as enclosed contours surrounding a depression or on the surface of the ground as low, wet areas that are difficult to cultivate. Following is a description of the aboriginal borrow pits so noted. These features are numbered according to the section of the 1966 UWM map in which they are located. Thus those borrow pits located in section 5, the most densely occupied and utilized area of the Cahokia site, are all numbered with the prefix 5 and with sequential numbers for each individual borrow pit (see Appendix 4).

Borrow Pit 5-1

The largest and most obvious of the borrow pits is an area extending from about S700 to S1100 and from W0 to about W450 on the UWM map (Figure 8.1). This large area is clearly visible on topographic maps and in numerous air photos. In the Goddard air photos of 1922, the pit shows up as a large, white area apparently completely filled with water. In recent years a large stand of trees and brush has grown up in it. Water stands in it in the spring and early summer.

Within the area labeled 5-1 were smaller sections completely enclosed by contour lines. The smaller sections are labeled A, B, etc. In the case of Borrow Pit 5-1, the larger area is enclosed by the 126.5-meter (415-foot) contour line. It includes some small areas previously thought to be outside the major borrow pit. Some were indicated by depressions on the USGS map, some appeared on the UWM map, and others were evident as low, wet areas. Using the area surrounded by the 126.5-meter line, Borrow Pit 5-1 encloses approximately 12.4 hectares (30.6 acres).

Borrow Pit 5-1A is the area enclosed by the 126-meter (413.4-foot) contour, or the area more traditionally thought of as the major borrow pit at the Cahokia site. Borrow Pit 5-1A includes 6.3 hectares (15.5 acres). Elevation in the central, more level portion of Borrow Pit 5-1A averages around 125.5 meters (411.7 feet) above sea level. This certainly does not represent the deepest extent of this borrow pit as there has undoubtedly been extensive silting and filling in recent times.

Tests of the borrow pit suggest that it may have had a depth of about 2 meters (6.8 feet) below the present ground surface. This was determined by James Porter with the use of a backhoe in 1965 and by Robert Hall using solid-core equipment in 1972 (information conveyed by personal communication to the author). In these tests, remnants of human remains as well as potsherds and other cultural debris were found. If one assumes an average depth of 2 meters for Borrow Pit 5-1A, about 125,000 cubic meters (163,400 cubic yards) of earth were removed from this borrow pit. This is nearly the equivalent of the volume of two mounds the size of Mound 48. Thus the soil removed from the area of 5-1A would have provided the material for only a very small portion of the mounds at the Cahokia site.

Aerial photographs taken in 1922 show the area of Borrow Pit 5-1 filled with water. The 1933 Dache Reeves aerial photos, however, show it without water and covered with vegetation, including what appear to be reeds, bushes, and trees. In the 1933 compilation map, this borrow pit is shown with a symbol for standing water. Some of the early descriptions of the area mentioned that this pit had water in it and people fished for small pan fish there. Oscar Schneider, a lifetime resident of the area, recalls that when he was a young man this borrow pit was a very popular for fishing and ice skating (personal communication, 1989).

Today, large trees and vegetation cover the area, but in extremely rainy years, water stands in the pond late into the spring and early summer. Water stood in the pond in the summer of 1973, which was noted for the extensive flooding in the Mississippi River valley. At that time there was a great deal of water in the pond; frogs, snapping turtles, a muskrat, and wading birds visited the area. It is possible that the borrow pits were used in precolumbian times to support fish, fowl, and mammals for food.

There is little or no evidence to suggest when soil was removed from Borrow Pit 5-1. Mound 72, on its eastern margin, dates to approximately A.D. 950 to A.D 1000. The earliest stage of construction consists of a heavy black clay that is common in the area. It lies just below the humus or plow zone. It is possible that the fill of Mound 72 came from this borrow pit when it was first opened, suggesting that the mound builders scooped up the soil nearest to the surface. Once the readily available material was used, later stages of mound construction required more deeply dug soil, which is more sandy. The later phases of Mound 72 are composed of this much more sandy material. This may suggest that the first use of this large borrow was ca. A.D. 1000.

Moorehead advanced a similar idea when he said that a variety of mounds were composed of this black hard clay, which he called buckshot gumbo. He suggested that mounds built of it were the earliest mounds at the site (1929: 104-105).

The larger borrow pit was probably the product of several small pits enlarged to encompass the entire area that we see today. There are many mounds on the periphery of this huge borrow pit, including Mounds 59, 60, 67, 68, and 72. Around the edge of Borrow Pit 5-1 are small peninsulas, or promontories, extending out into the lower area. Some of these have slight elevations, which indicate they may be mounds. If so, the number of mounds immediately surrounding the pond is much larger than supposed. Whether these represent mounds or some natural feature is not known because thorough testing of these small lumps has not been carried out.

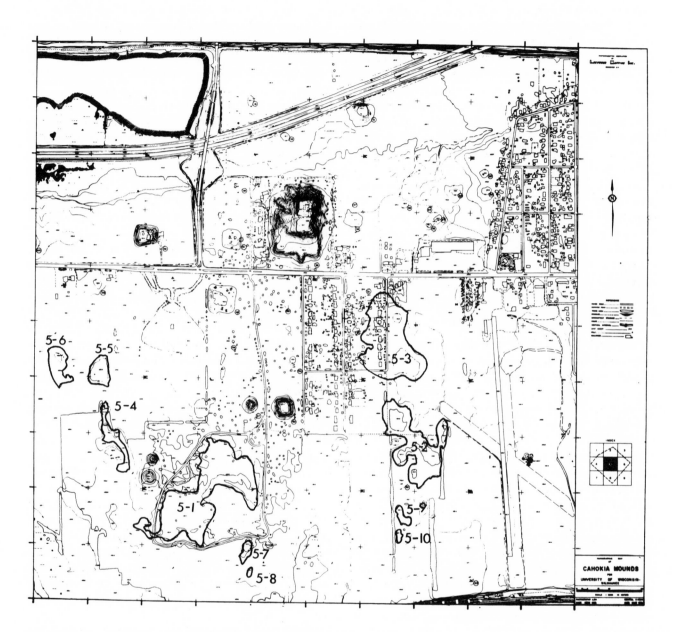

Figure 8.1. Borrow pits in section 5 of the UWM map.

Borrow Pit 5-2

The second largest borrow pit—Borrow Pit 5–2—is centered at approximately S600E600 (Figure 8.1). It, too, may be a series of small borrow pits joined together. These smaller areas show up quite clearly today in air photos and in the topography of the area. Early maps, such as the Patrick map and the 1931 USGS map, suggest that the larger area was completely filled with water. This larger area is enclosed by the 126-meter (413.4-foot) contour line. In wetter seasons the area within the 126-meter contour line is saturated, with standing water in the lower portion. Most of it, however, is dry enough through the growing season for crops such as wheat and corn.

The 1922 Goddard photos also show this 126-meter area completely filled with water. The Patrick map of the 1870s shows it as a large, water-filled area with two associated mounds, Mounds 61 and 62. These mounds are still visible today, although both have been plowed down to a much lower height than in Patrick's day. Mound 61 is more-or-less centrally located in the Borrow Pit 5-2 area and is surrounded on three sides by the borrow pit and water. Mound 61 is a ridge mound with its major axis in an east-west direction, although Patrick (in one of the two mistakes in his map) shows it running north-south. Mound 62 is at the southwest edge of Borrow Pit 5-2. It appears today to be round, although it may have been a rectangular platform before cultivation.

Extending northeastward from Mound 62 is a topographic peninsula with a maximum elevation of 126.4 meters (414.7 feet) extending out into the borrow pit. It is similar to, but more extensive than, some of the promontories extending into Borrow Pit 5-1. Mound 95 on the northeast side of the borrow pit appears to have been a ridge-topped mound running in a northwest-southeast direction. This mound is also surrounded on three sides by Borrow Pit 5-2.

The area of Borrow Pit 5-2 enclosed by the 126-meter contour is 3.6 hectares (8.9 acres). Within this larger area are smaller depressions enclosed by the 125-meter (410.1-foot) contour line. The most northern of these is area A—Borrow Pit 5-2A—which encompasses about 0.3 hectares (0.7 acres). Other depressions are Borrow Pit 5-2B, a little greater than 0.1 hectare (0.2 acres); 2C, which includes approximately 0.5 hectares (1.2 acres); and 2D, 0.06 hectares (0.15 acres). The areas enclosed and the coordinates of these borrow pits and the others discussed in this report are shown in Appendix 4.

Borrow Pit 5-3

To the north of Borrow Pit 5-2 is another low area, Borrow Pit 5-3, encompassed by the 127-meter (416.7-foot) contour within which are two lower areas, A and B (Figure 8.1). The larger area is bigger than the area proposed for Borrow Pit 5-2, but its boundaries are somewhat less distinct. Areas A and B are below the 126-meter (413.4-foot) contour line, and they remain moist today, making cultivation difficult.

The margins of the larger area had not been previously defined, but Harriet Smith reports that when she was digging in Mound 55 she moved just slightly to the east to do a standard test pit outside of the mound area and found that she was in a borrow pit (personal communication, 1989). The 1931 USGS contour map also suggests that this larger area was indeed a depression, and it is indicated on that map as a low, moist area.

Borrow Pit 5-3 encloses an area of 5.1 hectares (12.6 acres) and for the most part it is less than 1 meter (3.3 feet) in depth. Borrow Pit 5-3A, which stands to the north, encompasses 0.70 hectares (1.7 acres), while 5-3B includes 0.1 hectares (0.25 acres).

Paralleling the western limits of Borrow Pit 5-3 are four mounds: 51, 50, 54, and 55. Due to their proximity, it is possible that these mounds may have been constructed from the earth in this area. Between these mounds and the borrow pit, according to the aerial photographs, is the eastern palisade that once partially enclosed the central area of the Cahokia site. Borrow Pit 5-3 may also have been a source for the clay or earth that was used to plaster this large palisade. Mound 51, as already mentioned, was built over a filled borrow pit.

Examination of air photos and the topographic map of the southeastern area of the Cahokia site—the location of Borrow Pits 5-2 and 5-3—suggests that a much larger area is low and marshy. For instance, to the west of Borrow Pit 5-2 on the 1931 map are several suggested swamp areas. One of these is just to the southeast of Mound 60 and due south of the palisade and Mound 55.

If the 126.5-meter (415-foot) contour is interpolated on the UWM map, a much larger area is enclosed, including Borrow Pits 5-9 and 5-10 to the south of Borrow Pit 5-2. This whole area is low and swampy, suggesting that it may have been a source of earth for the construction of mounds, palisades, and houses. However, there is insufficient data to make a stronger case for this 126.5-meter "super" borrow pit.

Part of the layout of the Cahokia site was the central area of nearly 20 mounds surrounded by a large palisade (see Chapter 9). Just to the south and east of the palisade there was an extensive low, wet area that served first as a source of earth for construction and secondarily as a source of water and aquatic food. Narratives of the de Soto expedition described moats around palisaded towns (cf. Hudson 1976:79, 112-116). The more or less interconnecting borrow pits were not moats, but they may have served a somewhat similar function for the fortified central city.

Although the western line of the palisade cannot be clearly defined by excavations or air-photo interpretation, it may parallel the eastern palisade and run just to the west of Mounds 57, 58, 41, and 39. If this is the case, Borrow Pit 5-1 is just to the southwest of the palisade line and slightly further to the west is a series of borrow pits that exist in a context and arrangement similar to those of 5-2 and 5-3.

Borrow Pit 5-4

The largest of these, labeled Borrow Pit 5-4, is centered at approximately S620W500. If the 126.5-meter (415-foot) contour is used as the enclosing elevation, the pit encompasses an area of approximately 1 hectare (2.47 acres). Within it are two smaller pits defined by the enclosed 126-meter (413.4-foot) elevation. Pit 4A is approximately 0.2 hectares (0.5 acres) and 4B about 0.02 hectares (0.05 acres) (Figure 8.1).

Borrow Pit 5-4 is long and narrow, running approximately north-south. In the southern portion is a peninsula defined by the 127-meter (416.7-foot) contour line that extends into the borrow pit, nearly cutting it off. This peninsula reaches an elevation of 128.3 meters (420.9 feet) and may well represent an area of mound construction. This area has been designated Mound 93. The southern end of this borrow pit is not clearly defined and may extend further south, connecting with Borrow Pit 5-1 to make one large borrow pit in the southwest area of the central portion of the Cahokia site. If the borrow pit were defined by the 127-meter (416.7-foot) contour, it would include not only 5-1 but a large area of low, swampy ground southwest of the palisaded area. This is probably too extensive. The major extent of these low areas southeast and southwest of central Cahokia is undoubtedly the remnant of now extinct channels of the Mississippi River. Borrow pits were undoubtedly dug into these areas.

There are three mounds associated with Borrow Pit 5-4. Mounds 67 and 68 are a conical and platform mound much in the same pattern as Fox and Round Top mounds. They are located between Borrow Pits 5-

1 and 5-4. The third mound is Mound 93, which is located on the west side of Borrow Pit 5-4. These three mounds and Borrow Pit 5-4 are a mirror image of the relationships of Mounds 61, 62, and 95 and Borrow Pit 5-2 on the east side of central Cahokia. These two cases, Borrow Pits 5-1 and 5-4, are the best examples at the Cahokia site of the close association of mound and residential areas with these artificial ponds. In these cases the borrow pits are the central focus of the subcommunity.

Borrow Pit 5-5

At S380W560 is one of the deeper and more sharply defined borrow pits at the Cahokia site, Borrow Pit 5-5. The area enclosed in this borrow pit is 0.7 hectares (1.7 acres), and the deepest point located in present mapping is 125.2 meters (410.8 feet) below sea level. This borrow pit, in its present condition, is more than 1.8 meters (5.9 feet) in depth. It undoubtedly was deeper in precolumbian times and has filled in through silting (Figure 8.1).

Borrow Pit 5-6

Centered on grid coordinates S3700W720 is another clearly delineated borrow pit completely enclosed by the 127-meter (416.7-foot) contour. Borrow Pit 5-6 encloses 0.8 hectares (2.0 acres). Its deepest point, in the northern section, is at 125.9 meters (413.1 feet) (Figure 8.1).

Borrow Pits 5-7, 5-8, 5-9, and 5-10

South of Borrow Pit 5-1 are two small borrow pits defined by the 126-meter (413.4-foot) contour line. Borrow Pit 5-7 is centered at S1020W20. It encloses 0.3 hectares (0.7 acres). Its deepest point, at 124.9 meters (409.8 feet), is in its northern half. Just to the south of this, at S1100W5, Borrow Pit 5-8 is defined by the 126-meter contour line that encloses 0.08 hectares (0.17 acres).

There is an area east of Borrow Pit 5-7 that was, at the time the 1966 UWM map was made, marked as a flooded area, and it may be included in the borrow pit area (Figure 8.1). There is a similar area to the east of Borrow Pit 5-8, indicated as a swampy area on the UWM map, that might also be included in the borrow pit. These pits may have been encompassed in a larger area, which can be defined by interpolating the 126.5-meter (415-foot) contour.

In this case, a larger area would be implied, one separated from the borrow pits on the east by a ridge above the 127-meter (416.7-foot) contour line, which appears to be a causeway extending from just south of Mound 60 and east of Mound 72 southward as far as the Rattlesnake Mound (Mound 66). Some suggest that the causeway was built to cross over this very swampy area to the south of the main Cahokia site. This large swampy area may have been created during construction of mounds. It would have extended all the way across the southern portion of the Cahokia site south of and paralleling the east side of the palisaded central area. It would, however, take extensive soil testing to demonstrate this, and this discussion is restricted to the more limited definition of the borrow pits.

South of Borrow Pit 5-2, as mentioned above, are two other borrow pits: 5-9 and 5-10. Borrow Pit 5-9 is located at S880E560, and the area bounded by the 126-meter contour line is 0.2 hectares (0.50 acres). Borrow Pit 5-10, located at S960E540, encloses 0.15 hectares (0.38 acres) (Figure 8.1).

Borrow Pits 8-1, 8-2, 8-3, 8-4, and 8-5

The few borrow pits located in section 8 are the vicinity of the Rattlesnake Mound (Mound 66) and Mound 65, which is almost due east of Rattlesnake. There are three obvious depressions there that are probably borrow pits. Major modern construction, the railroad tracks, and the drainage ditch may have altered the ground considerably. These alterations have either made the limits of the borrow pits more restricted, or cut off larger drainage patterns, leaving depressions that may not be aboriginal borrow pits.

Borrow Pit Number 8-1 is located at S1360E300 (Figure 8.2). Defined by the 125-meter (410.0-foot) contour, this depression covers 560 square meters (0.14 acres) and is relatively shallow today. It is very possible that this borrow pit was once much larger but has been partially covered by construction of railroad tracks. If the 126-meter (413.4-foot) contour line is used as the limits rather than the 125-meter line, this borrow pit would probably have been ten times larger, covering an area of 5,560 square meters (1.47 acres). Even this is probably much less than originally, since the northern portions of this borrow pit were probably also covered over by railroad construction.

North and east of Mound 65 are four other borrow pits defined by the 126-meter (413.4-foot) contour line. Borrow Pit 8-2 is located at S1480E800 and encompasses an area of 1,840 square meters (0.45 acres). The deepest portion of this borrow pit is at 124.8 meters

(409.5 feet), making its depth 1.2 meters (3.9 feet). Just to the north of this, at S1430E800, is Borrow Pit 8-3. It covers an area of 840 square meters (0.21 acres). Just to the right of that borrow pit is 8-4A, which is best defined by the 125-meter (410.1-foot) contour line and encloses 320 square meters (0.08 acres). However, the 126-meter (413.4-foot) contour line seems to define the true margins of the upper area of this borrow pit and extends over a much greater area. This larger area encompasses 0.8 hectares (2 acres). It is difficult to tell if the larger area is truly the extent of this borrow pit because it has been disrupted by the digging of a drainage ditch, suggesting modern grading rather than an aboriginal borrow pit (Figure 8.2).

Borrow Pit 8-5, located at S1400E850, is just north of 8-4 and may indeed be a portion of that pit. It is one of the smallest areas I have suggested for a borrow pit at Cahokia. The enclosed 125 contour line includes an area about 25 m in diameter or about 625 square meters. Due to the ground conditions in the area, there was no way to determine depth.

On the other hand, the four small borrow pits in this area may be but the deepest portion of a larger borrow pit that can be defined using the 126.5-meter (415-foot) contour. This entire area is below 127 meters (416.7 feet) and could be similar to the larger borrow pits in section 5 described above. It is also lower than the northern portions of the site, giving the appearances of an extensive swampy area, which includes remnants of long-extinct river channels and drainage systems. Therefore, the current description of borrow pits is limited to those that are well defined by the 126-meter (413.4-foot) contour line.

Borrow Pit 4-1

What appears to be a large, shallow borrow pit is located at S300W1300 in section 4. This borrow pit is defined by an extensive loop in the 127-meter (416.7-foot) contour line that encompasses an area of 2.39 hectares (5.9 acres). It connects with a trough-like depression that runs from the northwest to the southeast through that area of the Cahokia site. This appears to be a drainage channel formed by an extinct channel of the Mississippi River. However, it is much more regular than most of the other low-lying drainage areas, suggesting it was modified by aboriginal reworking. Thus this borrow pit may be part of a much more extensive area from which soil was scooped for the building of the mounds. This area is close to Mounds 44 and 45, and it may have been a source of soil for their construction (Figure 8.3).

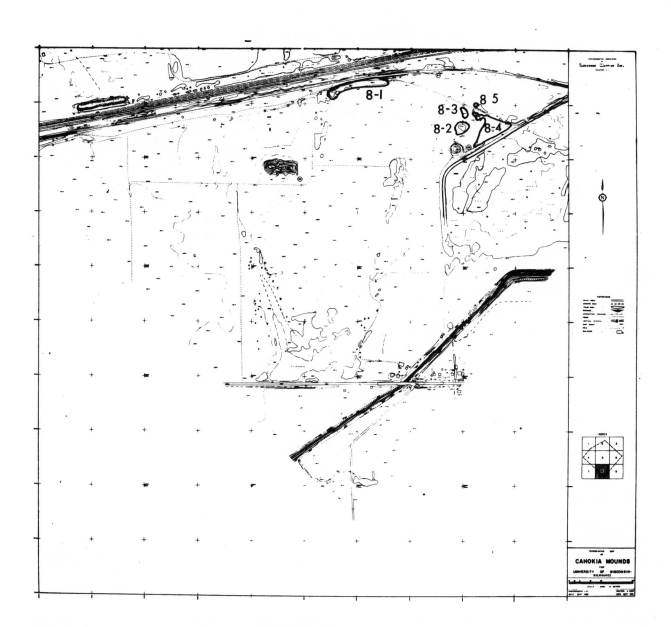

Figure 8.2.   Borrow pits in section 8 of the UWM map.

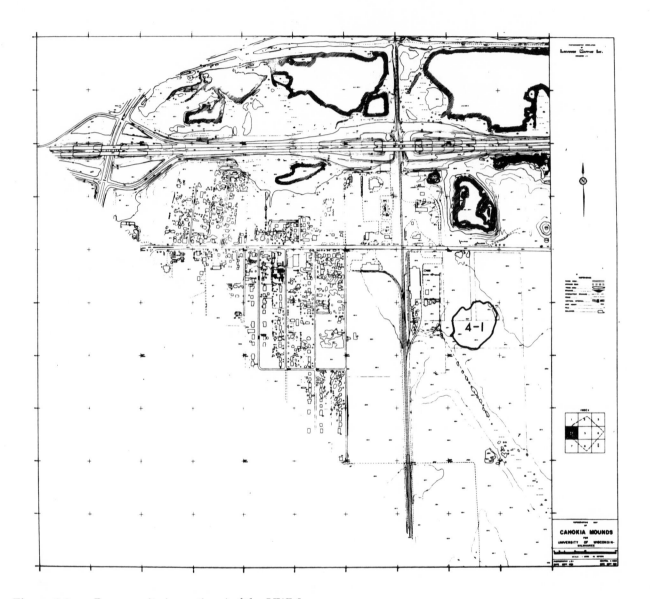

Figure 8.3.   Borrow pits in section 4 of the UWM map.

There are other depressions in the general area of Borrow Pit 4-1, but it is difficult to tell whether they represent aboriginal borrow pits so they have not been assigned borrow pit numbers.

Just to the north of Borrow Pit 4-1, between Interstate 55-70 and Highway 40, is a modern borrow pit that was dug for construction of Interstate 55-70. It is a good example of the general nature of borrow pits that existed in aboriginal times. Before current owners began filling it in with rubbish, it held water.

Borrow Pits 2-1, 2-2, 2-3, and 2-4

There are several depressions in section 2 that appear to be aboriginal borrow pits (Figure 8.4). Borrow Pit 2-1 is located at N148E0. It is obvious from the ground and in air photos, but was not shown on the contour map of the area. Ground reconnaissance and interpolation of the map suggest the 125.5-meter (411.7-foot) contour as the area of closure. If this is the case, then the area consists of about 0.1 hectares (0.3 acres). The original borrow pit was probably larger than this, but the data are unclear since this is an area of what appears to be natural levees or ridges and ditches. Without further detailed surveying or archaeological excavation, the actual limits of this borrow pit are difficult to determine. Just to the south of Borrow Pit 2-1 is Mound 89. It is possible that this mound was created from the fill taken from 2-1 (Figure 8.4).

There are several depressions in the area of N1200E400. They are in the low area to the south and east of Mound 6, which was originally the valley of Cahokia Creek. The area was greatly disturbed by construction of the drainage canal that replaced Cahokia Creek, and these slight depressions in the vicinity of Mound 6, which are labeled Borrow Pits 2-2, 2-3, and 2-4, may not be borrow pits but rather remnants of the meander pattern of Cahokia Creek. The depressions, however, are not typical of the other mapped areas of Cahokia Creek, suggesting the possibility that they are borrow pits (Figure 8.4).

Borrow Pit 2-2 covers an area of 0.2 hectares (0.5 acres); Pit 2-3, 0.1 hectares (0.3 acres); and Pit 2-4, 0.15 hectares (0.4 acres). The many low spots seen on the map suggest that there are other borrow pits in this section. However, extinct Cahokia Creek channels, natural levees, and modern construction make interpreting the full extent of aboriginal features difficult.

Discussion

At least 20 large borrow pits have been located at Cahokia. They are identified on the basis of closed contours and, in some cases, interpolated contours that enclose an area. Within the larger borrow pit areas are often deeper depressions that are well defined by contour lines. These smaller areas are the ones that are most obvious on the contour maps today and suggest the deeper borrow pits.

The whole problem of interpreting borrow pits is complicated by the buildup of soil since the time when the borrow pits were first excavated. There has been extensive alluvial filling and silting in the borrow pits so that their present depth is much shallower than in the past. Excavation underneath the area of Mound 51 by the University of Illinois suggests another reason why the original depth of the borrow pits may not be apparent today. The big borrow pit under Mound 51 extended to a depth of 2.1 meters (6.9 feet) below the base of the mound (Chmurny 1973:1). Some unpublished test excavations of Borrow Pit 5-1A area suggest that it, too, was about 2 meters (6.6 feet) deep. None of the borrow pits today show this great a depth. According to the University of Illinois study, the borrow pit under Mound 51 had been rather rapidly filled in by the Native Americans throwing trash into the area. Many of the borrow pits may have been used for this same purpose.

The area encompassed by the borrow pits has been estimated by interpreting their boundaries from the maps. The total area included in those borrow pits is 236,752 square meters (58.5 acres). Assuming, for these larger areas, an average depth of only 1 meter (3.3 feet), the borrow pits provided only 236,752 cubic meters (309,480 cubic yards) of fill for construction purposes. Looking only at the smaller areas within the large borrow pits, they encompass approximately 83,800 square meters (20.7 acres). Even if the smaller pits were excavated another meter deeper (for a total of 2 meters [6.7 feet]), the volume represented by the visible borrow pits totals no more than 320,552 cubic meters (419,022 cubic yards) of soil. Although no one has calculated the total volume of earth represented by all of the known mounds at the Cahokia site, it is obvious that this represents only a small portion of the amount of earth needed for construction at Cahokia. Monks Mound alone contains over 600,000 cubic meters (nearly 800,000 cubic yards) of fill.

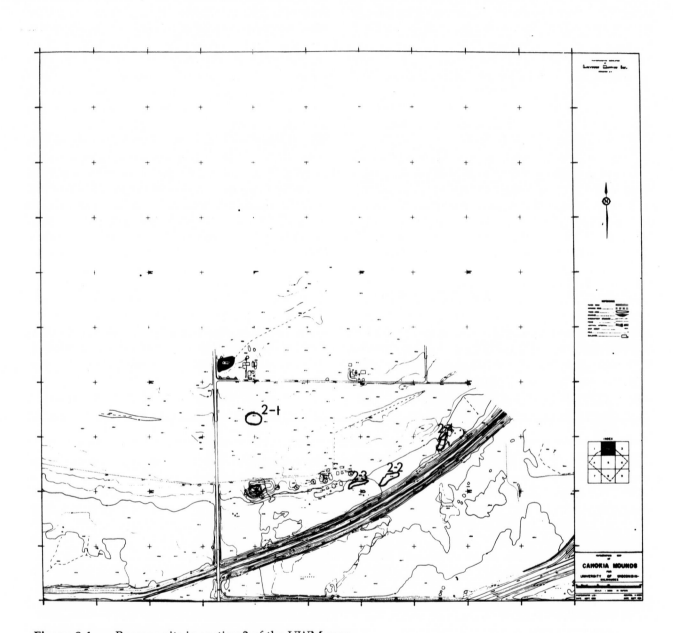

Figure 8.4.   Borrow pits in section 2 of the UWM map.

The borrow pits may have encompassed even larger areas and reached greater depths. However, I doubt that Cahokians dug deeper than 2 meters (6.7 feet) because of practical reasons. In the deep post pit in Mound 72, a little more than a meter below the surface was a stratum of silty clay that had a high water content and slumped very easily. During 1967 we had to shore up the Mound 72 post pit excavation to prevent it from slumping. The following year we attempted to excavate the rest of the post pit but found it impossible. A heavier than normal rainfall raised the water table to a dangerous level, increasing the chances of collapsing walls. The inhabitants of Cahokia probably encountered a similar problem in digging borrow pits much deeper than 2 meters. The alternative would have been to excavate larger areas at a shallower depth.

There are undoubtedly other areas with buried borrow pits like the one under Mound 51 (Chmurny 1973). The locations of the borrow pits were influenced by the expansion of the Cahokia site. In Emergent and Early Mississippian times (see Figure 1.7), the site may have been restricted to the central area, and the borrow pits excavated near the mound under construction. For example, it is possible that the borrow pit below Mound 51 was created during early stages of the construction of Monks Mound. As the population expanded, central portions of the site had to be put to different uses. Borrow pits were filled in with trash and other materials, and the area reclaimed for mound construction or habitation.

If we could test greater areas of the Cahokia site, we might find that much of the central area was originally borrow pits that were later filled in. A large distribution of shallow borrow pits is suggested by the borrow pits in section 5. Many of the larger borrow pits were probably connected, and the area south of the central portion of the Cahokia site may have been one vast borrow pit. In that case, the south end of the palisade was likely surrounded by man-made swamps and ponds.

The only way to determine the full extent of borrow pits is through judicious archaeological testing. Cross sections should be excavated to determine the depth and margins of the borrow pits. Included in these studies, of course, should be an analysis of the soils in the borrow pit fill, a determination of their origins, and identification of the pollen rain in the areas as the pits filled in. We know that at least one borrow pit was filled with trash, suggesting that the data recovered from these borrow pits might be unique and interesting. We might also expect those materials to be well preserved if they were waterlogged and unoxidized. Excavating and testing the borrow pits should be as significant a research project as those involving the mounds and habitation areas.

9

CAHOKIA AS A COMMUNITY

Since Brackenridge's discovery of the Cahokia site in 1811, more than a century and a half of historical, archaeological, and more casual investigations of the area have taken place. These inquiries have produced maps of the zone, descriptions of the mounds, air photos, and artifacts, as well as biological and cultural data from excavations. Most of the reports published by the myriad of investigators have included interpretations of the significance and nature of the Cahokia mounds. Some of these have been merely wild speculations, whereas others have been more reasoned statements based upon observations of the mounds and comparisons with what was known at the time of both the history and prehistory of the area. Whatever the nature of these interpretations, observation of this vast archaeological zone and its grandiose mounds has stirred the imagination. What must it have been like when people lived at Cahokia? How many people were here? What kind of society could have organized these people to construct the giant earthworks?

These are the kinds of questions Brackenridge dealt with at the time of his visit to the Cahokia mounds and in the years thereafter. Even though more recent investigators have also struggled with these problems using the large quantities of information that have accumulated since the early nineteenth century, these concerns and others can never be completely answered. Although modern archaeological investigation is the closest system to a time machine that is available to us, it is not the same as participating in the actual events. All that can be currently achieved is a closer and closer approximation of understanding.

Some types of questions are more amenable to analysis with the kinds of archaeological data that are most abundant. Only a small fraction of a percent of the Cahokia site has been excavated. These excavations have dealt with very specific problems, and they contribute only limited insights into the overall nature of the prehistoric Cahokia community. Much more

data exist on the above-ground remnants of Cahokia, such as the mounds, borrow pits, and surface debris. Over the decades of the nineteenth and twentieth centuries, students of Cahokia have described the mounds, made maps of the site, and discussed their interpretations. The surface data are particularly amenable to presenting interpretations of the character of Cahokia at its peak of occupation.

There are problems, however, in using these data for such purposes. A major limitation is that we do not know how much of the area was utilized at any given time. Moorehead recognized this problem when he stated:

> The question arises whether all of this extensive village was inhabited at one time. Were there several periods of occupation? . . . It is scarcely conceivable that so large a village—verily a city in extent—existed as a unit in a given time epoch. . . . Is it not likely that the Cahokia folk established camps from time to time at different points along the two creeks? Was not the region inhabited for several hundred years? These questions are important. At present we cannot answer them (1929:25).

The questions are as important today as they were when Moorehead was pondering them. It is now known that indeed the Cahokia mounds area was occupied for "several hundred years." In this atlas, I have discussed over 100 earthen mounds. Were these mounds all used at the same time? Does their distribution represent the pattern and organization of the functioning community? Without a systematic program to excavate widespread areas of the site, these questions can never be convincingly answered. The discussion of radiocarbon dates presented in Appendix 1 is a partial answer to this problem. The dates suggest that all areas of Cahokia thus far investigated were used throughout the total time range of Cahokia's development, although there were undoubtedly different intensities of utilization, as well as changing land use, through time.

There are some data to suggest partial answers to the questions. Based upon these limited answers, some assumptions can be made to direct the inquiry. Nearly everywhere archaeological excavations have been conducted at Cahokia, evidence for the Emergent and Early Mississippian periods has been recovered. In some cases data for later periods are missing in certain areas. This would seem to indicate that in the earlier periods, roughly A.D. 900 to A.D. 1100, Cahokia covered the area defined by the distribution of mounds, but in later periods it may have had a more limited extent.

For example, Harriet Smith's excavations into the Murdock Mound (55), in the center of the site near Monks Mound, gave evidence of the entire known sequence for Cahokia (Smith 1969). The UWM and other excavations in Monks Mound produced a similar sequence of occupations (Reed et al. 1968; Williams 1972, 1975). The earliest stage of Monks Mound was apparently in the Early Mississippian period as well.

What little is presently known of the peripheries of the site provide similar information. The best evidence for the periphery comes from the Powell Mound (86) area. Salvage excavations, spanning the 40-year period from 1933 to 1970, have recovered material from the entire Cahokia time span (Ahler and DePuydt 1987; Kelly 1933; O'Brien 1969a, 1969b, 1972a; Titterington 1938).

Unique among mounds excavated to date is Mound 72; its total span is limited to the Early Mississippian period, or the time around the end of the tenth century. This, however, is a very special case in that this mound and the associated Mound 96 were part of a ceremonial complex; they commemorate in elaborate burial ceremonials one of the early leaders of Cahokia. Someday examination of other mounds may isolate similar special functions of Cahokia. Mound 72 indicates that mound building was a feature of early Cahokia.

Another interesting indicator of the widespread early usage of the Cahokia site comes from excavations in the borrow pit under Mound 51, the Persimmon Mound (Chmurny 1973). The earliest premound fill of this borrow pit is contemporary with Mound 72. This suggests that the Mound 51 borrow pit had been dug, abandoned, and partially filled by Early Mississippian times. This borrow pit may have been the source for the material used in the early stages of Monks Mound. In other words, considerable activity was going on, at least in the central parts of Cahokia, before and during the tenth century A.D.

The above are only some selected examples of the data indicating that the distribution of mounds at Cahokia today is fairly representative of the extent of the Cahokia community in the Precolumbian past. These data do not tell us that all mounds were used at the same time. I think there are sufficient indications that many of the mounds at Cahokia were built in stages over relatively long periods of time. Further, there are data that indicate mound construction started in the Early Mississippian period and possibly earlier, during the Emergent Mississippian.

We can operate, then, on the assumption that the observed distribution of mounds is representative of the prehistoric extent and layout of the community. While all portions of this area may not have been occupied simultaneously, the concepts which dictated the organization of space are indicated by the distribution of the man-made features, primarily the mounds.

I have discussed in previous chapters the details of all of these observable features as well as some of the data that have been recovered from excavations. A summary of this vast quantity of information is now presented. This summary takes the form of an interpretive or idealized reconstruction of the Cahokia community. This model is not intended to be a factual representation of Cahokia at a specific moment in time, but rather an outline of the general nature of Cahokia.

CAHOKIA POPULATION

From the discovery of Cahokia to the present day, one of the major questions about the site has been how many people lived there. Brackenridge (1962 [1814]:189) compared it to the Philadelphia of his time. Thomas inferred a population of "ten or twelve thousand" (1907:364). Later investigators have varied greatly in their estimates. All these concerns have been dependent on the then-current attitudes regarding Native Americans, their hypothetical mound-builder ancestors, and both popular and anthropological prejudices.

There are several ways to estimate the population of a prehistoric community. Whatever the method applied, it should be kept in mind that it cannot provide an actual census of the population. The limits of both the methods applied and the restricted nature of archaeological data mandate that only approximations of population can be reached. As data increase and more sophisticated demographic insights are gained, we should ultimately be able to come closer to an approximation of the actual population. For the time being, we must deal in orders of magnitude.

One approach is in terms of the burials related to a given site. If there is a cemetery or a large number of burials at a site, indicating a normal or complete demographic profile, it is possible to project the total number of deaths over the period of the site's occupation. Then an average population can be estimated. There are, of course, limitations to this method. Can one be sure that burial is the only method of disposal of the dead or that a cemetery represents the entire community? In smaller sites this is more approachable, but in a site as large and complex as Cahokia, this is a serious problem.

Data on burials and cemeteries at Cahokia are very limited. Brackenridge (1962 [1814]:186) mentioned "an astonishing quantity of human bones, everywhere dug up" but gave no specifics as to these locations. Moorehead, on his various maps, located various cemeteries and burial areas within the Cahokia site, but no specific excavations or analysis of these have been reported. McAdams (1882:62) discovered an extensive "tomb or burial place" near Monks Mound. However, only a portion of the scores of pottery vessels from this discovery has been preserved. The skeletons were cast aside, so no analysis is possible. Nearly 300 burials were discovered in Mound 72. However, with its unique ceremonial and social context within the Early Mississippian community at Cahokia, Mound 72 cannot be considered representative of the overall population. The persons of most importance buried in the mound must have come from a very select segment of the population. Those sacrificed to be buried with them were probably also very carefully chosen from within the community and from other communities outside of Cahokia. Whereas the extant burial data can tell us a lot about the people of Cahokia, they are not of the quantity or nature to allow any inferences as to numbers.

Another method of estimating Cahokia's population might be called the labor-force approach. What size population could have supported a labor force sufficient to construct the many public and domestic structures-mounds, palisades, civic buildings, and residences-at Cahokia? This is the approach that McAdams (1882) used, albeit in a very intuitive and unsophisticated way. Nelson Reed (1969) has also applied this method to Cahokia. After estimating the volume of the many mounds and the number of logs that would have been needed for the palisade and other structures, Reed estimated the size of labor force necessary for these works and the size of the support-

ing population needed to provide the subsistence needs of the workers. Reed concluded that a population of about 10,000 would have been adequate to construct the Cahokia site. However, this does not necessarily mean that such a number represents the people living at the Cahokia site. Labor for public works may well have come from villages and farmsteads outside of the site itself.

A third, and perhaps more reliable, method is to consider the number of residential units there may have been at Cahokia at any one time. The number of persons per household can be hypothesized and from this a total population estimate made. Some areas of several acres have been excavated at Cahokia, most notably Tracts 15A and 15B (Fowler, ed. 1962, 1963, 1964; Vogel 1964a, 1964b, 1975). Data from these areas were utilized to make a population estimate (Gregg 1975a) for Cahokia. When this application was carefully prepared, it indicated a Cahokia population of ca. 30,000. Some archaeologists accept that figure as representative, while others think it much too high (cf. Ford 1974:406; Muller 1987). Again, we have no assurance that these houses were all occupied at one time nor do we know how long a residential structure might have existed. The population estimate of 30,000 may be erring toward the upper end, but dividing this by four probably errs in the other direction.

There is no question that all of these provocative estimates need to be challenged with new data and more sophisticated techniques. However, it seems to me that the best order-of-magnitude population estimate is more than 10,000 rather than in the thousands. Even if not as great as 30,000, the population at Cahokia was the largest in prehistoric times for any community within the present boundaries of the United States of America. To put it another way, Cahokia was not only physically the largest community, it was also the most densely populated.

COMMUNITY ORGANIZATION

The large number of mounds at Cahokia offers a picture of confusion and random scatter over the landscape to the person attempting to sense some order in this enormous archaeological complex. Yet the amount of labor involved in building these mounds, certainly the larger ones such as Monks Mound, indicates a coordination of community effort to accomplish these many works. Was there also coordination and planning in regard to the overall organization of the community?

All mounds are not the same in size and form. Separating the mounds in terms of these differences in form helps to place some order over the seemingly random distribution. The assumption is that the shapes of the mounds can be a basis for inferring the functions they served. One must assume that the shapes of mounds were deliberately chosen by the builders to suit the purpose for which they were being constructed. Examining the placement of these structures in relationship to each other can lead to some understanding of community order.

Analysis of the many maps of Cahokia, numerous aerial photographs, published descriptions of the mounds, and excavations in them, as well as on-the-spot examination of the remaining mounds, has led to a classification of the mound forms represented at Cahokia. Of the total of 104 numbered mounds, 52 have been identified as to form (see Appendix 2).

Platform Mounds

The most common mound form, 36 of the 52 mounds identified, is square to rectangular at the base with a flat top or surface (Figure 9.1a). These mounds are in the form of a truncated pyramid. They have been referred to over the years as flat-topped, pyramidal, substructure, and temple mounds. Mounds of this form were common in sites first visited by the de Soto expedition and later by French and English explorers and colonists in the Southeast. These early observers described this mound form as platforms upon which various types of buildings were placed. These buildings served a variety of functions, including residences, storehouses for community goods, charnel houses, and so-called temples.

The sizes of platform mounds and their locations probably imply their relative importance in the community. For example, many of the residences of the bulk of the population were built on low platforms. Such platforms were observed by Brackenridge (1811) with attendant residential debris. Other residential structures are found on the top of higher platforms and may therefore be the domiciles of community leaders. Harriet Smith (1969) concluded from her excavations in the Murdock Mound (55) that the area had first been a residential area with some structures built on low platforms. Later a large mound was built over the area with a structure on it. Her interpretation was that this changed from a general residential area to an "elite" residence and finally to "temple" location on top of the mound.

The placement of the various platform mounds within the community also is undoubtedly indicative of their relative importance. Thus Monks Mound (38) is not only the largest structure at Cahokia, it is also located near the geographic center of the mound distribution. It also had on its uppermost terrace or platform the largest building yet uncovered at the Cahokia site. This was undoubtedly the central focus of the community. Part of Smith's interpretation of Mound 55 as an elite residence is its proximity to Monks Mound, as well as its orientation, which lines up precisely with the east edge of Monks Mound.

There are variations on the basic platform mound. The most common variation is of a multiple, terraced mound. Monks Mound is a unique example of this variant in that it has four different terraces or levels. Most of the terraced platform mounds have only two terraces.

Another variation is what I refer to as Tee mounds, after their shape in the form of the letter "T" The first of these identified is the Mackie Mound (79). A second such mound was identified in the survey of previously unnumbered mounds: Mound 96, located just to the southwest of Mound 72. In my classification of mounds (see Appendix 2), I have listed these as platforms but made note of their special shape. A Tee mound was found as a primary or submound in Mound 72. Much of its platform surface was exposed, but no evidence of a structure was found. This platform was associated with the large marker post placed in the mound. It may be that these mounds are special platforms without structures built on them.

Conical Mounds

A much less common form of mound at Cahokia is that sometimes referred to in the past as a chocolate-drop mound. This refers to the fact that they are usually circular in base outline and rise to a point (Figure 9.1b). There is no platform surface on top that could have served as a foundation for a structure. In this book I refer to these as conical mounds. Only 11 such mounds have been identified at the Cahokia site.

The best preserved is Round Top (59). There appears to have been little or no leveling of this mound as it was never cultivated. Mound 59 has been consistently measured over the years as being over 12 meters (about 40 feet) in height and nearly twice that in diameter. Another large, conical mound is Mound 33, the James Ramey Mound. This mound has been greatly deflated by plowing and removal of earth from its summit to fill in nearby low spots. It is estimated that it was originally 10.5 meters (35 feet) high. Moorehead's

a

b

c

Figure 9.1. Typical (a) platform mound (Mound 42), (b) conical mound (Mound 59), and (c) ridge-top mound (Mound 86). Sources: (a) Cahokia Mounds Museum, Illinois Historic Preservation Agency; (b) and (c) Department of Anthropology, University of Illinois at Urbana-Champaign.

excavations produced some human remains from the mound as well as debris. The debris probably comes from the earth scooped up to build the mound and not from burial offerings. The Jondro Mound (78) was partially excavated by Moorehead (1929:51-52). Forty complete burials were uncovered as well as fragmentary human remains.

Another characteristic of conical mounds is that seven of the 11 examples were found in association with platform mounds. It appears that paired mounds were either built on a common platform or with a ramp or causeway connecting the two. Mounds 59 and 60 represent one of the clearest examples of this. An unusual association is the connection of Mounds 61 (Tippetts Mound) with Mound 62 by a long causeway. This causeway is shown only on the Patrick map, but some evidence for it can be seen in the contours of the area today.

The association of conical and platform mounds indirectly strengthens the hypothesis that conical mounds are burial mounds. In the early historic period of the Southeast, there are eyewitness accounts of the practice of storing human remains in charnel houses. These mortuary warehouses were emptied and the remains of the individuals were buried in mounds at intervals. My hypothesis is that the platform mounds represent the location of charnel structures and the associated conical mounds were the burial mounds. The limited number of the conical mounds and their direct association with platforms suggest that they may represent the final resting place of select portions of the total society.

There are several smaller mounds that might be identified here as conical mounds but which may have served functions other than for burial. Examples of these are Mounds 77 and 40, located between platforms 39 and 41, and 50 and 54, located between platforms 51 and 55. These mounds are either directly associated with or are close to platforms. There is some evidence that burials were included in Mound 77, but there are no data in this regard for the others mentioned. The unusual offertory pit found in Mound 77 leads me to suggest that these may be special dedicatory mounds relating to the activities carried out on the nearby platforms. In these cases the platforms may have been the residences of important people, and the small conicals nearby contained offertory pits and perhaps wooden posts or monuments dedicated to those persons. For the present, I include these types of mounds within the conical classification. Further research may indicate a separate category of dedicatory mounds.

Ridge-Top Mounds

Because they are rectangular in base outline and rise to a ridge "too narrow on top for large wigwams or temples" (Moorehead 1929:104), some mounds were often referred to as "hayrick" mounds (Peterson and McAdams 1906 map; Titterington 1938:15).

Eight possible examples of this form are noted for the Cahokia site (Figure 9.1c). Some of these are very clearly defined because they were so large that they did not get plowed over. The two best examples are Mounds 66 (Rattlesnake Mound) and 86 (Powell Mound). This latter mound was mostly destroyed for land fill in 1931, but fortunately air photos made in 1922 show its undisturbed form. The other six examples are smaller mounds that have been cultivated. Their basic form is determined from the fact that they have an elongated basal outline and a ridged top.

Other than the fact that their ridged tops mitigated against their use as platforms, these mounds had other unique characteristics. Five of the eight examples are at the extreme limits of the mound area; they are mostly located over 1,000-2,000 meters (3,000-6,000 feet) from Monks Mound. One ridged-top mound, Red Mound (49), however, is located slightly less than 150 meters (492 feet) from Monks Mound.

Another characteristic of mounds of this form is their alignment that each other and with Monks Mound. Rattlesnake (66), Mound 72, and Red Mound (49) form a north-south alignment that intersects at Monks Mound with an east-west alignment formed by Powell (86) and Mound 2.

Because of these two characteristics, which may of course just be fortuitous, I propose that one of the functions of ridged mounds was as marker mounds at the peripheries of the site and at other critical points within the community. This hypothesis is supported by the placement of a large post in Mound 72 (Fowler 1969a, 1974a, 1975) on the proposed north-south centerline.

Most of the mounds at Cahokia are oriented approximately to the cardinal points. Half of the mounds identified as ridge-tops are oriented northwest-southeast or southwest-northeast. In its final form, Mound 72 was oriented 30° from an east-west axis. Two other mounds (2 and 95) are approximately in this orientation. However, since they have not been as precisely mapped and have been more extensively cultivated, it is not possible to speak of precise orientations for these mounds. Mounds 2 and 85 have interesting similarities in their placement and orientation. Mound 2, at the eastern edge of the site, is oriented northwest-southeast. Mound 85, at the western limit of the site, is oriented southwest-northeast. Both of these mounds are ovoid and on the banks of Cahokia Creek. The uncommon orientations of four of the eight ridge-top mounds is further argument in favor of their being marker mounds.

Three of the proposed ridge-top mounds have been excavated. All contained interior primary mounds that were added to to form the final mounds, as well as burials and other features. The most complete of these excavations was the work in Mound 72. This indicated that, besides the marker post location, the mound had been made up of a series of primary or submounds. These mounds had been later covered over to make the final ridge-top mound. Within the submounds and the final mound were many burials. A few of these seem to have been of especially important individuals. The others were, in effect, offerings dedicated to these individuals. This does not mean that the interpretation of this mound form as community marker mounds is incorrect. It is probable that the burials included were also dedicated to the significant point in the community being marked. The presence of the burials and dedicatory artifacts only stresses the importance and significance of the locale within the community. The *primary* function of ridge-top mounds was as markers, just the the *primary* function of conical mounds was mortuary.

The Palisade

One body of information relevant to the organization and planning of Cahokia comes from both aerial photographics and excavation. This is the discovery that an extensive wall or fortification had been built around the central portion of the site (Anderson 1969). This wall was first noted in the 1922 Goddard aerial photographs, but it was also observed in later photos (Fowler 1977). Excavations east of Monks Mound and south of Fox Mound (60) confirmed that the soil marks were associated with a palisade. In fact, there had been several such walls in this locality built over a period of time. At regular intervals along this wall were watchtowers or bastions (Figure 9.2).

The eastern portions of this palisade were clearly indicated on the air photos and in the limited excavations. Several locations have been proposed for the western part of the palisade. Unfortunately, there were no indications on the aerial photographs of the palisade west of Monks Mound. It is possible, however, that the palisade was symmetrical around a north-south axis, and the western portion would have been a mirror image of the established eastern section. The proposed center line based upon the alignments of Mounds 66, 72, 49, and Monks Mound is probably close to the axis of symmetry for the palisade.

Figure 9.2.   A reconstructed section of the palisade around the Monks Mound area. Source: Cahokia Mounds Museum, Illinois Historic Preservation Agency.

With this proposed west area, the palisade would have begun northeast of Monks Mound on the banks of Cahokia Creek, or between Mounds 17 and 18 (see Figure 10.1). From there it went in a direction slightly west of south to a point near the eastern edge of the Murdock Mound (55). At that point, the line of the wall veered southwest to an area south of Fox Mound (60). At that juncture, the line went due west crossing the north-south centerline. The western half probably went north just west of Mound 48 and just east of the current location of Sand Prairie Lane. There is no evidence to date of a palisade along the north side of Monks Mound, but it is probable that such a north wall did exist. Thus proposed, the palisade enclosed an area of approximately 83 hectares (205 acres) with 18 mounds inside the wall. In the north-central portion of this enclosed area was Monks Mound.

Radiocarbon dates on materials from features cut by construction of the east wall of the palisade indicate that the wall was built after A.D. 1100, or in the later part of the Stirling phase at Cahokia (see Figure 1.7). This dates only the first palisade; subsequent replacements of the wall were somewhat later in time, perhaps extending into the thirteenth century. At any rate, the palisade and the area it surrounded were prime areas at Cahokia during the Mississippian period (ca. A.D. 1100 to 1300).

There are other soil marks on the air photos which clearly indicate that those lines tested are only a small portion of the many walls constructed at Cahokia.

Some of these appear to branch off from the palisade wall, and they may represent additions and modifications to the proven palisade. Other lines are parallel to and west of the mapped and excavated east wall. If these marks represent another palisade, the north-south line would have been near the present eastern edge of Monks Mound and the total area within this inner wall would probably have been about half that proposed for the tested palisade. As with the outer palisade, there is little or no evidence for a western half of the inner wall.

The inner line may represent an earlier palisade. If so, the central portion of Cahokia around Monks Mound may have been walled in several times. As the community grew in size, the central area was expanded. Areas outside the palisade in the earlier phases were incorporated into the palisaded area. For example, a house discovered in excavations east of Monks Mound was cut through and destroyed by the building of the outer palisade (Figure 9.3). The house may have been part of a residential area associated with, but outside of, the earlier inner stockade. Murdock Mound (55) presents a similar picture of changing use. In the time of the proposed inner wall, the Mound 55 area was residential. By the time this locality was surrounded by the outer stockade, the platform mound had been built.

Only future archaeological testing can substantiate, reject, or modify these hypotheses. There is no question that the central area of the Cahokia site was en-

Figure 9.3.   House 4 and the portion of the palisade that cuts across it. Source: Cahokia Mounds Museum, Illinois Historic Preservation Agency.

compassed by a great wall. The area included inside
this wall was highly important to the overall community, an area worthy of protection. The fact that there
may have been an earlier wall surrounding a smaller
area only emphasizes the point that this central precinct was highly significant throughout much of the
Mississippian occupation at Cahokia.

10

Downtown Cahokia and Its Satellites

To the modern visitor at the Cahokia Mounds State Historic Site, Monks Mound is the dominating feature and the central focus of the area. Its imposing size and central location draw one's interest and attention immediately. It must have also been so at the time of Cahokia's occupation by Native Americans. It was probably built in this central location and to its towering height exactly for the purpose of centering attention on it. Any consideration of the community organization at ancient Cahokia must take heed of this fact. Monks Mound and the area around it were the center of the community and undoubtedly the seat of control. Surrounding it were points of lesser focus, the residences of lesser functionaries, and the satellite communities they controlled.

DOWNTOWN CAHOKIA

The palisade at Cahokia enclosed an area of about 205 acres, which contained Monks Mound and 17 other mounds (Figure 10.1). It is obvious from the bastions, or watchtowers, that the palisade was for defensive purposes, but it also defined or delimited the central area of the Cahokia community. The area within the palisade undoubtedly was not only the seat of power but also the residential area for Cahokia's elite. This area has often been referred to by archaeologists working in the region as "downtown" Cahokia. Years ago, downtown Cahokia was thought of as the entire Cahokia site. This was based upon some suggestions by earlier investigators that the American Bottom was one large community. I prefer to retain this term only for the palisaded portion of Cahokia proper. It was surely

also the central city in the sense of being the focus of community activities.

The 17 mounds are located just inside the palisade in rows along the east and west walls. The two exceptions to this are Mounds 49 (Red Mound) and 56 (Jesse Ramey Mound). Red Mound is the only ridge-top mound inside the palisade. As noted previously, this mound is on the proposed north-south center line of the site. Mound 56 is centered between the east and west walls of the palisade. Both of these mounds are important in defining the main plaza of Cahokia.

A common characteristic of Mississippian sites in the southeastern United States at the time of European contact was a plaza that served as the central focus of the community. These plazas were surrounded by platform mounds supporting the important public buildings of the community and the residence of the ruling personage. An open area that may be such a plaza is south of Monks Mound (Figure 10.1). The north-south dimension of this plaza is the area between Monks Mound and the Jesse Ramey Mound (56), or about 300 meters (984 feet). The east-west limits are between the Persimmon Mound (51) and Mound 48, or about 400 meters (1,312 feet). This plaza appears to have been centered in the area included within the palisade. Very near the geometric center of the plaza is Red Mound (49). Red Mound may be a relict of an earlier era, perhaps a marker mound used in the early layout of the community. If so, it was also a marker for the center of the plaza in later eras.

Facing the north side of this plaza is Monks Mound. The south ramp on the first terrace more-or-less centers on the plaza. If this ramp was the stairway leading to the upper levels of Monks Mound, this would have been the major access from the plaza to the most important structure at Cahokia. The Jesse Ramey Mound (56) is centered along the southern edge of the

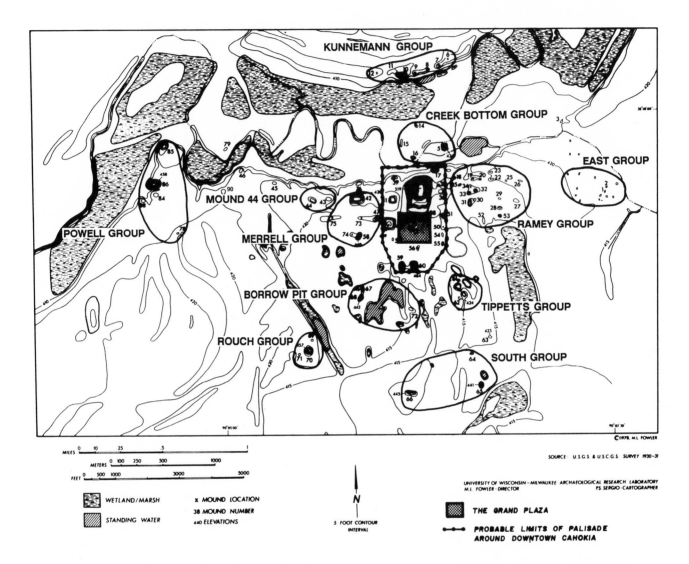

Figure 10.1.   Major subdivisions of the Cahokia site. The base map of mound distribution is the 1931 USGS compilation map. Not all mounds are shown because many of the smaller ones were not visible or identified when the survey was made. The following mounds are not shown: Kunnemann Group, Mound 89; East Group, Mounds 97-104; Creek Bottom Group, Mound 13; Tippetts Group, Mound 95; South Group, Mounds 82-83; Borrow Pit Group, Mounds 93-94, 96; Powell Group, Mound 87; Mound 44 Group, Mounds 91-92. The course of the palisade around downtown Cahokia is extrapolated from excavated portions and air photos.

plaza. A line through the center of the upper terraces of Monks Mound and the south ramp intersects the center of Mound 56. The contours of the Jesse Ramey Mound indicate that it was oriented with its long axis north-south. Surrounding this is a contour extending beyond the edges of the mound, which has its greatest extent to the north. This may represent a platform upon which Mound 56 was built or it may reflect a distribution of the mound material from cultivation. The orientation of this mound, and perhaps the foundation upon which it was built, was toward Monks Mound. These two great mounds face each other across the Grand Plaza of Cahokia.

The east side of the plaza is defined by four mounds just inside the palisade. At the northeast corner of the plaza is the Persimmon Mound (51). This is a platform mound. Its upper levels were hauled away for fill dirt before detailed study could be made, so its orientation is not clear. At the southeast corner of the plaza is the Murdock Mound (55). Excavated in 1941 by Harriet Smith (Smith 1969), its form and orientation have been reconstructed as a double-terrace mound facing to the west. Between 51 and 55 are two small mounds, 50 and 54, whose form and functions are not clearly definable. They may be examples of the conical dedicatory mounds described in Chapter 9, similar to Mound 77.

The west side of the proposed plaza is dominated by a large, square platform mound (48). Of the 18 mounds inside the palisade, only Monks Mound is larger. No excavations have been carried out on this mound, so we have no idea what type of building it supported or what activities were carried out on its surface. A line through its center and the long axis of Red Mound would bisect the plaza area. There is no doubt that Mound 48 would have dominated the west side of the Cahokia plaza. About 100 meters (328 feet) south of Mound 48 is Mound 57. This mound has been cultivated for many years so little can be said about its form. The 128-meter (419.9-foot) contour surrounds both of these mounds, which may indicate that they were associated on a platform.

On the basis of much the same data cited above, many earlier investigators have proposed this area as the great plaza of Cahokia. However, no excavations have been carried out to test this proposal. The plaza area was under cultivation for decades, and since the 1920s it has been park land. Therefore, it has not been possible to do surface surveys to see if there is any cultural debris in the area indicating past usage. However, the data described above and the placement of mounds are a good basis for proposing that the area described was the Grand Plaza of Cahokia and, as

such, was a major focal point of the greater Cahokia community.

Throughout the Cahokia site, there are at least nine examples of associations of conical mounds with platform mounds. The largest such pairing is Round Top (59) and Fox (60) mounds. Among the best preserved mounds at Cahokia, as they were probably never cultivated, the shapes of these mounds are very much as they were in Patrick's time and probably at the time of the Cahokia occupation. Fox Mound is a classic example of a platform mound, and Round Top is a classic conical. These two mounds are located just inside the southern edge of the palisade and to the south of Mound 56. They were both built on a single earthen platform. There is a slight ridge between the two, which may be artificial or it may be the fusing of the erosional slope wash of the two mounds. These two mounds are clearly associated. Fox Mound could have been a charnel-house mound, and Round Top its affiliated burial mound. I propose that these mounds represent the mortuary precinct for the leaders of Cahokia who lived on the other platform mounds within the palisaded area.

There are seven mounds within the palisade in the vicinity of Monks Mound. Along the west side of Monks Mound are Sawmill (39) as well as Mounds 77, 40, and 41. Mounds 39 and 41 are platform mounds, whereas 77 and 40 are small conical mounds. Mounds 77 and 39 are connected by a platform. There is a similar relationship between Mounds 40 and 41, but no platform has been demonstrated archaeologically. The pattern of these four mounds and their relationships to each other is nearly identical to the row of mounds—51, 50, 54, and 55—on the east side of the Grand Plaza.

Located approximately in the center of the area between the east side of Monks Mound and the northeast section of the palisade is Mound 36, a platform. The 1922 Goddard air photos clearly indicate that Mound 36 was a double-terrace mound. The higher terrace was on the south, and a narrower, lower terrace was along the entire northern edge. Connected to the northwest corner of Mound 36 is a small conical mound, 37. The location of these two mounds in the area east of Monks Mound is similar to the positioning of Mounds 48 and 57 on the west side of the Grand Plaza.

Mound 17, near the northeast corner of Monks Mound, is the only other mound within the palisade. This mound has no parallels at Cahokia. Patrick illustrated it as if it were two abutting but slightly offset platforms. The later USGS map (Figure 10.1) shows it as an oval mound with its long axis east-west. No excavations have been documented for this mound, and it has long since been plowed or eroded away. It must remain an enigma.

Analysis of the distribution of mounds and other features in downtown Cahokia provides a refinement of the proposal for community organization for this area. The palisaded area can be subdivided into three precincts:

1. The *Monks Mound Precinct* takes up the northern one-third of downtown Cahokia and is centered on Monks Mound. On the east side is a platform mound and its associated conical mound. On the west side is a row of four mounds, two platforms and two conicals.

2. Covering the central one-third of the palisaded area is the *Grand Plaza Precinct*. The focal area of this precinct is the Grand Plaza, with a ridge-top mound close to its center. Central to the west side of the plaza is a large platform mound. Fronting the east side of the plaza is a group of four mounds, two platforms and two conicals.

3. Composed of a platform mound and a conical mound built upon a large support platform, the *Mortuary Precinct* is in the southern portion of the central city of Cahokia. Even though there are other paired mounds within the palisade that may or may not include burials, I propose that the Mortuary Precinct is where the elite persons of Cahokia were buried. This is based upon the size and location of these mounds. No other paired mounds, either within or outside the palisade, are comparable to Fox and Round Top in size or in proximity to Monks Mound, the central focus of Cahokia.

Besides the residences of elite persons on the large platform mounds, there were probably other houses and associated buildings within the palisade. Excavation data indicate that the palisade cut through a residential area east of Monks Mound. This had apparently been a residential area throughout the prepalisade history of Cahokia. The palisade excavations, being limited to the area of the wall itself, do not tell us much about residential activity inside of and contemporary with the wall. Controlled surface collections within the eastern portion of the Monks Mound Precinct provided further data supporting this same sequence. The surface collections also provided evidence that there may have been a walled residential compound to the northeast of Mound 36.

Excavations in the Murdock Mound indicated a long period of use for this area. The earlier periods were residential, but later a platform mound was built over the locality. Harriet Smith (1969) interpreted this as a shift from an elite residential compound to what she labels a "temple" mound. Whether any building on top of Mound 55 was a temple or a residence is undeterminable.

Moorehead's map (1929:25-32) indicates "village site" locations for the areas southeast of Mound 36, between Mounds 51 and 50, and between Mounds 39 and 77. These were designated as village (that is, habitation), areas because of surface debris and test excavations. These areas are within the palisade. There were probably residential structures distributed along the east and west walls of the palisade. I do not imagine that there were residential structures within the Mortuary Precinct or adjacent to Monks Mound. These areas would have been too significant for residential use.

THE SUBURBS, SATELLITES, OR BARRIOS

Only 18 mounds were inside the palisade; the remaining 86 numbered mounds are scattered over the nearly 13 square kilometers (5 square miles) of area defined as the Cahokia site. The greatest number of them are within 1-kilometer (0.6-mile) radius of Monks Mound. Based on study of the various maps of Cahokia, the mounds appear to be distributed in clusters. Within the groups are usually both platform and conical mounds and, in some cases, ridge-top mounds. In certain instances the mounds are around open areas or plazas. I suggest that these discrete mound and plaza configurations represent subcommunities of Cahokia. These are the satellites of downtown Cahokia.

I have designated 11 clusters of mounds as representing separate subcommunities or suburbs (Figure 10.1). Some of these are designated as such because the mounds are around an open area suggesting a plaza. Others are indicated because they are obviously distinct from other groups, but they do not always manifest a plaza arrangement. These latter clusters are usually separated from others by some distance. The plaza-oriented groupings are found within 1 kilometer of downtown Cahokia. The separated mound clusters are at the margins of the site well beyond the 1-kilometer range. In effect these form concentric rings around the central city. One ring is close to central Cahokia. There appears to be empty space-at least few, if any, mounds-and then an outer ring of distinct subcommunities. The suburbs of Cahokia are about evenly divided between these two rings, with five in the outer circle and six in the inner ring. The discussion of these subcommunities deals first with the outer circle and then with the inner. The groups have been assigned numbers starting with the Kunnemann group on the north as Group I, proceeding clockwise around the outer circle, and then continuing with the inner circle.

I. Kunnemann or North Group

Composed of seven mounds (6, 7, 8, 9, 10/11, 12, and 89) linearly arranged along the north bank of Cahokia Creek, the Kunnemann group has been used to define the northern limits of the Cahokia site. In terms of the Cahokia grid coordinates, this group is found between N1215 to N1400 and W170 to E360. The largest mound of this group is Mound 10/11, which Patrick numbered as two mounds but which is more likely a two-terraced mound with the lower terrace (10) facing east. To the east of this large mound are two sets of paired mounds consisting of a platform and conical mound connected by a platform or causeway. About 280 meters (919 feet) north of Mound 10/11 is a small mound (89) near a borrow pit. This mound, unmentioned by Patrick or Moorehead, has been cultivated and its form is indistinct. Mound 12, about 200 meters (656 feet) west of Mound 10/11, was probably a conical mound but has been greatly plowed down. Titterington (1938:7) reported that a group of unfinished stone celts was found in this mound.

There is no indication of a plaza, unless the space between Mounds 10/11 and 89 is one. This lineal mound arrangement is somewhat unusual for Cahokia. There is surface evidence for a widespread distribution of habitation debris along the north bank of Cahokia Creek, which suggests that the Kunnemann suburb was much more extensive than just the area of the mounds. Differential distribution of special artifacts and other material gave rise to the hypothesis that the west area of the Kunnemann community was a shell-bead manufacturing area (Mason and Perino 1961).

II. East Group

Mound 1, on the west bank of Canteen Creek just below its juncture with Cahokia Creek, is usually considered the easternmost limit of the greater Cahokia site. This platform mound is just south of a small ridge-top mound (2). A group of mounds about 500 meters (1,640 feet) west of Mound 1 was identified from air photos (Mounds 97 to 104). Although traces of these mounds still exist, there is not sufficient evidence to determine their forms. The group may or may not be related to Mounds 1 and 2. However, I include them as part of this cluster for descriptive convenience. Further research may lead to better definition of the East group.

To the north-northwest of the East group is Mound 3. This mound has totally disappeared, and we have no data as to its form or function. It may relate to the Cahokia occupation or it may relate to an earlier period. At present, we cannot consider it effectively in discussing community organization at Cahokia.

III. Rattlesnake or South Group

At the south end of the area defined as the Cahokia site is the largest of the ridge-top mounds, the Rattlesnake Mound (66). At the western edge of Mound 66 are Mounds 82 and 83. These were apparently very small conical mounds, perhaps dedicatory mounds, although Moorehead's excavation into them did not produce evidence of burials. Air photographs show soil marks similar to these mounds completely around Mound 66. This large marker mound may have been surrounded by small dedicatory mounds similar to those mentioned inside the palisade.

In the vicinity of Mound 66 are two other fairly large mounds, another ridge-top (64) and a platform (65), located near a borrow pit. Moorehead shows three other mounds (63, 80, and 81) in this vicinity. However, details are lacking as to their form. The South group could be divided into two groups: IIIA, made up of Rattlesnake Mound and its associated dedicatory mounds, and IIIB, made up of Mounds 64 and 65 and the small mounds nearby. Neither of these subgroupings appears to be organized around a plaza. Rattlesnake Mound, and its associated dedicatory mounds, is such an unusual feature of the site due to its shape and positioning that it must be considered a special-function area. It may be a marker mound for the north-south axis of the site.

IV. Rouch Group

This group, composed of Mounds 69, 70, and 71, is isolated from the other groups; the nearest mounds are over 1 kilometer (0.6 miles) to the north and east. The largest mound (70) is a well-defined platform. North and west are small mounds of undefined form. Mound 70 is among the largest at the Cahokia site. It must have been the foundation for a fairly important structure. The group is located between grid coordinates S1100 to S1300 and W800 to W950.

V. Powell or West Group

The dominant feature of the West group is the Powell Mound (86). This large ridge-top is considered the marker mound for the western limit of the Cahokia site. There are two mounds (84 and 87) of indistinguishable form just south of the Powell Mound. To the west of 87 is Mound 88. About 350 meters (1,148 feet) north of Mound 86 is a large ridge-top mound (85). About 500 meters (1,640 feet) to the southeast of the Powell Mound is the Jondro Mound (78). Mounds 85 and 78 might well be considered as isolated mounds since they are so far away from the main Powell group. However, for the present I include them in the discussion of the West group.

There is little question that the focus of the West group is the Powell Mound. Excavations were carried out in the Powell Mound area during the construction of Interstate 55-70. Extensive habitation materials, including the entire range of time for Mississippian culture and its immediate predecessors, were forthcoming from that work (O'Brien 1972a, 1972b). The Powell group is concentrated between grid coordinates N50 to N250 and W2300 and W2450.

VI. Creek Bottom Group

This northernmost group of the inner circle is composed of five mounds (5, 13, 14, 15, and 16) enclosing an area that might have been a plaza. These mounds are located about 300 meters (984 feet) north of Monks Mound, between grid coordinates N470 to N725 and W20 to E500, in the bottoms of Cahokia Creek. Mound 5 is clearly distinguishable today due to its height of 6 meters (20 feet) or more. The other mounds are not very clear because they have been cultivated and nearly covered by the sediments left by extensive flooding. The surface on which these mounds were built is probably buried a meter or two below the present surface (Moorehead 1929:27). Proper archaeological testing might determine if these mounds, apparently built around a plaza, form a distinct group or subcommunity. Moorehead, based upon his study of McAdams's reports and his own experience, described the filling in of the creek bottoms and proposed a testing program as follows:

> [T]he drainage commission has had one or two deep canals dug through swamp lands north of Monks Mound. . . . The result is the gradual filling of Cahokia Creek and the lower portions of Canteen Creek. . . . In order to make a careful study of the village and

its relationship to the *first creek bed*, it is suggested that . . . a trench some three hundred feet in width be carried for a distance of one thousand feet (1929:27, emphasis added).

VII. Ramey Group

Just east of the palisade (S70 to N350 and E290 to E1100) is the largest cluster of mounds at the Cahokia site. This is referred to as the Ramey group after the family who owned much of central Cahokia before it became state property. This group is made up of 21 mounds surrounding an open area of about 4 hectares (10 acres); this open area is probably a plaza. The numerous mounds include many platforms and conicals and several examples of these in association. Some mounds within this group, including the James Ramey Mound (33) and Mound 34, have been excavated by Moorehead and others (Moorehead 1929:44-51; Griffin and Spaulding 1951; Perino 1957, 1959). Not much evidence has been accumulated on habitation areas associated with this group. If this is a unified group, that is if it represents a subcommunity, it is larger than many other Mississippian sites in the Midwest. It is certainly the largest, in terms of the number and variety of mounds and areal extent, of the subcommunities of greater Cahokia.

VIII. Tippetts Group

Perhaps the most unusual mound group in the inner ring is the Tippetts group just to the southeast of the Murdock Mound (55) and the southeast section of the palisade (S610 to S770, E50 to E670). This group is made up of Mounds 61, 62, and 95, all located on the banks of Borrow Pit 5-2. The mounds are a platform (61), a conical (62), and a ridge-top (95) forming an inverted L pattern, with 61 and 62 in a north-south alignment and 95 due east of 61. Patrick mapped a causeway connecting 61 and 62.

Extending northeast from Mound 62 is a peninsula into the borrow pit. This tongue of higher ground terminates in a square area with the sides oriented to the cardinal points. The square is about 35 meters (114.8 feet) on a side. The center of this square is at the geometric center of the Tippetts group. This peninsula is a deliberately constructed feature and served as the plaza for the Tippetts group. Both Moorehead and recent surveys suggest that there is extensive habitation to the north of the Tippetts group.

IX. Borrow Pit Group

Five mounds are located near the banks of the largest borrow pit (5-1) at Cahokia. There is no pattern to these mounds that suggests they represent a subcommunity of greater Cahokia. However, because of the special characteristics of some of the mounds in this group, it is possible that the area around the borrow pit and south of the stockade may have been a special-use area rather than a community per se. In this regard it might be compared to the Mortuary Precinct inside the palisade.

IXa. Mound 72 Group. One subgrouping of the borrow-pit mounds consists of Mounds 72 and 96. Mound 72 is a marker mound with commemorative burials within it. Mound 96 is a Tee mound associated with Mound 72. The post pits in Mound 72 and the placement of Mound 96 suggest that these two mounds may have been part of an early Woodhenge at Cahokia similar to those found by Wittry in Tract 15A. The ceramic data and radiocarbon dates indicate that Mound 72 was used for a short period of time at about A.D. 1000. There is a small mound (94) about 250 meters (820 feet) north of these two mounds that might be part of this complex.

IXb. Another subdivision of the Borrow Pit Group are three mounds to the west of Borrow Pit 5-1 (S650-775, W375-520). The two major mounds in this area are a conical (67) and an associated platform (68). These two mounds are on a north-south axis and appear to have been built on a connecting platform. There are nearly identical to but smaller than Fox (60) and Round Top (59). Mounds 67 and 68 are also probably representative of a charnel-house and burial-mound complex. Two hundred meters (656 feet) west of Mound 67 is Mound 93. The contours defining this mound are irregular but suggest that it may have been oriented with its long axis northeast-southwest. The relationship of Mound 93 to Mounds 67 and 68 and Borrow Pit 5-1 is very similar to the arrangement of mounds and borrow pit in the Tippetts group (VIII). This includes being built around a borrow pit.

X. Mound 44 Group

This group is composed of four mounds (43, 44, 91, and 92) around a small plaza in the area between grid coordinates N20 to N150 and W740 to W820. This is the smallest but probably the best defined of the proposed satellite communities. Mound 44 is the largest of the group and was a rectangular platform. The other three mounds are small and, due to continuous cultivation for over 150 years, are not well enough defined

to classify by shape. They surround a small open area about 70 meters (230 feet) square. A controlled surface collections was made of the Mound 44 area by archaeologists from Washington University of St Louis. The amount of material found between the mounds was much less than that found outside. This may indicate that this area was indeed a plaza and not used for habitation.

Moorehead, probably based upon surface materials, marked the area just east of Mound 43 as a "village"—habitation—area. Excavations just to the west of Mound 44 revealed extensive living areas representing much of the total time range of Cahokia (Vogel 1964a, 1964b, 1975; Wittry 1969; Wittry and Vogel 1962). A major find from those excavation was the Woodhenges. Wittry proposed that one of these circles of posts was covered over by the construction of Mound 44. However, some of the Woodhenges may have been contemporary with the Mound 44 group. Thus, Group X includes four mounds around a plaza, a habitation around this mound grouping, and sun calendars or Woodhenges.

XI. Merrell Group

The largest mound of this grouping is the Merrell Mound (42), a large rectangular platform; it is oriented with its long axis east-west and has a higher platform on its southwest corner. Over 150 meters (492 feet) south of the Merrell Mound is a large conical mound (58). Associated with Mound 58 is a smaller mound (74), which has been interpreted as either a small conical mound or a west platform extension of 58. Moorehead identified and numbered Mound 74, but he presented no strong data as to its form. Moorehead did state that Mound 58 was one of the "very large mounds of the group." Bisecting a line between Mounds 42 and 58 is an east-west axis defined by Mounds 75 and 47. Both of these mounds have been extensively cultivated so that appraisal of form is not possible. At the center of the area defined by Mounds 42, 47, 58, 74, and 75 is Mound 73. The formality of the arrangement of these five mounds and there alignments argue strongly for considering them as a group. To the north of the Merrell Mound is another small mound (76), which, because of its alignment with 42, 73, and 58, should be considered as part of this group.

Isolated Mounds

Several mounds at Cahokia cannot be directly associated with any of the defined groups. If they form any pattern, it is that they are located on the south bank of Cahokia Creek between downtown Cahokia and the Powell group. This is true of Mounds 45 and 46, which have long since been destroyed or buried under highway construction. These mounds are shown on both the Patrick map and the 1931 USGS plot on the banks of Cahokia Creek overlooking swampy bottomlands and meander channels of Cahokia Creek. Because no recorded excavation was done in the areas of these two mounds, little can be said about what they might have been.

A recently discovered and numbered mound (90) is also shown on the 1931 USGS map southwest of Mound 46 just on the bank of Cahokia Creek. Another mound which might be considered in this category is Mound 85, which has already been discussed under the Powell group. A similar context is noted for Mound 76, which, due to its proximity to and alignment with Mound 42, was included in the discussion of the Merrell group.

The location of these mounds (76, 45, 46, 90, and 85) at regular intervals along the south bank of Cahokia Creek is very similar to the situation mapped by Patrick between the Powell group at the western edge of the Cahokia site and the 40 or more mounds reported by Brackenridge in East St. Louis. The highest ridge of ground in the region is along the south bank of Cahokia Creek. This was undoubtedly the major pedestrian traffic route as Cahokia Creek was the most important water route. These isolated mounds may have served as monitoring points or way stations along these avenues leading to downtown Cahokia.

Another isolated mound is the Mackie Mound (79) located northwest of Mound 46 in the swampy bottoms of Cahokia Creek. This mound is unusual not only for its location but also for its Tee shape. The only other mounds in the Cahokia Creek bottoms are those in Group IV, the Creek Bottom group. These mounds may represent some occupation of the creek bottoms before siltation covered the area.

11

Cahokia Yesterday, Today, and Tomorrow

The large concentration of mounds at what is now known as Cahokia Mounds State Historic Site has been a place of unique importance for over a thousand years.

To the Native Americans who lived there around A.D. 1100, Cahokia was a booming, bustling center for tens of thousands of people. The city was organized around a very exclusive and impressive center. This center was screened off from the rest of the community by a large wall. Within this wall was the focal point of the community and countryside—a large earthen platform 100 feet high, Monks Mound. On the mound's summit was the largest building ever seen or heard about by the inhabitants. This large structure was probably the location of the palace or focus of power of the paramount ruler of ancient Cahokia. Inside the great wall were residences of lesser chiefs and other community leaders, an extensive plaza where public ceremonies and markets may have been held, and the burial temple and mound of this elite group. Outside the wall were smaller but significant communities. These suburbs contained peoples from different areas who had been drawn to Cahokia by its economic and political prowess.

There was nothing like Cahokia for hundreds of miles, and even then its rivals were but pale reflections. People from as far away as the banks of the Wisconsin River to the north and the Red River to the south, the southeastern edge of the Great Plains, the southern Appalachians, the Ohio River valley, and the upper reaches of the great Missouri River all came to Cahokia with their special goods to trade or to pay homage to the power and rulers of Cahokia.

By the time of the coming of Europeans to the Cahokia area, in the latter part of the seventeenth century, Cahokia was no longer the major center of Native American culture in the Midwest. The early French explorers such as Louis Jolliet made no mention of the site. It had apparently been abandoned some generations before, and the population and power scattered throughout the central Mississippi Valley and the lower Ohio River region. The French settlers of the American Bottom built a small chapel and trading post on Monks Mound, but the main focus of their settlement was at the towns of Cahokia and Prairie du Rocher in the southern part of the American Bottom. A small group of Indians lived around the chapel. The area we now know as Cahokia mounds, however, was of minor importance to the overall settlement of the countryside—it was but a small outpost on the northern frontier of the French community.

In the early years of the nineteenth century the Cahokia mounds were discovered by Euro-Americans. This was primarily the result of the investigations of Henry Brackenridge, who visited the area in 1811. His published notes and commentaries as well as his correspondence called attention to the mounds and the scattered debris attesting to the fact that this had once been the location of a populous community. Brackenridge was followed by many others, and during the 1800s there was an increasing number of visits to the site by travelers, artists, and scholars. It was a time of increasing awareness of North American scholars about the mounds. The only systematic investigations carried out were under the instigation of Dr. John J. R. Patrick, who, in the 1870s, made a detailed map of the locations, sizes, and shapes of 70 mounds in the Cahokia group, and who also mapped the mound groups in East St. Louis and Dupo, Illinois.

The nineteenth century is best characterized as the time of discovery and description at Cahokia. The twentieth century, on the other hand, has been the time of exploration and explanation.

In 1921 Warren K. Moorehead began the first intensive excavations at the Cahokia site. For a decade or more our understanding of the importance of Cahokia was based primarily upon his work. A significant turning point in archaeological research at Cahokia came in 1950 with foundation-supported, problem-oriented research directed by James B. Griffin. In the 1960s major salvage operations were carried out in conjunction with the construction of Federal Interstate Highways 55 and 70, which cut an east-west swath through the central axis of the archaeological zone just north of Monks Mound. This produced an incredible amount of controlled archaeological data. Never before or since had such a large area of the site been exposed to the scrutiny of skilled archaeologists. Much of our understanding of the nature of Cahokia today comes from these excavations.

This was followed in the late 1960s and the 1970s with National Science Foundation-supported research at Cahokia by archaeologists from the University of Wisconsin-Milwaukee. This project produced a detailed topographic map of the site, the first since Patrick's map of nearly a century earlier. Specific problem-oriented excavations were conducted, which provided information on site organization, social status, and the economic ties of Cahokia, and which added to the growing amount of data on the temporal periods and evolution of Cahokia as a prehistoric community.

Since 1950 many institutions have sponsored work at the Cahokia site. Archaeologists from the University of Illinois (both Urbana-Champaign and Chicago Circle), Washington University, the Illinois State Museum, Beloit College, the University of Wisconsin-Milwaukee, and Southern Illinois University (both Carbondale and Edwardsville) have all worked on major projects contributing to our understanding of Cahokia.

The result of all of this work is that the significance of Cahokia has been increasingly recognized by archaeologists, the public, and governmental agencies and administrators. In the 1990s we see the site very much as it was regarded in the eleventh and twelfth centuries: Cahokia is unique. There is nothing else like it, either in size or complexity, representing Native American achievements within the boundaries of the present United States. Cahokia is anthropologically significant because it presents a rare opportunity to understand how human societies developed complex civilizations in a part of the world where such complex societies were not previously thought to have developed.

The state of Illinois took cognizance of this increasing understanding beginning in the 1960s when a land acquisition program was begun; it has increased the size of the archaeological zone from a little more than 100 hundred acres to the nearly 3,000 acres of today. Further recognition by the state came in the building of the Interpretive Center, which makes it possible for the public to come to the site and see and learn about this unusual group of mounds.

National recognition of the Cahokia Mounds State Historic Site was formalized by nominating Cahokia Mounds to the National Register of Historic Places. International recognition of the areas is symbolized by the placing of Cahokia on the World Heritage Site list of UNESCO.

Cahokia stands today as the preeminent archaeological site within the United States. The importance Brackenridge hoped the people of St. Louis and the country would understand and accept has been achieved. This has taken over 160 years of increasingly intense investigation. In this book, I have sought to describe that work and the major features of the Cahokia Mounds State Historic Site. I have also sought to show something of our current understanding and interpretation of Cahokia.

These summaries and interpretations are not the final word on Cahokia. They should be considered only as shadowy outlines of a detailed and complex structure whose total understanding can only be achieved by research directed at specific questions. There are several such problems that come to mind when reviewing what we have learned until now about Cahokia.

First of all, our discussion of both the population size and the organization of prehistoric Cahokia is based upon the assumption that all of the site was inhabited at one time. This is necessary in order to look for patterns in the distribution of mounds and to make estimates of the order of magnitude of the population. There is evidence to support this assumption in that data representing all periods of occupation have been found in a majority of the areas excavated to date. However, techniques of research, both in the field and in the laboratory, should be developed to enhance our comprehension of this problem.

In terms of population size, more research should be undertaken on defining household or family residential units. Ethnographic accounts demonstrate that a household unit can be made up of several structures, including residences, kitchens, storehouses, and shrines. Most previous studies at Cahokia have assumed that each structure represents a residential unit. Definition of household units might be accomplished by examination of the distribution and associations of structural features and the types of artifacts and debris associated with structures. Such an analysis could be carried out with existing data, such as that from

Tracts 15A and B and the Interpretive Center Tract (e.g., Collins 1990; Pauketat 1991). Some analysis of this type is already in progress and promises to give interesting results. From these analyses should come new insights that will give focus to new excavations directed specifically to refining our understanding of households and the population of Cahokia.

The contemporaneity of the several structures within a household unit or compound should be no problem. Careful archaeological excavation, paying particular attention to living floors and association of materials with the structures, should be sufficient to infer contemporaneity. There are problems with some of the earlier excavated materials as these were recovered under less than ideal conditions. Later excavations have been able to apply more sensitive techniques and have greater resources available to do the job more thoroughly. Any new excavations at Cahokia should be undertaken only if the resources are available to apply the most scrupulous excavation and analytic methods.

A common approach to the question of contemporaneity has been the use of ceramic analysis, that is, dividing the time span of the site's occupation into units based upon stylistic and technical variation observable from potsherds. This method has been greatly improved over the years, and ceramic specialists working with data from Cahokia and surrounding sites have confidence in ceramic periods or phases of 50 years' duration. This is probably close enough for most problems of temporal association.

Ceramic manufacturing at Cahokia was probably an individual or family industry and not a standardized factory production. This is probably true whether the pots used at Cahokia were actually made there or at some smaller town or village some distance away. New ceramic studies to find idiosyncratic features should be conducted. Attention should be paid to special clays used in manufacture, individual variation of style and form, and other factors that might be "trademarks" of the potters. Identifying such idiosyncratic vessels in different structures might provide the best possible data for dealing with contemporaneity. At present, studies of this type have not been made. There is, however, a large enough corpus of data now available for them to begin.

I proposed in Chapters 9 and 10 that Cahokia was organized as a walled central city with suburbs or smaller individual communities surrounding the center. There are several problems that need to be solved taking this model or hypothesis of community plan as a starting point.

First, how many of the mounds were in use at approximately the same time? I have often thought that this problem might be solved by excavating test trenches into the edges of mounds. These trenches would have to extend into the mound far enough to get past the wash or recent erosional fill around the base in order to identify at least the earliest surface of the mound, and they would have to be deep enough to find the surface upon which the mound was built. Materials from this premound surface should help to fix the time period when the mound was begun. Another small trench could be dug on the top of the mound to locate its latest preserved surface. Materials collected from the premound surface and the upper surface could be compared to give an indication of the time span included in the mound's history. A series of mounds could be tested in this way to develop a better understanding of contemporaneity. Productive data could be gained from relatively small excavations so that the main portions of each of the mounds tested would be undisturbed.

Data along these lines could also be gathered from mounds already excavated. For example, within the palisaded portion of Cahokia, excavations have been made into Monks Mound, Mound 51, Mound 55, and Mound 56. The first three of these have been at least partially published and summaries can be made from the data about the span of time covered and contemporaneity. Mound 56 was trenched by Moorehead but the data from it is not well described in the literature. Why not reopen Moorehead's excavation trench and examine the profiles to collect whatever data could be gleaned? The other mounds within the palisade could be tested as described above. All these data taken together should tell us a great deal about not only the contemporaneity of mound construction but also changing land use within the most important part of the Cahokia site.

Another approach to examining the problem of how much of the Cahokia site was occupied at one time would be in the application of current site surveying and systematic sampling techniques. Within the past decade techniques for examining archaeological sites on the basis of surface-material distribution have been greatly refined. Shovel testing, statistically valid sampling strategies, and electromagnetic surveys have all been applied successfully to these archaeological problems.

The first controlled surface collections at the Cahokia site were carried out in 1967 in the Ramey Field area just east of Monks Mound. Further controlled surface collections were made in the Mound 44 plaza and the Dunham Tract west of Monks Mound (Bareis 1967a; Benchley 1981; Vander Leest 1980). These surveys provided interesting information on the period of occupancy of these areas, and the distributions of artifacts allowed interpretation of residential patterns. When compared with the data recovered from large excavations such as those in Tract 15A, Tract 15B, and the Interpretive Center Tract, highly important conclusions can be reached about the nature of and contemporaneity of the greater Cahokia community.

To make such a study feasible for Cahokia as a whole, the overall site needs to be broken into manageable units or strata. In this book I have proposed that the Cahokia site was subdivided into several subcommunities. These smaller units could be used as strata for examining the entire site. Each proposed subcommunity could be set up in a grid of small, collectible units. It would not be economically feasible to collect 100 percent of these units, so a statistically significant sample would be randomly selected for collection. Those units selected would need to be plowed to expose the artifacts that might be present, and within each unit all visible cultural materials would be collected.

Electromagnetic surveys could also be made of these subcommunities to determine the dimensions of mounds and perhaps to map below-surface features. A further aspect of this type of project would be the collating and analysis of all of the data pertaining to the analytical area from previous excavations and studies.

These data, taken together with the controlled surface collections, would make it possible to make several statements about the subcommunities. First of all, some knowledge of their extent and organization would be gained. Second, information would be forthcoming on the temporal span of the area tested. Third, comparisons could be made between the site divisions to gain a fuller picture of the overall site extent and dating.

The approaches proposed above are all largely "noninvasive" in terms of their impact on the site. Investigations involving excavation would be left to a later phase of examining the site. Problems appropriate to excavation would undoubtedly be defined in the carrying out of the above program of research. This project would certainly be a long-term one requiring a lot of time and personnel to accomplish and would perhaps be best handled in segments. The results, however, would be rewarding in terms of our increased understanding of the nature of Cahokia. They would provide a corpus of information upon which plans for the future development of the site could be made. And, as mentioned above, the information would define more meaningful research problems for future investigations.

Many other approaches to the future of Cahokia research could be defined. Those briefly outlined are an outcome of my particular approach and interests in attempting to understand Cahokia as a community. They are, to me, a logical result of the preparation of this atlas and the history of the Cahokia site. Other equally important topics could be developed based upon different perspectives. These I leave to other investigators to propose. However, the future of archaeological research at Cahokia will depend upon the interaction of persons of differing perspectives working together to ultimately bring about a detailed understanding of the people of Cahokia and their accomplishments.

Archaeologists have been intrigued by Cahokia from the days of Brackenridge to the present, but they have not always had great success in communicating this interest to the public. Brackenridge lamented:

> [After] . . . I examined . . . [Monks Mound] . . . in 1811, . . . I . . . published an account in the newspapers of St. Louis, detailing its dimensions, describing its form, position &c. but this, which I . . . considered a discovery, attracted no notice (1813:155).

In time, the Cahokia site became fairly well known among scholars at Harvard University, the Bureau of American Ethnology, and a few other public and private institutions. Some attempts were made to interest the public and politicians in recognizing Cahokia and establishing it as a public park. Noteworthy in these efforts was John Francis Snyder, who, from the mid-1800s to the early 1900s, was particularly active in this mission. It was not until Moorehead's work of the 1920s, however, that some measurable success was accomplished. At that time the state of Illinois purchased Monks Mound and the area immediately around it for a park.

A one-room museum was established in the park headquarters building near the southwest corner of Monks Mound. This museum was largely only shelves with artifacts that may or may not have related to Cahokia. In the early 1960s this museum was improved under the direction of the Illinois Department of Conservation. By 1970 the Illinois State Museum entered into an agreement with the Department of Conservation to take over the interpretive program for Cahokia. James Anderson was hired as the interpreter and William Iseminger as his assistant. From that time on the presentation of Cahokia to the public has vastly improved. New exhibits were prepared for the museum, which by this time had been expanded into the entire structure, and programs of public lectures and school tours increased. Later the interpretive program reverted to the Department of Conservation. And recently Cahokia Mounds State Historic Site has come under the aegis of the Illinois Historic Preservation Agency.

Tremendous improvements have been made at Cahokia in the past two decades. Hundreds of acres of ground have been purchased to expand the site and preserve most of the remaining mounds. Modern subdivisions have been removed from the center of the site. Landscaping has greatly improved the area so that it is now possible to see well-kept mounds and site areas, and the maintenance and interpretive staff has been expanded.

Many years of effort by scholars, governmental agencies and officials, and the increasingly active public culminated in the building of the Interpretive Center and the installation of up-to-date, state-of-the-art exhibits to tell the history of Cahokia. This facility makes it possible for the first time to adequately present to the public the Cahokia story. Groups and individuals can come to the site and see and understand the complexity and grandeur of this unusual Native American experiment.

In the exhibits, lectures, and the well-groomed mounds and other features, the visionary concepts of Brackenridge and other early explorers are being fulfilled. This is the result of the work of Patrick, Snyder, Bushnell, Moorehead, Titterington, Griffin, and of the many investigators who have worked at Cahokia in the past 30 years. The foundations have been put in place. The future of Cahokia is assured as the preeminent archaeological site in the United States of America. Future generations of archaeologists and laypersons will build on these foundations and contribute wisely and with greater understanding to approximate the grandeur that was Cahokia a thousand years ago.

APPENDIX 1

RADIOCARBON DATING

Almost every project at Cahokia has collected carbonized material and submitted samples for C-14 assay. From this has come a corpus of data relative to the time over which Cahokia was occupied and when certain areas were occupied in relationship to other sections of the site. Table A1.2 lists all of the dates available to this author either through publications or communications from specific investigators. The table is organized by listing the dates by areas of the site and then chronologically within each area. The first dates for each site area are the closest to the present. The areas of the site are listed in the following sequence:

Monks Mound
Powell Tract
Tract 15A
Tract 15B
Merrell Tract
Ramey Field - Stockade
South Stockade
Ramey Field - Mound 34
Mound 72
Mound 51
Mound 55
Interpretive Center Tract (ICT)
Airport Area

LIMITATIONS

There are many problems and limitations in using raw radiocarbon dates without careful consideration of the context from which the samples came, possible sources of alteration or contamination of the organic material, and atmospheric and chemical factors involved in the production of radioactive isotopes of carbon. In consideration of the problem of context, I have resolved it by accepting the statement of the investigator who collected the sample. The samples were selected and submitted because they came from well-documented contexts. Another assumption which I have made is that there were no contaminants in the sample either from the period of time the carbonized material was lying in the earth or introduced in handling the sample.

Recent research has demonstrated that there has been variation in the amount of radioactive carbon in the atmosphere through time. Various programs have been designed to calibrate the raw radiocarbon data in terms of this variation. These programs compensate for the difference in radiocarbon years and sidereal or calendar time. I have not applied this calibration to the Cahokia radiocarbon data set, as I want to present the raw information. My concern is in the broad temporal patterns. For those concerns the uncalibrated assays are sufficient.

Another problem is in the use of carbonized grass, nuts, and seeds rather than wood samples. One must take into consideration the process of isotopic fractionation in dealing with these types of samples. In this listing, I have relied upon the excellent analysis done by Donald Blakeslee (Blakeslee n.d.) and have used his dates corrected for isotopic fractionation, such as those from the pit underneath Mound 51. There are some other samples where correction for isotopic fractionation might have been useful but was not applied. This is particularly true of one sample (GX 860A and 860B) of carbonized material from inside a pot found in a burned structure cut by the palisade. These dates came out much too early for the associated materials and the other dates from these same contexts. However, since it is not really known what the carbonized material was, perhaps maize processed with lime, there is no way of manipulating these dates. Although they are listed in the table, they should not be used in analysis.

It is probable that the Cahokians reused logs and poles in rebuilding structures. It is also probable that they burned wood salvaged from earlier constructions. Thus, even taking a sample from a burned beam of a structure or charcoal from a well-defined fire place might yield a C-14 assay not in congruence with the associated ceramic materials. This may well be the case with the dates from the ICT area, where "only a few of the thirteen radiocarbon assays were judged reliable" (George Holley, personal communication, 1988).

Some of the carbonized wood samples submitted for radiocarbon assay from the ICT were cedar. This is a material that resists decay and therefore lasts a long time in a structure and could be reused many times. The radiocarbon date tells us when the cedar tree was cut, not necessarily when it was last used. One of the samples from Mound 72 (W 575) was from a cedar pole that was part of the stretcher on which a body was carried to the burial site. The date from this assay was closer to the expectations. It is probable that this was not a recycled pole but one prepared for this special event.

Another aspect of cedar is that it is slow growing and long lived. A small piece of cedar, such as charcoal from a fire, might be from the inner growth rings, which could be hundreds of years older than the outer growth rings. An example of this is the assays run on inner and outer growth rings from a bald cypress log containing 191 growth rings found at the Mitchell site:

Inner three rings: (W 229) 1110 ± 60 B.P.
Inner three rings: (TX 198) 990 ± 90 B.P.
Between (?) inner and outer rings: (M 1305) 1000 ± 75 B.P.
Outer three rings: (W 220) 900 ± 55 B.P.

The Texas date (TX 198) is not in agreement with the Wisconsin Laboratory date (W 229) on the same growth rings. The other dates, however, are consistent. The assays on the inner and outer growth rings indicate a life of the tree of about 210 years, which is strikingly close to the 191 growth rings counted.

With these reservations in mind, how does one consider radiocarbon dates? If they are to be considered as precise "dates," then a variety of atmospheric, chemical, and taphonomic factors have to be taken into consideration. Some of these problems are manageable while others are not. If one is more concerned about relative time and general indications of when areas were subject to human activity, then a less specific approach can be taken. When a large body of radiocarbon assays are available for a given site, the distribution of these through radiocarbon time can give a good assessment of the length of time a site was oc-

cupied and when the peak of this occupation took place. Given the distribution of the assays over the site geographically, then dates from the different areas can be considered indicative of the portion of time that those areas were used. The concern of this analysis is with the general temporal and spatial picture of Cahokia and not specific, fine-tuned chronological problems.

CAHOKIA DATES AND PERIODS OF OCCUPATION

At the present time, 95 radiocarbon assays have been run on samples submitted from the Cahokia site. These are from wide areas of the site and thus represent a fair geographic distribution. However, their collection was more opportunistic than planned in terms of an adequate sampling strategy. They were not collected as part of an overall plan to provide dates from the various areas of the site, but instead represent samples from numerous salvage and research projects obtained to date specific features and archaeological phases.

When all radiocarbon assays from Cahokia are plotted (Figure A1.1), nearly half of the dates (n = 45, 47%) fall between A.D. 950 and 1150 (A.D. 900-1300: n = 75, 79%). One quarter (n = 24, 25%) fall between A.D. 1050 and 1150. The implication of this is that the most intense occupation of the Cahokia site was from A.D. 900 to 1300, with the century from A.D. 1050 to 1150 being the peak. These dates probably represent the Mississippian culture at Cahokia. There are several (14) radiocarbon assays from Cahokia falling before A.D. 900. There is a significant decrease in these. The earliest ones plotted on the graph, between A.D. 600 and 700, are aberrant dates, two of which came from the material inside the pot from House 4 (GX 860A and 860B) and should probably be eliminated from consideration. There are a few dates (four) from Cahokia that fall between A.D. 1300 and 1500.

These dates can be used to divide the Cahokia occupation into three temporal eras (Table A1.1). Era I, between A.D. 700-900, represents the gradual increase in the use of the Cahokia site by Late Woodland and Emergent Mississippian peoples. There is indication of an increasing, but modest, intensity of the use of the Cahokia area. In Era IIa, A.D. 900-1000, there is a dramatic, if not sudden, increase in the use of Cahokia. This reaches its peak between A.D. 1000 and 1100, Era

TABLE A1.1.

Eras of Utilization of Cahokia site Areas and Mounds

Years A.D.	Era	Habitation areas	Palisade	Mounds
850				
	I	Powell Tract Merrell Tract Tract 15A Interpretive Center Tract		pre-Monks Mound
950				
	IIa	Powell Tract Tract 15A Interpretive Center Tract	pre-Palisade	Monks Mound Mound 72 Mound 34 ?
1050				
	IIb	Tract 15A Merrell Tract Tract 15B	pre-Palisade	Monks Mound Mound 72 Mound 34? pre-Mound 51
1150				
	IIc	Tract 15A Tract 15B Airport	Palisade	Monks Mound Mound 34 Mound 51
1300				
	III	Tract 15B		post-Monks Mound Mound 55 ? Mound 34 ?
1500				

IIb. In Era IIc, A.D. 1100-1300, there appears to have been a decrease. Era II, in these terms, is the height of Mississippian occupation. After 1300, Era III, there is a sharp decline in radiocarbon dates and the inferred density of occupation of the site. Era III is the time of the Late Mississippian use of the area.

MONKS MOUND

Assays of radiocarbon come from different areas of Monks Mound and from different contexts (see Table A1.2), including stages in the building of Monks Mound and data from before and after its construction. These dates give a good indication of the time in which Monks Mound was built. However, they do not give an indication of the intensity of activity. The bulk of the assays come from the final surfaces or terraces that were built, because these are the most available for archaeological investigation. The fact that nearly two-thirds (n = 11) of all the dates (n = 17) fall between A.D. 1000 and 1300 and that only five assays are earlier only indicates where the most intensive excavations were carried out. The dates do, however, give a representative picture of when the mound was built.

The total range of time indicated for Monks Mound itself is from A.D. 900 to 1300 or Era II (Table A1.1). There is one date (W 587) from the east lobes area that is earlier, but this is from a pre-Mississippian strata pertaining to Era I. The date (I 2308) obtained from coring on what appears to be an early stage of Monks Mound suggests that mound construction was begun in Era IIa between A.D. 900-1000. The dates from the fourth terrace indicate Era IIb, A.D. 1000-1100, and the dates on the first terrace, Era IIc, A.D. 1100-1300. It is probably not parsimonious to use the assays in this way to indicate specific ages for specific feature construction. At present, the radiocarbon dates from Monks Mound do indicate when it was begun (ca. A.D. 900), and when it was completed in the form we know it today (no later than A.D. 1300).

OTHER MOUNDS

Radiocarbon assays were determined for several other mounds at Cahokia. The most tightly controlled samples came from Mound 72. All of these are from specific feature contexts either from before mound construction or during the building of the final mound.

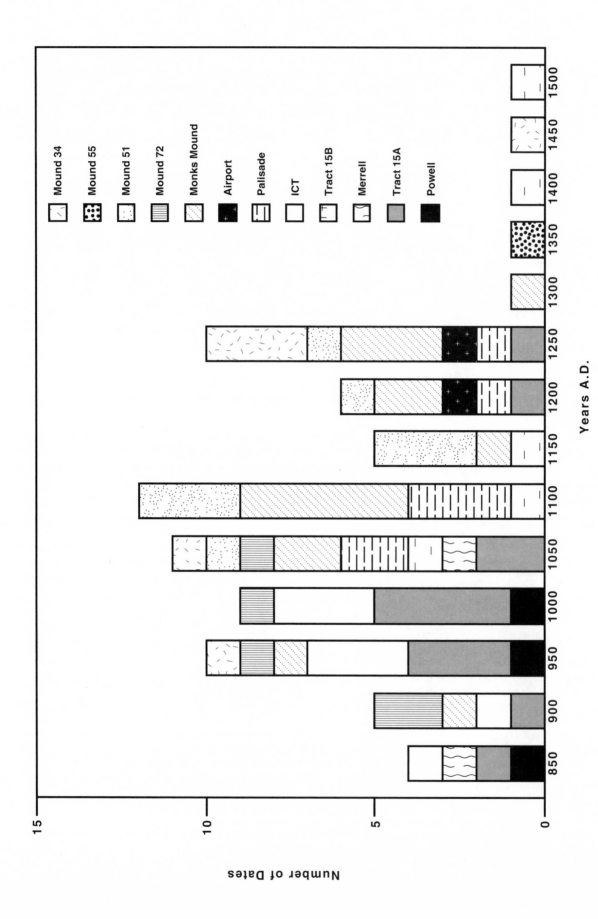

Figure A1.1. Cahokia radiocarbon dates.

The results of the radiocarbon assays are also tightly clustered. The activities of Mound 72 were confined to Era IIa, or between A.D. 950 and 1050.

Another mound with dates from a premound context is Mound 51. The bulk of the samples assayed came from fill of a large borrow pit dug out and refilled before the mound was constructed. This fill material could have been brought from wide areas of the site or could have been already-mixed debris. However, the pit was probably filled in rapidly to prepare the area for the building of the mound. The assays range from about A.D. 800 to ca. A.D. 1300. The largest number of the dates fall between A.D. 1050 and A.D. 1299. On the basis of this, I would suggest that Mound 51 was built after A.D. 1200, perhaps during Era IIc, and that most of the assays indicate use of the area in the eleventh and twelfth centuries A.D. and earlier for nonmound activities.

One radiocarbon assay was derived from Mound 55 (M 1290). This was from charcoal that had apparently eroded down from the final structure on top of the mound. Thus the date of about A.D. 1350 may indicate the final use of the mound in the early part of Era III. There was a detailed sequence of structures and other habitation activity under Mound 55, but unfortunately no C-14 dates were obtained from those levels. However, it appears that there was use of the Mound 55 area contemporary with pre-Mound 51 activity and preceding the construction of Mound 55.

Several samples were collected in the vicinity of Mound 34. Most of these were from contexts around and near Mound 34. The assays range in time from ca. A.D. 1000 to after A.D. 1400. Many of the samples were run with the solid carbon method and others were not corrected for fractionation. Because of this and the uncertainties regarding the contexts, it is difficult to make even general statements about the time period of Mound 34. It seems probable, however, that the area was being used as early as A.D. 1000 and later than A.D. 1300, that is during Era II. Mound 34 itself may have been built after A.D. 1200, but this is only surmise.

period preceding the construction of the wall when the area was used for residential construction. These dates range from A.D. 1050 to A.D. 1150, or Era IIb.

Only one date was determined for a post in the stockade itself (W 444). This was from the latest wall in the sequence and dated to A.D. 1200, or during Era IIc. There is no indication of whether this sample came from inner or outer rings of the post. It is of course possible that the outer rings were missing and the actual cutting of the tree was later than this date indicates. Another late date (W 359) of about A.D. 1250 was obtained from the stockade area. These later dates are certainly consistent with the dates on the prepalisade habitation areas. The palisade construction must therefore have began as late as or later than A.D. 1150, or Era IIc.

HABITATION OR RESIDENTIAL AREAS

The Powell Tract and Tracts 15A and 15B were excavated in conjunction with highway construction. The ICT was excavated in preparation for construction of the new interpretive center. The Merrell Tract was excavated to test some hypotheses that developed out of the Tract 15B excavations. The Airport data came from a small salvage project preparing for some additions to the Collinsville Airport. With the exceptions of the ICT and the Airport, all of these areas are in the western half of the Cahokia site, so data on nonmound use of the Cahokia site is skewed to the western portions. Other limited data on habitation comes from excavation of premound surfaces, such as the east lobes area of Monks Mound and under Mound 55, as well as from the structures that were disturbed by construction of the palisade.

THE PALISADE

Most of the radiocarbon assays pertaining to the palisade came from features, both wall-trench and single-post houses, which were cut through by the palisade trenches. Therefore, these dates indicate the

TABLE A1.2.

Cahokia Radiocarbon Dates by Area of Site and Chronological Order[a]

Lab no.	Site area	Years B.P.	Years A.D.	Comments
WIS 586	Monks Mound East lobes	640 ± 55	1310	N168.9
WIS 443	Monks Mound First terrace	670 ± 55	1280	Feature 113. Post No.1 Centered at N72.23E103.19 Below platform mound.
M 1637	Monks Mound West edge	670 ± 100	1280	Late Mississippian walltrench house on top of slope wash from Monks Mound.
WIS 362	Monks Mound First terrace	690 ± 50	1260	Burned floor. Below platform mound.
WIS 549	Monks Mound First terrace	720 ± 55	1230	Burned wood in matrix of ash from burned basin. Feature 149 predates primary mound. N78-80 E100-101
WIS 545	Monks Mound First terrace	740 ± 55	1210	Charcoal from Fea. 139. Burned building on top of platform mound. Burned post.
I 2947	Monks Mound First terrace	760 ± 95	1190	Fill above primary mound. Date corrected 422 years for fractionation (4.25 factor). (Blakeslee n.d.:Table 8)
WIS 546	Monks Mound First terrace	805 ± 60	1145	Log 24 lying on floor of Fea. 113. Large burned building.
WIS 547	Monks Mound First terrace	825 ± 60	1125	Log 1 lying on burned floor of Feature 114. Burned building under primary mound.
M 1636	Monks Mound Fourth terrace	840 ± 150	1110	
WIS 365	Monks Mound First terrace	840 ± 55	1110	Post 2 of burned structure.
M 982	Monks Mound First terrace	850 ± 100	1100	Below primary mound.
W 525	Monks Mound Fourth terrace	879 ± 55	1071	
W 527	Monks Mound Fourth terrace	890 ± 60	1060	
W 970	Monks Mound Fourth terrace	970 ± 65	980	
I 2308	Monks Mound ISM core	1020 ± 100	930	Sample from coring Monks Mound - 29 feet above basal coring sediments. First stage of Mound construction (?).
I 2309	Monks Mound ISM core	1110 ± 70	840	Precedes Monks Mound. Late Woodland occupation.
WIS 587	Monks Mound East lobes	1150 ± 60	800	Burnt thatch layer with ash lenses interspersed. East lobes N150-152.
ISGS 140	Powell Tract	950 ± 75	1000	Period III. Fea. 331.
ISGS 130	Powell Tract	950 ± 75	1000	Period III. Fea. 331.
WIS 58	Powell Tract	1000 ± 65	950	Period IV. Fea. 227. Date suggested as ca. 300 years early (Blakeslee n.d.:Table 2).
M 1292	Powell Tract	1055 ± 75	895	Period III. Fea. 234.
M 1294	Powell Tract	1125 ± 75	825	Period V. Fea. 217.

Lab no.	Site area	Years B.P.	Years A.D.	Comments
ISGS 163	Powell Tract	1170 ± 80	780	Period V. Fea. 198.
M 1293	Powell Tract	1190 ± 75	760	Period IV. Fea 227. Dates seem too early.
ISGS 131	Powell Tract	1200 ± 150	750	Period III. Fea. 331. Carbonized corn. Correction of 420 years added (Blakeslee n.d.:Table 2).
M 1295	Powell Tract	1915 ± 150	35	Unassociated material
M 1339	Tract 15A	685 ± 100	1265	House 35.
M 1338	Tract 15A	725 ± 100	1225	House 32 east of Circle 2. Intrudes into Circle 1 post pit 112. Therefore must date later than Circle 1.
I 2069	Tract 15A	875 ± 105	1075	Pit feature 153. Mississippian refuse pit.
I 2071	Tract 15A	890 ± 135	1060	Features 371 and 369. Mississippian refuse pits.
M 1337	Tract 15A	905 ± 100	1045	House 2. Wall-trench structure associated with Ramey Incised ceramics.
M 1341	Tract 15A	905 ± 120	1045	Features 174 and 369. Posts from Woodhenge.
I 2012	Tract 15A	910 ± 100	1040	Southeast of Circle 2. Woodland refuse pit.
I 2013	Tract 15A	920 ± 100	1030	Pit Feature 297.
I 2016	Tract 15A	980 ± 90	970	Feature 338. Mississippian refuse pit inside Circle 2.
I 2070	Tract 15A	990 ± 135	960	Feature 368. Mississippian refuse pit.
I 2014	Tract 15A	1000 ± 100	950	Feature 289. Mississippian refuse pit.
M 1340	Tract 15A	1025 ± 110	925	Floor of house 74. Single post construction.
I 2015	Tract 15A	1060 ± 90	890	Feature 108. Mississippian wall-trench structure.
M 1334	Tract 15B	385 ± 90	1565	Feature 59. Sand Prairie phase structure.
M 1332	Tract 15B	515 ± 100	1435	Feature 43. Sand Prairie phase structure.
M 1335	Tract 15B	765 ± 200	1185	Feature 77. Acculturated Late Woodland (?).
M 1333	Tract 15B	825 ± 100	1125	Feature 44. Acculturated Late Woodland (?).
M 1336	Tract 15B	885 ± 200	1065	Feature 113. Acculturated Late Woodland (?).
ISGS 276	Merrell Tract	855 ± 75	1095	Feature 306 C. Early Fairmount.
ISGS 281	Merrell Tract	1085 ± 75	865	Feature 306. Early Fairmount.
ISGS 283	Merrell Tract	1220 ± 75	730	Feature 306. Floor. Early Fairmount.
WIS 359	Ramey Field	690 ± 55	1260	Stockade. E461.64-461.70 N336.80. 40-80 cms below surface.
WIS 444	Ramey Field	750 ± 55	1200	Feature 28. Burned post. E461.80-461.87.
WIS 493	Ramey Field	810 ± 45	1140	House 4. Support beam. N315.38-315.48.
GX 859	Ramey Field	815 ± 85	1135	Charcoal. E461-462 N277- 279. House feature previous to palisade construction.
WIS 495	Ramey Field	850 ± 50	1100	House 4. Timber on floor. N315.80-215.90.
WIS 494	Ramey Field	900 ± 55	1050	Structural timber.
GX 860A	Ramey Field	1310 ± 65	640	House 4. Carbonized material from inside vessel 2. Too early. Treated with hot dilute HCL and NaOH.
GX 860B	Ramey Field	1350 ± 85	600	House 4. Too early.

Lab no.	Site area	Years B.P.	Years A.D.	Comments
WIS 366	South Stockade	890 ± 55	1060	South Stockade area southeast of Fox Mound. 100 cm below surface.
M 672	Ramey Field	480 ± 200	1470	Same context as M 670. Date more recent than expected.
M 636	Ramey Field	660 ± 200	1290	Sample "should date with Mound 34 in time" (Crane and Griffin 1959:181).
M 670	Ramey Field	960 ± 250	990	Associated material identified as Trappist complex. Date much too old for associated material.
M 635	Ramey Field	670 ± 200	1280	Carbon from "ceremonial fire" next to ramp on west side of Mound 34. (Crane and Griffin 1959:81).
M 33A	Ramey Field	700 ± 300	1250	Charred plant material from pit under mound 34. Solid carbon method.
M 33B	Ramey Field	900 ± 300	1050	Same as M 33 A.
WIS 492	Mound 72	900 ± 45	1050	Feature 227. Central midden.
WIS 575	Mound 72	920 ± 60	1030	Fea. 229. Portion of cedar litter pole from burial #210. S865-865.3.
WIS 293	Mound 72	970 ± 50	980	Feature 1. Cribbing Log B materials from bottom of post pit. S865-E.83.5.
WIS 447	Mound 72	1015 ± 60	935	Feature 205. North midden
WIS 29	Mound 72	1020 ± 55	930	Feature 1. Cribbing log A from bottom of post pit.
W 355	Mound 51	680 ± 60	1270	Deer bone - corrected for fractionation Stratum G.
W 350	Mound 51	750 ± 50	1200	Deer bone - corrected for fractionation. Stratum E.
I 2573	Mound 51	760 ± 95	1190	Charred thatch - corrected for fractionation. Stratum F.
W 351	Mound 51	780 ± 60	1170	Deer bone - corrected for fractionation. Stratum F.
W 352	Mound 51	800 ± 65	1150	Deer bone - corrected for fractionation. Stratum H.
W 356	Mound 51	810 ± 50	1140	Deer bone - corrected for fractionation. Stratum D 1.
W 360	Mound 51	815 ± 60	1135	Deer bone - corrected for fractionation. Stratum D 2.
W 391	Mound 51	850 ± 65	1100	Nut hull - corrected for fractionation. Stratum D 2.
W 390	Mound 51	890 ± 65	1060	Nut hull - corrected for fractionation. Stratum G.
W 389	Mound 51	900 ± 50	1050	Nut hull - corrected for fractionation. Stratum H.
M 1784	Mound 51	910 ± 110	1040	Charred thatch - corrected for fractionation. Outside pit.
GX 950	Mound 51	1145 ± 65	805	Charred thatch - Corrected for fractionation. Stratum F. Out of line with other dates and stratigraphy.
M 1290	Mound 55	600 ± 75	1350	Debris washed down from last "temple" on mound.
B 19491	Interpretive Center Tract	800 ± 80	1150	Moorehead phase.
B 19484	Interpretive Center Tract	930 ± 80	1020	Late Stirling phase. Date seems too early for ceramic phase associations.
B 19478	Interpretive Center Tract	940 ± 80	1010	Late Stirling phase. Date seems to early for ceramic phase associations.
B 19480	Interpretive Center Tract	950 ± 60	1000	Late Stirling phase.
B 19473	Interpretive Center Tract	960 ± 100	990	Lohmann phase.
B 19485	Interpretive Center Tract	960 ± 60	990	Lohmann phase.
B 19474	Interpretive Center Tract	970 ± 60	980	Lohmann phase.

Lab no.	Site area	Years B.P.	Years A.D.	Comments
B 19490	Interpretive Center Tract	1010 ± 60	940	Moorehead phase. Date seems too early for ceramic phase associations.
B 19474	Interpretive Center Tract	1030 ± 70	920	Late Stirling phase.
B 19487	Interpretive Center Tract	1050 ± 70	900	Early Stirling phase. Date seems too early for ceramic phase associations.
B 19492	Interpretive Center Tract	1050 ± 70	900	Early Stirling phase. Date seems too early for ceramic phase associations.
B 19475	Interpretive Center Tract	1100 ± 70	850	Late Stirling phase. Date seems to early for ceramic phase associations.
B 19486	Interpretive Center Tract	1320 ± 80	630	Early Stirling phase. Date seems too early for ceramic phase associations.
M 1297	Airport area	675 ± 75	1275	Charcoal and charred maize from refuse pit with Sand Prairie ceramics. Not corrected for isotopic fractionation.
M 1296	Airport area	725 ± 75	1225	Wall-trench structure.

[a] Dates are grouped by site area. Years B.P. gives the radiocarbon years before present with the standard deviation. Years A.D. are uncorrected calendrical dates with 1950 as the base year.

APPENDIX 2

KEY TO THE 1966 UNIVERSITY OF WISCONSIN-MILWAUKEE CAHOKIA MAP

The 1966 map—at a scale of 1:2,000—was much too large to have been placed on a single sheet. The finished map was divided into sections of 2,000 meters square. These nine sections were numbered beginning in the upper left had corner extending in a row across the top of three continuing likewise across the with the second and third rows. Following is a list of the grid coordinates for each section.

Section 1	N800 to N2800	W2800 to W800
Section 2	N800 to N2800	W800 to E1200
Section 3	N800 to N2800	E1200 to E3200
Section 4	S1200 to N800	W2800 to W800
Section 5	S1200 to N800	W800 to E1200
Section 6	S1200 to N800	E1200 to E3200
Section 7	S3200 to S1200	W2800 to W800
Section 8	S3200 to S1200	W800 to E1200
Section 9	S3200 to S1200	E1200 to E3200

Monks Mound and other major features of the Cahokia site are in section 5. The 0:0 point of the Cahokia grid is also in this section just southwest of Monks Mound. Section 5 encompasses the area we have referred to as downtown Cahokia in Chapter 9.

The rest of the mounds of the Cahokia site are in sections 2, 4, 6, and 8. Sections 1, 3, 7 and 9 include only very small sections of the site as we have bounded it. They include no major features and are heavily areas built over by recent construction.

For convenience of location within the larger sections, they were subdivided into smaller units of 400 meters on a side, giving 25 subsections to each larger section. These subsections were designated alphabetically starting in the upper left hand corner with the letter A. The letters were assigned in sequence as follows.

First row	A	B	C	D	E
Second row	J	I	H	G	F
Third row	K	L	M	N	O
Fourth row	T	S	R	Q	P
Fifth row	U	V	W	X	Y

For example, section 8H of the map refers to the area between 0 and East 400 and South 1600 to South 2000.

In most of the discussion of locations in the atlas reference is made only to the larger sections. For example, the borrow pits were assigned numbers by first reference to the section in which they were located with an additional number designating the specific borrow pit within that section. The largest borrow pit in section 5 is designated as Borrow Pit 5-1.

In discussing specific locations of mounds, reference is sometimes made to the subsections. Monks Mound is located in subsection 5H. Usually, however, reference to the location of a specific feature such as Monks Mound is given in terms of specific grid coordinates. The point of reference in this case is a point at the geometric center of the feature or the highest point. In this case Monks Mound is given the coordinates of N400E200.

APPENDIX 3

MOUND NUMBERS, LOCATIONS, AND FORMS

This appendix gives the group (as defined in Chapter 10), grid coordinates, and section for the UWM map, form, and comments where appropriate for each mound. Group DT is downtown Cahokia; "?" signifies isolated mounds or those with uncertain associations.

Mound	Group	Mound name	UWM map section	Grid coordinates	Form	Comments
1	II		6H	N200E2066	Platform	
2	II		6H	N253E2058	Ridge top	NW-SE orientation.
3	II		3Y	N852E1628	Conical?	
4	VI		5E	N524E992		
5	VI		5C	N568E392	Platform	
6	I	Kunnemann 6	2R	N1288E360	Conical	Associated with Mound 7.
7	I	Kunnemann 7	2R	N1243E266	Platform	Associated with Mound 6.
8	I	Kunnemann 8	2R	N1236E190	Platform	Associated with Mound 9.
9	I	Kunnemann 9	2R	N1226E144	Conical	Associated with Mound 8.
10	I	Kunnemann 10	2R	N1222E52	Platform	Combined with 11 as two-terraced mound?
11	I	Kunnemann 11	2Q	N1216E10	Platform	Combined with 10 as two-terraced mound?
12	I		2Q	N1230W164	Conical?	
13	VI		5B	N702W16		
14	VI		5C	N722E122		
15	VI		5B	N592W18		
16	VI		5C	N472E110		
17	DT		5H	N342E324	Platform	
18	VII		5I	N262E500		
19	VII		5I	N290E664		
20	VII		5I	N278E744	Platform	
21	VII		5J	N260E810		
22	VII		5J	N280E858	Platform	
23	VII		5J	N344E850		
24	VII	Edwards mounds	5J	N286E910		
25	VII	Edwards mounds	5J	N286E988		
26	VII		5J	N276E1094		
27	VII		5J	N96E1062		
28	VII		5J	N34E294	Platform	
29	VII		5J	N116E932		
30	VII	Grandpa's	5I	N76E686	Platform	
31	VII	Schmidt	5I	N70E630	Platform	
32	VII		5I	N156E648	Platform	Connected to Mound 33.
33	VII	James Ramey	5I	N184E684	Conical	Connected to Mound 32.
34	VII		5I	N224E644		Apron on west side.
35	VII		5I	N228E554		
36	DT		5H	N172E366	Platform	Terraced.
37	DT		5H	N225E346	Conical	Associated with Mound 36.
38	DT	Monks Mound	5H	N200E200	Platform	Four terraces.
39	DT	Sawmill	5G	N294W77	Platform	Connected to Mound 77?
40	DT		5G	N177W74	Conical?	Associated with Mound 41.
41	DT		5G	N99W76	Platform	Associated with conical Mound 40? by platform.
42	XI	Merrell	5F	N100W414	Platform	Mound on SW corner.
43	X		5F	N102W673		
44	X		4J	N80W816	Platform	Near Tract 15A.
45	?		4I	N206W1138	Platform	
46	?		4I	N332W1542	Platform	
47	XI		5L	S90W244		

Mound	Group	Mound name	UWM map section	Grid coordinates	Form	Comments
48	DT		5L	S125W127	Platform	True Monks Mound ?
49	DT	Red Mound	5M	S142E104	Ridge top	E-W orientation.
50	DT		5M	S132E385	Conical?	
51	DT	Persimmon	5M	S32E388	Platform	
52	VII		5N	S100E798	Platform	
53	VII		5O	S74E923		
54	DT		5M	S238E396		
55	DT	Murdock	5M	S286E404	Platform	Terrace on west side? Conical mound?
56	DT	Jesse Ramey	5M	S334E144	Platform	
57	DT		5L	S246W122		
58	XI		5K	S264W422	Conical	
59	DT	Round Top	5Q	S496W2	Conical	Associated with Mound 60.
60	DT	Fox	5R	S498E110	Platform	Associated with Mound 59.
61	VIII	Tippetts	5S	S623E536	Platform	Associated with Mound 62.
62	VIII		5S	S766E552	Conical	Associated with Mound 61.
63	III		5Y	S1114E814		
64	III		5Y	S1270E688	Ridge top	Original Rattlesnake Mound ? E-W orientation.
65	III		8D	S1566E772	Platform	
66	III	Rattlesnake	8G	S1630E80	Ridge top	Original Harding Mound. Sub mounds.
67	IX		5Q	S696W360	Conical	Associated with Mound 68.
68	IX		5Q	S760W376	Platform	Associated with Mound 67.
69	IV		4Y	S1162W832		
70	IV	Rouch	7E	S1258W800	Platform	
71	IV		7E	S1294W948		
72	IX		5W	S860E66	Ridge top	Multiple sub mounds.
73	XI		5L	S74W376	Platform	
74	XI		5K	S232W448		Terrace on west of Mound 58?
75	XI		5K	S68W570		
76	XI		5G	N228W402		
77	DT		5G	N22W64	Conical?	Connected to Mound 39.
78	V	Jondro	4L	S188W2070	Conical	Sub mound.
79	?	Mackie	4I	N462W1610	Platform?	Tee mound.
80	III		8D	S1240E840		
81	III		8D	S1356E690		
82	III		8G	S1672E24		
83	III		8G	S1640E21		
84	V		4G	N148W2310		
85	V		4B	N580W2150	Ridge top?	Sub mound.
86	V	Powell	4G	N232W2314	Ridge top	Sub mound.
87	V		4G	N75W2302		
88	V		4G	N50W2438		
89	I		2R	N1400E0		
90	?		4H	N154W1660		
91	X		5F	N140W780		
92	X		5F	N20W746		
93	IX		5P	S665W510		Associated with Borrow Pit 5-4 and Mound 67.
94	IX		5Q	S680W55		

Mound	Group	Mound name	UWM map section	Grid coordinates	Form	Comments
95	VIII		5S	S616E665	Ridge top?	Associated with Borrow Pit 5-2 and Mound 61.
96	IX		5W	S933W35	Platform?	Tee mound. Associated with Mound 72.
97	II		6A	N520E1584		
98	II		6B	N510E1660		
99	II		6B	N634E1610		
100	II		6F	N102E1548		
101	II		6G	N165E1652		
102	II		6G	N218E1658		
103	II		6G	N355E1715		
104	II		6G	N410E1914		

APPENDIX 4

BORROW PITS

This appendix gives data on the borrow pits (see Chapter 8 for discussion and maps).

Central Borrow pit	(meters above coordinates	Base elevation (meters above sea level)	Area Square meters	Hectares	Acres
Section 2					
2-1	N1480E0	125.5	1,400	0.14	0.35
2-2	N1250E500	124.0	1,880	0.19	0.46
2-3	N1230E400	124.0	1,240	0.12	0.31
2-4	N1390E710	124.0	1,500	0.15	0.37
Section 4					
4-1	S300W1300	127.0	23,920	2.39	5.91
Section 5					
5-1	S800W200	126.5	123,960	12.40	30.62
5-1A	S800W200	126.0	62,960	6.30	15.55
5-2	S600E600	126.0	35,356	3.56	8.78
5-2A	S550E500	125.0	3,640	0.36	0.90
5-2B	S600E710	125.0	1,240	0.12	0.31
5-2C	S680E600	125.0	5,400	0.54	1.33
5-2D	S740E600	125.0	600	0.06	0.15
5-3	S200E500	127.0	50,680	5.07	12.52
5-3A	S350E550	126.0	7,040	0.70	1.74
5-3B	S180E530	126.0	560	0.06	0.14
5-4	S620W500	126.5	10,040	1.00	2.48
5-4A	S580W530	126.0	1,960	0.20	0.48
5-4B	S500W540	126.0	200	0.02	0.05
5-5	S380W560	127.0	6,760	0.68	1.67
5-5A	S380W560	126.0	4,480	0.45	1.11
5-6	S370W720	127.0	7,720	0.77	1.91
5-6A	S330W710	126.0	760	0.08	0.19
5-7	S1020W20	126.0	2,560	0.26	0.63
5-7A	S1000W10	125.0	1,160	0.12	0.29
5-8	S1100W5	126.0	760	0.08	0.19
5-9	S880E560	126.0	2,016	0.20	0.50
5-10	S960E540	126.0	1,520	0.15	0.38
Section 8					
8-1	S1360E300	125.0	560	0.06	0.14
8-2	S1480E800	126.0	1,840	0.18	0.45
8-2A	S1480E800	125.0	520	0.05	0.13
8-3	S1430E800	126.0	840	0.08	0.21
8-4	S1480E900	126.0	7,960	0.80	1.97
8-4A	S1450E850	125.0	320	0.03	0.08
8-5	S1400E850	126.0	625	0.07	0.14

APPENDIX 5

CURRENT RESEARCH (1984–1989)

William I. Woods and George R. Holley

Since 1984 archaeological field investigations within the confines of the National Historic Landmark Boundary of the Cahokia Mounds State Historic Site have been almost exclusively conducted by the Contract Archaeology Program and the Department of Geography and Earth Science of Southern Illinois University at Edwardsville (SIUE) and sponsored and funded by the Illinois Historic Preservation Agency. These SIUE investigations have resulted in a series of generalizations concerning the occupation of the Cahokia site, as well as the elucidation of specific problems, and are individually summarized below. The location of each project is indicated in Figure A5.1. Completed project reports are cited for each discussion, and it is anticipated that these and future reports will be published by the Illinois Historic Preservation Agency.

INTERPRETIVE CENTER TRACT II (ICT-II)

This large-scale endeavor encompassed a series of projects (Collins 1987; De Mott 1989; Gums 1989; Holley 1987; Kelly 1988; Lopinot 1988; Milner and Paine 1987; Woods 1984) designed to provide recommendations for the positioning of the new Interpretive Center and associated facilities within an area termed the ICT-II and to mitigate the impact of the resultant construction activities. The field investigations were conducted between 1984 and 1986. During 1984 a program consisting of controlled surface collection, machine stripping, and feature definition was completed. In 1985 and 1986, additional controlled

surface collections were made and the area to be affected by the center (5,833 square meters) was exposed by machine stripping and all 466 identified features were excavated. Subsequent fieldwork in 1986 provided additional information on areas to be developed for parking lots, roadways, and the utility corridor paralleling Ramey Street.

Based on an analysis of the results of these investigations, the initial occupation occurred during the Lohmann phase (see Table 1.2). It consisted of a community with structures oriented along the cardinal directions. A large borrow pit, located to the west of this community, was filled during this phase. A small platform mound, situated immediately beyond the southern end of the mitigated area, was probably also constructed during Lohmann times. Although visible on early aerial photographs and evident as slight rises in the field, this and another small mound nearby had not been previously identified.

A reorganization of the Lohmann community plan occurred during the early portions of the Stirling phase. Throughout the Stirling phase, structures were placed around a central plaza and rebuilding in place was typical, suggestive of residential stability. A possible palisade trench to the west of the tract, on the filled borrow pit, may also relate to the Stirling phase.

During the succeeding Moorehead phase, the number of structures declined markedly and the occupation was concentrated along the higher elevations of the tract to the east. In addition, structures exhibited shallower basins, square rather than rectangular plans, and narrower wall trenches, indicative of wood scarcity.

Structure frequencies for both the Lohmann and Stirling phases are fairly equivalent, and large sections of the tract were not occupied; at most 11% of the excavated area contained features. For the Moorehead

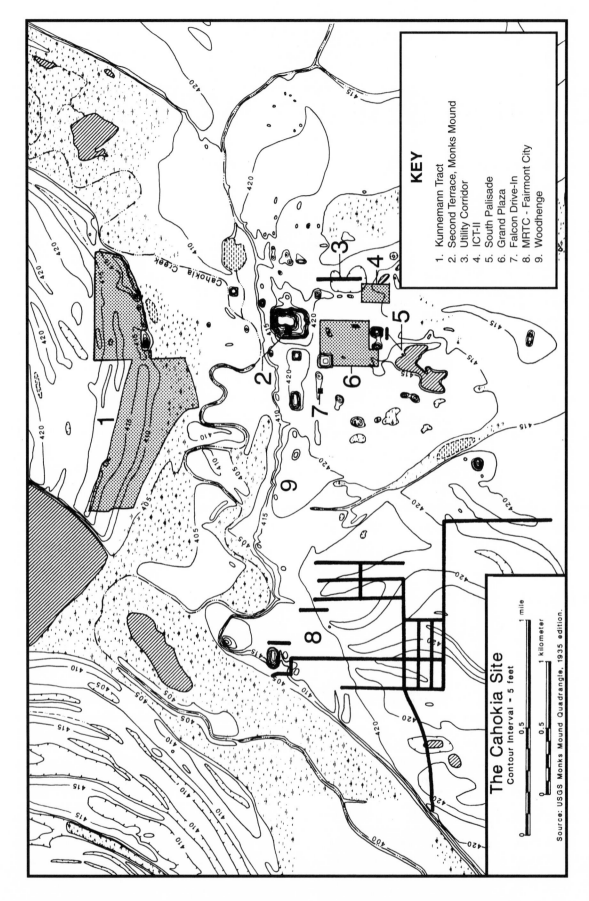

Figure A5.1.   Locations of recent (1984–1989) archaeological projects at Cahokia.   Source: USGS Monks Mound Quadrangle, 1935 edition.

KEY

1. Kunnemann Tract
2. Second Terrace, Monks Mound
3. Utility Corridor
4. ICT-II
5. South Palisade
6. Grand Plaza
7. Falcon Drive-In
8. MRTC - Fairmont City
9. Woodhenge

The Cahokia Site
Contour Interval = 5 feet

Source: USGS Monks Mound Quadrangle, 1935 edition.

phase only 3% of the tract was occupied by structures and pits.

Utility Corridor

A 5-meter-wide (16.4 feet) corridor (Collins 1987) to the east of and parallel to Ramey Street was plowed and subjected to a controlled surface collection, resulting in a collection area of 0.1 hectares (0.25 acres). Ceramics from the controlled surface collection date from the Emergent Mississippian through the Mississippian periods. Shell-tempered ceramics outnumber all other temper types.

Based upon topography and artifact density, seven areas were selected for plowzone removal and examination of the subsurface. Four of the blocks yielded evidence of features. Of those features containing ceramics, most date to the Stirling phase. Deep test trenches were placed at two locations. One revealed cultural fill extending to 2.5 meters (8.2 feet) below the surface.

In the utility corridor, as with the ICT-II, the disparity between the time span of occupation identified below the surface and that inferred from the material collected on the surface underscores the degree to which trash was broadcast across the Cahokia landscape. This and the presence of deeply buried cultural deposits also point to the clear necessity for at least limited excavation in order to interpret properly a controlled surface collection at the Cahokia site.

Monks Mound

Another project involved limited test excavation on the upper portion of the second terrace of Monks Mound during the winter of 1985-1986 (Collins, Chalfant, and Holley 1986). This investigation was initiated in response to a massive slump that had occurred on the west face of the mound earlier in the year.

Testing procedures included topographic mapping, excavation of a 6 x 4-meter (19.7 x 13.1 feet) block, and mapping of the exposed scarp profiles. Three distinct strata were identified within 80 centimeters (2.6 feet) of the surface. Two of these represent culturally derived fill, while the surface stratum consists of postoccupation colluvium. The uppermost cultural

zone is a sandy loam cap applied sometime during late Stirling or Moorehead times. A pit filled with domestic refuse was defined in this zone. The lower cultural zone exhibited basket loading and formed a dome-shaped feature, interpreted as a buttress constructed during Lohmann or early Stirling times. A deep post pit was associated with this lower surface.

Kunnemann Tract

In 1985 a controlled surface collection was conducted on a large tract of land to the north of Cahokia Creek that had recently been acquired by the state. A total of 1,503 20 x 20-meter blocks (65.6 x 65.6 feet) in an area of cultivated land (covering approximately 60 hectares [148 acres]) surrounding the Kunnemann mound group was collected.

Approximately 30 hectares (74 acres) of the project area yielded artifacts, with most coming from the prominent sand ridge bordering the Cahokia Creek floodplain. Artifacts recovered indicate occupations spanning the Middle Woodland through Mississippian periods. The Middle Woodland occupation is minimal and dates relatively late within the period. A negligible Late Woodland presence was also identified. The most significant occupation occurred during the Emergent Mississippian period and early in the Mississippian period. These components appear to be spread uniformly along the sandy ridge. Based on the presence of diagnostics alone, the Stirling phase would appear to represent the peak period of occupation. Moorehead materials are confined, in the main, to the northeastern section of the ridge and mark a significant reduction from the previous Stirling phase distribution. In addition, fragments of human bone were collected from scattered locations, indicating burials along the ridge.

One significant result of the controlled surface collection was the documentation of the well-known microdrill industry, which was confined primarily to the Mound 12 area. Microdrill debitage (cores, rejuvenation flakes, and blades) and drills were abundant in an area of approximately 1.5 hectares (3.7 acres). Notably, very few shell beads and little shell debitage were recovered; this absence may be attributable to poor preservation in the sandy soil. Ceramics in the microdrill area date from the Emergent Mississippian period through the Lohmann and Stirling phases of the Mississippian period.

SOUTHERN PALISADE

The first SIUE field school at the Cahokia site was directed toward an examination of the southern course of the palisade, directly south of Fox Mound, during the summer of 1988 (Dalan 1988; Holley et al. 1989). These investigations used a remote sensing program directed by Rinita Dalan, an analysis of previous excavations by the University of Wisconsin-Milwaukee and Washington University in the area, and excavation to assess the course of the palisade. The remote sensing project resulted in the identification of the palisade course and other anomalies. Three excavation units confirmed the route of the palisade and identified the presence of an area of differential fill, consisting of sand, that was also noted during remote sensing. This area of differential fill contained a buried platform of prepared clay, indicating a complex situation of construction and fill in this section of the site.

It appears likely that the area of the southern palisade was first filled to raise the surface at least 1 meter (3.3 feet), perhaps in conjunction with the plaza or the Twin Mounds complex (Mounds 59 and 60 south of the Grand Plaza). All four identified stages of the palisade trend east-west in the area of investigation and appear to merge into two courses with rebuilding in the same location. The location of a western wall remains problematic, although the southern section of the western course may have been identified by the remote sensing investigations. Additional evidence for bastions was also recovered, as was a light scatter of pits and structures. The palisade course in the south appears to have been constructed during the Stirling and Moorehead phases.

The interpretation of land filling in the southern portion of the central precinct of the site led to the inference that perhaps the Grand Plaza, to the north, was also created as an artificially ordered landscape, which involved filling to create a level surface from south of Monks Mound to the Twin Mounds complex.

PLAZA EXCAVATIONS

A coordinated research program was devised to explore the Grand Plaza for the second field school program by SIUE during the summer of 1989. Prompting this research was the atypical level surface of the plaza, contrasting with the surrounding ridge and swale topography, and results from the 1988 field school that appeared to indicate the southern terminus of the central area was artifically raised. An electromagnetic survey, traversing the sections of the plaza not disturbed by modern housing, revealed, among other anomalies, a prominent feature interpreted as a buried sand ridge. The ridge angles northwest to southeast and is located under Mound 48 and the northern portion of Mound 56 and is similar in orientation to other ridges evident to the west in the Dunham Tract.

Subsequent test excavations at five localities in the plaza documented that this ridge and adjacent swales have been subjected to anthropogenic cut-and-fill modifications. Although clear evidence of basket loading was uncommon, overlying sediments lack natural soil-formation characteristics and contain prehistoric artifacts, indicating that at least 75 centimeters (2.5 feet) of fill was added to attain the present surface. The large-scale earth moving necessary to create the plaza occurred during the terminal stages of the Emergent Mississippian period and ranks as one of the largest artificial landforms in the United States. Although mound construction at the Cahokia site has not been documented for the Emergent Mississippian period, it appears likely that given the scale of the plaza creation, there is no doubt that other construction activities were undertaken at this time.

The plaza also contains a number of borrow pits, evident on a 20-centimeter (7.9-inch) contour map of the plaza, most located adjacent to the small mounds. One of these was excavated, to the west of Mound 56, revealing the presence of at least 2.8 meters (9.2 feet) of fill. The fill of the borrow appears to date to the same time as the erection of the Grand Plaza.

MRTC AND FAIRMONT CITY

Two pipeline projects were subject to field investigations in the western portions of the Cahokia site during 1988 (Gums et al. 1989; Lopinot, Brown, and Holley 1989). The first, termed the MRTC project, involved the excavation of a 3-meter-wide (9.8 feet) trench along 3 kilometers (1.9 miles) of the site. This project identified two occupation areas yielding features within the Cahokia site. The southern occupation, part of the previously identified Mackie site, comprised two single-post structures and associated pits dating late during the Emergent Mississippian period. To the north, near the Fingerhut cemetery previously identified by Charles Bareis, the second occupation consisted of two wall-trench structures dating to the Stirling phase. Based on proximity to the previously excavated cemetery and the contents of the structures—sparse domestic debris but significant quantities of marine shell and other exotic items—it is likely that these structures functioned in association with the cemetery, perhaps as temples or guardian/caretaker facilities.

The Fairmont City pipeline, which was located along streets within the present-day community, involved the examination of ca. 5.7 kilometers (3.6 miles) of the western portion of the site within a 1-meter (3.3 feet) trench. An important contribution of this research was the demonstration that, in many cases, modern development has merely covered rather than destroyed prehistoric subsurface remains. This is quite significant because it implies that the large sections of the site under streets and in residential and commercial use may not be greatly disturbed. A number of Lohmann and Stirling structures and pit features were identified in the profiles of the pipeline trenches. Based on the distribution of the features, it appears that Mississippian occupational intensity declines toward the western margins of the present limits of Fairmont City.

Additional data collected from the western margins of the Fairmont City project point to the location of another microdrill concentration similar to, but perhaps smaller than, that recovered from the Kunnemann Tract, as well as human remains. Also at this location, a small scatter of Sand Prairie ceramics was recovered, suggesting that the on-site occupation during this period was quite dispersed.

The Fairmont City project points up an intriguing implication that bears further scrutiny concerning the location of specialized activities at the margins of the Cahokia settlement. Two microdrill concentrations and nearby burial areas have been identified at the northern and western site margins. It is possible that these activities are interrelated.

FALCON DRIVE-IN

During 1988 a small area (67 square meters [720 square feet]) was excavated before the construction of a picnic facility in the vicinity of the abandoned Falcon Drive-In. Below the historic overburden, a complex juxtaposition of fill and pit features and structures

was revealed. Numerous wall trenches indicating rebuilding were identified. Terminal Emergent Mississippian and Lohmann phase ceramics are the most common, with Stirling materials also present. The intensity of the early Mississippian occupation revealed in this testing contrasts with that of Tract 15B immediately to the north, which was transformed from domestic to public use during this period.

WOODHENGE

The Cahokia Mounds Museum Society Field School excavated in Tract 15A in 1985 (Iseminger 1985), to locate the three remaining post pits for Wittry's Circle 2/Woodhenge 3 that had been missed in the 1961 and 1963 excavations, so that reconstruction of the Woodhenge would be complete. All three post pits were identified within centimeters of their predicted locations, although upper portions had been partially removed by salvage work in the early 1960s. One post pit superimposed the northeast corner of a wall-trench structure that probably dates to the Lohmann phase.

IMPLICATIONS OF RECENT RESEARCH

The Emergent Mississippian occupation within the Cahokia site was confined to ridges near water and concentrated along the levee deposits of Cahokia Creek. Planning and execution of the center originated during terminal Emergent Mississippian. Although no definitive evidence for on-site mound construction during this period exists, this seems a foregone conclusion given the large-scale efforts obviously expended in the creation of the Grand Plaza.

During the Lohmann phase, mound construction accelerated and the central precinct was functional. These developments resulted in displacement of habitation outward from the Emergent Mississippian core. The resultant Lohmann subcommunities exhibit formalized orientation of structures. The retention of deep basins for structures and the presence of large pit features suggests a continuity between the Emergent Mississippian period and the Lohmann phase.

Clear differentiation into smaller subcommunities characterized the succeeding Stirling phase occupation. Perhaps the peak population was reached early during this phase. At this time evidence for site occupation terminates immediately to the north of the Kunnemann mounds and south of the Rattlesnake mound complex. Toward the east and the west, however, habitation continued in an attenuated form and was confined to southern levee deposits of Cahokia Creek. Indeed, to the west the site could be said to have extended to the East St. Louis mound group. Continued mound construction and the erection of the central palisade marked community-wide endeavors during the Stirling phase.

Although palisade construction continued, there is clear evidence for decline in site population and contraction of settled areas during post-Stirling times. Where present, Moorehead occupations were confined to higher elevations. The distribution of the sparse Sand Prairie habitation mirrors that of the Emergent Mississippian period and appears to have been concentrated in the Monks Mound area and lightly scattered across other portions the site.

APPENDIX 6

CURRENT RESEARCH (1990–1995)

George R. Holley, William I. Woods,
Rinita A. Dalan, and Harold W. Watters, Jr.

Since the last summary of research at Cahokia, prepared in 1989 (see Appendix 5), work has continued at the Cahokia site. Annual field schools as well as mitigation related to minor construction activities associated with the park have been carried out by the local Office of Contract Archaeology, Southern Illinois University at Edwardsville (SIUE). Other individuals at the University of Oklahoma (UO), University of New Mexico (UNM), and Washington University (WU) have also contributed to the study of the Cahokia site during the period 1990-1995.[1]

A number of publications and reports dealing with work conducted during the 1984-1989 period have emerged subsequent to the publication of Appendix 5 and include the series devoted to the ICT-II (Collins 1990; De Mott, Marcucci, and Williams 1993; Gums 1993; Holley 1989; Lopinot et al. 1991; Woods 1993a) and a variety of other projects (Collins and Chalfant 1993; Emerson and Woods 1990, 1993; Holley 1995; Holley, Dalan, and Smith 1993; Holley et al. 1989; Iseminger et al. 1990; Lopinot, Brown, and Holley 1993). Three edited volumes that deal in part with the Cahokia site have also appeared, offering descriptions of previous fieldwork and new interpretations relating to the site (Barker and Pauketat 1992; Emerson and Lewis 1991; Stoltman 1991).

This update of the 1990-1995 investigations is organized following Fowler's (Chapter 10) proposed functional division of the site between the palisaded downtown and the outer margins. The general sequence of occupational history for the Cahokia site identified in the previous summary of investigations

remains intact on the basis of this new research. Explaining the social and political forces behind this history has kept pace with these findings and can be gleaned in the vast number of references provided in this summary. The location of these investigations are presented in Figure A6.1.

DOWNTOWN CAHOKIA

As in past investigations, much work has been invested in the center of the Cahokia site. Nearly all of the prominent elements comprising downtown Cahokia have been the subject of investigations during the period from 1990 to 1995. The most extensive of these investigations was associated with ongoing SIUE investigations of the *Grand Plaza*. In her doctoral dissertation and elsewhere, Rinita Dalan (1991, 1993a, and 1993b; Dalan and Banerjee 1995) incorporated data from earlier SIUE investigations along with extensive coring during the 1991 SIUE Field School (Dalan and Ollendorf 1991) to offer a synthetic model of landscaping in the plaza and elsewhere at the site. Dalan developed a comprehensive approach to understanding created landscapes by merging field and laboratory geophysical methods with archaeological methods. The immensity and novelty of landscape creation at the Cahokia site has yet to be fully appreciated. For example, within the Grand Plaza, Dalan documented

---

[1] Since these works are of recent vintage and in some cases ongoing, publications are often incomplete or absent. A reference for these investigations is provided only if it is published or if a final report is available from the IHPA. We have relied on personal communication with the principal investigators for information relating to these projects.

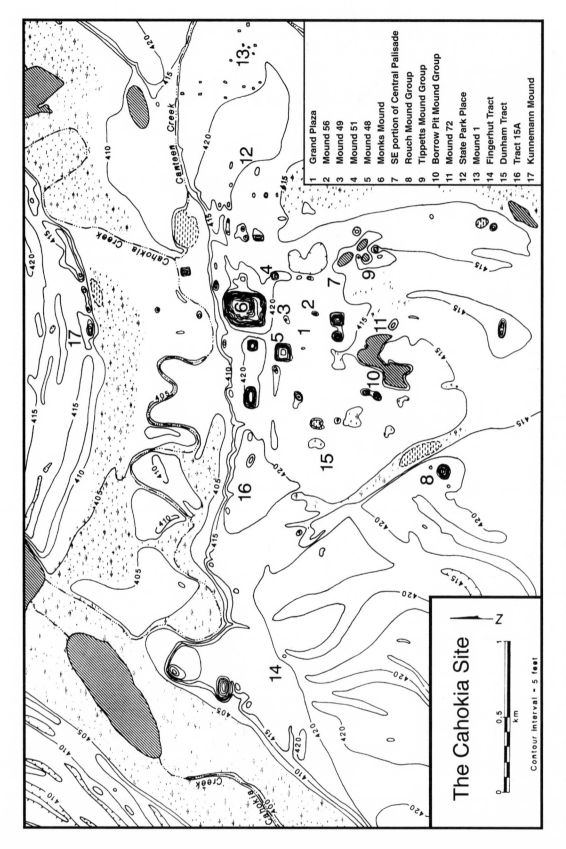

The Cahokia Site

N

Contour Interval = 5 feet

0   0.5   1
        km

1	Grand Plaza
2	Mound 56
3	Mound 49
4	Mound 51
5	Mound 48
6	Monks Mound
7	SE portion of Central Palisade
8	Rouch Mound Group
9	Tippetts Mound Group
10	Borrow Pit Mound Group
11	Mound 72
12	State Park Place
13	Mound 1
14	Fingerhut Tract
15	Dunham Tract
16	Tract 15A
17	Kunnemann Mound

Figure A6.1. Locations of recent (1990-1995) archaeological projects at Cahokia.

that at least four hectares of surface deposits were stripped, probably for use in early mound construction, and that this area was subsequently refilled. Discrete borrow pits have also been identified. To a significant extent, major remolding of the landscape appears confined to downtown Cahokia and its immediate margins.

In an outgrowth of this approach, Dalan and Harold Watters (1994) developed a method for evaluating the shape of a prehistoric mound utilizing fine-scale topographic mapping and laboratory soil magnetic analyses. Testing this method on known flat-top and conical mounds (see Fowler's descriptions of mound types in Chapter 9), they also extended the approach to poorly known or unique mound shapes. Two of the mounds in the plaza were investigated (Mound 49, a ridge-top, and Mound 56, a platform mound). Mound 49 had been interpreted as being dissimilar along the major and minor axes, both topographically (by Fowler) and in its magnetic signature (by Dalan and Watters), and thus similar to what is implied by a ridge-top mound. More importantly, they demonstrated that Mound 56 was a two-tiered mound, a shape initially proposed during SIUE investigations at the mound during the 1993 Field School (see below).

SIUE investigations into *Mound 56,* during the 1993 Field School (Dalan, Holley, and Watters1993), were intended to address the extent to which Warren Moorehead's extensive excavations during the 1920s could be salvaged. Moorehead's work at the site was either scantly published or unpublished. We reasoned that by exposing one of his excavations we would be able to derive a profile of a mound and retrieve materials for dating construction. Using remote sensing, coring, reconnaissance, and topographic mapping, we were able to identify Moorehead's trench on the southern portion of the mound.

Our exposure of this trench indicated that Moorehead either did not excavate the mound in a manner that preserved a vertical face or that the infilling process destroyed the walls. Thus our goal of obtaining a profile of the mound was not possible. However, a large amount of prehistoric material was retrieved by screening, which was unexpected. This material likely represents a combination of trash deriving from summit occupations and from fill during the occupation of the mound. Included within the debris recovered was a host of exotics, among which was a bead manufactured from a shark centrum. We date the occupation of the mound within the Stirling phase. Stray Emergent Mississippian sherds recovered may derive from an earlier occupation or, likely, from fill for the mound.

The small but interesting ridge-top mound located within the Grand Plaza, Mound 49, was investigated by Timothy R. Pauketat, of the University of Oklahoma, during 1994 as part of his larger Early Cahokia Project aimed at understanding the emergence of Cahokia. This work, which exposed portions of the mound in two 5 x 2-meter trenches, revealed complex architectural elements and indications earlier flat-topped mound stages. Pauketat and associates (1993) are also re-examining the well-preserved archaeological specimens retrieved by Charles J. Bareis, of the University of Illinois, from the fill of a borrow pit under Mound 51 that flanks the eastern margin of the Grand Plaza. Their ongoing analyses have revealed stark differences between early Cahokia refuse and that of outlying support communities.

Mound 48, a large platform mound on the western margins of the Grand Plaza, was investigated by a combined SIUE and UNM field school during 1995. This work, under the direction of William Woods and Robert Santley, consisted of topographic survey, coring, and the excavation of 2 x 2-meter test units on the colluvial slopes of the mound. Coring results revealed the presence of an Emergent Mississippian village occupation immediately to the north of the mound, suggested that the mound was not accretional, and confirmed Dalan's prior interpretations of preplaza topography and surficial stripping of this surface for plaza construction. This interpretation was also supported by the test excavations, one of which revealed a late Edelhardt phase structure superimposed on the stripped surface. Among other identified features were a ramp extending from the mound's northeast corner and a wall trench identified in three units along the southern side of the mound. This wall trench is interpreted as representing a fence or screen erected during the early Mississippian period. Most of the mound's erosion was found to have occurred during its prehistoric occupation, when this feature was not covered by vegetation. Emergent Mississippian materials are found throughout the fan deposits and likely derived from fill procured to construct the mound. In contrast, little debris dating to the Lohmann-Stirling periods was recovered from the colluvium. Primary refuse disposal was only evident in a series of loading episodes exposed in the southwesternmost excavation unit, dating from the Moorehead-Sand Prairie time periods.

Archaeological work pertaining to the massive failures that occurred on the east and west slopes of *Monks Mound* in 1984 has been discussed elsewhere (see Appendix 5 and Emerson and Woods 1990, 1993). In the spring of 1995, large-scale slumping again took place along the western slopes of the second terrace. A geotechnical study has been undertaken and recommendations for remediation of the current failure zones employing recently developed technologies have been made. The only fieldwork conducted concerned topographic mapping and a series of cores emplaced on the fourth terrace (Woods 1993b). This study confirmed the previous excavation locations, found that modern fill extended up to 2 meters in depth, and identified the unexcavated northeast portions of the terrace.

Finally, additional investigations were conducted in the southeastern portion of the *central palisade* by John Kelly (1993) in response to the replacement of septic facilities for the park. This work appears to substantiate our 1988 findings (Holley et al. 1990) that, within the southern section, the first of the four curtains of the central palisade had a different course and likely enclosed an area larger than the final three stages.

MARGINS

An ongoing focus of the SIUE research field school concerns the nature of mound groups located outside of Cahokia's downtown. That is, we are interested in identifying the spread and timing of occupation around the mounds and the internal configuration of the mounds comprising the isolated mound groups.

Four field seasons (1991, 1993, 1994, 1995) have been invested at the *Rouch, Tippetts, and Borrow Pit mound groups.* This work has involved reconnaissance, topographic survey, remote sensing, coring, and test excavations (Dalan et al. 1994; Holley, Dalan, and Watters 1992; Holley et al. 1995). Our objectives were to gather data relating to the occupation and organization of these mound groups in a manner that limited the impact upon the cultural resources. Excavations were minimal and involved the scattered placement of 1 x 1-meter units that were excavated to a depth of only 20 cm below surface. Occasionally, units were excavated to greater depths to address specific questions regarding subsurface deposits.

To a significant extent, domestic occupation at these tracts was displaced from the margins of the mounds. Lighter occupation debris was present on and around the mounds that could have derived from mound fill. Settlement was initiated in these groups during the Emergent Mississippian period, at least marginally so, and was definitely well established by Lohmann and Stirling times. Later occupation during the Moorehead phase appears confined to the margins of downtown

Cahokia and was not found at the most isolated Rouch mound group.

A significant finding of our work derived from the mapping of the mounds and examining their alignments. Axial alignments were pronounced and uniquely expressed at each mound group. New and interesting construction activities were revealed at all groups that continues to expand the lexicon of Cahokian earthworks. At the Rouch mound group (see Figure 6.27) we identified a borrow pit to the immediate north of the main mound and have subsequently surmised that the smaller mounds (69 and 71) were linked by raised causeways to the main mound. A much more complicated pattern is evident at the Tippetts mound group (see Figure 6.17). At this location we have identified a central plaza feature that was constructed by sculpting (borrowing) earth to form a square plaza. This feature is roughly equidistant between the two mounds, which are joined by a large earthwork causeway to the west. The plaza feature was devoid of occupation and clearly ceremonial in function.

Work at the Borrow Pit mound group (see Figure 6.25) during the 1995 SIUE Field School revealed that the main mounds were joined by a common platform, confirming Fowler's hypothesized platform. Construction events appear to have been initiated during the Lohmann-Stirling time periods. To the immediate north of these mounds we recovered a sufficient density of debris to suggest the location of village occupation.

Melvin Fowler (1994) has investigated a proposed Woodhenge that would have encompassed two of the large postmolds previously identified within Mound 72. Three field seasons were conducted in the vicinity of the mound, employing topographic survey, remote sensing, and excavation. These investigations resulted in the identification of subsurface soil disturbances interpreted as evidence for the arc defining the Woodhenge 72.

Few investigations have been conducted on the eastern margins of the site, an area that remains poorly understood because of extensive urban development. Pipeline emplacement in the community of *State Park Place* (Wells, Skele, and Holley 1991), in the area between Interstate 55-70 and Collinsville Road, revealed that several mounds are present amid the streets. Sparse material evidence for occupation recovered appears to span the early portions of the Mississippian period. Likewise, Gayle Fritz's WU field school has (Iseminger, Kelly, et al. 1991, 1994) conducted testing at *Mound 1,* conventionally assumed to represent the eastern terminus of the site. These excavations, prompted by removal of a condemned modern house on the mound, revealed a small prehistoric mound under the larger modern house mound, which dated from the Mississippian period.

In addition to work at the Rouch mound group and extensive work reported for the 1984-1989 period, two mitigation projects related to highway construction and golf course construction were initiated in the extreme western limits of the site, which has been identified as the *Fingerhut Tract.* Witty (1993) conducted limited machine stripping in areas planned for construction. This area was located adjacent to the Fingerhut cemetery excavated during 1962 by Charles Bareis (Bareis and Porter 1965) and the SIUE investigations (Gums et al. 1989). Witty identified a small cemetery adjacent to that excavated by Bareis, both of which likely span the Lohmann-Stirling portion of the Emergent Mississippian period. A Lohmann phase household cluster was also identified.

The second project was conducted by John Kelly (1995) for the Illinois Department of Transportation and involved the excavation of a Moorehead phase structure immediately to the east of Illinois Route 11. Washington University field schools, under the direction of John Kelly, have conducted survey and testing in the Fingerhut area in 1992, 1994, and 1995. The surface collection and limited testing indicated discontinuous use of the area temporally and spatially from Lohmann through Moorehead phases. The surveys also revealed evidence of craft production in the form of microdrills and basalt residue, which are related to activities on the Powell Tract to the north. The intensity of occupation appears to mirror the occupational history on the Powell Tract. This work also led to the remapping of the Jondro Mound (78).

Closer to downtown, Pauketat analyzed materials from previous excavations in three areas—*Dunham Tract, Tract 15A,* and the *Kunnemann Mound*—which formed the basis for his doctoral dissertation (1991) concerning the evolution of the Cahokia site (see also Pauketat 1993a, 1993b, 1994). Pauketat's analysis places Woodhenge within the revised Cahokia sequence as occurring during the Stirling phase. Its erection disrupted a domestic setting that was initiated during the Emergent Mississippian period. Domestic occupation returned during the Moorehead phase but was considerably reduced in frequency. At the Kunnemann Mound (11), Pauketat (1993a) interpreted the materials recovered by Preston Holder as relating to elite activities adjacent to and on the main mound of this group. His analysis of this, the best documented mound excavation currently available, demonstrated that shell bead and necklace making was an elite-subsidized craft. Holder's mound excavations also illustrated that during the Stirling phase mound building entailed many mantle layers and repeated construction of associated temples and elite residences.

BIBLIOGRAPHY OF CAHOKIA ARCHAEOLOGY

Anonymous
1820   *History of North America*, vol. 2. Davies and Company, Leeds, England.
1873   *Illustrated Encyclopedia and Atlas Map of Madison County (Illinois)*. Brink, St. Louis.
1881   *History of St. Clair County, Illinois*. Brink, McDonough, and Company, Philadelphia.
1887   Early Books which Treat of Mounds (Editorial). *The American Antiquarian* 9:239–242. Chicago.
1889   *East St. Louis Journal*. On microfilm at the East St. Louis (Illinois) Library.
1891   Archaeological Notes: The Patrick Collection. *The American Antiquarian* 13:245. Chicago.
1908   Cistercians in America. *Catholic Encyclopedia*, vol. 3, p. 787. The Encyclopedia Press, Inc., New York.
1909   The Great Cahokia Mound to be Sold. *Journal of the Illinois State Historical Society*, 2 (2):19–20. Springfield.

Adams, Robert McCormack
1941   *Archaeological Investigations in Missouri, 1939-40*. Transactions of the Academy of Sciences of St. Louis, Vol. 30, No. 5. Springfield.
1949   Archaeological Investigations in Jefferson County, Missouri. *The Missouri Archaeologist* 2(1):18–28.

Ahler, Steven R., and Peter J. DePuydt
1987   *A Report on the 1931 Powell Mound Excavations, Madison County, Illinois*. Illinois State Museum Reports of Investigations, No. 43. Springfield.

Anderson, James
1969   A Cahokia Palisade Sequence. In *Explorations into Cahokia Archaeology*, edited by Melvin L. Fowler, pp. 89–99. Illinois Archaeological Survey Bulletin, No. 7. University of Illinois, Urbana.

Atwater, Caleb
1820   *Description of the Antiquities Discovered in the State of Ohio and Other Western States*. Transactions and Collections of the American Antiquarian Society, Vol. 1. Printed by William Manning, Worcester.

Avebury, John Lubbock, 1st Baron
1913 [1869]   *Pre-Historic Times, as Illustrated by Ancient Remains, and the Manners and Customs of Modern Savages*. 7th ed. Henry Holt and Company, New York.

Baker, Frank C.
1923   The Use of Molluscan Shells by the Cahokia Mound Builders. *Transactions of the Illinois State Academy of Science*, Vol. 16, pp. 328–334. Springfield.
1930   The Use of Animal Life by the Mound Building Indians of Illinois. *Transactions of the Illinois State Academy of Science*, Vol. 22, pp. 41–64. Springfield.
1931   Additional Notes on the Mound Builders of Illinois. *Transactions of the Illinois State Academy of Science*. Vol. 23, pp. 231–235. Springfield.
1941   A Study in Ethnozoology of the Prehistoric Indians of Illinois. *Transactions of the American Philosophical Society*, Vol. 32, Part 2, pp. 51–77. Philadelphia.

Bareis, Charles J.
1964a   Meander Loops and the Cahokia Site. *American Antiquity* 30:89–91. Salt Lake City.
1964b   University of Illinois Projects. In *Third Annual Report: American Bottoms Archaeology, July 1, 1963–June 30, 1964*, edited by Melvin

L. Fowler, pp. 4–10. Illinois Archaeological Survey, Urbana.

1967a   *Interim Report on Preliminary Site Examination Undertaken in Archaeological Section A of FAI 255 South of Business 40 in the Interstate Portion of Area S-34-4 of the Cahokia Site, St. Clair County, Illinois.* Department of Anthropology Research Reports No. 1. University of Illinois, Urbana.

1967b   *Report on Preliminary Site Examination Undertaken at the Faust Site (S-69) on FAI 64, St. Clair County, Illinois.* Illinois Archaeological Survey, Urbana. (Mimeographed).

1968   *Report of Salvage Work Undertaken at the Faust Site (S-169) on FAI 64, St. Clair County, Illinois.* Illinois Archaeological Survey, Urbana. (Mimeographed).

1970   *Final Report on Salvage Work Undertaken at the Knoebel Site (S-71) on FAI 64, St. Clair County, Illinois,* Illinois Archaeological Survey, Urbana. (Mimeographed).

Bareis, Charles J., and Donald Lathrap
1962   University of Illinois Projects. In *First Annual Report: American Bottoms Archaeology, July 1, 1961–June 30, 1962,* edited by Melvin L. Fowler, pp. 3–9. Illinois Archaeological Survey, Urbana.

Bareis, Charles J., and James Warren Porter
1965   Megascopic and Petrographic Analyses of a Foreign Pottery Vessel from the Cahokia Site. *American Antiquity* 31:95–101. Salt Lake City.

Bareis, Charles J., and James Warren Porter (editors)
1984   *American Bottom Archaeology.* University of Illinois Press, Urbana.

Barker, Alex W., and Timothy R. Pauketat (editors)
1992   *Lords of the Southeast: Social Inequality and the Native Elites of Southeastern North America.* Archaeological Papers of the American Anthropological Association, Washington, D.C.

Barrett, Samuel A.
1933   *Ancient Aztalan.* Bulletin of the Public Museum of the City of Milwaukee, Vol. 13.

Baum, Rev. Henry Mason
1903   Antiquities of the United States: The Cahokia Mounds. *Records of the Past,* Vol. 2, pp. 214–222. Washington, D.C.

Beck, Lewis C.
1823   *A Gazetteer of the States of Illinois and Missouri.* C.R. and G. Webster, Albany.

Bell, Robert
1951   Dendrochronology at the Kincaid Site. In *Kincaid: A Prehistoric Illinois Metropolis,* by Fay-Cooper Cole et al., pp. 238–292. University of Chicago Press, Chicago.

Benchley, Elizabeth D.
1972   The First Terrace of Monks Mound. In *The University of Wisconsin-Milwaukee Cahokia Archaeology Project,* edited by Melvin L. Fowler, pp. 70–74. Report prepared for the National Science Foundation (G1098, GS2119, and GS3006), Washington, D.C. Copies available from the Department of Anthropology, University of Wisconsin-Milwaukee.

1974   *Mississippian Secondary Mound Loci: A Comparative Functional Analysis in a Time-Space Perspective.* Unpublished Ph.D. dissertation, Department of Anthropology, University of Wisconsin-Milwaukee.

1975   Summary Report of Excavations on the Southwest Corner of the First Terrace of Monks Mound: 1968, 1969, 1971. In *Cahokia Archaeology: Field Reports,* edited by Melvin L. Fowler, pp. 16–20. Illinois State Museum Research Series, No. 3. Springfield.

1976   *An Overview of the Prehistoric Resources of the Metropolitan St. Louis Area.* Cultural Resource Management Studies, National Park Service, U.S. Department of the Interior, Washington, D.C.

1981   *Summary Report on Controlled Surface Collections of the Ramey Field Cahokia Mounds Historic Site Madison County Illinois.* University of Wisconsin-Milwaukee Archaeological Research Laboratory Report of Investigations, No. 51. Milwaukee.

Benchley, Elizabeth D., and Peter DePuydt
1982   *Final Report of 1980 Excavations at the Interpretive Center Tract, Cahokia Mounds Historic Site.* University of Wisconsin-Milwaukee Archaeological Research Laboratory Report of Investigations, No. 61. Milwaukee.

Bennett, John W.
1945   *Archaeological Explorations in Jo Davies County, Illinois.* University of Chicago Press, Chicago.

Black, Glenn A.
1944 *Angel Site, Vanderburgh County, Indiana: An Introduction.* Prehistory Research Series, Vol. 2, No. 5. Indiana Historical Society, Indianapolis.
1967 *Angel Site.* 2 vols. Indiana Historical Society, Indianapolis.

Blakeslee, Donald
n.d. Radiocarbon dating of the Cahokia Site. Research paper on file at the Archaeological Research Laboratory, University of Wisconsin-Milwaukee.

Bleed, Peter
1970 Notes on Aztalan Shell-Tempered Pottery. *The Wisconsin Archeologist* 51 (1) (new series):1–20. Milwaukee.

Bluhm, Elaine A. (editor)
1959 *Illinois Archaeology.* Illinois Archaeological Survey Bulletin, No. 1. University of Illinois, Urbana.

Brackenridge, Henry Marie
1811 Unsigned article in *The Missouri Gazette*, 9 January. St. Louis.
1818a On the Population and Tumuli of the Aborigines of North America. In "A letter from H.M. Brackenridge, Esq. to Thomas Jefferson. Read Oct. 1, 1813." *Transactions of the American Philosophical Society*, 1 (new series):151–159. Philadelphia.
1818b Brief Report on the Cahokia Mounds. *Analectic Magazine*, p. 328. Philadelphia.
1962 [1814] *Views of Louisiana Together with a Journal of a Voyage up the Missouri River, in 1811.* Pittsburgh. Reprint. Quadrangle Books, Inc., Chicago.

Brandt, Keith
1972 American Bottoms Settlements. In *The University of Wisconsin-Milwaukee Cahokia Archaeology Project*, edited by Melvin L. Fowler, pp. 63–69. Report prepared for the National Science Foundation (G1098, GS2119, and GS3006), Washington D.C. Copies available from the Department of Anthropology, University of Wisconsin-Milwaukee.

Brown, James A. (editor)
1961 *The Zimmerman Site.* Illinois State Museum Reports of Investigations, No. 9. Springfield.

1975 *Perspectives in Cahokia Archaeology.* Illinois Archaeological Survey Bulletin, No. 10. Urbana.

Buck, Solon J.
1967 *Illinois in 1818.* University of Illinois Press, Chicago.

Bushnell, David I., Jr.
1904 The Cahokia and Surrounding Mound Groups. *Papers of the Peabody Museum of American Archaeology and Ethnology* (1904–1913), Vol. 3, No. 1, pp. 3–20. Harvard University, Cambridge Mass.
1917 The Origin and Various Types of Mounds in Eastern United States. *Proceedings Nineteenth International Congress of Americanists, Washington 1915*, pp. 43–47. Washington, D.C.
1922 Archaeological Reconnaissance of the Cahokia and Related Mound Groups. Explorations and Field Work of the Smithsonian Institution in 1921. *Smithsonian Miscellaneous Collections*, Vol. 72, No. 15, pp. 92–105. Washington, D.C.

Caldwell, Joseph R.
1958 *Trend and Tradition in the Prehistory of the Eastern United States.* Illinois State Museum Scientific Papers, Vol. 10. Springfield.
1959 The Mississippian Period. In *Illinois Archaeology*, edited by Elaine A. Bluhm, pp. 33–39. Illinois Archaeological Survey, Bulletin No. 1. University of Illinois, Urbana.
1964 Interaction Spheres in Prehistory. In *Hopewellian Studies*, edited by Joseph Caldwell and Robert Hall, pp. 133–143. Illinois State Museum Scientific Papers, Vol. 12. Springfield.

Carr, Lucien
1893 The Mounds of the Mississippi Valley, Historically Considered. *Annual Report of the Board of Regents of the Smithsonian Institution, July, 1891*, pp. 503–605. Washington, D.C.

Charlevoix, Pierre Francois
1761 *Journal of a Voyage to North America*, Vol. 2. R. and J. Dodsley, London.

Chmurny, William
1973 *The Ecology of the Middle Mississippian Occupation of the American Bottom.* Ph.D. disser-

tation, University of Illinois. University Microfilms, Ann Arbor.

Cole, Fay-Cooper, and Thorne Deuel
1937   *Rediscovering Illinois.* University of Chicago Press, Chicago.

Collins, James M.
1987   *Archaeology of the Cahokia Mounds, ICT-II: Features.* Report submitted to the Illinois Historic Preservation Agency, Springfield.
1990   *Archaeology of the Cahokia Mounds, ICT-II: Site Structure.* Illinois Cultural Resources Study No. 10. Illinois Historic Preservation Agency, Springfield.

Collins, James M., and Michael L. Chalfant
1993   A Second-Terrace Perspective on Monks Mound. *American Antiquity* 58:319-332.

Collins, James M., Michael L. Chalfant, and George R. Holley
1986   *Archaeological Testing of the Slump Area on the West Face of Monks Mound, Madison County, Illinois.* Report submitted to Illinois Historic Preservation Agency, Springfield.

Conant, A. J.
1879   *Foot-Prints of Vanished Races.* Chancy R. Barns, St. Louis.

Conrad, Lawrence A., and Alan D. Harn
1972   *The Spoon River Culture in the Central Illinois River Valley.* (Mimeographed.)

Crane, H. R., and James B. Griffin
1958   University of Michigan Radiocarbon Dates V. *American Journal of Science Radiocarbon Supplement* 1:173–198.
1959   University of Michigan Radiocarbon Dates VI. *American Journal of Science, Radiocarbon Supplement* 1:173–198.
1964   University of Michigan Radiocarbon Dates IX. *Radiocarbon* 6:1–24.
1968   University of Michigan Radiocarbon Dates XII. *Radiocarbon* 10:61–114.

Crook, A. R.
1915   Origin of Monks Mound. *Bulletin of the Geological Society of America* 26:74–75. New York.
1916   The Composition and Origin of Monks Mound. *Transactions of the Illinois Academy of Science,* Vol. 9, pp. 82–84. Springfield.

1918   Additional Note on Monks Mound. *Bulletin of the Geological Society of America* 29:80–81. New York.
1922   *The Origin of the Cahokia Mounds.* Bulletin of the Illinois State Museum (May). Springfield.

Dalan, Rinita A.
1988   *Geophysical Investigations of the Prehistoric Cahokia Palisade Sequence.* Master's thesis, Environmental Studies Program, Southern Illinois University at Edwardsville.
1991   Defining Archaeological Features with Electromagnetic Surveys at the Cahokia Mounds State Historic Site. *Geophysics* 56:1280–1287.
1992   *Landscape Modification at the Cahokia Mounds Site: Geophysical Evidence of Cultural Change.* Unpublished Ph.D. dissertation, University of Minnesota, Minneapolis.
1993a   *Landscape Modification at the Cahokia Mounds Site: Geophysical Evidence of Cultural Change.* Ph.D. dissertation, University of Minnesota. University Microfilms, Ann Arbor.
1993b   Issues of Scale in Archaeogeophysical Research. In *Effects of Scale in Archaeological and Geoscientific Perspectives,* edited by Julie K. Stein and A. Linse, pp. 67–78. Geological Society of America, Boulder, Col.
1997   The Construction of Cahokia. In C*ahokia: Domination and Ideology in the Mississippian World,* edited by T. R. Pauketat and T. E. Emerson. University of Nebraska Press, Lincoln.

Dalan, Rinita A., and Subir K. Banerjee
1997   *Soil Magnetism, an Approach for Examining Archaeological Landscapes.* Geophysical Research Letters. In press.

Dalan, Rinita A., George R. Holley, and Harold W. Watters, Jr.
1993   *An Assessment of Moorehead's Investigations at Mound 56, Cahokia Mounds State Historic Site.* Unpublished report submitted to the Illinois Historic Preservation Agency, Springfield.

Dalan, Rinita A., and Amy L. Ollendorf
1991   *Report on the 1990 SIUE-Cahokia Mounds Field School in Geoarcheology.* Unpublished report submitted to the Illinois Historic Preservation Agency, Springfield.

Dalan, Rinita A., and Harold W. Watters, Jr.
  1994   *Determining the Original Form of Mississippian Mounds.* Unpublished report submitted to the Illinois Historic Preservation Agency, Springfield.

Dalan, Rinita A., Harold W. Watters, Jr., George R. Holley, and William I Woods
  1994   *Sixth Annual Cahokia Mounds Field School: Understanding Mound Construction.* Unpublished report submitted to the Illinois Historic Preservation Agency, Springfield.

DeHass, W.
  1869   Archaeology of the Mississippi Valley. *Proceedings of the American Association for the Advancement of Science. 17th Meeting Held at Chicago, Illinois, August, 1868,* pp. 288–302. Joseph Lovering, Cambridge.

Deiner, Paul
  1968   *The Demographic Dilemma of Food Producing Revolutions: Hopewell.* Paper presented at the Annual Meeting of the Central States Anthropological Society. Detroit.

De Mott, Rodney C.
  1989   *Archaeology of the Cahokia Mounds, ICT-II: Lithics.* Report submitted to Illinois Historic Preservation Agency, Springfield.

De Mott, Rodney C., Derrick J. Marcucci, and Joyce A. Williams
  1993   Chipped Lithic Materials. In *The Archaeology of the Cahokia Mounds ICT-II: Testing and Lithics.* Illinois Cultural Resources Study No. 9. Illinois Historic Preservation Agency, Springfield.

Dick, George C.
  1955   Incised Pottery Decorations from Cahokia. *The Missouri Archaeologist* 17(4):36–48. Columbia.

Dickens, Charles
  1842   *American Notes for General Circulation,* vol. 2. London.

Eggan, Fred
  1951   The Ethnological Cultures and Their Archaeological Backgrounds. In *Archaeology of Eastern United States,* edited by James B. Griffin, pp. 35–45. University of Chicago Press, Chicago.

Emerson, Thomas E.
  1982   *Mississippian Stone Images in Illinois.* Illinois Archaeological Survey Circular, No. 6. Urbana.
  1995   Settlement, Symbolism, and Hegemony in the Cahokian Countryside. Ph.D. dissertation, University of Wisconsin, Madison. University Microfilms, Ann Arbor.

Emerson, Thomas E., and R. Barry Lewis (editors)
  1991   *Cahokia and the Hinterlands: Middle Mississippian Cultures of the Midwest.* University of Illinois Press, Urbana.

Emerson, Thomas E., and William I. Woods
  1990   The Slumping of the Great Knob: An Archaeological and Geotechnic Case Study of the Stability of a Great Earthen Mound. In *6th International Conference on the Conservation of Earthen Architecture: Adobe 90 Preprints,* edited by Neville Agnew, Michael Taylor, and Alejandro Alva Balderrama, pp. 219–224. The Getty Conservation Institute, Los Angeles.
  1993   Saving the Great Nobb. A Case Study in the Preservation of Cahokia's Monks Mound Through Passive Management. *Illinois Archaeology* 5:100–107.

English, Thomas H.
  1921   The Cahokia Indian Mounds: A Plea for Their Preservation. *The Geographical Review* 2 (2):207–211. New York.

Fairbanks, Charles H.
  1956   *Archaeology of the Funeral Mound, Ocmulgee National Monument, Georgia.* Archaeological Research Series, No. 3. National Park Service, U.S. Department of Interior, Washington, D.C.

Farnsworth, Kenneth B.
  1973   *An Archaeological Survey of the Macoupin Valley.* Illinois State Museum Reports of Investigations, No. 26. Springfield.

Featherstonhaugh, G. W.
  1844   *Excursion through the Slave States,* vol. 1. Harper, London and New York.

Fecht, William G.
  1960   Cahokia Mounds Serpent Pottery. *Central States Archaeological Journal* 7 (1):34–35. Fayetteville.

Fenneman, N. M.
    1911   *Geology and Mineral Resources of the St. Louis
            Quadrangle Missouri-Illinois.* U.S. Geological
            Survey Bulletin, No. 438. Department of the
            Interior, Washington, D.C.

Flagg, Edmund
    1838   *The Far West: or, A Tour Beyond the Mountains,*
            vol. 1. Harper and Brothers, New York.

Flint, Timothy
    1826   *Recollections of the Last Ten Years, Passed in
            Occasional Residences and Journeyings in the
            Valley of the Mississippi, from Pittsburgh and
            the Missouri to the Gulf of Mexico, and from
            Florida to the Spanish Frontier; in a Series of
            Letters to the Rev. James Flint, of Salem, Mas-
            sachusetts.* Cummings, Hilliard, and Com-
            pany, Boston.

Ford, Richard I.
    1974   *Northeastern Archaeology: Past and Future
            Directions.* Annual Review of Anthropology,
            vol. 3. Annual Reviews Inc., Palo Alto.

Fowke, Gerard
    1910   Antiquities of Central and Southeastern
            Missouri. *Bureau of American Ethnology,* Bul-
            letin No. 37, pp. 5–7. Washington, D.C.

Fowler, Melvin L.
    1952   Ware Groupings and Decorations of Wood-
            land Ceramics in Illinois. *American Antiquity*
            20:213–225. Salt Lake City.
    1959   *Summary Report of Modoc Rockshelter: 1952,
            1953, 1955, 1958.* Illinois State Museum Re-
            ports of Investigations, No. 8. Springfield.
    1962   John Francis Snyder: Pioneer Illinois Archae-
            ologist. In *John Francis Snyder: Selected Writ-
            ings,* edited by Clyde C. Walton, pp. 181–273.
            Illinois State Historical Society, Springfield.
    1969a   The Cahokia Site. In *Explorations into Cahokia
            Archaeology,* edited by Melvin L. Fowler, pp.
            1-30. Illinois Archaeological Survey Bulle-
            tin, No. 7. University of Illinois, Urbana.
    1969b   Middle Mississippian Agricultural Fields.
            American Antiquity 34:365–375. Salt Lake
            City.
    1974a   *Cahokia: Ancient Capitol of the Midwest.*
            Addison Wesley Module in Anthropology,
            No. 48. Addison Wesley Publishing Com-
            pany, Reading, Mass.
    1974b   Prehistoric Urban Evolution in North
            America. In *Human Cultural Development,*

            Indiana Historical Society Lectures 1973–1974,
            pp. 23–44. Indianapolis.
    1975   A Precolumbian Urban Center on the Mis-
            sissippi. *Scientific American* 23(2):92–101.
    1977   Aerial Archaeology at the Cahokia Site. In
            Aerial Remote Techniques in Archaeology, ed-
            ited by Thomas R. Lyons and Robert K.
            Hitchcock, pp. 65–80. Reports of the Chaco
            Center No. 2. Albuquerque.
    1978a   Cahokia and the American Bottom: Settle-
            ment Archaeology. In *Mississippian Settle-
            ment Patterns;* edited by Bruce D. Smith, pp.
            455–478. Academic Press, New York.
    1978b   The Temple Town Community: Cahokia and
            Amalucan Compared. In *Urbanization in the
            Americas from its Beginnings to the Present,*
            edited by Richard P. Schaedel, Jorge E.
            Hardoy, and Nora Scott Kinzer, pp. 175–184.
            Mouton, The Hague.
    1994   *The Woodhenge 72 Project: A Summary Report
            of the 1991, 1992, and 1993 Fieldwork.* Report
            of Investigations No. 119. Archaeological
            Research Laboratory, University of Wiscon-
            sin-Milwaukee.

Fowler, Melvin L. (editor)
    1962   *First Annual Report: American Bottoms Archae-
            ology, July 1,1961–June 30, 1962.* Illinois Ar-
            chaeological Survey, Urbana.
    1963   *Second Annual Report: American Bottoms Ar-
            chaeology, July 1,1962–June 30, 1963.* Illinois
            Archaeological Survey, Urbana.
    1964   *Third Annual Report: American Bottoms Ar-
            chaeology, July 1, 1963–June 30, 1964.* Illinois
            Archaeological Survey, Urbana.
    1969   *Explorations into Cahokia Archaeology.* Illinois
            Archaeological Survey Bulletin, No. 7. Uni-
            versity of Illinois, Urbana.
    1972   *The University of Wisconsin-Milwaukee Ca-
            hokia Archaeology Project.* A Symposium Pre-
            sented at 37th Annual Meeting of the Society
            for American Archaeology. Milwaukee.
            (Mimeographed).
    1975   *Cahokia Archaeology: Field Reports.* Illinois
            State Museum Research Series, No. 3.
            Springfield.

Fowler, Melvin L., Elizabeth D. Benchley, and Peter
DePuydt
    1980   *Final Report of the 1979 Archaeological Inves-
            tigations at the Interpretive Center Tract, Ca-
            hokia Mounds Historic Site.* Report of
            Investigations No. 40. Archaeological Re-

search Laboratory, University of Wisconsin-Milwaukee.

Fowler, Melvin L., and Robert L. Hall
1972 *Archaeological Phases at Cahokia.* Illinois State Museum Research Series, Papers in Anthropology, No. 1. Springfield.
1975 Archaeological Phases at Cahokia. In *Perspectives in Cahokia Archaeology*, pp. 1–14. Illinois Archaeological Survey Bulletin, No. 10. University of Illinois, Urbana.
1978 Late Prehistory of the Illinois Area. In *Handbook of North American Indians*, Vol. 15, edited by Bruce G. Trigger, pp. 560–568. Smithsonian Institution, Washington, D.C.

Garcilaso de la Vega
1951 *The Florida of the Inca*, translated and edited by J. R. Varner and J. J. Varner. University of Texas Press, Austin.

Gardner, William M.
1973 Ecological or Historical Determinants in Cultural Patterning among the Prehistoric Occupants of the Upper Kaskaskia River Valley, Illinois. In *Variation in Anthropology: Essays in Honor of John McGregor*, edited by Donald W. Lathrap and Jody Douglas, pp. 189–197. Illinois Archaeological Survey, Urbana.

Garraghan, Gilbert J.
1934 *Chapters in Frontier History.* Bruce Publishing Company, Milwaukee.

Gergen, Robert D., and William R. Iseminger
1986 Testing of Mound 50 at Cahokia Mounds State Historic Site, 11S-34. Cahokia Mounds Museum Society. Ms. on file at Cahokia Mounds State Historic Site and IHPA.
1987 Testing of Mound 50 at Cahokia Mounds State Historic Site, 11S-34. Cahokia Mounds Museum Society. Ms. on file at Cahokia Mounds State Historic Site and IHPA.

Goddard, George
1969 *Overview.* Doubleday and Company, New York.

Gregg, Michael
1971 *A Structure of Human Society and State Level Integration with Population Consideration for Cahokia.* Master's thesis, Department of Anthropology, University of Wisconsin-Milwaukee.

1972 Biological Resource Base and Area Ecology. In *The University of Wisconsin-Milwaukee Cahokia Archaeology Project*, edited by Melvin L. Fowler. Symposium presented at the 37th Annual Meeting of the Society for American Archaeology, Milwaukee. (Mimeographed).
1975a A Population Estimate for Cahokia. In *Perspectives in Cahokia Archaeology*, pp. 126–136. Illinois Archaeological Survey Bulletin, No. 10. Urbana.
1975b *Settlement Morphology and Production Specialization: The Horseshoe Lake Site, a Case Study.* Unpublished Ph.D. dissertation, Department of Anthropology, University of Wisconsin-Milwaukee.

Griffin, James B.
1941 Report on Pottery from the St. Louis Area. *The Missouri Archaeologist* 7(2):1–17. Columbia.
1949 The Cahokia Ceramic Complexes. *Proceedings of the Fifth Plains Conference for Archaeology*, pp. 44-58. Notebook No. 1, Laboratory of Anthropology, University of Nebraska, Lincoln.
1952 Some Early and Middle Woodland Pottery Types in Illinois. In *Hopewellian Communities in Illinois*, edited by Thorne Deuel, pp. 93–129. Illinois State Museum Scientific Papers, Vol. 5, No. 3. Springfield.
1960 A Hypothesis for the Prehistory of the Winnebago. In *Culture in History, Essays in Honor of Paul Radin*, edited by Stanley Diamond, pp. 852–862. Columbia University Press, New York.
1961 Some Correlations of Climatic and Cultural Change in Eastern North American Prehistory. *Annals of the New York Academy of Sciences* 95:710–717.
1967 Eastern North American Archaeology: A Summary. *Science* 156 (3772):175–191.
1977 The University of Michigan Excavations at the Pulcher Site in 1970 (sic 1950). *American Antiquity* 42:462–490. Salt Lake City.
1978 Foreword. In *Mississippian Settlement Patterns*, edited by Bruce Smith, pp. 15-22. Academic Press, New York.

Griffin, James B., and Albert C. Spaulding
1951 The Central Mississippi Valley Archaeological Survey, Season 1950—A Preliminary

Report. *Journal of the Illinois State Archaeological Society* 1(3) (new series):74–81. Fairbury, Illinois.

Grimm, R. E. (editor)
1949   *Cahokia Brought to Life: An Artifactual Story of America's Greatest Monument.* The Greater St. Louis Archaeological Society. Wellington Printing Company, St. Louis.

Gums, Bonnie L.
1989   *Archaeology of the Cahokia Mounds, ICT-II: Groundstone Tools and Modified Rock.* Report submitted to Illinois Historic Preservation Agency, Springfield.
1993   Groundstone Tools, Modified Rock, and Exotic Materials. In *The Archaeology of the Cahokia Mounds ICT-II: Testing and Lithics.* Illinois Cultural Resources Study No. 9. Illinois Historic Preservation Agency, Springfield.

Gums, Bonnie L., Rodney C. De Mott, Neal H. Lopinot, George R. Holley, and Lucretia S. Kelly
1989   *Archaeological Investigations for the Mississippi River Transmission Corporation Alton Line in Madison and St. Clair Counties, Illinois.* Report submitted to Illinois Historic Preservation Agency, Springfield.

Hair, James T. (compiler and publisher)
1866   *Gazetteer of Madison County.* S.V. Crossman and Company, Printers, Alton, Illinois.

Hall, Robert L.
1962   *The Archaeology of Carcajou Point,* 2 vols. University of Wisconsin Press, Madison.
1966   *Cahokia Chronology.* Paper prepared for distribution at the Annual Meeting of the Central States Anthropological Society in St. Louis, Missouri. Illinois State Museum. (Mimeographed).
1967a   The Mississippian Heartland and Its Plains Relationships. *Plains Anthropologist* 12(36):175–183. Lincoln.
1967b   Northern Mississippi Valley. *American Antiquity* 32(4):571. Salt Lake City.
1968   The Goddard-Ramey Cahokia Flight: A Pioneering Aerial Photographic Survey. *The Wisconsin Archeologist* 49(2) (new series):75–79. Milwaukee.
1975   Chronology and Phases at Cahokia. In *Perspectives in Cahokia Archaeology,* pp. 15-31.

Illinois Archaeological Survey Bulletin, No. 10. Urbana.

Harn, Alan D.
1970   *Notes on the Mississippian Occupation of the Central Illinois River Valley.* Paper presented at the 69th Annual Meeting of the American Anthropological Association, San Diego.
1971a   An Archaeological Survey of the American Bottoms in Madison and St. Clair Counties Illinois. In *An Archaeological Survey of the American Bottoms and Wood River Terrace,* pp. 19–39. Illinois State Museum Reports of Investigations, No. 21. Springfield.
1971b   *Comments on Spatial Distribution of Late Woodland and Mississippian Ceramics in the General Cahokia Sphere.* Paper presented at the Cahokia Ceramic Conference. (Mimeographed).
1973   *Cahokia and the Mississippian Emergence in the Spoon River Area of Illinois.* Paper presented at the 52nd Annual Meeting of the Central States Anthropological Society. St. Louis.

Harris, Thaddeus Mason
1805   *The Journal of a Tour into the Territory Northwest of the Alleghany Mountains; Made in the Spring of the Year 1803.* No. 2. Manning and Loring, Cornhill, Boston.

Higgins, George B.
1938   In *The Cahokia Mound Group and Its Village Site Material,* by Paul F. Titterington, p.16. St. Louis.

Holley, George R.
1987   *Archaeology of the Cahokia Mounds, ICT-II: Ceramics.* Report submitted to the Illinois Historic Preservation Agency, Springfield.
1989   *The Archaeology of the Cahokia Mounds ICT-II: Ceramics.* Illinois Cultural Resources Study No. 11. Illinois Historic Preservation Agency, Springfield.
1995   Microliths and the Kunnemann Tract: An Assessment of Craft Production at the Cahokia Site. *Illinois Archaeology* 7:1–68.

Holley, George R., Rinita A. Dalan, and Philip A. Smith
1993   Investigations in the Cahokia Site Grand Plaza. *American Antiquity* 58:306–318.

Holley, George R., Rinita A. Dalan, and Harold W. Watters, Jr.

1992 *Archaeological Investigations at the Rouch Mound Group, Cahokia Mounds State Historic Site.* Unpublished report submitted to the Illinois Historic Preservation Agency, Springfield.

Holley, George R., Rinita A. Dalan, Harold W. Watters, Jr., and Julie N. Harper
1995 *Investigations at the Tippetts Mound Group, Cahokia Mounds State Historic Site.* Unpublished report submitted to the Illinois Historic Preservation Agency, Springfield.

Holley, George R., Neal H. Lopinot, Rinita A. Dalan, and William I. Woods
1989 *Southern Palisade Investigations, Cahokia Mounds State Historic Site, St. Clair County, Illinois.* Report submitted to the Illinois Historic Preservation Agency, Springfield.
1990 *South Palisade Investigations.* Illinois Cultural Resources Study No. 14. Illinois Historic Preservation Agency, Springfield.

Holley, George R., Neal H. Lopinot, William I. Woods, and John E. Kelly
1989 Dynamics of Community Organization at Prehistoric Cahokia. In *Households and Communities,* edited by S. MacEachern, D. J. W. Archer, and R. D. Gavin, pp. 339–349. Proceedings of the 21st Annual Chacmool Conference. The Archaeological Association, University of Calgary, Alberta.

Holmes, William H.
1883 Art in Shell. *Transactions of the Anthropological Society of Washington,* Vol. 2, pp. 106–107. Washington, D.C.
1903 Aboriginal Pottery of the Eastern United States. *20th Annual Report of the Bureau of American Ethnology,* pp. 1–201. Washington, D.C.

Howland, Henry R.
1877 Recent Archaeological Discoveries in the American Bottom. *Buffalo Society of Natural Sciences Bulletin* 3(5):204–211. Buffalo.

Hudson, Charles
1976 *The Southeastern Indians.* University of Tennessee Press, Knoxville.

Iseminger, William R.
1985 Summary Report for Field School Excavations at Woodhenge. Cahokia Mounds State Historic Site, 1985. Cahokia Mounds Museum Society. Ms on file at Cahokia Mounds State Historic Site and IHPA, Collinsville.

Iseminger, William R., John E. Kelly, Bonnie L. Gums, Gayle Fritz, and William Gartner
1991 *In over Our Heads: Excavations at Mound 1, Cahokia, 11-Ms-2/9.* Paper presented at the Midwest Archaeological Conference, La Crosse.
1994 *Summary of Investigations at Mound 1 (11-Ms-2/9), Cahokia.* Research Notes and Papers on American Bottom Archaeology No. 2. Central Mississippi Valley Archaeological Research Institute.

Iseminger, William R., Timothy R. Pauketat, Brad Koldehoff, Lucretia S. Kelly, and Leonard Blake
1990 *East Palisade Investigations.* Illinois Cultural Resources Study No. 14. Illinois Historic Preservation Agency, Springfield.

James, James Alton
1928 *The Life of George Rogers Clark.* University of Chicago Press, Chicago.

Judd, Neil M.
1948 "Pyramids" of the New World. *National Geographic Magazine* 93:105–128. Washington, D.C.

Keller, Kenneth J.
1996 A Summary of the Analysis of the Mound 50 Material. *Cahokian* (Spring). Cahokia Mounds Museum Society, Collinsville.

Kelly, A. R.
1933 Some Problems of Recent Cahokia Archaeology. *Transactions of the Illinois State Academy of Science* 25(4):101–103. Springfield.

Kelly, A. R., and Fay-Cooper Cole
1931 Rediscovering Illinois. *Blue Book of the State of Illinois 1931–1932,* pp. 328–334. Springfield.

Kelly, John E.
1993 *Recent Investigations in the Area of the Southeastern Palisade, Cahokia.* Unpublished report submitted to the Illinois Historic Preservation Agency, Springfield.
1997 Stirling Phase Socio–Political Activity at East St. Louis and Cahokia. In *Cahokia: Domina-*

tion and Ideology in the Mississippian World, edited by T. R. Pauketat and T. E. Emerson. University of Nebraska Press, Lincoln.

Kelly, Lucretia S.
1988   *Archaeology of the Cahokia Mounds, ICT-II: Faunal Remains.* Report submitted to the Illinois Historic Preservation Agency, Springfield.

Keplinger, John G.
1919   Who were the Mound Builders? *Illinois State Historical Society Journal* 12:45–52. Springfield.

Kirkpatrick, John E.
1911   *Timothy Flint, Pioneer, Missionary, Author, Editor 1780–1840: The Story of His Life among the Pioneer and Frontiersmen in the Ohio and Mississippi Valley and in New England and the South.* Arthur H. Clark Company, Cleveland.

Lahontan, Louis Armand, Baron de
1905 [1703]   *New Voyages to North America.* 2 vols. Reprint, English edition of 1703. Notes and Index by Reuben Gold Thwaites. A.M. McClurg and Company, Chicago.

Latrobe, Charles Joseph
1835   *The Rambler in North America*, vol. 2. Harper and Brothers, New York.

Leighton, M. N.
1929   The Geological Aspects of Some of the Cahokia (Illinois) Mounds. *University of Illinois Bulletin* 26(4):109–143. Urbana.

Lewis, Henry von, and George B. Douglas
1923 [1857]   *Das Illustrirte Mississippithal.* Reprints of Rare Americana No. 3. Schmidt and Gunther, Leipzig.

Long, Stephen H.
1905 [1823]   Account of an Expedition from Pittsburgh to the Rocky Mountains performed in the Years 1819, 1820. Compiled from the Notes of Major Long, Mr. T. Say, and other Gentlemen of the Party by Edwin James. In *Early Western Travels 1748–1846*, Vol. 14, edited by Reuben Gold Thwaites. Reprint. Arthur H. Clark Company, Cleveland.

Lopinot, Neal H.
1988   *Archaeology of the Cahokia Mounds, ICT-II: Archaeobotany.* Report submitted to the Illinois Historic Preservation Agency, Springfield.

Lopinot, Neal H., Alan J. Brown, and George R. Holley
1989   *Archaeological Investigations of the Proposed Sanitary Sewer Collection System, Eastern Portion of Village of Fairmont, St. Clair and Madison Counties, Illinois.* Report submitted to the Illinois Historic Preservation Agency, Springfield.
1993   Archaeological Investigations on the Western Periphery of the Cahokia Site. *Illinois Archaeology* 5:407-420.

Lopinot, Neal H., Lucretia S. Kelly, George R. Milner, and Richard Paine
1991   *The Archaeology of the Cahokia Mounds ICT-II: Biological Remains.* Illinois Cultural Resources Study No. 13. Illinois Historic Preservation Agency, Springfield.

Mason, Richard Lee
1915   *Narrative of Richard Lee Mason in the Pioneer West 1819.* New York City.

Mason, Ronald J., and Gregory Perino
1961   Microblades at Cahokia, Illinois. *American Antiquity* 26(4):553–557. Salt Lake City.

McAdams, Clark
1907   The Archaeology of Illinois. *Transactions of the Illinois State Historical Society for 1907*, pp. 35–47. Springfield.

McAdams, William
1881   Ancient Mounds of Illinois. *Proceedings of the American Association for the Advancement of Science.* 29th Meeting held at Boston, Massachusetts, August, 1880, pp. 710–718. Salem.
1882   Antiquities. In *History of Madison County, Illinois*, pp. 58–64. W.R. Brink and Company, Edwardsville, Illinois.
1883   *Antiquities of Cahokia or Monks' Mound in Madison County, Illinois.* W. R. Brink and Company, Edwardsville, Illinois.
1887   *Records of Ancient Races in the Mississippi Valley.* C.R. Barns Publishing Company, St. Louis.

1895 Archaeology. *Report of the Illinois Board of World's Fair Commissioners at the World's Columbian Exposition.* H.W. Rokker, Printer and Binder, Springfield.

McDermott, John Francis
1949 *Old Cahokia: A Narrative and Documents Illustrating the First Century of Its History.* Buechler Publishing Company, Belleville, Illinois. (Copyright by the St. Louis Historical Documents Foundation.)

McGimsey, Charles R., and Michael D. Wiant
1984 *Limited Archaeological Investigations at Monks Mound (11-MS-38): Some Perspectives on Its Stability, Structure, and Age.* Illinois Historical Preservation Agency Studies in Illinois Archaeology, No. 1. Springfield.

Mehrer, Mark
1988 *The Settlement Patterns and Social Power of Cahokia's Hinterland Households.* Unpublished Ph.D. dissertation, Department of Anthropology, University of Illinois, Urbana.

1995 *Cahokia's Countryside: Household Archaeology, Settlement Patterns, and Social Power.* Northern Illinois University Press, DeKalb.

Meiners, Ray, and Robert Grimm
1942 Uncovering an Ancient Village Site. *Hobbies—The Magazine for Collectors* 47(7):99–100.

Melbye, F. Jerome
1963 *The Kane Burial Mounds.* Archaeological Salvage Report, No. 15. Southern Illinois University Museum, Carbondale.

Messenger (surveyor)
1808 Field notes for the south edge of Town 9 north, range 3 west of the third principle meridian. Saturday, January 9, 1808. In *Illinois Land Records, Original Field Notes*, vol. 12. Illinois State Archives, Springfield.

Milner, George R., and Richard Paine
1987 *Archaeology of the Cahokia Mounds, ICT-II: Human Skeletal Remains.* Report submitted to the Illinois Historic Preservation Agency, Springfield.

Moorehead, Warren K.
1912 Archaeology of the Mississippi Valley. *Transactions of the Illinois State Historical Society for the Year 1910*, pp. 184–185. Illinois State Historical Library Publication No. 15. Springfield.

1921 *Help Save the Cahokia Mounds.* (Circular). August, 4 pages. Andover, Massachusetts.

1922a The Cahokia Mounds: A Preliminary Report. *University of Illinois Bulletin* 19(35). 24 April. Urbana.

1922b Preservation of the Cahokia Mounds. *The Wisconsin Archeologist* 1(1)(new series):25–27. Milwaukee.

1923 The Cahokia Mounds: Part 1, A Report of Progress by Warren K. Moorehead and Part 2, Some Geological Aspects by Morris M. Leighton. *University of Illinois Bulletin* 21(6). Urbana.

1929 The Cahokia Mounds. *University of Illinois Bulletin* 26(4). Urbana.

Morrison, Anna R.
1914 [1840] Diary of a Journey from New York to Jacksonville (November 11, 1840 to March 1, 1841). *Journal of the Illinois State Historical Society* 7(1):34–51. Springfield.

Muller, Jon
1987 Salt, Chert, and Shell: Mississippian Exchange and Economy. In *Specialization, Exchange, and Complex Societies*, edited by Elizabeth M. Brunfiel and Timothy K. Earle, pp. 10-21. Cambridge University Press, Cabridge.

Munson, Patrick J.
1971 An Archaeological Survey of the Wood River Terrace and Adjacent Bottoms and Bluffs in Madison County, Illinois. In *Archaeological Surveys of the American Bottoms and Adjacent Bluffs, Illinois*, pp. 100-120. Illinois State Museum Reports of Investigations, No. 21, Pt. 1. Springfield.

1973 The Origins and Antiquity of the Maize-Beans-Squash Agriculture in Eastern North America: Some Linguistic Implications. In *Variation in Anthropology: Essays in Honor of John McGregor*; edited by Donald Lathrap and Jody Douglas, pp. 107–135. Illinois Archaeological Survey, Urbana.

1974   Terraces, Meander Loops, and Archaeology in the American Bottoms, Illinois. *Transactions of the Illinois State Academy of Science*, Vol. 67, No. 4, pp. 384–392. Springfield.

Munson, Patrick J., Paul W. Parmalee, and Richard A. Yarnell
1971   Subsistence Ecology of Scovill, A Terminal Middle Woodland Village. *American Antiquity* 36(4):410–431. Salt Lake City.

Nassaney, Michael S., Neal Lopinot, Brian Butler, and Richard W. Jeffries
1983   *The 1982 Excavations of the Cahokia Interpretive Center Tract, St. Clair County, Illinois.* Southern Illinois University Archaeological Salvage Report, No. 23. Carbondale.

Obrecht, Rev. Father
1905   Letter to Clark McAdams regarding the Cahokia Mounds. In *The Archaeology of Illinois*, by Clark McAdams, pp. 39–41. Transactions of the Illinois State Historical Society for 1907.   Springfield.

O'Brien, Patricia J.
1969a   *A Formal Analysis of Cahokia Ceramics: Powell Tract.* Ph.D. dissertation. University of Illinois. University Microfilms, Ann Arbor.
1969b   Some Ceramic Periods and Their Implications at Cahokia. In *Explorations into Cahokia Archaeology*, edited by Melvin L. Fowler, pp. 100–120. Illinois Archaeological Survey Bulletin, No. 7. University of Illinois, Urbana.
1972a   *A Formal Analysis of Cahokia Ceramics from the Powell Tract.* Illinois Archaeological Survey Monograph, No. 3. Urbana.
1972b   Urbanism, Cahokia, and Middle Mississippian. *Archaeology* 25 (3):188–197.

Oliver, William
1924 [1843] *Eight Months in Illinois; with Information to Emigrants.* William Andrew Mitchell, Newcastle upon Tyne. Reprint. The Torch Press, Cedar Rapids, Iowa.

Orr, Kenneth G.
1951   Change at Kincaid: A Study of Cultural Dynamics. In *Kincaid: A Prehistoric Illinois Metropolis* by Fay-Cooper Cole et al., pp. 291–359. University of Chicago Press, Chicago.

Parmalee, Paul W.
1957   Vertebrate Remains from the Cahokia Site, Illinois. *Transactions of the Illinois State Academy of Science*, Vol. 50, pp. 235–242. Springfield.
1958a   Evidence of the Fisher in Central Illinois. *Journal of Mammology* 39(1):135.
1958b   Marine Shells of Illinois Indian Sites. *Nautilus* 71(4):132–139.
1958c   Remains of Rare and Extinct Birds from Illinois Indian Sites. *Auk* 71(4):132–139.
1975   A General Summary of the Vertebrate Fauna from Cahokia. In *Perspectives in Cahokia Archaeology*, pp. 137–155. Illinois Archaeological Survey Bulletin, No. 10. Urbana.

Parrish, Randall
1906   *Historic Illinois: The Romance of the Earlier Days*, 2nd ed. McClurg and Company, Chicago.

Pauketat, Timothy
1991   *The Dynamics of Pre-State Political Centralization in the North American Midcontinent.* Unpublished Ph.D. dissertation, Department of Anthropology, University of Michigan, Ann Arbor.
1993a   *Temples for Cahokia Lords: Preston Holder's 1955–1956 Excavations of Kunnemann Mound.* Memoir No. 28, Museum of Anthropology. University of Michigan, Ann Arbor.
1993b   Preliminary Observations of Building Density at Cahokia Tract 15A and Dunhman Tract. *Illinois Archaeology* 5:402–406.
1994   *The Ascent of Chiefs: Cahokia and Mississippian Politics in Native North America.* University of Alabama Press, Tuscaloosa.
1997   *The Archaeology of Downtown Cahokia: The Tract 15A and Dunham Tract Excavations.* Studies in Archaeology No. 1. Illinois Transportation Archaeological Research Program, Department of Anthropology, University of Illinois, Urbana.

Pauketat, Timothy R., and Thomas E. Emerson (editors)
1997   *Cahokia: Domination and Ideology in the Mississippian World.* University of Nebraska Press, Lincoln.

Pauketat, Timothy R., Gayle J. Fritz, Lucretia S. Kelly, and Neal H. Lopinot
1993   *Early Cahokia: A New Research Project in the American Bottom.* Paper presented at the

Midwestern Archaeological Conference, Milwaukee.

Peale, T. R.
1862 Ancient Mounds at St. Louis, Missouri, in 1819. *Annual Report of the Smithsonian Institution 1861*, pp. 386–391. Washington, D.C.

Peck, John Mason
1834 *Gazetteer of Illinois*. R. Goudy, Jacksonville.
1840 *The Travelers Directory for Illinois*. J.H. Colton, New York.

Peet, Stephen D.
1890 Phallic Worship and Fire Worship. *The American Antiquarian* 12:352–356. Chicago.
1891a The Great Cahokia Mound. *The American Antiquarian* 13(1):3–31. Chicago.
1891b Note. *The American Antiquarian* 13(1):58-59. Chicago.

Perino, Gregory
1947 Cultural Problems at Cahokia. *Illinois State Archaeological Society Journal* 4(3):14–17. Springfield.
1957 Cahokia. *Central States Archaeological Journal* 3(3):84–88. Quincy.
1959 Recent Information from Cahokia and Its Satellites. *Central States Archaeological Journal* 6(4):130–138. Quincy.
1963 Tentative Classification of Two Projectile Points and One from West-Central Illinois. *Central States Archaeological Journal* 10(3):95–100. Quincy.
1966 *Three Late Woodland Projectile Point Types from Illinois*. Descriptions prepared for distribution at the 24th Plains Conference in Lincoln, Nebraska, on November 24-26.
1971 The Mississippian Component at the Schild Site (No. 4), Greene County, Illinois. In *Mississippian Site Archaeology in Illinois, Vol. 1*, pp. 1–148. Illinois Archaeological Survey Bulletin, No. 8. Urbana.

Perrin, T. H.
1872 Mounds near Anna, Union County, Illinois. *Annual Report of the Smithsonian Institution 1872*, pp. 418–420. Washington, D.C.

Peterson, C. A.
1902 *The Mound Building Age in North America*. Read on 15 February 1902 before the Missouri State Historical Society, St. Louis.

Pfeiffer, John
1974 Indian City on the Mississippi. *1974 Nature Science Annual*. Time Inc., New York.

Pidgeon, William
1858 *Traditions of De-Coo-Dah and Antiquarian Researches*: Comprising Extensive Explorations Surveys, and Excavations of the Wonderful and Mysterious Earthen Remains of the Mound-Builders in America: The Traditions of the Last Prophet of the Elk Nation Relative to their Origin and Use; and the Evidences of an Ancient Population More Numerous Than the Present Aborigines. Horace Thayer, New York.

Porter, James Warren
1969 The Mitchell Site and Prehistoric Exchange Systems at Cahokia: A.D. 1000±300. In *Explorations into Cahokia Archaeology*, edited by Melvin L. Fowler, pp. 137–164. Illinois Archaeological Survey Bulletin, No. 7. University of Illinois, Urbana.
1974 *Cahokia Archaeology as Viewed from the Mitchell Site: A Satellite Community at A.D. 1150-1200*. Ph.D. dissertation, University of Wisconsin-Madison. University Microfilms, Ann Arbor.

Priest, Josiah
1833 *American Antiquities and Discoveries in the West*, 5th ed. Hoffman and White, Albany.

Putnam, F. W., and J. J. R. Patrick
1880 *Twelfth Annual Report of the Peabody Museum*. Reports of the Peabody Museum of American Archaeology and Ethnology in Connection with Harvard University, 1876–79, vol. 2. Cambridge, Mass.

Ramey Family
1916 *The Mound Builders: The Greatest Monument of Prehistoric Man, Cahokia or Monks Mound*. Private printing.

Randall, Emilius Oviatt
1908 *Masterpieces of Ohio Mound Builders*. Ohio State Archaeological and Historical Society, Columbus.

Rau, Charles
1867 Indian Pottery. *Annual Report of the Smithsonian Institution, 1866*, pp. 346–355. Washington, D.C.

1869   A Deposit of Agricultural Flint Implements in Southern Illinois. *Annual Report of the Smithsonian Institution, 1868*, pp. 401–407. Washington, D.C.

Reed, Nelson
1964   Cahokia. *The St. Louis Magazine: Bicentennial Issue* 1(9):47ff. St. Louis.
1969   Monks and Other Mississippian Mounds. In *Explorations into Cahokia Archaeology*, edited by Melvin L. Fowler, pp. 31–42. Illinois Archaeological Survey Bulletin, No. 7. University of Illinois, Urbana.

Reed, Nelson, John W. Bennett, and James Warren Porter
1968   Solid Core Drilling of Monks Mound: Technique and Findings. *American Antiquity* 33:137–148. Salt Lake City.

Reeves, Dache M.
1936   Aerial Photography and Archaeology. *American Antiquity* 2:102–107. Salt Lake City.

Reynolds, John
1879   *My Own Times: Embracing also the History of My Life*. Chicago Historical Society. Fergus Printing Company, Chicago.

Rowe, John Howland
1953   Technical Aids in Anthropology: A Historical Survey. In *Anthropology Today*, edited by Alfred L. Kroeber. University of Chicago Press, Chicago.

Russell, John
1831   Western Antiquities. *Illinois Monthly Magazine*. March. Vandalia, Illinois.

Salzer, Robert
1975   Excavations at the Merrell Tract of the Cahokia Site: Summary Field Report, 1973. In *Cahokia Archaeology: Field Reports*, edited by Melvin L. Fowler, pp. 1–8. Illinois State Museum Research Series, No. 3. Springfield.

Schoolcraft, Henry Rowe
1825   *Travels in the Central Portions of the Mississippi Valley: Comprising Observations on its Mineral Geography, Internal Resources, and Aboriginal Population*. Collins and Hannay, New York.

Shalkop, Robert L.
1949   *The Jersey Bluff Archaeological Focus*. Master's thesis, Department of Anthropology, University of Chicago.

Shelford, V. E.
1963   *The Ecology of North America*. University of Illinois Press, Urbana.

Shetrone, Henry Clyde
1930   *The Mound-Builders*. D. Appleton and Company, New York.

Shipp, Barnard
1897   *The Indian and Antiquities of America*. Sherman and Company, Printers, Philadelphia.

Short, John T.
1880   *The North Americans of Antiquity*. Harper and Brothers, New York.

Silverberg, Robert
1968   *Mound Builders of Ancient America: The Archaeology of a Myth*. New York Graphic Society Ltd., Greenwich, Conn.

Smith, Hale G.
1951   *The Crable Site, Fulton County, Illinois*. Anthropological Papers, No. 7. Museum of Anthropology, University of Michigan, Ann Arbor.

Smith, Harlan Ingersoll
1902   The Great American Pyramid. *Harper's Monthly Magazine* 104:199–204. New York.

Smith, Harriet M.
1942   Excavation of the Murdock Mound of the Cahokia Group. *Journal of the Illinois State Archaeological Society* 1(1):13–18. Springfield.
1969   The Murdock Mound: Cahokia Site. In *Explorations into Cahokia Archaeology*, edited by Melvin L. Fowler, pp. 49–88. Illinois Archaeological Survey Bulletin, No. 7. University of Illinois, Urbana.

Snyder, John Francis
1894   An Illinois "Teocalli." *The Archaeologist* 2(9):259–264. Waterloo, Indiana.
1895   A Group of Illinois Mounds. *The Archaeologist* 3(3):77–81. Waterloo, Indiana.
1900   The Field for Archaeological Research in Illinois. *Transactions of the Illinois State Histori-*

cal Society for 1900, pp. 21–29. Springfield.

1909 Prehistoric Illinois. Certain Indian Mounds Technically Considered. *Journal of the Illinois State Historical Society* 1 and 2:31–40, 47–65, 71–92. Springfield.

1911 Prehistoric Illinois. Its Psychozoic Problems. *Journal of the Illinois State Historical Society* 4:288–302. Springfield.

1912 The Kaskaskia Indians. A Tentative Hypothesis. *Journal of the Illinois State Historical Society* 4:231–245. Springfield.

1913 *The Prehistoric Mounds of Illinois.* Pamphlet published by "The Monks of Cahokia."

1914 Prehistoric Illinois—The Great Cahokia Mound. *Illinois State Historical Society Journal* 6:506–508. Springfield.

1917 The Great Cahokia Mound. *Illinois State Historical Society Journal* 10:256–259. Springfield.

1962 [1904] Certain Indian Mounds Technically Considered. In *John Francis Snyder: Selected Writings*, edited by Clyde C. Walton, pp. 230–273. Illinois State Historical Society, Springfield.

Squier, E. G., and E. H. Davis
1848 Ancient Monuments of the Mississippi Valley: Comprising the Results of Extensive Original Surveys and Explorations. *Smithsonian Contributions to Knowledge*, Vol. 1. Washington, D.C.

St. Louis Daily Globe–Democrat.
1888 The Monk's Mound: A Prehistoric Marvel in Madison County, Illinois. 5 February:16.

St. Louis Post Dispatch
1931 Ancient Tumulus Leveled to Make Truck Farm Discloses Evidence of High Civilization. 4 March.

Stoltman, James A. (editor)
1991 *New Perspectives on Cahokia: Views from the Periphery.* Monographs in World Archaeology No. 2. Prehistory Press, Madison, Wisc.

Stuart, George C.
1972 Who were the Mound Builders? *National Geographic* 142(6):783–801.

Sutter, J. R.
1891 Inscription with Date of 1676 near St. Louis. *American Antiquarian* 13:350–351. Chicago.

Thomas, Cyrus
1894 Report on the Mound Explorations of the Bureau of Ethnology. *12th Annual Report of the Bureau of Ethnology, 1890-91*, pp. 131–134. Washington, D.C.

1907 Cahokia or Monks Mound. *American Anthropologist* 9 (new series):362–365. Menasha.

Throop, Addison J.
1928 *The Mound Builders of Illinois.* Call Printing Company, East St. Louis, Ill.

Titterington, Paul F.
1933 The Cahokia Mound Group and Its Surface Material. *Wisconsin Archaeologist* 13 (1):7–14. Milwaukee.

1935 Certain Bluff Mounds in Western Jersey County, Illinois. *American Antiquity* 1(1):6–46. Menasha.

1938 *The Cahokia Mound Group and Its Village Site Material.* St. Louis, Missouri.

1942 The Jersey County, Illinois, Bluff Focus. *American Antiquity* 19:240–245. Menasha.

Townley, E. C.
1927 Some Mound Builders in Illinois. *Art and Archaeology* 24(6):234–238. Washington, D.C.

Tucker, Sara Jones (compiler)
1942 *Indian Villages of the Illinois County, Vol. 2, Scientific Paper, Illinois State Museum.* Part 1, *Atlas.* State of Illinois, Springfield.

Udden, J. A., and E. W. Shaw
1915 *Geologic Atlas of the United States: Belleville-Breese Folio No. 195 Illinois.* U.S. Geological Survey, Washington, D.C.

Vander Leest, Barbara J.
1980 *The Ramey Field, Cahokia Surface Collection: A Functional Analysis of Spatial Structure.* Unpublished Ph.D. dissertation, Department of Anthropology, University of Wisconsin-Milwaukee.

Vogel, Joseph O.
1964a *A Preliminary Report on the Analysis of Ceramics from the Cahokia Area at the Illinois State Museum.* University Microfilms, Ann Arbor.

1964b *A Preliminary Report on the Analysis of Ceramics from the Cahokia Area at the Illinois State Museum.* A 1964 revision of the original 1964 manuscript xeroxed for participants of the 1971 Cahokia Ceramic Conference.

1975 Trends in Cahokia Ceramics: Preliminary Study of the Collections from Tracts 15A & 15B. In *Perspectives in Cahokia Archaeology*, pp. 32–125. Illinois Archaeological Survey Bulletin, No. 10. University of Illinois, Urbana.

Wagner, Robert W.
1959 *An Analysis of the Material Culture of the James Ramey Mound*. Master's thesis, Department of Anthropology, University of Illinois at Champaign-Urbana.

Walthall, John A., and Elizabeth D. Benchley
1987 *The River L'Abbe Mission*. Studies in Illinois Archaeology No. 2. Illinois Historic Preservation Agency, Springfield.

Walton, Clyde C. (editor)
1962 *John Francis Snyder: Selected Writings*. Illinois State Historical Society, Springfield.

Warner and Beers
1874 *Illustrated Historical Atlas of St. Clair County, Illinois*.

Weber, Jessie
1912 Report of the Secretary of the Illinois State Historical Society, May 14, 1909 to May 5, 1910. *Transactions of the Illinois State Historical Society for the Year 1910*. Illinois State Historical Library Publication No. 15. Illinois State Journal Company, State Printers, Springfield.

Wells, Christy, Mikels Skele, and George R. Holley
1991 *Investigations Relating to the State Park Place Water Main Emplacements, Cahokia Mounds Historic Site*. Unpublished report submitted to the Illinois Historic Preservation Agency, Springfield.

Whitlock, W. H.
1933 Who Built Monks' Mound? *Illinois State Historical Society Journal* 26:51–161. Springfield.

Wild, J. C.
1841 *The Valley of the Mississippi; Illustrated in a Series of Views*. Chambers and Knapp, St. Louis.

Williams, Kenneth
1972 Preliminary Summation of Excavation at the East Lobes of 38. In *The University of Wisconsin–Milwaukee Cahokia Archaeology Project*, edited by Melvin L. Fowler, pp. 75–77. A symposium presented at the 37th annual meeting of the Society for American Archaeology, Milwaukee. (Mimeographed).

1975 Preliminary Summation of Excavations at the East Lobes of Monks Mound. In *Cahokia Archaeology: Field Reports*, edited by Melvin L. Fowler, pp. 21–24. Illinois State Museum Research Series, No. 3. Springfield.

Williams, Stephen
1954 *An Archaeological Study of the Mississippian Culture of Southeastern Missouri*. Unpublished Ph.D. dissertation, Department of Anthropology, Yale University, New Haven.

Williams, Stephen, and John M. Goggin
1956 The Long-nosed God Mask in Eastern United States. *The Missouri Archaeologist* 18 (3):1–72. Columbia.

Witty, Charles O.
1993 The Fingerhut (11S34/7) Cemetery Three Decades Later. *Illinois Archaeology* 5:402-433.

Wittry, Warren L.
1964 An American Woodhenge. *Cranbrook Institute of Science News Letter* 33(9):102–107. Bloomfield Hills, Michigan.

1969 The American Woodhenge. In *Explorations into Cahokia Archaeology*, edited by Melvin L. Fowler, pp. 43–48. Illinois Archaeological Survey Bulletin, No. 7. University of Illinois, Urbana.

Wittry, Warren L., and Joseph O. Vogel
1962 Illinois State Museum Projects. In *First Annual Report: American Bottoms Archaeology, July 1, 1961–June 30, 1962*, edited by Melvin L. Fowler, pp. 15–30. Illinois Archaeological Survey, Urbana.

Woods, William I.
1984 *Archaeological Testing at the Cahokia Mounds Interpretive Center Tract-Location II, St. Clair County, Illinois*. Report submitted to the Illinois Historic Preservation Agency, Springfield.

1993a ICT-II Phase II Testing. In *The Archaeology of the Cahokia Mounds ICT-II: Testing and Lithics.* Illinois Cultural Resources Study No. 9. Illinois Historic Preservation Agency, Springfield.

1993b *Monks Mound 4th Terrace Coring Report.* Unpublished report submitted to the Illinois Historic Preservation Agency, Springfield.

Worthen, A. H.
  1866 *Geological Survey of Illinois*, Vol. 1. Illinois Geological Survey, Urbana.

Wray, Donald E.
  1952 Archaeology of the Illinois Valley: 1950. In *Archaeology of the Eastern United States*, edited by James B. Griffin, pp. 152–164. University of Chicago Press, Chicago.

INDEX

Note: Page numbers in italics refer to figures and figure captions. References to specific maps in chapters 4-8 (descriptions of mounds and borrow pits) have not been indexed; most of the mounds and borrow pits appear on one or more maps, as indicated by the subheading "maps of." A distinction has been made between "archaeological investigations" (including documentary research, survey, controlled surface collection, testing, and excavation) and "excavations."